Quest for your Empowered Self

Life Skills to Help You Live, Thrive, and Produce Like Never Before

1st Edition

Thomas Ventimiglia

M.A. in Counseling
M.A. in Higher Education
B.A. in Business Administration

WESTBOW PRESS
A DIVISION OF THOMAS NELSON & ZONDERVAN

Website: tappingintowellness.com
Email: tomventi@verizon.net

All illustrations except the "Sea of Success" provided by David Mintz.

WestBow Press books may be ordered through booksellers or by contacting:

WestBow Press
A Division of Thomas Nelson & Zondervan
1663 Liberty Drive
Bloomington, IN 47403
www.westbowpress.com
1 (866) 928-1240

ISBN: 978-1-4908-2683-7 (sc)
ISBN: 978-1-4908-2682-0 (e)

Library of Congress Control Number: 2014903092

Printed in the United States of America.

WestBow Press rev. date: 04/30/2014

Quest for your Empowered Self

Life Skills to Help You Live, Thrive, and Produce Like Never Before

TABLE OF CONTENTS

EMPOWERED INNER SELF: **LIVE** LIKE NEVER BEFORE

Page

Acknowledgments

I want to acknowledge my wife, Kathy, for teaching me to look beyond the simple and my family and relatives for providing a strong foundation from which I could more easily grow. To my three daughters, Emily, Olivia, and Sophia who always seem to be able to take me away from the world of stress and bring me back into their world of play and laughter.

Introduction

Quest for your Empowered Self

We as human beings have gone to the moon, split the atom, unraveled the genetic code, probed the birth of the universe, and achieved technological triumphs with impressive, blinding brilliance. Yet, I wonder if achieving inner triumphs within our selves is just as important. Isn't it strange that we can split the atom and go to the moon, but we can't feed the physical, emotional, and spiritual starvation of others and our selves? But, isn't the pursuit of knowledge the key to advancing our evolution? We see this today with the technology of the Internet and how it can supply almost any bit of information we want. However, don't we have generations of people stressed, depressed on Prozac, lonely, confused, leading meaningless lives, and addicted to everything from food and television to drugs and alcohol? The fastest growing addiction today is the computer and the Internet. Perhaps the focus should not be so centered outside of our selves, but rather within.

Is it so painful to spend some time each day silently going inside our inner mind and conducting an "inner ritual" to access knowledge, insight, and direction like you would the Internet? One might say, "But, I don't have the time!" The average person fills most gaps of silent space with a barrage of stimulation. For example, he/she may get into the car and listen to the radio on the way to work. On the lunch hour, he/she may read a paper. When arriving at home, this same person turns on the television for up to four hours. When it is time for bed, the stimulated mind is still online, making it difficult to go to sleep. This may go on for the next 40 years. Yet, we say we are looking for more purpose, meaning, excitement, and balance in our lives even though we stuff our selves with a multimedia smorgasbord on a daily basis.

When we take the time to become clearer about our values, we then become clearer about our life decisions. By responding to the following four questions, one is well on his/her way to a more meaningful life: Who am I? (Identity), Where am I going? (Direction), Why am I going there? (Purpose), and How will I get there? (Strategy). Many people today are miserable, unhappy, and confused as a result of bad decisions based on outer gain, self-gratification, or their woundedness. The following statistics exemplify this. Over 50% of people indicate that they wish they were in another job; over 50% of people are in the wrong relationship; and as a community college counselor and professor, I know that over 50% of students are in the wrong major. So, why do we make these poor choices and decisions? It does not help that we are living in a society that brainwashes us into thinking that true happiness and sparkling health are attained by something outside of ourselves--a product, a service, or an expert. Advertisements, doctors, movies, songs, magazines, television, and radio are all scrambling to get you to believe that their viewpoint or product is *best* for you. We are bombarded with the "You would be happy if" advertisements. Many people fall into the philosophical trap of, "If I just had more money, material possessions, fame, etc., I'd be happy." You may get the hot sports car, but you wake up the next morning and say, "I'm still a miserable person but with a really great car." So, what good is it? It's as if we have an electrical plug and determine that if we stick the plug into a certain food, person, drink, or product, we would be happy. However, research shows that our attitude even after traumatic or exciting events like winning the lottery, basically stays the same a few months after such events. So, regardless of outside circumstances, we need to take that plug and insert it into our inner selves if we are to obtain an empowered self.

This book was written to <u>empower</u> the reader to make wise decisions affecting many aspects of their lives. The word "Empower" means in this book to make one stronger and more confident especially in one's ability to control one's life and claiming one's rights. It also means to give inner authority and power back to oneself instead of giving it to others under pressure and/or wasting it away to the chaotic, lazy mind. Quest means to search within oneself for that power that is waiting for one to take advantage of it and use it responsibly.

It is beyond imagination that we can go through 12 years of education and not receive one day of instruction on how to draft a goal-setting plan, make excellent decisions based on quantifiable and intuitive methods, manage a financial budget, bring balance into our lives, identify a dominant style of learning to maximize comprehension of any educational material, manage relationships, enhance communication skills, change our negative beliefs and attitudes, develop compassion for others and ourselves, discipline ourselves to overcome obstacles, and take full responsibility for our actions. Most schools and personal growth programs exclude these life skills in their structure. So, as we become adults, we are often unaware why we behave the way we do and, eventually, we fall into a rut. Do you ever ask yourself the following questions: Why am I afraid to speak up? Why do others take advantage of me? Why am I so self-critical or critical of others? Why can't I motivate myself? Why do I procrastinate? (Or haven't you gotten around to doing that yet?) Why am I always late? Why do I say yes when I mean no? Why do I end up with the wrong person all the time? Why am I addictive? Why do I stress myself out so much? Why is it so hard to get out of this rut I'm in? Why do I fear failure or fear success? This book, particularly the first two chapters, will help you answer these questions. However, in order to lead a full life and advance your personal growth, the above *life skills* must be learned and incorporated into a life plan. This book encompasses those life skills.

In order to obtain an empowered self, the individual must learn these life skills under a self-empowerment model I developed. It consists of eight elements of the self that make up the titles of the eight chapters in the book. The Eight Elements of the empowered self are listed below with a note as to their order and their purpose. To provide clarification, a parallel is made between the self-empowerment model and the rules of driving an automobile.

1. **Self-Identity –** You must have a clear sense of where you are, where you're going, and why you're going there. That is, you must discover your inner purpose and core values that make up your identity so you can choose a path in life that will provide ultimate meaning for you.

2. **Self-Understanding** – First, you must know the operations of your car before you drive. That is, you must understand how and why the mind operates before attempting to improve it. Its purpose is to help you access your "True Self" so that you head off in the best direction.

3. **Self-Observation** – Observe and self-correct when you fail to stay in the car lane. You must observe and self-correct thoughts and behaviors when they veer from your target goals. Its purpose is to help you achieve success by strengthening positive thoughts and behaviors.

4. **Self-Compassion** – Drive when you are secure, alert, and in a stable frame of mind. You must have self-compassion to successfully confront and cope with life's challenges. Its purpose is to heal low self-worth so that you can express yourself freely while loving others.

5. **Self-Advancement** – Acquire *driving skills* to go to your chosen destination. You must acquire lifelong *strategic skills* to advance your goals, health, and life. Its purpose is to help you learn the goal planning process necessary for faster, more efficient goal attainment.

6. **Self-Integrity** – For a successful journey, integrate the "rules of the road" using proper driving skills. You must integrate the "rules" of communication and conduct in developing a strong character. Its purpose is to bring wholeness and to achieve respect from others and yourself.

7. **Self-Discipline** – Stay on course by being disciplined to resist enticing stimulations on the road. You must be disciplined to resist the urge to gratify yourself in the short-term to achieve long-term gain. Its purpose is to keep you aligned with your life mission and achieve success.

8. **Self-Assertion** – Assert your actions to let other drivers know what you want. You must assert yourself to let others know what you feel, desire, and need. Its purpose is to help you communicate effectively to enhance your relationships and spur goal achievement.

It might be easy to jump to the conclusion that this is a selfish oriented program since it has, as its focus, the eight elements of empowering the Self. On the contrary, the Eight Elements of Self-Empowerment are designed to help the individual and student to be a "force for good" by providing service to the local and world community as well as to the Self. Self-esteem alone is too narrow in scope and not noble enough. For example, members of the Nazi party in World War II had very high self-esteem. However, they were arrogant murderers. Therefore, the aim of this program is to develop a sense of service to others accompanied by a sense of service to the Self.

It is ineffective to develop only one (or a few) of the Eight Elements of the empowered self, especially if we are deficient in a particular area. For example, if we only worked on self-understanding and self-observation, we may never take the necessary action to advance our lives. If we only developed self-compassion, we may be eligible for the clergy or convent, but we would not necessarily be offering all of our gifts to a world that needs our contribution. If we only worked on our self-assertion skills like Amy Weinstein, Anna Nicole Smith, Heath Ledger, Whitney Houston, John Belushi, River Phoenix, Curt Kobain, and Charles Keating, we may achieve success. However, if not congruent with our inner selves, our outer persona can create disastrous results. Notice how the lives of the people who are mentioned above took a nose dive because their focus was on outer approval instead of inner approval. However, if not congruent with our inner selves, our outer persona can create disastrous results. It is important that the individual can connect with his/her own essence or core Self. This part of our selves is deeper than the socialized or cultural influences that have tried to shape us.

Live, Thrive, and Produce

Look at the table of contents in the book. The "***Live*** Like Never Before" section presents the inner psychological work that is needed to become clear and empowered. Attention is directed primarily toward having the student look within him/herself for insight, guidance, support, life answers, and wholeness. When we are able to perform this inner work, we more successfully thrive and produce, which is presented in the second half of the course. The "***Thrive*** Like Never Before" section assists the student to master the life skills that help the student become educated on developing character-strength such as ethics, morals, tolerance, and self-responsibility. The other set of life skills help the student plan and craft a comprehensive goal-setting plan that can be used for any goal they want. Attention is primarily directed toward having the student now, look outward to master key life skills through integrating moral and logical thinking as well as self-responsibility into one's actions. The "***Produce*** Like Never Before" section is designed to have the student practice and acquire self-discipline behaviors necessary for gaining control over one's life. Furthermore, self-assertion and communication skills are learned to enhance goal attainment and personal success. This success should be congruent with the true desires of the student's core self and values rather than what society deems successful.

Chapter 4 (Self-Compassion), Chapter 6 (Self-Integrity), and Chapter 8 (Self-Assertion) of the book emphasize assisting individuals of multicultural backgrounds and of disadvantaged groups to identify their own values apart from the multiple value systems they straddle. Simultaneously, this part encourages non-disadvantaged individuals to have compassion, respect, and understanding of those who have not had the same privileges in the American culture.

Each individual who completes the program will have completed an assessment to discover his/her learning style, personality style, love modality, intellectual style, Type A or B personality temperament, emotional intelligence, lifelong value system, stress level, Enneagram personality, and boundary setting score.

You will find 56 high-powered *strategies* that are presented in bold print. These strategies will empower you to gain valuable life skills and take action. In addition, you will find 168 *exercises and assignments* to enhance your personal growth in various areas: time management; creativity; managing stress, anxiety, depression, and the grieving process, brainstorms; problem solving; decision making; money management; learning style identification; emotional IQ, the seven intelligences; taking responsibility; identifying thought/reasoning distortions in logic; raising self-esteem; diversity; getting support from others; drafting a goal plan strategy; meditations and guided imagery; developing compassion for others and self; transactional analysis; changing negative attitudes and beliefs; clarifying cultural, family, religious, and societal value systems; life balance; a proven method for goal attainment; how to attract to the right person; communication strategies; dealing with difficult personalities; personality style inventory; resolving conflict for win/win solutions; and much more. All of the assignments listed under Exercise 1 are beginning level, those assignments listed under Exercise 2 are intermediate level, and those listed under Exercise 3 are advanced level.

<u>Teachers</u>

I recommend that you only choose three or four lessons or strategies from each chapter if you are teaching a semester length course. Completing all of the exercises along with test taking and so forth may be too overwhelming for students. The exercises can be performed in class or outside of class. You will probably want to choose exercises that relate more to the objectives within the curriculum that you are teaching from. ***The pages have been perforated to make it easier for students to tear out their assignments and exercises and hand them in to be graded.***

Explanation of the Sea of Success Picture

On the following page is an illustration of the inner journey that is taken as one charts his/her course towards success in life. The sailboat represents our thinking mind and the eight areas of the empowered self, (Self-Identity, Self-Understanding, etc.). As the navigator, you use your mind and these eight skills to sail your life toward your own Sea of Success. You alone should define what success is to you. Along the way, there are mental island traps that tempt us to become shipwrecked. Some people stay there a lifetime while others move on toward their Sea of Success. The more time you allocate toward accessing the "Heart-Mind" (see Values lesson in the first chapter) and mastering the book's life skills, the easier it will be to avoid these mental island traps and reach your Sea of Success.

The water represents a lifetime of past, present, and future experiences. Some people's experiences have been stormier than others. The moon represents the four life areas (the spiritual, physical, aspirational, social---see Week 2 on Sunday). We know the moon has a gravitational pull on the sea. When we spend at least 15 minutes a day in each life area, we become more balanced which will calm the storms in our life for smoother sailing toward the Sea of Success. See an explanation of the mental island traps below.

Mental Island Traps

Some people ignore their "heart" voice—they deny problems in their relationships, job, and with their family; they deny any prejudice inside themselves; they deny that their actions are causing their own suffering. It's their "heart" they need to **dial.** These people usually sail themselves to the
Isle of Denial.

Some people want to stay fixed in their beliefs and never forgive others. Their need to always be right; not taking responsibility is usually their **aim.** These people usually sail themselves to the **Beach of Bitterness and Blame.**

Some people after experiencing setbacks get angry, depressed, and **retreat.** These people usually sail themselves to the **Harbor of Bad Feelings and Self-Defeat.**

Some people have the ego-driven, good paying job, but it's mundane. They don't use their talents; the deadline, stress, and repetitive job environment is trying and a **pity**. These people usually sail themselves and their lives to **Burnout City.**

Some people live their lives apart from their "heart" voice. With every failure they experience, they listen to their negative, internal voice that tells them they are not worthy, they will never be successful. They truly **mope.** These people usually sail themselves to the **Cape of No Hope.**

And then there are some people who listen to their "heart" voice. They live balanced lives, are open to self-improvement, and create harmony within themselves and with others, even under **stress.** These people usually sail themselves to their **Sea of Success.**

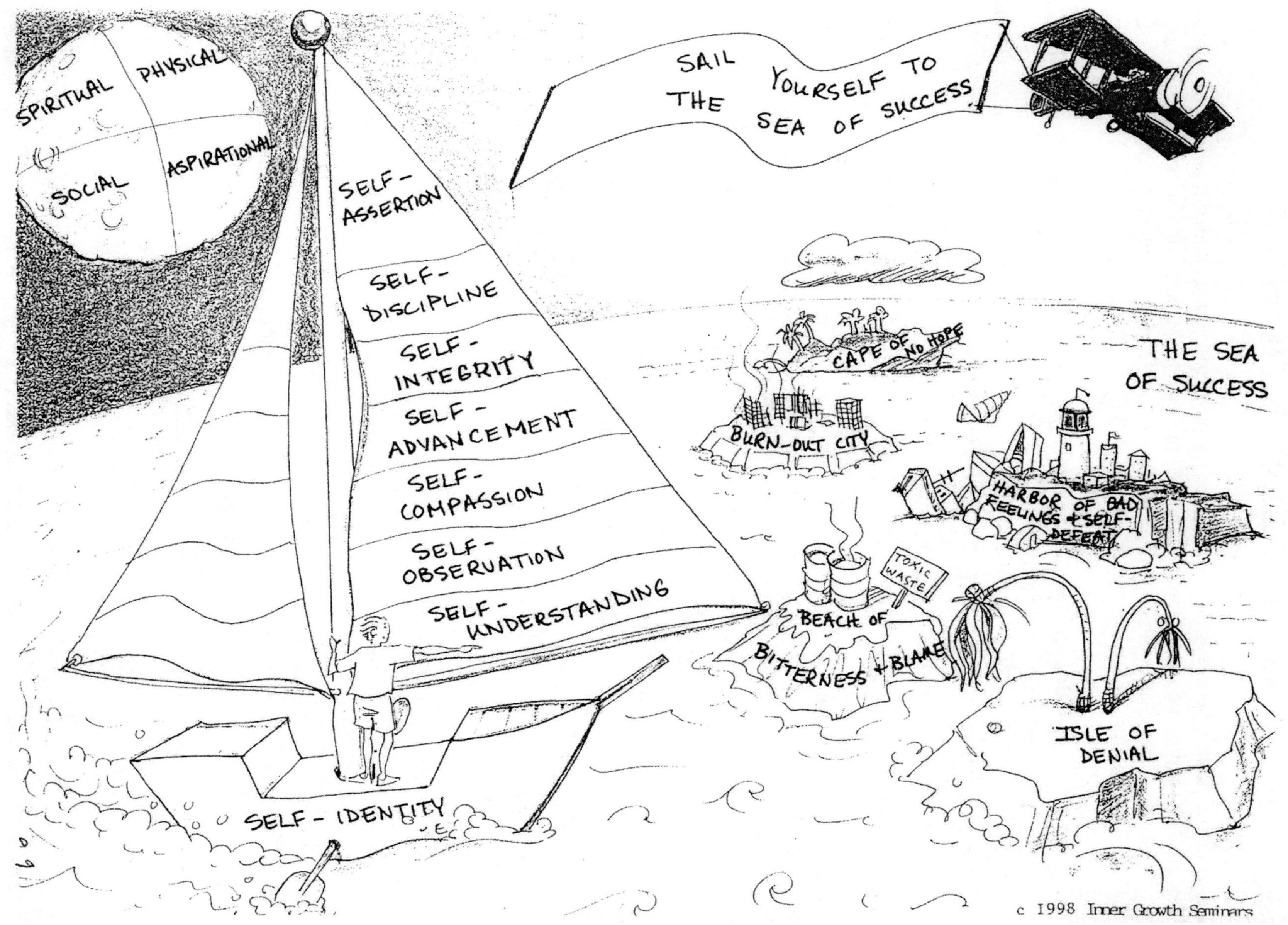
SPIRITUAL
PHYSICAL
SOCIAL
ASPIRATIONAL
SAIL YOURSELF TO THE SEA OF SUCCESS
SELF-ASSERTION
SELF-DISCIPLINE
SELF-INTEGRITY
SELF-ADVANCEMENT
SELF-COMPASSION
SELF-OBSERVATION
SELF-UNDERSTANDING
SELF-IDENTITY
CAPE OF NO HOPE
BURN-OUT CITY
THE SEA OF SUCCESS
HARBOR OF BAD FEELINGS + SELF-DEFEAT
TOXIC WASTE
BEACH OF BITTERNESS + BLAME
ISLE OF DENIAL
c 1998 Inner Growth Seminars

Pre-Post Life Skills Assessment

Complete the following assessment to see where your strengths and challenges lie. Then complete it again at the end of the semester (or if you are not in a class, when you've completed the book) to see if you've made progress in each of these life areas. This assessment is not a picture of who you are. It is a picture of how you view yourself in only the following areas.

1 - Not at all 2 – Somewhat 3 – Average 4 – Pretty Strong 5– Strongly

1. How well do you know and understand your personal attributes (strengths, weaknesses, interests, personality, family history, values, etc.,) and their impact on your behavior and success?
   Semester start__________________________ Semester end______________________________
2. Do you know what motivates you and how strongly can you motivate yourself?
   Semester start__________________________ Semester end______________________________
3. How clear are you on your major and the career you should pursue?
   Semester start__________________________ Semester end______________________________
4. How clear are you on what your core values are?
   Semester start__________________________ Semester end______________________________
5. How clearly do you know your purpose and mission in life?
   Semester start__________________________ Semester end______________________________

Total Score: (1) Self Identity Semester start__________ Semester end__________

1. Are you able to use your intuition and/or access the spiritual realm to help guide your life?
   Semester start__________________________ Semester end______________________________
2. Do you believe you have the personal qualities to lead a successful, meaningful life?
   Semester start__________________________ Semester end______________________________
3. Today, do you believe your future is shaped by your internal forces (desire, self-control, discipline, hard work, attitude)
   Semester start__________________________ Semester end______________________________
4. How well do you manage your emotions?
   Semester start__________________________ Semester end______________________________
5. When you consider your social, spiritual, physical, and mental health, how well balanced are you?
   Semester start__________________________ Semester end______________________________

Total Score: (2) Self-Understanding Semester start________Semester end_____

1. When you need to make an important decision, how well do you <u>not</u> jump to conclusions, gather the facts, test ideas, weigh alternatives, and decisively choose what's best in long run?
   Semester start__________________________ Semester end______________________________
2. How well can you control your emotions, substances, habits, and reactions to others?
   Semester start__________________________ Semester end______________________________
3. How healthy are your reasoning and thinking patterns? Can you resist personalizing things or blaming others?
   Semester start__________________________ Semester end______________________________
4. Can you resist the use of denial, lying, or suppression when trying to make your self feel better?

Semester start__________________________ Semester end______________________________

5. Do your personal issues contribute to your success? Answer 1 or 2 if you are overly critical, feel unworthy, stupid, inadequate, guilty, shame, arrogant, controlling, anxious, etc.
   Semester start__________________________ Semester end______________________________

Total Score: (3) Self-Observation Semester start________ Semester end_________

1. Do you accept and are you proud of who you are?
   Semester start__________________________ Semester end______________________________
2. Do you spend enough time pampering yourself with self-care activities?
   Semester start__________________________ Semester end______________________________
3. How well do you deal with stress in your life?
   Semester start__________________________ Semester end______________________________
4. How worthy do you feel as a person? How would you rate your self-esteem?
   Semester start__________________________ Semester end______________________________
5. Do you not need approval from others to help you feel good about yourself?
   Semester start_________________________________ Semester end_____________________________

Total Score: (4) Self-Compassion Semester start_________Semester end________

1. How confident are you, when setting a goal, that you will achieve it in a timely manner?
   Semester start__________________________ Semester end______________________________
2. How knowledgeable are you in drafting a goal plan?
   Semester start__________________________ Semester end______________________________
3. How well are you able to solve personal dilemmas in your life? (identifying the source not the symptom of your problems, taking steps to manage the problems effectively, seeing the pros and cons objectively)
   Semester start__________________________ Semester end______________________________

4. When you have to make a decision between two or more things, how confident are you in making the right decision? Do you use a logical and intuitive method to help you decide?
Semester start______________________________ S Semester end______________________________

5. How well do you learn and understand information? Semester start_______Semester end_________

Total Score: (5) Self-Advancement Semester start________Semester end_______

1. How much of a moral or ethical person are you?
   Semester start__________________________ Semester end______________________________
2. How honest are you in all of your dealings?
   Semester start__________________________ Semester end______________________________

3. How much do you accept and appreciate people who are different than you? For example, differences regarding race, the disabled, the poor, gender, religion, homosexuality, elderly, etc.
   Semester start__________________________ Semester end______________________________

4. Do you take responsibility for many things in your life? Do you take on too much responsibility?
   Semester start__________________________ Semester end______________________________

5. How well can you say "no" to others and not worry too much about what they'll think?
   Semester start__________________________ Semester end______________________________

Total Score: (6) Self-Integrity Semester start___________Semester end________

1. When you face a setback in life, how well are you able to think in the long-run and have a positive attitude?
Semester start___________________________ Semester end______________________________
2. How well are you able to detach yourself from something that troubles you?
Semester start___________________________ Semester end______________________________
3. Can you discipline yourself to accomplish tasks in a timely matter without procrastinating?
Semester start___________________________ Semester end______________________________
4. When you fail at something, how good is your ability to not quit/persevere despite the odds?
Semester start___________________________ Semester end______________________________
5. How well do you use moderation in your life? Are you moderate with food, TV, alcohol, drugs, sex, shopping, gambling, etc?
Semester start___________________________ Semester end______________________________

Total Score: (7) Self-Discipline Semester start__________Semester end__________

1. How would you rate your ability to easily and effectively communicate your needs, feelings, and opinions to people around you?
Semester start___________________________ Semester end______________________________
2. Are you able to set boundaries with others? e.g. not allowing others to take advantage of you, abuse you, standing up for yourself, etc.
Semester start___________________________ Semester end______________________________
3. How do you rate the success of your current relationships?
Semester start___________________________ Semester end______________________________
4. How well do you handle difficult people? e.g. bullies, invalidators, negative types, gripers, etc.
Semester start___________________________ Semester end______________________________
5. How well do you resolve conflict and create win/win solutions?
Semester start___________________________ Semester end_________________

Total Score: (8) Self-Assertion Semester start__________ Semester end_______

Now shade in the areas below using your total score from each area to determine which chapters will help you most.

(1) Self-Identity		(2)Self Under-standing		(3)Self-Observation		(4) Self-Compassion		(5) Self-Advancement		(6) Self-Integrity		(7) Self-Discipline		(8) Self-Assertion	
Start	End	Start	End	Start	End	Start	End	Start	End	Start	End	Start	End	Start	End

Comments:____

____

CHAPTER 1

Self-Identity

Using your **Soul** to **Identify** with
your life mission and purpose in life.

Purpose: To know oneself and live life with meaning and purpose.

Rewards: Empowerment, Congruency, Happiness, Inner Strength

Obstacles: Listening to Others, Greed, Fear of Taking Risks, Ego/Pride

Consequence: Self-alienation, Being Lost, Confusion, Powerlessness

Symbol: Your Name

Related Web Sites: http://www.keirsey.com/cgi-bin/keirsey/newkts.cgi

http://www.bls.gov/oco

Self-Identity

The discovery of your core values and finding meaning in your life is essential to the achievement of identity and empowerment. The quest for identity involves a commitment to exploring the meaning and value of one's uniqueness. Many people lose their sense of self because they try to base their identity on acquiring material wealth, being approved of by everyone, and getting ahead at all costs. Whether you believe one's identity is inherited or constructed, it is important in the process of your quest for identity to let "parts of yourself die." In other words, you may need to shed old roles and immature identities that prevent you from growing. Often we need to go against our cultural or familial upbringing to create an identity that is congruent with our core values and true self. Though the struggle and resistance from loved ones and society can be painful, nothing can compare with the prize of happiness, fulfillment, peace, and empowerment one feels when aligned with one's true identity and purpose. Empowerment is important because this sense of power enables you to direct the course of your own life by the freedom to choose your destiny instead of seeing yourself as a passive victim of circumstances and conditions. Individuals develop strong identities when they seek answers to profound questions concerning their self and their purpose in life while seeking to understand and connect with the world of others. When one achieves a clear and strong identity, an empowered self is born.

Though we must have goals, life slowly unfolds in a way where we can't always see the future. Yet, when we're open to learning and growing, we can find meaning and insightful reasons into why things have happened to us in the past. The goals, purpose, and identity you have now can be much different five years from now. Instead of clinging to a certain way of thinking about yourself, it is critical to continually reinvent yourself if you are to develop yourself and your life. Life goals are not set once and for all. Over time, as you do this work, answers to the following questions will often be different: Who am I? What do I stand for? Where am I going? How do I get there?

This chapter and book will help you answer some of these questions. It helps you to do so by getting you to examine the following: your core values; thoughts on human nature and behavior; sources of your fears and motivations; personality characteristics; career interests; personal abilities, talents, aptitudes, and skills; self-reflective exercises; family expectations; your relationships with friends, parents, and siblings; cultural upbringing; dating experiences; gender roles; the values you place on marriage and children; religious views; sources of meaning in your life; critical turning points; how you see yourself and others; kind of life you want; and goals you'd like to achieve.

Part of shaping an identity requires an active search in trying to find your place in the world. We live in the American culture that programs its citizens to believe that the answers to key life questions and finding peace of mind as well as bliss are out there in some service, person, or product. Will you show the courage it takes to realize that this is an inside job?

Strategy 1.1

Increase self-awareness by clarifying your personal qualities, preferences, abilities, talents, accomplishments, knowledge, and experiences to better understand a piece of who you are.

The unexamined life is not worth living.
Socrates

Directing Awareness Within

When we don't take the time to be self-aware (reflect on our thoughts, feelings, behaviors, values), our struggles and pain repeat themselves in an endless circle. We then make bad decisions that affect every aspect of our lives. Most people use only their external cues and senses (seeing, hearing, touching) to make the key decisions in their life. Yet, like trying to hit a baseball with one hand, they are only using half of their abilities. Intuition and self-reflection are your inner senses of perception. They are the internal cues that usually give us very accurate feedback when we need insight for making important decisions. For example, if you are in the midst of making a decision and you feel a sense of heaviness, warning, or fear, you might need to slow down in order to delay a decision or to gain more information. So many times we push through our feelings, dismiss inner cues, and wind up making counterproductive decisions when we're hurried, angry, or tired. When we bring more awareness to our thoughts and feelings and we read the manual to our own mind, we can more easily control our life and learn how to live life according to our own wishes and desires.

The Benefits of Bing in Touch with Yourself

The following are some examples of why being in touch with yourself is so important.

- *To see that you medicate your anger with food, alcohol, drugs, etc., instead of processing the anger and to help heal the pain. You can vent anger by journal writing, screaming into a pillow, hitting the bed with a plastic baseball bat as you verbalize the anger, etc.*
- *To bring clarity to an important decision you need to make. Example: choice in career, marriage*
- *To gain clarity on issues and stances you need to take in your personal and professional life. Example: tell how you feel about somebody, how to confront the boss, how best to say what is needed to your mother, friend etc.*
- *To gain clarity on current events and social causes and take a position that reflects your core values. Example: health care policy, gay marriage rights, immigration policy, the war in Iraq, abortion, gun control, and so on*
- *To recognize how often you criticize yourself and rarely appreciate the struggles you've endured*
- *To identify what is triggering your fear of success or fear of failure that prevents success*

The Johari Window of Awareness

To help bring more awareness to your interactions with yourself and others, a model developed by Luft (1969) called the Johari Window can help. There are four windows of awareness as shown in the graphic below. *Window 1* is the area of free activity that contains factors known to self and known to others. *Window 2* is the blind area that contains factors perceived by others about you of which you are unaware. *Window 3* is the avoided or hidden area, which represents things you know but do not reveal to others. *Window 4* represents the area of unknown activity. Neither you nor others are aware of certain behaviors or motives that you have. Examine the Johari Window below.

	Known to Self	**Not Known to Self**
Known To Others	1 Openness (Open)	2 Unconscious Defense and Motives (Blind)
Not Known To Others	3 Conscious Defense and Motives (Hidden)	4 Unconscious Defense and Motives (Unknown)

When you are often operating in the awareness of Window 2, others may want to distance themselves from you. This is because many of your motivations can be selfish and greedy. For example, if at work there was one good chair among many mediocre ones at the conference table, and you always ran for the good chair at each meeting week after week, your behavior would be perceived as infantile and selfish. If you are unaware of how your selfishness is affecting others, you will continue to blatantly act out. Instead, if you were aware of it, you could work on curbing your selfishness or learn how to communicate your selfishness in combination with thinking of others. Feedback and insight from others about our selves is crucial to our personal growth. Often many people only see the "good side" of their personality while denying or repressing areas that need change.

When you are often operating in the awareness of Window 3, you may be distancing yourself from others and end up lonely with few friends. This is because intimacy and depth of friendship can only occur when you disclose or open yourself up to others and reveal some of your weaknesses, inadequacies, and vulnerabilities. Of course, you would only want to do this with somebody you trust and with whom you feel safe with. People who can laugh at themselves are usually very healthy people we want around because they make us feel at ease about ourselves.

They help us not to feel like we have to keep a wall around our emotions and motives. When emotions are bottled up, it turns into depression and illness.

When you are often operating in the awareness of Window 4, you may be making poor decisions in your life that are causing a lot of pain and failure. This is because you do not have the luxury of getting feedback from others. For example, you may sabotage your every chance of success (e.g. getting drunk at work before a promotion) because you fear the responsibility that will go with it. So instead of checking the accuracy of that feeling and problem solving it, you blindly behave in a way that blocks your ability to advance in this area of your life.

Insights about the Johari Window are as follows:

- Energy is depleted by hiding, denying, or concealing your motives.
- Your blind area may cause much difficulty for you and others.
- Your knowledge and awareness of yourself/others is always incomplete. There is always something going on that you do not know about or are aware of.
- There is much resistance and defense when you try to increase your awareness.

Identity and Identity Statuses

Definition: Identity refers to having a relatively clear and stable sense of who you are and what you stand for such as your values. It is also the personal characteristics that distinguish you from other people. Though, thoughts, feelings, and experiences may change, you remain familiar to yourself and the image you have of yourself mostly matches the image others have toward you. You have an individual identity and a social identity. Your **individual identity** is made up of characteristics which include: your name, gender, age, physical characteristics, talents, likes and preferences, emotions, beliefs, artistic activities, possessions, and educational interests. Your **social identity** is related to how you identify yourself in relation to the important people in your life, the roles you play, and the cultural, ethnic, and religious groups you belong to. Your **cultural identity** refers to the behaviors, ideas, attitudes, values, beliefs, ethics, ways of expression of self, and traditions shared by a large social group. Examples include: your family role as mother, father, son, etc., your romantic role, your occupational role, your friendship role, your nationality, your religion, political affiliation, devotion to country, social class, race, and so on.

According to psychoanalyst Erik Erikson (Weiten & Lloyd, 1997) identity emerges out a crisis that occurs over a period of time in adolescence. Decisions of committing to a life philosophy and identity are confronted. He studied four statuses that characterize a person's identity orientation at any particular time.

1. Identity Conformity (Foreclosure)

People in this category unquestioningly adopt the values, roles, beliefs, and expectations designated and prescribed for them by their parents and culture/society. They will pursue the same career choices as the parent or what the parent tells them to pursue. They conform to the parents' political leanings without questioning and trying to find the truth on their own. They stick to the same religion they grew up with without exploring others. Therefore, they make a lifelong commitment to this thinking.

RESULT

While strongly connected to their families, they stay sheltered in the family cocoon and do not enjoy the discovery of their potential and understanding the rest of the world. They are cognitively rigid and conservative in most things they do. If you are an artist with a talent but your parents have told you that you are to go into business, your artistic talent will unlikely or never become realized because you choose not to explore and discover your inner gifts due to conformity.

2. Identity Experimenting (Moratorium)

In the adolescent period between ages twelve and twenty, the necessary struggle to find one's identity intensifies though it does not end at age twenty. There are four factors that force the individual to reflect and experiment with different roles, beliefs, and values different from their parents/caretakers.

The four factors that help force people in this experimentation include: 1) the physical changes of puberty make people confront their own sexuality and self-image, 2) the start of Piaget's formal operations (the brain can now think abstractly at age twelve which promotes self-reflection, 3) the end of high school forces people to think about career choices and decisions about their future. 4) Peer pressure. Faced with many daily decisions, they have to decide, should they use drugs, date a particular person, become sexually active, become politically involved, go to college, etc. Attraction of rock music and rap stars, movie stars, and other charismatic figures provide a star like quality to which the person can relate and achieve some sense of personal identity apart from their parents. But, if the need to be accepted and liked is stronger than the need for self-respect, adolescents will find themselves being more "fake" and look to others to tell them what and who they should be. This is similar to Identity Conformity but in this status, there is no final commitment yet.

RESULT

A lot of struggling and pain occur because by experimenting and exploring different life philosophies, roles, and beliefs, they are not always accepted and are often ridiculed or shunned. Continually testing parental limits, they have a strong urge to break away and declare their uniqueness. By doing so, they often feel frightened and lonely, masking their fears with rebellion, while covering up their need to be dependent by exaggerating their independence. When parents can give the adolescent some distance as they try on different roles and values, the career and life decisions they make later on will likely be freely chosen and the adolescent turned adult will have more devotion and commitment to their decisions instead of feeling like they were forced into something. These early decisions are not to be lifelong and binding forever. And, parents are not to let their adolescents explore unwatched. There are life threatening dangers that can destroy a life such as AIDS and other sexually transmitted diseases, gangs, drug dealers, and so on.

3. Identity Apathy (Diffusion)

People in this category experience a lot of self-doubt and don't appear to be concerned about doing anything to change their circumstances. They are unable to make career and value commitments and "give up" in the process. If this "giving up" lasts too long, the following takes place.

RESULT

These people stay in a confused and stagnate state of being. Like being "stuck in first gear," they make no commitments in deciding on what their values are, what career should be chosen, what person they should marry, and where they stand on social and political issues. All of this often leads to unhappy and unproductive results.

4. Identity Achievers

People in this preferred category successfully pass through an identity crisis and now are able to make a commitment to a career, meaningful beliefs, lifelong/intimate partner, and a strong personal/political philosophy. Because they chose to experiment, research, observe both negative and positive influences, interacted with others, and tried to discover their own "inner" and worldly truths from a distance (not cut off) from the parent's expectations, they gain a

more clear sense of reality putting them in a position to reach their full potential. They are able to trust themselves enough to become open to new possibilities and listen to their inner selves.
RESULT
They are more cognitively flexible being able to accept and understand different cultures, religions, and philosophies, while remaining true to what they believe. They have a higher level of moral reasoning (knowing what is right and wrong), and have the capacity for more emotionally intimate relationships. They have not necessarily completely thrown away their parental expectations and values but have integrated one's own and one's parental value systems into a congruent sense of self and have consciously created their own identity. In fact, through their distancing from the parent to explore their inner and outer world, may come full circle and identify with many of their parents values and beliefs. It often becomes more empowering because instead of blindly accepting their parental values like individuals in the Identity Conformity/Foreclosure Status, Identity Achievers understand themselves as beings who have a past, present, and future that can always be challenged, strengthened, and changed for the better. Instead of looking to what others expect of them and seeking their approval, they ask: "Who is it that I want to become and what do I expect from myself?" They end up being better parents for their children in the future. Answer the following identity questions:
Am I able to trust others and myself?
Do I fear being rejected to a point where I don't risk in social situations?
Are most of my values similar to my parents or have I challenged most of the values I hold?
Do I accept myself as being OK, or do I seek too much confirmation outside of myself?
Am I hungry for approval from others? Do I dare make enemies or must I be nice to everyone?
How far will I go in my attempt to be liked? Do I need to be approved of by everyone?
Is there a God? What explains the inhumanity I see in the world? What should I do about it?

Achieving psychological separation from one's family is common in Western cultures. But in many indigenous and third world cultures, there is no adolescent phase. At puberty boys and girls are initiated into adult roles for which they have long been prepared. Identity selection is a luxury these cultures cannot afford. The cultural conflict can be tremendous when such families emigrate to the West and their children want to "find" or be themselves, become "teens," or "do their own thing."
Note the cultural value differences between a student I counseled and her parent's values. "Working for the family business, I wanted to take time off to relax and spend some money to buy myself nice things while trying to spend some leisure time enjoying life. Yet, I would be verbally attacked by my parents who accused me of, being selfish, wasting too much time on myself, and not devoting enough time to family obligations."
A double whammy occurs when people have to straddle value systems from two different cultures.

Adult Life Stages: What Stage Are You In?

In the following life stage descriptions, derived from a variety of research on adult life stages, they suggest that we have different needs at different times of our lives. Reviewing the life stage information below can help you gain and accept insight about your current life situation and what you may be experiencing emotionally. However, since the culture has changed so much in the past thirty years, there is no typical standard like before. Middle age has been pushed ahead to the fifties instead of the forties. There are a different set of conditions that affect people in their twenties than decades ago.

Late Adolescence (Ages 16-20)
This is a time some begin leaving home, detaching from family, and searching for a personal identity. Some of the stage activities include: finding a peer group, establishing a gender identity, finding an occupation, developing a personal world view, attempts at intimacy with others, loneliness which is numbed often by using drugs, clinging to another person yet rarely finding success in the relationship.

The Twenties: Provisional Adulthood (Ages 21 – 29)
Young adults often move away from the safe shelter of the family and confront insecurity about the future as they attempt to establish independence, which isn't always very stable. Life decisions are complex and personal. Examples of decisions include: choosing the security of staying home or the financial struggle of moving out; choosing to be single or getting married (worrying you will never find someone you can love who really loves you as well); choosing college or making money more quickly in a job; choosing a career that has security as opposed to a career that is meaningful or part of one's dream. Psychologically, proving competence to one's parents is common as well as getting their approval. Yet, a resentment of one's parents occurs because the parents have the financial hold on them. Single parent families struggle financially and depend on the twenty-something for family support.

The Thirties: Digging Down Roots (Ages 30-39)
From the late twenties to the early thirties, there is a questioning of values, beliefs, and early commitments to marriage and relationships as well as to a career. Inner turmoil increases about making commitments or not in marriage and in a career. There is something about age twenty-nine that is really felt, especially among women. Children are usually born during this time however, this is sometimes pushed back into the late thirties as the culture has valued more stimulation and careers. It is no longer as common for American women to grow up thinking they will get married, have children, live in a home with a white picket fence and be financially supported by their husband by the time they reach thirty. A college education has been the ticket to financial security and independence. Striking a balance between the two has been the dominant thinking for the past thirty years. For most, the decade of the thirties involves helping children grow, buying a home, psychoanalyzing the past, giving more attention to business matters, establishing a reputation at work, and asking the following questions: Will I have enough time to do it all? What do I really want to be? Is this all there is to life? What is missing from my life now? Men and women often feel restricted because of choices about family, children, career, and life priorities made in their twenties. Women who had children in their teens or early twenties will often begin their education and/or career in their thirties. A woman who has spent her adult life entirely on her career usually devotes most of her life at this time to being a mother. The decision then becomes, does she work full-time, part-time, or stay at home? Then the decision becomes for how long? Men start to question their previous external meaning of success and whether they want to pay the price of that success. Adjusting one's values is often very common.

The Forties: The Midlife (Ages 40-49)
From the late thirties to early forties, there is often an inner experience of great upheaval and midlife crisis. This is accompanied by, a feeling that there is something missing in life, further thoughts about raising a family, starting or changing a career, and/or a questioning, "Why am I here?" and "Where am I going?" Often feeling confined, men may venture out of their relationship and career and seek more stimulation to bring aliveness back into their "dead" lives. If not done in a responsible manner, regrets later on in their life often occur. This time can also be an opportunity to change lifestyles that concentrate on personal growth, becoming healthier, stronger, deeper, wiser, funnier, and freer even though age and slowness may start to set in. The ability to love well and work well helps one to feel happy as well as living life with meaning. Adults who fail to achieve a sense of productivity and creativity may begin to stagnate, become

bitter, and slip into negative, depressed, and self-centered states of mind. Most everyone feels that "time is slipping away" and that one is clearly alone even though there are loved ones in their lives.

Events that trigger a midlife crisis or transformation include:

- Realizing that our youthful dreams will never come about.
- Realizing that life is not necessarily fair and that we often do not get what we had expected.
  Marriage crisis: a spouse may have an affair or seek a divorce.
- The loss of some of our youthful physical qualities can be hard to face.
- Women confronted with menopause, which can be a crisis for some.
- Losing a job or being demoted because of age discrimination. Losing interest in one's job.
- The death of our parents drives home the truth that we are ultimately alone in this life.
- Our children grow up and leave home and parents may feel the "empty nest" syndrome.
- Confronted with taking care of our elderly parents around the time the kids leave home.

Ideas and solutions to some of these challenges include:

- Going back to school and starting a new career.
  Looking inward to get answers on creating a new life.
- Develop new talents and hobbies and change your lifestyle and day-to-day activities.
- Be open to the unconscious forces that influence you like paying attention to your dreams, desires, and express yourself through art, writing, music, journal writing, and poetry.
- Taking more risks in life to help express your true self.

The Fifties (Renewal) (Ages 50 – 59)

The fifties can be a satisfying time in one's life as one is often in one's peak in terms of status and personal power, and the process of preparing for older age begins. One may not have to work as hard as one did in the past and can use this time for reflecting, refocusing, and contemplating about how one now wants to use one's time. This can either be a time of calm, boredom, meaninglessness, and depression or a time to face new challenges and find love, meaning, fun, spiritual companionships, and sexuality. Women may experience menopause as their looks fade and they get depressed. It is recommended that menopause be seen as a gateway to a new stage of life that awakens the creative side of oneself. Men often feel their once highly satisfying goals and projects lack the pleasure it once held and get depressed when they realize that they've been pursuing empty dreams. This can be a time to tap another creative side of them, develop hobbies, and set new goals for retirement.

The Sixties and Late Adulthood (Ages 60 on up)

As life is extended and retirement is not mandatory, this period may become the true "golden years" of continued usefulness to society and growth for oneself. This can include opportunities for increasing social and civic activities in the community, volunteering, turning hobbies into businesses, and enjoying travel, family, and leisure time. Typical themes for people in late adulthood include: decreased physical capacities (not usually until the seventies and eighties); finding meaning in life; relate to the past without regrets; adjusting to the death of a spouse or friends; enjoying grandchildren; loneliness and social isolation; feelings of rejection and dependency uselessness, and despair; fears of death and dying; and accepting themselves and others as they are. Those who don't come to terms with themselves and their lives may yearn for another chance, feel they have wasted their lives and let valuable time slip by going into depression and die unhappy. Those who take good care of themselves and are fortunate enough to have good genes may live into their nineties and beyond. Studies of thousands of people who lived to be one hundred years of age show that the factor above genetics, surgery, diet, and exercise that helped them to live so long was that they felt wanted and loved by others around them. The American culture with its value on youth often neglects the elderly when they have a wealth of life experiences to hand down to generations. My (Tom) aunts and uncles (eight whom I've known) lived into their nineties and my Uncle Tony until just short of one hundred and five years old. All of them were mentally sharp with incredible memories of the past all the way up until their deaths. They were sacred to me and I learned more from them about life than I could have ever learned from a book. My hope is that you won't look at aging as a negative and rather, with a good attitude, form the picture of the life you would like to live, as you get older.

Our Past Experiences and Key People Who influenced Our Life

The exercises on the following pages help you to get in touch with past experiences, people, and events that helped form your identity. You will record four significant life events and four important people that have changed your life for the better or worse. These exercises are powerful and important for you to complete because they contribute to a big part of your identity. They have made you unique unlike anyone else, and they are actually secret indicators for you to heal and empower yourself. Once you identify the impact a life event had on you, you can then take steps to heal inner wounds and help achieve goals that you desire more successfully.
For example, one big life event for me was when I was between 16 and 18 years old. I worked in the grocery business as a courtesy clerk, bagging groceries and chasing carts in the parking lot. The boss was a mean-spirited man and I actually dreaded going to work. I said to myself as I entered college, "I will do whatever it takes to get a job I don't dread going to and find one I actually look forward to, that pays great, allows me enough time with my family, and that utilizes my talents. Yet it wasn't until after my bachelor's degree in my mid twenties that I picked counseling and teaching. That career had everything I wanted, helping others to reach their potential, ability to teach personal growth courses, an ideal work week, a community environment, and many other perks. I worked hard to obtain two master's degrees and work part time for several years before landing a full time contract position. I didn't want to go get an ordinary degree and eventually dread work. It took a lot of perseverance, desire, and discipline. Yet, I know that life event of working in the grocery store, gave me a lot of the motivation I needed to persevere during many obstacles that came along the way of my educational and occupational path. So think about the life events that have shaped you. Think about your family life, your work life, positive or negative experiences around other people, deaths, illnesses, or divorce, an achievement or award, or anything else you can think of. Record these in the exercises on the following pages.

Then, think about which key people in your life have been either a positive or negative influence on you. Both positive and negative influences shape who we are and we can learn important information about ourselves so that we can get clues about things like our career choice, our core values, or why we have a fear of success or failure which stops us from actually getting what we want in life. For example, one key person in my life was somebody who I never met. It was the author, Leo Buscaglia. As I read his books, he wrote so simply and powerfully on a subject that to me was more important than any other subject one could name; love. He wrote how a lack of love contributed to disease, depression, personality disorders, and all sorts of ailments that are prevalent in today's society. It was one of the key inspirations for writing my book, "Quest for the Empowered Self. "

For me, another example is the music of Jeff Lynne who wrote pop rock songs for the Electric Light Orchestra in the 1970's and 1980's. His music puts me in a good mood like nothing else can. He inspired me to write songs myself when nobody ever told me I had a talent to write music much less, sing. Today I have three CD's of personal growth songs that I sell at seminars and give out for free to people who can benefit. It is one of my life joys.

Who were the key people in your life? Was it a religious figure like Jesus, Mohammed, Buddah, or Confucius? Was it your mother or father, brother or sister, or a relative? Was it an author, teacher, neighbor, friend, boyfriend, girlfriend, pop culture figure? Write down who these people were and across from their name write how they affected you and how you can learn from it. Record these in Exercise 2C of this strategy.

The Left-Hand Path

When we increase our awareness and become clear about our motives, inner strengths, weaknesses, desires, purpose, and abilities, we are able to push through the ordinary and create the extraordinary. The questions on the next page will assist you to this end. Joseph Campbell, the great scholar of mythology, describes the evolutionary process of going beyond the known in what he calls "the left-hand path." In myths, the Hero traditionally chooses this path as the place where he will encounter new information and discover the truth. The right-hand path is the current dilemma or the status quo. To form a stronger identity, we must have the desire to take both a different inner and outer journey. Examples of the left hand path include, choosing a different career than your parents or culture wants you to choose, standing up to do the "right, ethical thing" at work when it might mean being fired, demoted, or being shunned, choosing a different religion or way of thinking that's different from your family, and so on. After the time period of struggle, one can come out the other end empowered, changed, stronger, and much more successful and happy. However, it's important to note that if one has the courage to choose the alternative, left path, one is likely to encounter both inner and outer resistance. This resistance can take the form of people who try to sabotage your success, or you may try to sabotage your own success so you don't have to struggle anymore. You may also fail many more times than you succeed causing many ego blows, as well as many other unpredictable forces that will try to throw you off course. Know that the effort is usually worth it if it is in line with your true identity, mission, and purpose in life. The following questions on the next page will start you on this exciting inner journey.

Exercise 1

Questions about your Experiences, Accomplishments, Abilities, Preferences, and Personal Qualities. *Transcribe your most important answers to pages 72 – 73, Exercise 2.*

1. When you look at your work life, what activities at work do you consider of greatest worth?

2. What results are you currently getting in your life that you don't like?

3. What results are you currently getting in your life that you do like?

4. People have always told me that I am very....

5. What things do you do well that seem to be difficult for most other people?

6. If I received an award it would probably be for.....

7. What activities have been most responsible for any success you have attained in your life?

8. What talents and abilities seem to come easily to you or that no one else really knows about?

9. What can you do best that would be of worth to others?

10. What things make you happy when you are doing them? (may give you goose bumps)

11. If you had unlimited time and resources, what would you do?

12. What have been your happiest moments in life and why?

13. I was probably born to....

14. I keep expecting....

15. The qualities I admire most in my self and others are....

16. My past preoccupations or recurring themes in my life are.... e.g. self-criticism, control, approval, overspending, security, a fear, conformity, physical image, lack of love, anger, guilt, anxiety, etc.

17. In the first column in the chart below, list the things you would really like to do or contributions you would like to make at some time in your life. Then check the age boxes of when you'll attain it

Future contributions and accomplishments you would like to achieve	**When** (approximate age)								
	20	25	30	35	40	45	50	60	70-
Notes:	Notes:								

Exercise 2

A. Referring to Window 2 of the Johari Window, ask somebody what comment they would make about you that you might be unaware of. Ask somebody who is safe and who you can trust. Write it below

____

____

____

Referring to Window 3 of the Johari Window, what are some things that you are hesitant about in showing others? Also, write down, why you are hesitant?

____

____

____

B. List 4 events in your life (positive and/or negative) that helped shape you into who you are today. What decisions did you make about yourself or life as a result?

Events	**Decisions Made About Self/Life**
Example 1: When my parents divorced *Example 2: When I worked in the fast food business and dreaded going to work.*	*1: Self: I believed I was bad because it was my fault. Life: The world is unpredictable and people are untrustworthy.* *2: I will work hard, go to college, and get a job I like so I never have to dread work like this again.*
1.	
2.	
3.	
4.	

C. List 4 people who have had a great impact on your life and your identity (positive or negative). Write across how they affected you?

People	**How They Affected You**
Example: Lisa Johnson (teacher)	*She helped me believe in myself by helping me to work hard, be creative, and do my best.*
1.	
2.	
3.	
4.	

Exercise 3

Which Identity Status do you think you are in right now? Write below changes you could make to become an identity achiever.

____

____

____

____

____

What life stage are you in right now? Write below which of the material applied to you. Also write what you have experienced that was not mentioned in the material in this chapter.

____

____

____

____

Strategy 1.2

Clarify and empower your core values and life views.

Definition of Values: A value is the relative worth or importance you place on different elements of life. What you deem important is a value. For example, if you value time with family, then you will make sure that you don't choose a job that requires you to work 60 hours a week. Values form the subset of your total thinking system. They affect and determine your identity, thoughts, and behavior.

The wisdom of many spiritual and cultural beliefs would say that you have an essence or spiritual self that you were born with. This essence or self is perfect the way it is. It comes with certain traits such as particular talents, aptitudes, ethnic race, propensities for specific abilities, and a personality. But, in the growing years, biological and social forces or influences shape it as you grow up. When you were young, you were conditioned through hormones and other biological forces as well as conditioned through social forces such as culture, religion, and education that shaped you into either something that makes that spiritual essence of yourself stronger or it distorted and/or wounded that self. Finding that core essence of yourself along with sorting out what influenced you through the years is the journey toward personal clarity and freedom. Identifying your values is a key step in making that happen.

These values, in addition to **you** or your core self shape your identity and drive your behavior. The graphic below illustrates that both internal and external forces shape your values.

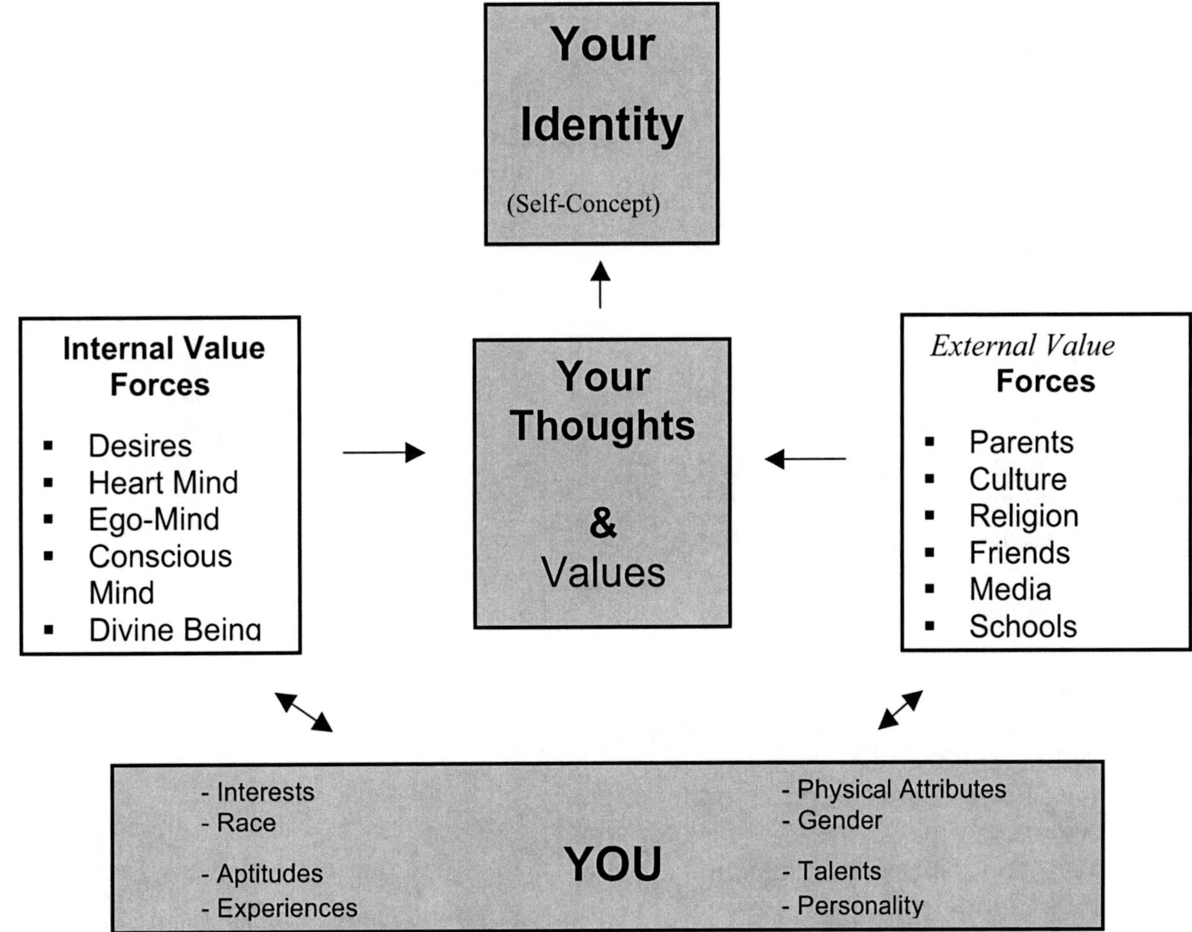

Your values determine all the decisions you make in your life. They will answer the following questions for you: Should I go to college? What major or career should I pursue? Who should I marry? Where should I live? What is moral? What kind of future do I want? Yet, if you are unclear about what you want out of life, you may not get what you want.

The first step is knowing what your values are. Below are a variety of values that are subcategorized for your understanding. Global Values relate toward how your values affect the larger society/world.

Circle up to six bullets under each title that relate to your highest values.

PERSONAL VALUES	**GLOBAL VALUES**
▪ Being a good parent ▪ Education ▪ Music or Art ▪ Sports ▪ Quiet time ▪ Health/nutrition ▪ Honesty ▪ Being positive ▪ Doing God's work ▪ Wisdom ▪ Exercise ▪ Leisure ▪ Other	▪ Volunteering ▪ Right to choose ▪ Giving to Charity ▪ Educating children ▪ Justice for others ▪ Compassion ▪ Good Citizenship ▪ Saving rainforests ▪ Ending Racism ▪ Other
Work Values ▪ Help others/society ▪ Money or material gain ▪ Work with others (teamwork) ▪ Work alone ▪ Make decisions ▪ Manage/Control Others ▪ Leadership: Influencing people ▪ Seek knowledge ▪ Create something (art, new programs) ▪ Variety and change ▪ Be secure and stable ▪ Fast-paced environment ▪ Gain recognition and status ▪ Feel excitement and have fun ▪ Be independent/Free time ▪ Be in right location (close to family) ▪ Control your own time ▪ Being honest, ethical, and moral ▪ Challenge ▪ Promoting fairness and justice ▪ Advancement	**Cultural/American Values** ▪ Competition ▪ Prestige ▪ Punctuality ▪ Job status ▪ Money ▪ Appearances ▪ Financial advancement ▪ Suppression of anger ▪ Independence ▪ The sensational ▪ Youth ▪ Self-reliance ▪ Hollywood

Internal Value Forces

The next step is understanding where your values came from. The Internal influences that help shape our values include the Heart, Ego, Divine Being (if you believe in one), and our thoughts.

Heart values are championed in many of the major religions. The list below contains many of these heart values. The heart can be accessed through meditation, prayer, journal writing, being in nature, or any inner ritual that helps you go to that deepest place inside you where you can receive insight to make important decisions. You do not have to be religious to access the heart. The heart is discussed in detail in the next chapter. Also, see the Heart-Ego Model on page 94.

Ego values are selfish in nature, relying on something external to be motivated and satisfied. We either consciously or subconsciously choose one of the two mindsets (heart or ego) that create thoughts and pieces of logic in our mind that drive our values and behavior.

People who are religious often believe in a **Divine Being**; something more powerful and good than they are. Some people call this nonphysical being one's Higher Power, God or Gods, the Life Force, the Great Spirit, etc. These people believe that their values are affected and their behavior is influenced by this Divine Being. Many people with strong addictions and diseases have been cured and brought back to health; they believe they could not have done it without this Divine Being. This therapy has the highest success rate of any other therapy in psychology. When discussing values, it is important to construct your own belief system in this area. Does your portrait of a God come from your own thoughts and study or did it come from your parental and religious upbringing? If it did come from your upbringing, is there anything about it that you would change? People often say when they get in touch with their "heart values" their personal, global, and work values become known.

Our thoughts also have a huge impact on our value system. Deep thought is vital in forming values for yourself. It will ensure that your values are based on logic, reason, and good common sense. Critical thinking is the basis of our educational system. Critical thinking will help you to think about issues more clearly and with a more in-depth analysis as opposed to oversimplifying things.

External Value Forces

The External influences that shape our values are our parents, culture, religion, friends, media, and schools. Values are transmitted through language, custom, religion, and tradition. Parents usually have the greatest influence on our development and our values. While it is important to learn from the above influences that have shaped your life, it is also necessary that you determine your own values while taking the good from the bad, the healthy from the unhealthy, and live in a manner that is consistent with them. For example, you may have grown up with the cultural value of giving your whole life to your parents' family business. However, your value system could incorporate going to college as well as working for the family business until you enter your own field of choice. If you also accept without thought the values that were handed down to you, you will likely end up going through life like a programmed robot, the programming coming from outside you, not within you.

How To Choose Empowering Values

Knowing your values is not enough. It is crucial to act consistently with your values and follow them. Values are what you do, not what you say. Also, you must make your values congruent with your goals. For example, if you value your health, but you smoke and live in a very smoggy city, you would probably be unhappy and feel like you say one thing but do another. When your values are incongruent, it feels like trying to drive a car with your foot on the brake. There are bad values as well as good ones. You may value getting approval from others, yet the detriment to your integrity and self-esteem becomes damaged because you will sacrifice your own needs to conform to the whim's of others. Developing your own value system instead of blindly accepting others will empower you like nothing else. To assist you in making good value decisions, learn to ask the six critical questions: who, what, where, when, how, and why. See the questions below for good examples. Be a good listener by being open to all the facts. Also, trust that your ability to cultivate your own value on an issue will be found after the searching process. Evaluate the pros and cons of various choices and positions. You may be asking yourself, "Is values clarification a purely selfish and amoral approach to make our selves happy and to hell with everyone else?" On the contrary, I believe that the needs and rights of others should always be a part of the values clarification process. To help, ask these questions when defining your values:

- What effect will this choice have on others around me?
- What is right or wrong, as I understand it?
- What is the ethical thing to do?
- If everyone followed my example, what kind of world would this become?

To develop your own values, use the following advice:

- Spend frequent time alone in reflective thought or journal writing about personal and social issues.
- Adopt an open attitude toward those whose value systems differ from yours and develop a willingness to test your own values.
- Use significant contacts with others who are willing to challenge your values and beliefs and
  the degree to which you live by them.
- Consider what meaning the fact of your eventual death has for you in the present timeframe.

When you finally have chosen a value in a specific area, it is suggested that you perform the following:

- cherish it,
- publicly affirm it when appropriate,
- ask how it might change other beliefs and values that you hold,
- be open to changing it as new information comes in
- act on it with a pattern of consistency and repetition.

Questions to Ponder to Clarify Your Values:

- If you could make one thing come true for all humans on the planet, what would it be?
- If you could have God's existence personally proved to you in one way, what would it be?
- If you were to go on a mission for any humanitarian or religious cause, what would it be?
- If you were to name what you think humankind's most positive and negative characteristics are, what would they be?
- If you spent 15 minutes a day just "thinking" to become stronger, which thoughts are best?
- If you were to articulate the most important thing missing from your life now, what is it?
- If you had to name the thing you are most curious about in another religion, what would it be?

Developing Your Own Definition of Success

There is no one way to define success. Webster's Dictionary defines it as, "a favorable or prosperous termination of attempts or endeavors. Some people define it as fortune, fame, winning awards, popularity, a prestigious job, and so on. For this author, success is a lifetime of learning, achievement, and fulfillment where others are helped not hurt. One could define success as getting pleasure anyway possible, even if it hurts others. So be careful in thinking about the consequences of your values. So, what is your definition of success? See Exercise 2.

Developing Your Own Theory on Human Nature and the Causes of Behavior

Have you ever asked yourself why you felt so strongly about a social issue you were voting for? Or why you believe your style of parenting (whether you are or not a parent) is best? Or why so many experts can believe and propose differing solutions to the same social issue? All social issues are rooted in human behavior. There are widely differing views on such social issues as capital punishment, abortion, gun control, teen pregnancy, education reform, corporate pollution, drug tests, a national health care plan, affirmative action, and same-sex couples parenting children. There are differing views because each individual has differing values and a different theory on the causes of human personality, human nature, and human behavior. If you are unclear about the causes of human behavior/nature such as, how to best help others to grow, then you are likely to be undecided and ambivalent about social issues you vote on, how people should parent children, and how one should conduct oneself. Many people are clearly ambivalent; others are clearly ignorant. In other words, they have not taken the time to think deeply about why humans behave the way they do. Why is this topic important? Your stance on human nature and how to best influence behavior forms the root thoughts that branch out into the stances you will take on social issues like how to parent and how one should live one's life. Consider the following example:

- Let's say you heard that a 30-year-old man was convicted of robbing a bank. You also discovered that he comes from poverty in the inner city and had an abusive parent. If you were on the jury, would you give the convicted man a lighter sentence because of his background? Or, would you believe that people need to be responsible for their decisions when they are adults and pay the penalty that is associated with that crime? If you believe human nature is basically good and that our environment has one of the biggest influences on human behavior, then you might be more sympathetic and give him a lighter sentence. If you believe that human nature is basically selfish and that one's values play a heavier role in influencing human behavior than environment, then you would probably give him the full sentence. Thus, the root theory you have on human nature (good or selfish, environmental or value-driven) will determine your stance on a social issue. It will also likely determine if you are on the political left or right. The left believes people are basically good and that one's environment shapes behavior most. The right believes people are basically selfish and one's value system determines conduct and will shape behavior most. This is why people on the left are usually against capital punishment (since the accused are good, they deserve a second chance to change) and people on the right are for capital punishment. Is our human nature good, bad, selfish, ungrateful, lazy, violent, and/or addictive? And if so, how can we best rise above our human nature to lead desirable lives? It is the hope of the author that this book will help you to accomplish that.

Words of Wisdom

You alone judge how you interpret the past, value the present, and shape the future.

Exercise 1

1. What are the three things you consider to be the most valuable and important in your life? (things you would fight for, stand up for, sacrifice for, etc.)

2. How would you spend your money if you won $10,000,000?

3. How would you spend your time if you learned you only had six months to live?

4. What have you always wanted to do but have been afraid to attempt?

5. What types of activities and what sort of circumstances give you your greatest feeling of importance, self-worth, and make you feel good about yourself?

6. If you received one wish, what would you want to accomplish if you knew you could not fail?

7. What books, magazines, CD ROM's, subjects in school, or bumper stickers appeal to you?

8. What qualities of character do you most admire in others?

9. Do your values match what you would like to do?

10. What is something you really want to learn before you die?

11. If you had unlimited funds, what charities or causes would you contribute to?

12. A problem in society that really concerns me is....

Exercise 2

A. By noting the list of values in the grid on the previous pages, write down your five Top Personal Values, Global or Cultural Values, Cultural, and Work Values that you hold and why you hold them. Write down one behavior that you do that conflicts with one value in each of the three areas. Example: If under your Personal Value, you value quiet time, one conflict might be the crowding of your schedule with daily activities that don't allow you to schedule some quiet time in your day.

Personal Values

Global or Cultural Values

Work Values

B. What words come to mind when you think of success? Write your definition of success below.

Describe two people you know who have achieved success the way you define it.

Exercise 3

Jot down a cultural or religious value, a family value, a societal value, and a personal value that you grew up with that you feel are responsible for ***preventing you*** from growing emotionally and psychologically. Give specific examples. Examples include:

- Cultural/Religious value: to stay in San Diego and work for the family business
- Family value: declare a law or medicine major to be a doctor or a lawyer
- Societal value: to get the highest paying job regardless of job fulfillment
- Personal value: I must get an 'A' grade on my test

For each of the four values, write down:
a) describe what the value is
b) a consequence of holding onto that value.
c) a benefit of that same value
d) your new value (how you might change or adjust the value to make it more appealing to you)
e) the consequence of your new value
f) the benefit of your new value
Remember to choose values below that are preventing you from growing. Then choose d) your value that would allow you to grow more progressively.

For example:
a) Personal Value: You need to be liked by everyone in order to feel worthy and happy.
b) Consequence: I'll get a lot of friends who want to manipulate me. My happiness is dependent upon others.
c) Benefit: I have a lot of friends.
d) Your new value: I want to be liked but I don't need to be. I will not change myself to suit others.
e) Consequence: Not everyone will show as much friendliness toward me.
f) Benefit: Less energy will go to adjusting my behavior to fit others approval and more energy will go to the people I care about most.

a) Cultural/Religious____

____

b)____

____

c) ____

____

d) ____

____

e) ____

____

f) ____

____

a) Family Value____

____

b)____

c) ____

d) ____

e) ____

f) ____

a) Societal Value________________________________

b)____

c) ____

d) ____

e) ____

f) ____

a) Personal Value________________________________

b)____

c) ____

d) ____

e) ____

f) ____

Strategy 1.3

Examine the messages, careers, birth order, beliefs, fears, traditions, and talents you acquired from your family and cultural background to get a clearer sense of who you are and where you come from.

Give me a child for the first seven years and you may do what you like with him afterwards.
Jesuit saying

The Tribal Family

No one begins life as a conscious individual with an identity; instead, we begin life as part of a tribe (family) connected to the societal culture, absorbing its strengths, weaknesses, beliefs, superstitions, and fears. Through our interactions with family and other groups, we learn the benefits of sharing a belief with other people as well as the painful, alienating consequences of being excluded from a group if we don't take on its belief systems. Thousands of years ago, tribal or group thinking was sacred because its purpose was to protect and bond a community from perceived outside catastrophes. Going against the group was perceived as lowering the strength of the group. What belief systems did you acquire from your family and culture?

Family Birth Order Patterns

We receive hundreds of messages about ourselves from our parents in our childhood and adolescent years. The messages often depend upon your birth order and/or cultural background. Were you the oldest, middle, or youngest child in your family? Or, were you an only child? The psychologist Alfred Adler was one of the first to introduce this birth order concept to modern psychology. Though the validity studies on birth order psychology and its effects on personality and social relationships are mixed (it is not an exact science), you may find typical patterns for each category that relates to you and your family. The implications for parents are important. The parent who says to the middle child, "why can't you be more like your older brother?" exacerbates the middle child's problem, which is to distinguish himself from his brother and carve his own identity. The following are characteristics that fit each birth order category.

OLDEST: Whatever the family hopes and expectations, the oldest has the pressure to fulfill them. The first child "had the stage" to himself/herself for a while. These children received the attention of their parents who were convinced they were the cleverest in the world when they said "Mama." Because of all the fuss, the first child is likely to have a persistent feeling of importance. However, they feel a lot of pressure and responsibility because parents fretted about each setback and pounced on every infraction. Hence, the child ended up worrying about whether they lived up to their parent's standards. They were encouraged to set a good example as well as help with the care of younger children. This teaching assists them to be natural leaders later on. They sometimes are so preoccupied with being good and doing things right that they forget how to enjoy life. The first borns specialize in defending the status quo while later borns specialize in toppling the status quo. Examples of oldest children include Bill and Hillary Clinton, J.K. Rowling, George W. Bush, Bill Cosby, Clint Eastwood, Steven Spielberg, Bruce Springsteen, Meryl Streep, and Bruce Willis. They are often ambitious, responsible, dominating, and sometimes vengeful. Culture also plays a part in birth order and gender roles. For example, in the Mexican culture, the oldest male is often expected to carry on the family responsibilities or be in charge of the family business. Firstborns from disrupted families and minority groups tend to wind up more like laterborns. Oprah Winfrey fits the mold—a rebellious teen, a social liberal, and an empathetic individual.

MIDDLE: Because they follow the oldest and the youngest follow them, middle children often end up being confused about their identity and have a hard time developing distinctive traits. They are forced to compete for attention with the older sibling. Since they have neither the rights of the oldest child nor the favors of the youngest, they often feel that life is unfair. They are sensitive to being left out or slighted. They are less capable of taking the initiative or thinking independently. In a crisis where the oldest would go home to get support, the middle child would often say, "That's the last place I'd go. I love my family, but I get my support from my friends." Whether they are the second, third, or later, they have the family's most ambiguous position. They can have a well-developed sense of empathy because they know what it is like to be the younger and older. Therefore, they become peacemakers and mediators. Or, they may become competitive; always assuming they'll have to fight to get their rightful "piece of the pie." Examples include: Jennifer Lopez, Miley Cyrus, Julia Roberts, Charles Darwin, Tom Selleck, Cyndi Lauper, Howard Stern, Madonna, Bill Gates, Malcolm X, Martin Luther King, Gloria Steinem and Jack Kevorkian. Clowning can attract attention from parents in a crowded family; wit becomes a great weapon against older siblings. Thus, Jay Leno, David Letterman, and Conan O'Brien are also middle or later borns. They can become social reformers, crusaders, or become open to radical new ideas as Bill Gates did in the computer industry. Science historian Frank Sulloway in his book "Born to Rebel" compiled biographical data on 6,566 people and found that middle children were 18 times more likely to take up left-wing, liberal causes than to get involved with conservative ones. Not surprisingly, Mahatma Gandhi, Martin Luther King Jr., Fidel Castro, Yasir Arafat, and Ho Chi Minh fit this type. Rush Limbaugh, George Wallace and Newt Gingrich are all firstborns. Second-born children often compete with the "can't do anything wrong oldest." They will seek some other way to be unique. If the first is known for getting good grades, the second needs to be known for something. And if they can't find it through their efforts, they may turn to mischief and become more rebellious by becoming good at being bad.

YOUNGEST: The youngest child, who doesn't have to worry about a younger sibling gaining from behind, usually grows up easygoing and carefree. They often have a well-developed sense of humor, show off, or become the "clown" in the family. They can play the victim role to their parents by referring to their older siblings being more powerful than they. Therefore, they depend on charm and manipulation to "get their way." The same parents who pressured the first child to be a "big boy" or "big girl" often want to prolong the babyhood of their last, so they may encourage him/her to be dependent and cute. When he/she does grow up, the youngest often harbors resentment when they don't get the respect that they believe they deserve. Youngest girls often are spontaneous, cheerful, playful, and adventurous. Yet, they can be messy and bratty. They feel closest to their mother. They usually have trouble making decisions while having an attitude of "wanting it all." Examples include: Jim Carrey Jay-Z, Cameron Diaz, Elizabeth Dole, Geraldine Ferraro, and Mary Lou Retton. The youngest boy is usually daring, headstrong, rebellious, and a less significant one of the boys. They are often compared unfavorably to older brothers and expected to be like them. They are often the comedians in the family-- Eddie Murphy, Billy Crystal, and Ronald Reagan.

ONLY CHILD: Because they grow up with the parents' undivided attention, an only child is often self-assured, secure, and self-reliant. However, because they didn't have to experience negotiating, empathizing, competing, and cooperating with other siblings, they are less relaxed with their peers and may only have two or three close friends. They tend to be less playful than others. They take on the characteristics of the "over-achieving oldest" and the "pampered youngest." Since they had to depend on themselves for play, they are excellent at using their imagination in fantasy play and finding ways to entertain themselves. They have highly developed verbal skills and act like miniature adults often to the delight of parents who think they are being cute as well as "good." Examples include Tiger Woods, Rudi Guiliani, Condoleeza Rice, Elvis Presley, Ted Koppel, Nancy Reagan, Brooke Shields, Frank Sinatra, and Danielle Steel.

Birth Order Considerations

Factors affecting birth order psychology include the sex of the child, the number of years between the births of siblings, and the sex of the siblings. With regard to sex of the child, boys and girls are socialized differently. If a parent doesn't believe girls should be competitive and scholarly because they are "going to become full-time mothers anyway," the older girl will less likely be the achiever type. With regard to number of years between the births of siblings, the smaller the age difference between siblings, the more influence they usually have on each other. The middle child who is closer in age to the oldest child usually develops more youngest child characteristics. If there are more than five or six years between siblings, each will have many of the characteristics of an only child. With regard to sex of the siblings, there is usually more jealousy between two brothers than between a brother and a sister. One study of 25 highly successful business women found that all were either oldest or only children and none had brothers.

Exercise 1

Complete the family history chart below. Put the name of the person on the line first. Then in the next parenthesis, write one word that describes that person's personality. Then write the occupation or avocation of that person. An avocation is a minor career or a hobby. For example, you could write social service for a homemaker who often volunteers time in a hospital. Also write in any stepparents that affected your life. If you are unsure about some of this information, get answers from relatives or other family members who can provide you with more information about your family background.

Maternal (Mother's Side of Family) **Paternal** (Father's Side of Family)

	Maternal			Paternal		
Sample	Hilda	(Outgoing)	(Homemaker)	Victor	(Reserved)	(Accountant)
Grandparents	______	( )	( )	______	( )	( )
	______	( )	( )	______	( )	( )
Aunts and	______	( )	( )	______	( )	( )
	______	( )	( )	______	( )	( )
Uncles	______	( )	( )	______	( )	( )
	______	( )	( )	______	( )	( )
Cousins	______	( )	( )	______	( )	( )
	______	( )	( )	______	( )	( )
Parents or	______	( )	( )	______	( )	( )
Step parents	______	( )	( )	______	( )	( )
You/	______	( )	( )	______	( )	( )

Siblings ________( )( ) ________( )( )

________( )( ) ________( )( )

________( )( ) ________( )( )

Exercise 2

Write below what family patterns, from exercise one, emerged in both the personality and occupational areas. For example, in the occupational area, do you come from a family of teachers, comedians, or mechanics? In the personality area, was there physical abuse or alcohol/drug abuse in your family lineage? Were there strong family values? Dig a little deeper. Was there a pattern of mental illness in the family? What common health problems do you notice in your relatives? What talents were inherited?

Then write how these forces impacted you through the years and what effect it had on your identity.

Emerging Occupational Patterns: ________

____

____

Emerging Personality Patterns: ________

____

____

The Family Values: ________

____

____

Health Problems: ________

____

____

Talents: ________

____

____

Impact on You: ________

____

____

Exercise 3

1. What belief patterns did you inherit from your family?

____

____

2. Which of those belief patterns that still have authority in your thinking can you acknowledge are no longer valid?

3. What roles, behavior, and attitudes in your family were reinforced for males? Females?

Males: Example: don't ask for help, be ambitious, etc.

Females: Example: marry well, take care of others, etc.

4. Do you have any unfinished business with your family members? If so, list the reasons that prevent you from healing your family relationships.

5. List all the blessings or positive experiences that you feel came from your family.

6. If you are now raising a family of your own, list the qualities that you would like your children to learn from you.

7. Is there anyone in your life today who can get you stirred up like your most difficult sibling? How?

8. What is your birth order? How did your parents handle your relationship with your siblings?

9. How did the gender of your other siblings impact your life? What comparisons were made by your parents between you and your siblings?

____

____

____

10. How has birth order impacted your life? Did your parents have favorites or show favoritism?

____

____

____

11. How important was your sibling relationship in terms of defining your own identity? How do you think you would be different if you had a different sibling position?

____

____

____

Exercise 1.4

Identify both your own internal and external sources of motivation and your needs to spur understanding of yourself/identity and behavior.

Definition of Motivation: the internal state of desires, needs, and fears that drives the individual to act. Its purpose is to relieve a state of tension that causes one to feel unsafe, imbalanced, or insecure.

Motivated by Defined Goals

What is the difference between a college student who dreads going to class and is close to dropping out and a student who looks forward to class and is driven to graduate despite any obstacles that may arise? The answer is motivation. But why are some students motivated and others not? As a college counselor, everyday I encounter students who are either undecided about their major/career or know exactly what major/career they are pursuing. If there were a scale to measure motivation, students who were clear on their choice of major would, if I were to estimate, measure between 70 to 100 on a 100-point scale. The students who are undecided almost always measure somewhere between 0 – 70. Their nonverbal cues tell the story. The undecided students have a hunched posture, show little to no emotion, have a monotone voice, and are on the verge of dropping out of college to go back to work full-time. The students with declared majors/careers usually have a smile, show enthusiasm, want to know other support classes/resources they can utilize that are related to their major, and are driven to stay in college until their degree is awarded. There is probably no better motivator than that of having a clear defined goal.

The ability to identify what motivates you to perform and to achieve is perhaps one of the most important pieces of knowledge in helping you to achieve your goals and attain success in life. There is a big difference between doing things we want to do as opposed to doing things we have to do. For example, many young college students often look at learning as a "have to" in order to advance their lives. When those same students drop out and return to college 10 or 20 years later, their motivation changes to a "want to" learn instead of a "jumping through the hoops" mentality. They have a "how can I relate this to my major" mentality. Their performance usually dramatically increases via a higher grade point average.

Internal and External Sources of Motivation

All motivation comes from either of two sources--internal or external. As you read about each one, ask yourself if you could use a few of these to help motivate you toward your next goal and substitute a more productive motivational source for the one you've been using. Remember, external sources are also valid ways to motivate you. It is important to state that one's motivation can be used for either destructive or constructive purposes. Motivation is not necessarily good in and of itself. On the next page, there are the TOP 25 Sources of Motivation.

Internal or Growth Sources of Motivation: this motivation to act comes from one's desire for learning, inner growth, or inner change. If a golfer lost a golf match but played one of his best games, his motivation would continue to be strong. If it were based on external factors such as recognition or money, his motivation and desire would diminish. Internal motivation can also be fear-driven but channeled to a positive outcome. The founding fathers of this country were driven out of fear of a repressive governmental system and created, out of their desire for growth and change, one of the best living document's ever written—the Constitution.

Internal Motivational Sources	Definition
1. Self-Actualization	Will act to fulfill their potential by moving in the direction of inner growth and good health.
2. Challenge	Will act to take joy in overcoming obstacles and testing strength. It keeps life interesting as opposed to becoming boring.
3. Competence	Will act to become highly satisfied when their skills are mastered and they excel in an area of competence. Occurs after a period of time and effort.
4. Self-Knowledge	Will act in order to find fulfillment from diving deeper into self-understanding and knowledge.
5. Enthusiasm for Learning	Will act in order to find enjoyment which occurs when learning fulfills a broader mission or goal they possess.
6. Desire to Help Others	Will act to feel good about contributing to individuals and/or to society as a whole.
7. Need for Self-Improvement	Will act to thrive in several areas of their life.
8. Identity	Will act to empower their purpose in life and become clear on who they are. Previous social roles or lack of cultural awareness may have prevented one from obtaining a clear identity.
9. Independence	Many people who have been too dependent upon someone will act to take charge and feel more in control of their lives.

External or Scarcity Sources of Motivation: this motivation to act is dependent upon a desired external result that will cause some type of pleasure or fulfillment. The desire to act often comes from a position of scarcity, either to avoid pain, experience pleasure, or in response to a fear. To act is not a guarantee that one will act for good purposes.

External Motivation Source	Definition
9. Fear	Will act to prevent the one thing they fear the most from happening. The fear could be a loss in employment, a divorce, being single, getting a bad grade, etc.
10. Pain or Pleasure	Will act to reduce any pain and/or increase pleasure in their lives. They may often see academic success as a means to reduce pain later on.
11. Approval	Will act to gain approval from others in order to feel stroked. Estimates that their own approval is not enough.
12. Unhappiness	Will act to obtain happiness in order not to feel the pain of unhappiness.
13. Materialism	Will act to gain material goods which are estimated to increase pleasure and happiness.
14. Failure of Others	Will act to avoid similar disappointments that they see others experiencing.
15. Proving Oneself	Will act to prove themselves to others. Often occurs when somebody "puts them down" by telling them they "don't have what it takes."

16. A Reward	They come in many forms both internal and external. Examples of external include: money, prestige, approval of others, etc. Internal rewards include: learning a new skill, the joy of a challenge, the love of ideas, etc.
17. Overcoming Inferiority	Will act to avoid the pain of feeling unworthy or less than.
18. Anxiety	Will act to relieve the uncomfortable feelings of stress. May want to achieve something so as not to feel like time is "running out."
19. Independence	Many people who have been too dependent upon someone will act in order to take charge and feel more in control of their lives.
20. To Fill an Empty Void	Will act to prevent feeling an inner emptiness. The unhealthy way to achieve this is fill it with food, alcohol, or drugs. The healthy way would be to fill it with supportive people, self-knowledge, and love of self.
21. To be Successful Like Others	Will act to feel respected and valued by others.
22. Recognition	Will act to feel important/validated by others.
23. Love	Will act from a place of feeling hollow and may go to healthy or unhealthy means to obtain this love.
24. Insecurity	Will act out of fear of losing security. The act may be harmful or helpful depending on the response.
25. Power	Will act to prevent feeling powerlessness. One may want to have power and control over others as well as to direct the course of one's own life.

Exaine Maslow's Hierarchy of Needs in the illustration on the next page. Humanistic psychologist Abraham Maslow theorized that we are motivated to adopt certain values to fulfill both psychological and physical needs. See the graphic below. Values will be covered in the next section.

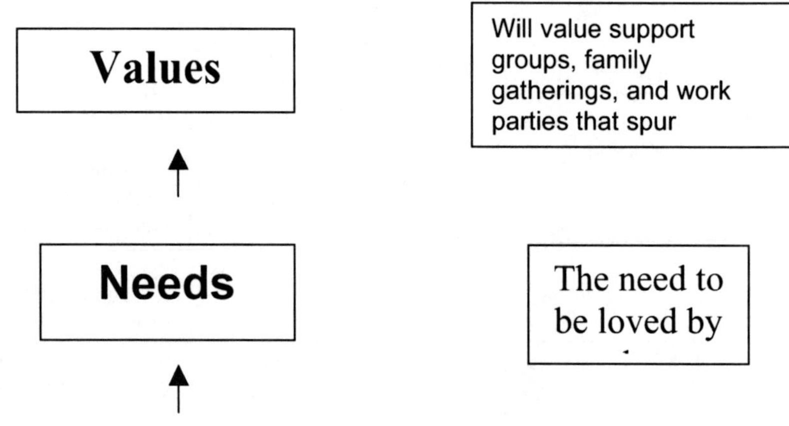

- Interests
- Aptitudes
- Experiences
- Fears

YOU

- Physical Attributes/Race
- Talents
- Personality
- Sex/Gender

He illustrated these needs and values in terms of a pyramid in which needs are organized in a hierarchy arranged from the most basic (bottom of pyramid) to the most complex (top of the pyramid). *The main idea is that you cannot rise to the next level of need until the lower level need is met first.* You can't skip levels. *In other words, when a person satisfies a level of need, this satisfaction automatically activates needs at the next level up.* For example, many missionaries go to other countries to spread their religion to people in poverty. Often they are turned down because the impoverished people have not had their lower needs met yet. The missionaries fail because these people are starving (biological need), and don't have a roof over their head (safety need). Once they have these needs met, then they can start to consider whether they want God in their lives or not. Or, if you have a great musical talent but must work as an accountant, your need for self-actualization will be prevented. *This is because you cannot skip from the safety level up to the self-actualization level.* You must fulfill your love needs first before moving to esteem and self-actualization needs. Notice the Top 25 sources of motivation on the previous page stem from the love needs on up because their physiological and safety needs have already been met. Self-actualizers have the need to fulfill their potential and to personally grow. They possess the following characteristics: they can tolerate uncertainty and criticism while caring for self and others, are inner directed as opposed to living by others' expectations, have a strong knowledge of right and wrong, experience times of being at one with the universe, have need for privacy and have a few deep intense relationships, strive for self-expression/creativity, can laugh at themselves and the human condition with good sense of humor. *If a need is in danger of not being met over a period of time, fears arise and often control one's behavior in a unhealthy way.*

Maslow's Hierarchy Of Needs

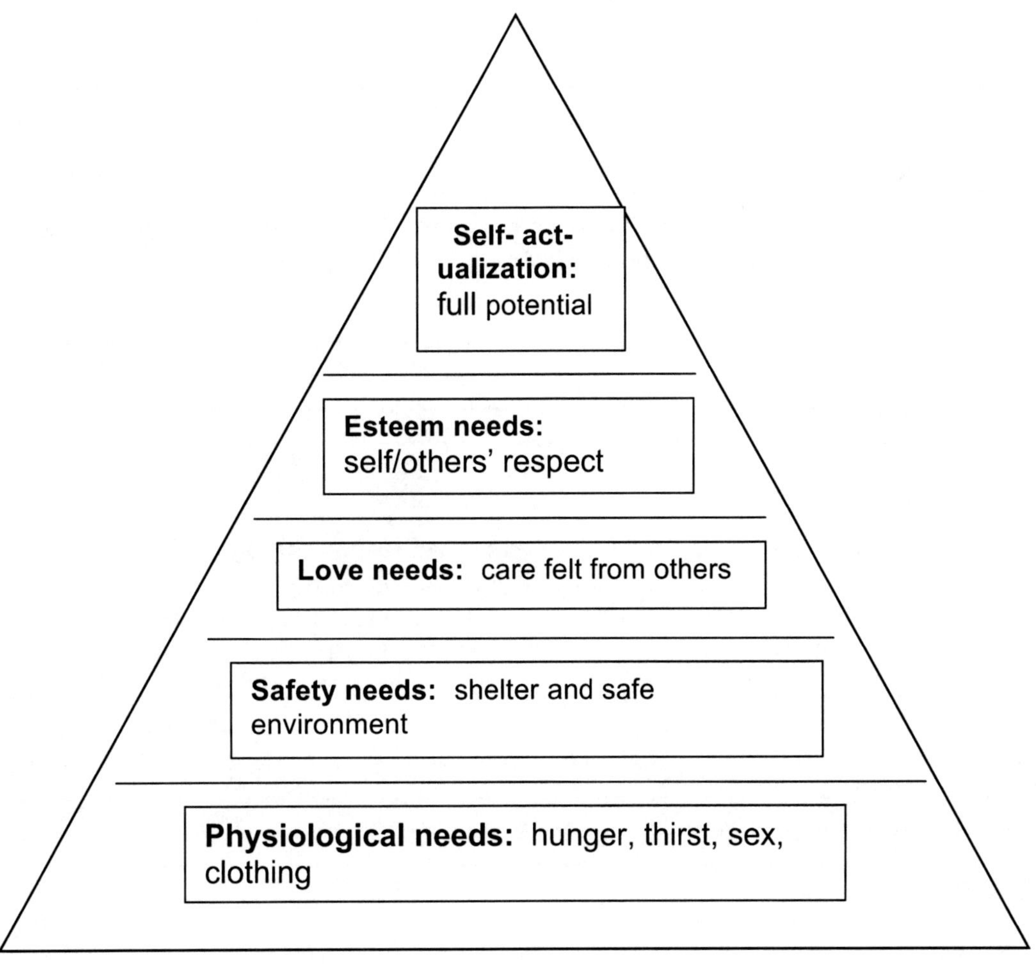

Take Personal Responsibility

It is often said that many people in today's generation feel entitled to get what they want in life and not have to work hard to get it. It is the philosophy that somebody or society owes one a job, a college degree, a retirement plan, etc., without much effort. The power of hard work and earning what you achieved builds character, self-esteem, and personal pride as opposed to it being handed to you easily. Most successful people from any profession will tell you they worked hard to become great at what they do. They are the Victors in life because they conquered their own human nature of laziness, selfishness, and excuse making to become a success. The opposite person is a victim. Victims blame others for what they don't have and often quit their goals. Most students who obtain a college degree hold the values of Victors. Most students who drop out hold the values of Victims. Taking responsibility for your future will turbo-charge your motivation to act toward any goal you desire. See Strategy 6.4 for more information. Complete the grid in Exercise 3

Exercise 1

Identify where you are on Maslow's Hierarchy at this time in your life. For example, if Sue was finally fulfilling her safety needs (her job was secure enough to pay for rent/house), and she could finally start to fulfill her love needs, then she would be at the Love need level. Using this example, remember Sue would not be able to skip to the Esteem level need because according to the theory, one can only move to the next level above the one they just fulfilled. Thus, Sue must feel love and a sense of belongingness from others before she would be able to feel significant levels of self-esteem and self-respect. After identifying the level you are at, write below how you intend to fulfill the next level of need on the hierarchy.

____

____

____

____

Exercise 2

Write below a goal you want to pursue in the next year. Then, identify two internal sources of motivation you could adopt to help you to stay motivated as you pursue this goal and write how you plan to implement it.

____

____

____

____

Exercise 3

A. Identify five external sources of motivation you have used in the past. Then substitute healthier internal or external sources for any of your current sources that may be unhealthy. Then write how you will implement this. For example, Joe substituted getting approval and support from others instead of the motivational source of filling an empty void using alcohol.

____

____

____

____

____

____

____

B. Complete the blanks in the rows below to better understand Victims and Victors.

Victim Talk	Victory Talk
VICTIMS, LIKE PESSIMISTS, BELIEVE THEIR RESULTS IN LIFE ARE BEYOND THEIR CONTROL AND DETERMINED BY LUCK OR BY OTHERS. THEIR LANGUAGE IS CHARACTERIZED BY MAKING EXCUSES, BLAMING, COMPLAINING, FEELING OBLIGATED, AND THEY OFTEN QUIT THINGS. THEY SEE THEMSELVES AS PAWNS IN THE CHESS GAME OF LIFE. ***FILL IN THE BLANKS***	*VICTORS, LIKE OPTIMISTS, BELIEVE THEIR RESULTS IN LIFE ARE MOSTLY DUE TO THEIR OWN CHOICES THEY'VE MADE AS A RESULT. THEIR LANGUAGE IS CHARACTERIZED BY OWNERSHIP, BEING ACCOUNTABLE, AND MAKING A PLAN OF ACTION. THEY SEE THEMSELVES AS THE CHESSMASTERS WHO CREATE THEIR OWN LIFE.* ***FILL IN THE BLANKS***
This professor is boring; I want to drop the class.	Since this professor is boring, I'll tape-record his lectures so I can listen to them a little at a time.
This professor gave me an F grade on the last test.	I got an F on the test because I didn't study enough. I'm going to study 8-11pm Monday through Friday.
I try to study but my kids are too noisy.	I'll study in the library after class and tell my kids not to come into my room until 5pm.
It's not my fault I am late.	I was late because I didn't wake up early enough. I'm going to set my alarm 20 minutes early from now on.
I can't pass math. I barely passed in high school because the teachers were lousy.	I'll find out who the good professors are and use the tutoring lab twice a week.
I'll probably have to drop out mid-semester because I don't have the money to pay for books next time.	I'll see if I can get grants and loans from financial aid. I'll also look into scholarships and see if I can work a few more hours. I'll cut down on my fast food costs.
I'm too busy to go to school. I have to juggle work, college, kids, bills, and taking care of my parents.	I'll get the kids to do more chores, take one less course, and ask my brothers and sisters to help with caring for my parents.
I'm easily distracted and socialize too much.	I will start to say "no" to invitations to socialize when I have to study.
I couldn't get to class on time because my last teacher kept us late.	
I would have called you but my daughter got sick.	
I couldn't come to your party like I said I would because my English teacher made me take a makeup test.	
I couldn't get the assignment because I was absent.	
You just can't pass a class when it's that hard.	
I cram for tests and study long hours.	
I hate being overweight.	
I didn't have time to do my homework.	
I lose concentration when I read. I hate reading.	
I procrastinate when I'm overwhelmed.	
	I use creative note-taking skills to keep my focus in class.
	I narrowed by major choices to Art and Psychology
	I practice my stress busters before the all tests.

Strategy 1.5

Identify your personal interests and aptitudes to help you make smart career decisions.

When work is a pleasure, life is a joy! When work is a duty, life is slavery
Maxim Gorky

Methods for Increasing Job Skills

Studies predict that the average worker will have 14 jobs and five different careers in a lifetime. It will be important for you to learn how to access and acquire knowledge, learn a second language, adjust to the changing job market, learn the skill of teamwork, enhance communication skills, and learn transferable skills.

You can upgrade your current job by learning new skills that will make you more productive at work and increase your value to your employer. Ask yourself, "What skill, ability, or piece of knowledge could I commit to learning this next month?" It could be taking a computer or Internet course, joining "Toastmasters," enrolling in a writing, memory, sales, or marketing course. Other skills include increasing logical skills, public speaking skills, communication skills, writing skills, math skills, memory skills, problem solving skills, computer skills, comprehending systems, decision making, acquiring knowledge in certain subject areas, etc. If you don't stay ahead of change, you risk becoming obsolete in your skills and to your employer or your own business--and that means bankruptcy!!!

The Search for a New Career

In a survey, over 70% of people indicated they would change their job if they had enough money. And over 50% indicated they would choose a job where they were helping others. Are you sure you want to stay in the career/job you are in? Take the interest inventory on the following pages to see where you stand. For a more in-depth analysis, complete career and personality tests at your local community college counseling office to see which field you would best be suited for. Talk to experts, professors, and others to help you decide on a major. Realize that these are just some tools among many in helping you decide. Often, people are not happy in their job because their values are in conflict with the nature of their job. What are your life values and how do they match with your current job?

If you decide to pursue a different career field, see a community college counselor to find out which lower division and general education courses you would need to complete in order to obtain a degree in your chosen field. If you're nervous about going to college, know that you can have grades discounted in most colleges and you can repeat a course in which you received a D or F grade for a better grade. There are also resources such as financial aid, child care, book grants, free tutoring, and plenty of programs and support services at the college to make your college experience more affordable, convenient, and possible.

If you believe that going to college would be too inconvenient, consider "Distance Learning Programs" where you can attend courses at your home through the use of your computer. An excellent book exists called, "Distance Learning in Higher Education (2008). Evaluate these distance learning programs, making sure they are accredited by the U.S. Dept of Education and CORPA (Commission on Recognition of Post-secondary Accreditation).

Sometimes, working a home business part-time can suddenly turn into full-time. Be aware of overlooked costs: computer, fax machine, telephone bills, electricity, paper, binders, rubber bands, etc. If you want to work for someone else, find a company that truly values employees by researching them in the library and making your own list of acceptance criteria. They do exist.

Exercise 1

To gain a better understanding of your career interests, put an X next to the statements below that relate to your personality type and interests. Total the X's under each type and write the number on the total line.

Creator Types

____Like to be different and strive to stand out from the crowd
____Are creative, expressive, original, intuitive, and individualistic
____Like creating artwork: music, painting, photography, acting, writing, dancing, decorating etc.
____Read magazines about art, music, drama or writing
____Tend to be uninhibited and nonconforming in dress, speech, and prefer to work without supervision.
____Find it difficult to function well in highly ordered, systematic situations.
____Place great value on beauty and aesthetic qualities Want attention and praise but are sensitive to criticism
____Are impulsive with their choices and in outlook
____Tend to be emotional and complicated

________Total

Investigator Types

____Not typically expressive emotionally and may not be considered friendly
____Tend to be reserved and have formal interpersonal relationships
____Interested in science, math, research environments, and getting an advanced degree
____Scholarly and scientific and tend to be pessimistic and critical about non-scientific explanations
____Explore new facts and theories and like to work alone
____Are original and creative often finding it difficult to accept traditional values and attitudes
____Are naturally curious and inquisitive
____Enjoy activities that require learning complex principles: sailing, scuba, chess
____Tend to lack leadership and persuasive skills
____Avoid highly structured, rule-oriented situations but well disciplined and precise

________Total

Relater Types

____Are friendly, enthusiastic, outgoing, and cooperative
____Like helping/facilitating roles like teacher, adviser, counselor, social services etc.
____Are understanding and insightful about others' feelings and problems
____Are considered to be kind, supportive, and caring
____Dislike working with machines, data, routine and repetitive tasks
____Like to deal with philosophical issues such as the purpose of life, religion, and morality
____Like problem solving, training, informing, and explaining in their occupation
____Have interest in improving the welfare of others

_____Like attention and enjoy being at or near the center of the group
_____Are idealistic, sensitive, and conscientious about life and dealing with others

_________Total

Operator Types

_____Tend to find it difficult to express their feelings and may be regarded as shy
_____Do not have strong interpersonal skills and are often uncomfortable with attention
_____Are attracted to outdoor, mechanical, physical activities, and occupations
_____Like to operate and use equipment to see tangible results
_____Like to read magazines about cars, airplanes, boats, or sports
_____Like to construct, restructure, and repair things around them
_____Think in absolutes, preferring not to deal with abstract or philosophical issues
_____Enjoy hunting, camping, fishing, or rock climbing
_____Like having a job where they can dress casually
_____Are industrious builders but seldom creative and innovative, preferring familiar methods

_________Total

Persuader Types

_____Are outgoing, self-confident, persuasive, and optimistic
_____Have interest in positions of leadership, power and status
_____Like to organize, direct, manage, and control the activities of groups
_____Are energetic and enthusiastic in initiating and supervising activities
_____Are adventurous, impulsive, assertive, and verbally persuasive
_____Dislike activities requiring scientific abilities and systematic and theoretical thinking
_____Avoid activities that require attention to detail and a set routine
_____Love attending conventions or working in a business or financial environment
_____Like to associate with well-known and influential people
_____Place a high value on status, power, money, and material possessions

_________Total

Organizer Types

_____Are well-organized, persistent, dependable, efficient, and practical
_____Excellent at keeping records, bookkeeping, and operating office machines
_____Like for things to go as planned and prefer not to change routines
_____Are status-conscious but usually do not aspire to high positions of leadership
_____Usually conform to expected standards and follow the lead of those in charge
_____Like to work indoors in pleasant environments and value material comforts
_____Enjoy work that is detailed and accurate like writing business reports or doing a financial analysis
_____Are self-controlled and low-key in expressing their feelings
_____Avoid intense personal relationships in favor of more casual ones
_____Tend to be conservative and traditional

_________Total

As you can see from your score, you are not just one personality type. In most people, one or two characteristics are dominant, two or three are of medium intensity, and one or two may be of low intensity. Write the totals under each type from highest to lowest on the side. Find one or two of your highest totals and correspond it to the interpretation to discover majors/careers that fit you.

Creator Types
Occupations: advertising executive, architect, commercial artist, interior decorator, medical illustrator, musician, photographer, public relations director, reporter, translator, acting/theater, creative writing, dance, fashion design/illustration, graphic arts, multimedia tech., stage design, corporate trainer, chef *Majors:* Dance, Music, Art, English, Culinary Arts, Graphic Design, Journalism, Fashion, Theater *Interests/Skills:* self/artistic-expression, art appreciation, composing, writing, creating visual art *Values:* beauty, imagination, originality, independence

Investigator Types
Occupations: biologist, chemist, veterinarian, science teacher, audiologist, college professor, computer programmer, systems analyst, dentist, doctor, geologist, mathematician, pharmacist, optometrist, psychologist, respiratory therapist, dietitian, pollution control and technology, chiropractor *Majors:* Biology, Chemistry, Physics, Mathematics, Medical Science, Computer Science, *Interests/Skills:* science, theories, ideas, data, lab work, math, writing, analysis, researching
Values: curiosity, learning, independence

Relater Types
Occupations: social worker, speech pathologist, athletic trainer, child care provider, teacher, counselor, minister, nurse, occupational therapist, parks and recreation coordinator, physical therapist, school administrator, probation officer, realtor, dental assistant, labor relations, dietician *Majors:* Psychology, Teacher Education, Social Science, Social Work, Health Sciences, Real Estate *Interests/Skills:* human welfare, community service, teaching, helping, listening, empathy *Values:* service to others, generosity, cooperation, teamwork, showing understanding,

Operator Types
Occupations: athletic trainer, auto mechanic, carpenter, electrician, emergency medical technician, engineer, military officer, police officer, radiologic technologist, photography, jewelry repair, optician, small business owner, plumber, groundskeeper, forester, farmer, cabinetmaker, building contractor *Majors:* Agriculture, Nature, Athletics, Engineering, Radiologic Technology, Criminal Justice *Interests/Skills:* the outdoors, machines, tools, physical coordination, building, repairing.
Values: tradition, practicality, common sense

Persuader Types
Occupations: banking and finance, engineer, business administration, travel agency management, marketing agent, salesman, lawyer, international relations, outdoor recreation, life insurance agent, realtor, buyer, store manager, restaurant manager, dental hygienist, flight attendant, florist *Majors:* Business, Political Science, Engineering, Law, Management, Public/Private Administration *Interests/Skills:* politics, leadership, influence, business, selling, persuading, motivate and direct others
Values: risk taking, status, competition, challenge, "moving up the ladder"

Organizer Types
Occupations: accountant, data processing, bookkeeping, building inspection, court reporter, library assistant, medical records technology, secretarial science, quality control technology, roofreader, banker, credit manager, food service manager, nursing home administrator, personnel clerk *Majors:* Office Information Systems, Administrative Assistant, Accounting, Data Management *Interests/Skills:* math, data analysis, record keeping, setting up procedures, attention to detail *Values:* accuracy, stability, efficiency, organization

Exercise 2

A. What abilities or aptitudes do you do well at? Circle the following. 1. *abstract reasoning* – can solve math, science, or physics problems in their head 2. *verbal reasoning* – excels at articulate speaking and how well you reason with concepts and words 3. *spatial relations* – excels in thinking in 3 dimensions and can mentally picture the position of objects 4. *numerical ability* – can reason with numbers quickly, solving math problems easily 5. *language ability* – excels at using language (English) such as grammar and punctuation 6 *clerical ability* – able to organize records, perceive small detail rapidly i.e. letters, symbols, numbers 7. *mechanical ability* – skilled with your hands, able to physically manipulate parts of a machine

B. Circle the skills you most enjoy using. explaining, being accurate, writing, reading, recording data, interviewing, operating equipment, building, being creative, repairing things, teaching, speaking, scheduling, helping others, entertaining, handling money, solving problems, taking risks, selling, negotiating, motivating, managing, counseling Write below with the help of a career counselor, which jobs utilize those skills. Put the most important items in the Mission Summary Box at the end of the chapter.

C. Write below with the help of a career counselor, the occupations that utilize these aptitudes. Put your top two aptitudes and occupations in the Mission Summary Box at the end of the chapter. Also use the websites shown on the first Self-Identity page. Especially try, http://www.bls.gov/oco for descriptions of thousands of occupations.

Exercise 3

After noting your personality type (creator, investigator, relater, operator, persuader, organizer), list below the books you could obtain, the workshops and seminars you could attend, the associations you could join, and the journals/magazines you could subscribe to, and the skills you could develop that relate to your field of interest. Also talk to a community college counselor or career counselor.

Books____

____

____

Workshops/Seminars/Associations______________________________________

____

____

Journals/Magazines____

____

____

Skills____

____

____

Strategy 1.6

Identify your dominant personality to strengthen your deficiencies and empower your strengths.

Definition of Personality: the pattern of characteristic thoughts, feelings, and behaviors that distinguishes one person from another. It is also the complex pattern of traits (aggressive, passive, possessive, independent, dramatic, structured, extroverted, logical, reserved, controlled, tender, emotional etc.) that are consistently expressed under certain conditions.

Where Does Personality Come From?

There are several theories that have been formed over many years by psychologists that help us to understand human nature and the causes of human personality and behavior. Psychologist Carl Jung believed that we were born with a predisposition for certain personality preferences. He believed that healthy development was based on the lifelong nurturing of inborn preferences rather than trying to change a person to become something different.

Human Nature and the Causes of Human Behavior

What do you believe about human nature and the causes of human behavior? This example might help. Let's say you are a parent and you want to teach your child how to be a successful person in life. You first have to ask yourself what a successful person is. Your values will determine that. Is it somebody that makes a lot of money? The mafia does that! Is it somebody that rises to a powerful position in life to control and persuade others? Adolf Hitler did that! Is it somebody that has high self-esteem? Saddam Hussein had that! Or, is it somebody that is always good to others? A lot of depressed and abused people have done that! You have to define it in greater, more specific detail for yourself. Then, model, as well as teach your children accordingly. How will you implement it? For instance, if you wanted to teach your children that doing their homework is one of the important steps in becoming successful, how would you motivate them to perform? Would you give them a positive, nurturing environment? Would you set up a combination of punishments and rewards to get them to do their homework? Would you convince them that they have what it takes to be successful and increase their self-esteem? Would you get the whole family excited about the pursuit of learning with the idea that they would naturally follow that desire to learn? After reading the theories below, you may choose one that you believe in, you may choose a combination of theories from below, or you may adopt your own. Make sure that if you adopt your own, you base it on the following factors: the experiences you have learned from others, not just your own experiences (if so, your theory may not apply to most people); good common sense; logic; intuition; and reliable and valid research published in reputable journals. Below, according to Phares (1988), are some of the most important theories on personality and human nature.

1. Psychoanalytic Theory: **(We are motivated by psychosexual forces)**
Sigmund Freud: Premise: Childhood experiences and unconscious motivations determine our thoughts, attitudes and behaviors. For example, growing up in a stressed home will make you a stressed adult. Also our entire mental life is determined.....a certain set of conditions will create paranoia and another will produce an anxiousness...we are captives of our biological and environmental forces. There are three personalities in one according to Freud.
1. Id – the dominant force in personality...deep, inaccessible part of personality that is devoid of values, ethics, and logic; it wants pleasure only.
2. Superego – the values of society presented to the child through punishments and rewards with the message of striving toward perfection

3. Ego- the manager of personality that is rational and juggles the outrageous demands of the other two.

Carl Jung: Our human nature seeks to constantly grow and become balanced. Our personality is determined both by who and what we have been and also by the person we hope to become. We do this by accepting the full range of our being....our good and dark sides (selfishness and greed). He gave a greater role to the ego in its ability to influence behavior instead of just the id controlling the show.

Eric Erikson: (Psychosocial forces)

We are motivated by our social world with eight critical stages that unfold in a genetically determined sequence. The ages vary from culture to culture but will still remain. He combined biological, psychological and social aspects of development to explain whether one grows or not. There are critical needs or turning points at each of the eight stages of life that we either satisfy or become frustrated and stagnate (we either go forward or backward). The resolution of the need or turning points leads to a successful or unsuccessful resolution like hope or fear. The ages and turning points include:

Trust vs. Mistrust (hope or fear) ages...0-1 Autonomy vs. Shame (will power or self-doubt) ages...1-3 Initiative vs. Guilt (purpose or unworthiness) ages...4-5 Industry vs. Inferiority (competency or incompetency) ages...6-11 Identity vs. Role confusion (fidelity or uncertainty) ages...12-20 Intimacy vs. Isolation (love or promiscuity) ages...20-24 Generativity vs. Stagnation (care or selfishness)

ages...25-65 Integrity vs. Despair (wisdom or meaninglessness) ages 65 and over.

2. Humanistic Theory: (We are motivated by our needs to grow personally and socially)

Carl Rogers: Premise: People have at their deepest core a positive goodness. People should be accepted and trusted and you will make them advance forward. By asking, Who am I? How can I become what I deeply wish to become? and accept ourselves, we will advance and grow.

Abraham Maslow: Premise: That people strive for growth but growth is not an automatic process. Because growth involves some pain, people struggle between desire for security/dependence and desire to experience the delights of growth. People are motivated to act only when a set of lower needs are fulfilled. See the next lesson on motivation.

Rollo May: The Existential approach:

As opposed to Freudian determinism, the past doesn't determine the present or the future--we have freedom of choice. So action and commitment are the key to positive behavioral change. If we are authentic, take responsibility and exercise good choices, we can free ourselves from the dominance of others and approach our potential.

Alfred Adler: He blended the ideas of the desire and need for self-actualization with the idea of that self-actualization could only occur when accompanied within one's social group since we are social creatures. Birth order plays a part in determining personality. One can shape one's own life.

3. Eastern and Native Cultures:

If you enhance the well-being of the group through unification, you will have individual well-being. Self-actualization is not needed. As long as harmony, interdependence, and socially relevant oriented goals are achieved, the ultimate good occurs to the individual and the group.

4. Behavior Theory

B.F. Skinner: Our conditioning or the rewards and punishments used to shape our behavior determines our behavior and personality. The environment is the biggest factor in changing behavior. Reinforcing behavior like that on an animal will equally work as well on humans. People are motivated by their needs being met.

5. Social Learning Theory

Julian Rotter and Albert Bandura: Behaviorism ignored the role of cognitive factors such as we think, we plan, we believe, and we imagine…even during reinforcement. Social Learning Theory or SLT believes people are motivated by a) how they value a goal and how much they need it and b) their expectation or likelihood of achieving the goal. People are motivated by needs similar to Maslow's.

Example: If a student was told about the rewards of going to UCSD with a major in chemistry because it was one of the best schools, the behaviorists would say that this person would be motivated to go to UCSD. SLT would say if the person didn't believe he/she had the academic skills to get the required high g.p.a. to transfer, he/she would probably choose another less demanding school because the expectation of getting accepted at UCSD was low. So we must look at one's judgments, beliefs, and expectations to understand their motivation and predict behavior.

6. Trait/Type Theory

Gordon Allport and Raymond Cattell: Personality traits and types come from both heredity and childhood experiences. One could be extroverted or introverted, pessimistic or optimistic, structured or carefree, controlled or impulsive, moody or easygoing, etc. Types are composed of traits, which in turn are comprised of numerous habits. Many psychologists only 30 years ago thought socialization caused boys to be more aggressive than girls. Yet, many studies since then have confirmed a biological link to make aggressiveness. Years ago many believed if you gave boys dolls to play with instead of guns, they would be more passive like girls. What they consistently found was that boys often constructed catapults to fling the dolls far distances to their death. So much for socialization. Examples of personality type tests include the Myers Briggs and the Enneagram which is explained on the next page.

Note:

It is amazing that these theories, besides eastern/native cultures, are only about 60 years old. In other words, through the thousands of years of human history, people didn't entertain the notion that their behavior and emotional stability could have been a result of early childhood experiences and influences. To complete personality inventories and get results, go on the Internet and visit this site: http://www.personalitypage.com In studying many behavioral systems that attempt to explain human behavior, I have not found any system that fulfills this complex task better than that of the Enneagram.

Exercise 1

Which theory or theories do you agree with and why?____________________________________

____

____

____

How could you use this information in your life?_______________________________________

____

____

____

What personality or behavioral theories do you have of your own? _______________________

____

____

____

____

The Enneagram

The Enneagram, a new technology of self-discovery, delineates nine fundamental personality types of human nature. Combining ancient traditions with modern psychology, it has no exact origin but is thought to be about 2500 years old. The Christian mystics used it to convert vices into virtues. It was the cornerstone of Sufi ethical training for 1400 years. Known only by sages and spiritual leaders, it was brought to Europe in the 1920's by a mystic named, G. I. Gurdjieff. The transpersonal psychologists brought it to the United States in the 1960's. There have been over 40 books published on the topic and over one million books sold in several languages. People often say the Enneagram teaches them more about personality than all the psychology courses they took in college. The Enneagram teaches us how to work best with each personality type, shows us obstacles that prevent us from gaining a fuller more graceful life, expands our consciousness to concerns broader than our own, helps us walk in the shoes of others by approaching them in a non-judgmental, compassionate way, teaches us how to avoid unnecessary conflicts and how to create openings for better communication.

The nine personality types are not rigid boxes; they're fluid and flexible like real people are. Though there are nine types, we adopt a main type that was formed from childhood that helped us cope with life challenges. For example, when the "Helper" type personality received the message of "don't disagree with me or else," or "take care of me," the Helper coped by ignoring their own needs, and their whole consciousness switched to only serving others' needs. Each type has a fear; when they tame it and accept the consequences of it, they obtain true health and happiness. If they give into their fear and resist it by overcompensating, then they become unhappy, depressed, and mentally unstable. Though we have one dominant personality type of the nine, the other eight are potentials for us to develop so that we become more well-rounded and balanced. The Enneagram is just a tool and like any tool can be used for either good or bad. We can use it for bad by labeling others and categorizing them into boxes and judging them as inferior. Or, we can use it for good by accepting types that are different than us, and finding the value of each person as their type manifests itself. By seeing that every type has a set of fears, values, and desires, we see how much we have in common.

Exercise 2

Determine your Enneagram personality below and read the interpretations on the following pages. There are several ways that you can determine your Enneagram personality.

1. You can read each personality below and identify the one closest to your personality. Or,

2. You can get on the world wide web and type in enneagraminstitute.com and complete the shortened 36 question version of their inventory. Click on free RHETI Sampler. Or,

3. You can call the Enneagram Institute and obtain their 144 questionnaire at (212) 932-3306. O

4. Find Enneagram information and inventories on the Internet or any large bookstore in your town.

Exercise 3

After determining your Enneagram personality, pick ten items from the following pages of your type and state if each item applies to you or not. Also state why it does or does not apply to you. For example: "It says a hot button for the Enthusiast is negative people. You may say, "This is true because, I find myself feeling resentful when I am around people who are negative." Word process this assignment on a separate sheet of paper with your Enneagram type as the title.

Type 1: THE REFORMER

(alias: the judge, perfectionist, purist, the organized person)

HEALTHY

They emphasize strong principles, morals, integrity, ethics, moderation, high standards, discernment, and are wise and strong on their convictions. They are agents for social change. They focus on what is wrong with things and how they can be improved. They know the best thing to do in most circumstances and strive to be fair.

AVERAGE

They are orderly, idealistic, dissatisfied with reality feeling that it is up to only them to improve everything. Thorough, neat, organized, sense for right/wrong and good/bad, they feel their values are worth dying for. They rely on conscience to determine their morality. They are afraid of making a mistake and can become workaholics, anal-compulsives, and critical of self and others.

UNHEALTHY

They distrust authority due to bad experiences. Inflexible, impersonal, rigid, highly critical, makes severe judgments of others while rationalizing their own actions, they can become condemnatory, punitive and cruel so they can rid themselves of what is disturbing them. They are often bitter and have problems with anger at themselves for not living up to their own standards. They can have nervous breakdowns, become suicidal, or highly depressed.

AS CHILDREN

They learned to postpone their rewards until their work was done. They were praised for adult-like behaviors as a child, and felt, "If I don't do it, nobody will." Tried to transcend the family rules by creating their own, more rigorous code of ethics so they could avoid being criticized and be blameless. Received messages of, “be perfect, work hard, don’t be a child.” They feared the parental protective figure or they feared God - being sent to hell for their own immoral acts.

VALUES

Conscience, truth, honesty, values, logic, justice, self-discipline, rightness, fairness, correctness.

DESIRE →	FEAR →	RESPONSE →	RESULT
Healthy Level To be good, have integrity, strive for the ideal, judge objectively	*Of being corrupt, evil, and defective*	Being objective, prudent, discerning, hopeful, noble, kind, uplifting, fair, truthful, modest	Wise, discerning, lets others be themselves, accepts their flaws, is truthfully objective
Average Level To admonish others and self for not meeting their ideals/standards	Of others messing up their order and balance they have achieved. Their ideals are wrong.	Being rigid, sarcastic, badgering, picky, uncompromising, critical, opinionated, self-pitying	Never satisfied with anything unless it is done according to their liking. Becomes self-righteous.
Unhealthy Level To control their irrational impulses and rid themselves of their emotional disorder.	That they are losing all control of themselves and becoming irrational, flawed, and wrong.	Merciless, hysterical, attacking, cruel, fixated, hypocritical, wrathful.	*Basic fear realized: they are corrupted, evil, defective and imbalanced.*

FAMOUS REFORMERS

Michelle Obama, Al Gore, Hillary Clinton, Thomas Jefferson, Margaret Thatcher, The ‘Church Lady’ (SNL), Mr. Spock from Star Trek, Ghandi, Dennis Prager, George Will, Rudolph Guiliani, Jane Fonda, Tom Brokaw, Leslie Stahl, Jerry Brown, Dr. Joyce Brothers, George Harrison, Ralph Nader, Bill Maher.

THEIR MAIN PROBLEM AND HOT BUTTONS

They impose a rigid order on their drives, emotions, and impulses which causes them to repress their desires; they become defeated and angry at themselves/others for not living up to the ideal. They see themselves as higher than others. Those who disagree with their "truth" are condemned. People who are excessively tardy anger them.

TO IMPROVE YOUR RELATIONSHIP AND HELP A REFORMER

1. Be logical and objective with them. 2. Offer support and information 3. Get work done first, with little small talk, then play. 4. Admit to your own mistakes 5. Let them know they are likable even when they aren't perfect. 6. Remind them the goal of growth is to be whole, not perfect. 7. Admit your own mistakes.

RECOMMENDATIONS FOR GROWTH

1. Learn to relax and let go of some responsibility 2. Don't expect others to change immediately 3. Know how much to say and how to say it--let your wisdom be your guide, not rightness. 4. Don't impose an order on your irrational side because it will always resurface. 5. Learn to allow minor errors without self-blame. 7. Notice your thinking in terms of either/or, right/wrong and include more sides to your point. 8. Forgive.

CAREERS

People-oriented ones = Teachers, politicians, religious work, journalists, and spokespersons.
Analytical ones = found in management, law, science careers, consumer advocates, authors, and critics. Work best in jobs requiring detail e.g. accounting, finance, science/technology. They have problems with jobs where rules change often (e.g. start-ups, marketing high-tech products), etc. They model ethical idealism and are best in high responsible jobs (e.g. operating rooms, inspection teams, and referees.

WINGS OF THE REFORMER

9 WING: "The Idealist"

They are wise, discerning, scholarly, generous, idealistic, and more gentle. They are less involved with making concrete changes. They are more cerebral and impersonal, being an outside evaluator of the culture. There is a mystical side to them and are attracted often to nature, art, and animals more than to humans. They can often distance themselves from others.

2 WING: "The Advocate"

They are more involved with making changes in the trenches. They are more extroverted, like debating, and focus on the needs of others and relationships. They can be more irritable, vocal about discontents, and firey. They are more warm and empathetic towards others. They are often kind and good-humored. They may manipulate others with guilt for being less than they should be.

DEFENSE MECHANISM / ADDICTION / MENTAL DISORDERS

Reaction formation / Perfection / Compulsive and Depressive personality disorders.

MOTTO / SIGNALS THEY SEND

Find the rules and master them / "I'm right and you're not," under criticism falls back on the letter of the law.

TO MAKE INNER CHANGES FOR HEALTHIER BEHAVIOR, REPEAT OUT LOUD

<u>I now release:</u>

- holding myself and others to impossible standards
- obsessing about things I can't change
- feeling angry, impatient, and easily annoyed
- believing I'm in a position to judge myself and others
- allowing my desire for order/efficiency to control my life
- that it is up to me to fix everything
- rationalizing my own behavior
- all bitterness/disappointment in the world
- my fears of ever being wrong
- ignoring my emotional/physical stress
- focusing on what's wrong with things

<u>I now affirm:</u>

- that I can allow myself to relax and enjoy my life
- being grateful that others have many things to teach me
- my feelings are legitimate and I have a right to feel them
- that I'm gentle and forgiving with myself
- the best I can do is good enough
- I can make mistakes without rebuke
- I treat others with respect and kindness
- I'm compassionate/forgiving of others

Type 2: THE HELPER

(alias: the giver, cheerleader, supporter)

HEALTHY

They are empathetic, generous, can skillfully empathize with feelings of others, compassionate, unselfish, give with no expectation of return, remember your name, birthdays, allergies etc. They are dedicated and supportive of others as they bring out the best in them. They are truly joyful, gracious, selfless, nurturing and warm hearted

AVERAGE

They become overly intimate and intrusive. They engage in "people pleasing" in order to be closer to others. They use flattery and kindness to get others to like them. Becomes a "martyr" for others.

UNHEALTHY

They are people pleasers, use flattery and gifts since they don't know if they are loved in return. They use self-deception and manipulation to hold onto people. They may coerce others to get their needs met. They will often manipulate and play on guilt and shame and will call on past favors to get what they want. Thus they instill guilt and manipulation to make others feel indebted to them. They often abuse food/medications to stuff feelings and get sympathy. They become domineering, coercive, and feel entitled to get anything they want from others while being bitter and resentful. They have chronic health problems that often surface.

AS CHILDREN

They may have grown up in a family that raised the younger kids or got praise for helping parents. But when they parent their friends and spouse, then it's not appreciated and becomes belittling. They learned to put the needs of others before their own and feel they must give to others before getting anything back. They learned to manipulate to get affection. They often received messages of "take care of me, don't think, don't disagree with me, and don't feel important."

VALUES

Giving, generosity, empathy, open communication, serving and loving others.

DESIRE →	FEAR →	RESPONSE →	RESULT
Healthy Level Unconditional love from others	*Being unworthy, unloved, and unwanted.*	Caring, unselfish, humble, forgiving, serving, sympathetic, affectionate	Helpers who are altruistic. They can give with no ulterior motives.
Average Level To be close to others and feel needed and acknowledged	Others will love someone else more than them. That they are being taken for granted and driving others away.	Manipulation, smothering, guilt-instilling, discoursing, blaming, jealous, worry, gossip, self-sacrificing.	People pleasers who hover, intrude, and control in the name of love.
Unhealthy Level To get love from anyone in any way they can.	That they have permanently estranged loved ones. That they are Bad, selfish, and violated others.	Recklessness, obsessiveness, sexually act-out, insatiable, remorseless, destructive. Vengeful	*Domineering and coercive. Basic fear realized: they have become unwanted and unlovable.*

FAMOUS HELPERS

Josh Groban, Arsenio Hall, Paula Abdul, the music of "Journey",Leo Buscaglia, Bill Cosby, Mother Theresa, Eleanor Roosevelt, Pope John 23rd, Luciano Pavarotti, Marilyn Monroe, Dolly Parton, Barbara Bush, Alan Alda, and the "Jewish/Italian" Mother stereotype.

THEIR MAIN PROBLEM AND HOT BUTTONS

They ignore their own needs and then become angry which they suppress. Always serving others makes others feel in debt. They want to be consulted on others affairs and become possessive. They hate being taken for granted.

TO IMPROVE YOUR RELATIONSHIP AND HELP A HELPER

1. Let them help you 2. Do something for them and tell them your feelings so they can be open with theirs 3. Tell them you like and appreciate what they do and who they are. 4. Don't ask what they need, just do something for them. 5. Be sincere and speak from your own emotions. 6. Mirror back what they say.

RECOMMENDATIONS FOR GROWTH

1. Give without expecting a return 2. Resist the urge to suppress your own needs and wants. 3. Learn to put your needs first and then give to others. 4. Make time to be alone and bring your attention back inside before focusing out again. 5. Tell people what you need, and allow them to give it to you. Enjoy receiving.

CAREERS

They become teachers, ministers, and healers in the medical, emotional, and physical arenas. They excel in jobs with a high interpersonal component: receptionist, human resources, health care professions, service industries, sales representatives, and social work. Jobs that lack people such as tax auditor or forest ranger will depress them. Extroverted twos are often found in the limelight as actresses, actors, salespersons, and motivational speakers.

WINGS OF THE HELPER

1 WING: "The Servant"

Communicates warmth, understanding, and is the good samaritan type. Takes on things others usually avoid, can be self-critical, and their emotional life is like driving with the brake and the accelerator on. They become martyrs. They start charities and want to give the best possible service to others. Make excellent teachers.

3 WING: "The Host/Hostess"

Are more intimate and values personal qualities more than service. They are charming and entertaining, but, can have a forced friendliness and exaggerated empathy. Less task driven and critical of self. They are free spirited.

DEFENSE MECHANISM / ADDICTION / MENTAL DISORDERS

Repression / Service or Manipulation / Histrionic or Dependent personality disorder, Hysteria

MOTTO / SIGNALS THEY SEND

Every successful person relies on a good Giver / I will dump you if you don't respond properly.

TO MAKE INNER CHANGES FOR HEALTHIER BEHAVIOR, REPEAT OUT LOUD

<u>I now release:</u>

- all feelings of rage and resentment toward others
- all desires to make others love me
- not wanting to acknowledge my negative feelings
- all physical ailments, aches, and complaints
- doing things for others to make myself needed
- my fear that I'm unwanted and unloved
- expecting others to repay my help in the way I want
- feeling possessive of loved ones
- calling attention for what I've done for others
- making others feel guilty for not meeting my needs

<u>I now affirm:</u>

- that I own all of my feelings without fear
- I'm lovable for who I am
- I can let go of loved ones
- The joy of warmth that fills my heart
- I'm honest and clear about my motives
- That my happiness does not depend on pleasing others
- That I nurture my growth/development
- That I love others without expecting anything in return

Type 3: THE ACHIEVER

(alias: the motivator, performer, promoter, instant expert)

HEALTHY

They are success oriented, self-assured, attractive, pragmatic, value self-improvement, and becomes outstanding in many areas of life. They are authentic, role models for others, inspire others, distinguish themselves from others, believe they are desirable and admirable. They are charming, poised, good representatives and spokespersons. They are energetic, diplomatic, and ambitious to improve themselves.

AVERAGE

They are too competitive and driven for success. They feel they have to be the best and look to formulas to get the job done quickly. They need a lot of attention, promote themselves, very image conscious, and can become Supermom/dad. They are often found in seminars, health clubs, and classes sharpening their skills.

UNHEALTHY

Fearing failure and humiliation, they distort the truth of their accomplishments and become exploitative, pathological liars, extremely hostile while sabotaging people in order to triumph over them. They become relentless about destroying whoever reminds them of their own shortcomings and failures.

AS CHILDREN

They got elected on teams, were the family heroes and mascots, had few discipline problems, and became competent in an area to gain recognition, praise, and status. They were the most responsible in their class. They may have felt too much pressure from parents to perform at a high level. They received messages of "be a winner," and "don't feel your feelings."

VALUES

Popularity, self-improvement, achievement, reputation, success, recognition, physical appearance, uses presentation skills to advance worthy causes.

DESIRE →	FEAR →	RESPONSE →	RESULT
Healthy Level To feel valuable, desired, accepted, and worthwhile.	*Being worthless and rejected*	Being genuine, self-accepting, esteemed, other-directed, confident, charitable	Accept themselves for who they are without the need for applause or admiration.
Average Level To create a favorable impression of themselves to convince others of their greatness.	Of losing positive regard of others and will be humiliated for failing.	Rehearsed, "showing off," arrogant, jealous, competitive, inflating accomplishments.	Present themselves according to the expectations of others. Loses sense of self and out of touch with feelings.
Unhealthy Level To destroy whoever threatens them or reminds them of what they lack.	That there is nothing about them people will admire. That their emptiness will be exposed and they'll be ruined.	Exploitative, betraying, sabotaging, scheming, lying, remorseless, malicious, sadistic	*Basic fear realized: they are rejected as worthless*

FAMOUS ACHIEVERS

Tiger Woods, Oprah Winfrey, Lady Gaga, Bill Clinton, Mitt Romney, Arnold Schwarzenegger, Whitney Houston , Tony Robbins, Gloria Steinem, Paul McCartney, Tom Cruise, Shania Twain, Kathie Lee Gifford, Denzel Washington, Kathie Lee Gifford, Taylor Swift, Justin Bieber, Will Smith, Courtney Cox, Madonna.

THEIR MAIN PROBLEM AND HOT BUTTONS

They may have problems with intimacy--if someone gets too close, they fear that others may see their inadequacies and therefore get rejected. They develop image rather than real self. Feel threatened when others are more successful than they are. They project style over substance, develop grandiose goals, and value sexual conquests.

TO IMPROVE YOUR RELATIONSHIP AND HELP AN ACHIEVER

1. Don't ignore or criticize them 2. Match their energy level 3. Praise both performance and inner qualities.

RECOMMENDATIONS FOR GROWTH

1. Be truthful about your weaknesses and resist impressing others 2. Encourage and support others 3. Develop spiritual life 4. Forget other's approval, your worth lies within 5. Allow your need for down time and accept your limitations 6. Don't take yourself too seriously 7. Stop from time to time and ask, "What am I feeling?"

CAREERS

Many are actors, sales representatives, marketers, advertisers, teachers, managers, business, law, politics or any competitive environment with a ladder to climb. They thrive in jobs that require efficiency, rapid turnaround and streamlining. They have problems in jobs requiring inactivity/sitting and discussing ideas. Work Style: "If you don't want footprints on your back, get outta my way."

WINGS OF THE ACHIEVER

2 WING: "The Star"
They accept limitations, don't take self too seriously. They are tender, genuine, and affectionate. Outstanding personal qualities, spontaneous, and can turn on the charisma, but can lose self in the process. Actors, models, and singers are often this type because they can "turn it on."
4 WING: "The Professional"
They put more attention on work, are disciplined, serious, put entire self worth on the line with every project they take on. They have more potential for developing their emotional/artistic sides. They are more terrified of failure.

DEFENSE MECHANISM / ADDICTION / MENTAL DISORDERS

Identification / Efficiency / Manic-depression & Narcissistic personality disorder

MOTTO / SIGNALS THEY SEND

I am what I do / Goals may appear to matter more than people. Others often feel exploited. Assumes leadership without consulting: Someone's either on board or out.

TO MAKE INNER CHANGES FOR HEALTHIER BEHAVIOR, REPEAT OUT LOUD

I now release:

- feeling jealous of others and their good fortune
- feeling that I must conceal my mistakes and limitations
- betraying my own integrity to get the admiration of others
- using arrogance to compensate for my own insecurity
- desiring to impress others with my performance
- driving myself relentlessly to be the best
- my fear of failing and being humiliated
- closing down feelings to function
- grandiose expectations I have of me
- craving constant attention/affirmation
- comparing myself with others

I now affirm:

- that I have value regardless of my achievements
- that I can reveal my real self without being afraid
- that I'm responsible to those who look up to me
- I develop my true talents by accepting who I am
- that I'm centered/emotionally available
- that I take in the love that others give me
- I'm happy to work for the good of others
- that I delight in the success of others

Type 4: THE ARTIST

(alias: the romantic, individualist, elitist, connoisseur)

HEALTHY
Intuitive, self-aware, expressive, gentle, creative, and they can turn a painful experience into a meaningful one for themselves. They have a witty view of life and of self. They are emotionally honest and romantic while being profoundly creative, expressing the personal and the universal. They are often engaged in a "search for self." They enjoy creating something beautiful.

AVERAGE
They hold on to feelings/moods and think that's who they are. They take a romantic orientation to life. They often feel different from others. They can become self-indulgent, decadent, and they dislike the ordinary. They can be very moody and envy others and think they're better off. They personalize things becoming self-absorbed, hypersensitive, and self-conscious.

UNHEALTHY
Vulnerable to depression, they can't go on with life until their emotions are worked out which could take days, weeks, or years. They hold themselves back and then complain that people leave them out. They commonly feel misunderstood and find the self through feelings, not reality. They stay withdrawn to protect their self-image. They often feel hopeless and become self-destructive abusing substances to escape. This can lead to an emotional breakdown or suicide.

AS CHILDREN
They felt disconnected from their parents. They had either an unhappy or solitary childhood as a result of marital problems, illness, or disinterested parents. They couldn't identify with a parent figure so they looked to themselves in aloneness to form their elusive identity. Thus, they began to inventory all the ways they were unlike others. Feeling abandoned and rejected, they turned to self-knowledge in hope of finding self-esteem to prevent feeling so different from others. They received messages of "don't count on my being here for you, don't be close."

VALUES
Creativity, beauty, personal freedom, deep feeling, self-awareness, the artistic, fantasy, the personal/universal.

DESIRE →	FEAR →	RESPONSE →	RESULT
Healthy Level *To find themselves and their significance*	*That they have no identity or personal significance*	Redemptive, honest with self, self-aware, authentic, inner-directed, gratitude,	Able to transform all their experiences into something valuable.
Average Level To shut out intrusions by intensifying their mental activity	That others are invading them and that they won't find a place in the world or with people	Withholding, aloof, sulking, possessive, envious, dismissive, pretentious, demanding	Moody, plays "hard to get" but still feels like an outsider, self-pity and envy are prominent.
Unhealthy Level To reject and punish anyone/thing that doesn't support their emotional demands. To escape it all.	That they are cut off from others and life. Their situation is hopeless and they are abandoned.	Emotionally blocked, self-sabotaging, tormented, hopeless, crimes of passion, accusatory, parasitic	*Basic fear is realized: they have lost their identity and personal significance*

FAMOUS ARTISTS
Michael Jackson, Angelina Jolie, Yoko Ono, Paul Simon, Virginia Woolf, Bob Dylan, Edgar Allen Poe, Judy Garland, Tchaikovsky, Joni Mitchell, Johnny Depp, Stevie Nicks, Cher, Nicolas Cage, Kate Winslet, Prince.

THEIR MAIN PROBLEM AND HOT BUTTONS
Self-pity. They hold on to hostility, which makes them depressed. If someone says "You look great" they think, she/he thinks I'm ugly. Other people look more interesting when they're distant, less so when they're present.
Don't give them advice, "fix it", or talk them out of something.

TO IMPROVE YOUR RELATIONSHIP AND HELP AN ARTIST
1. Be sensitive to their feelings. 2. Encourage them to express and stand up for themselves. 3. Let them know you won't abandon them. 4. Listen to their feelings and believe them–but don't buy into them, help let their emotions work through them. 5. Tell them your own feelings and reactions. 6. Appreciate their authenticity.

RECOMMENDATIONS FOR GROWTH
1. Realize that your feelings don't determine your identity. 2. Express your feelings to others. 3. Stand up for yourself. 4. Take up a body-based activity to learn to ground yourself. 5. Focus more on the here and now as opposed to what is missing. 6. See the extraordinary in the ordinary. 7. Honor your empathic skills.

CAREERS
Artists (music, fine art, dancing), writers (poetry, novels, journalism), teachers or anything where they can create the outrageous or beautiful. Many will bring out the best in people as psychologists or counselors. They accept mundane jobs to support their creative pursuits. Some take pride in the small businesses they own.They often gravitate toward distinctive work: advertising, product design, modeling, and performance arts.

WINGS OF THE ARTIST
3 Wing: "The Aristocrat"
More sociable and goal oriented. They are practical, image oriented, upbeat, ambitious, competitive, and strive toward attaining their self-ideal through their imagination and feelings. They can be ambitious, accomplished, yet more resentful.
5 Wing: "The Bohemian"
They are the most creative of all types, introverted, attracted to the exotic, intellectual, reserved, and depressed. They are mysterious. Pondering their torment leads to nihilism, distorted thinking patterns, self-hatred, and isolation.

DEFENSE MECHANISM / ADDICTION / MENTAL DISORDERS
Introjection & Artistic sublimation / Elitism / Manic-Depression, Avoidant & Narcissistic personality disorder

MOTTO / SIGNALS THEY SEND
Fill the half-empty glass / You are too ordinary and not flamboyant or bizarre enough.

TO MAKE INNER CHANGES FOR HEALTHIER BEHAVIOR, REPEAT OUT LOUD
I now release:
- turning my anger and aggression against myself
- the fear that I'm unimportant and undesirable
- being distraught, fatigued, and inhibited
- all unrealistic expectations of myself and others
- all self-indulgence in my emotions and behavior
- protecting myself and withdrawing from others
- all feelings of hopelessness and despair
- feeling misunderstood by others
- feeling that people always let me down
- needing to be treated differently
- dwelling on the past to prolong feelings

I now affirm:
- that I'm not defined by my feelings
- that I open myself up to people and the world
- the goodness of my life, my friends, and myself
- that I'm transforming my life into something higher
- that I'm bringing something good and beautiful into the world
- only feelings I act on express who I am
- that I use all my experiences to grow
- that I love myself and treat myself gently
- that I'm free of the damage of my past

Type 5: THE THINKER

(alias: the analyst, observer, philosopher, sage)

HEALTHY
They are alert, curious, ask thoughtful questions, have a high ability to concentrate and focus, inventive, deep, avid reader, perceptive, make pioneering discoveries, extraordinary perceptiveness and insight, and experts in their field.

AVERAGE
They often forget to eat, disappears in their projects, become detached, secretive, and remote. They will minimize emotional needs since it interferes with their projects. They are cynical and would probably say "Stay away so I can work and follow my investigations." They feel they must always have some new insight or new piece of knowledge. They are most talkative when the discussion is about their chosen field or passion. They can't allow themselves to play or act silly because they feel they must always be doing something intelligent.

UNHEALTHY
They become loners, retreating into their heads. They may pursue one college degree after another without graduating or getting a job. They can get obsessed with dark and disturbing subjects and not come out of it. They become antagonistic toward others and shock them with strange viewpoints. They "burn bridges" and jump to conclusions. They become eccentric and nihilistic. They get obsessed with threatening ideas becoming horrified and are prey to phobias and distortions.

AS CHILDREN
They may have been quiet, played a musical instrument, played with insects, or computers. They perceived that there was no role/place in the family to fit in and be needed. They may have felt intruded on by their parents or nurtured erratically, perhaps, in a disturbed or alcoholic way, or caught in a loveless marriage were love was not dependable. They attempt to resolve this by mastering a piece of knowledge/skill that is unexplored. So they go to their room and strike a unstated bargain with parents like "Don't ask too much of me, and I won't of you." Received messages of "don't be close, don't belong."

VALUES
Knowledge, intelligence, specifics, openness, originality, perception, discovery, independence.

DESIRE →	FEAR →	RESPONSE →	RESULT
Healthy Level To be competent and capable and have something to contribute.	*Being helpless, useless, incapable*	Compassionate, trusting, curious, alert, objective, inventive, creative, whimsical, open-minded	Attain skillful mastery of their desired interest, have incredible foresight, and vision.
Average Level To shut out intrusions and scare off anyone who threatens their workings.	That others are attacking their workings. Never be able to find their place in the world or with people	Intense, cynical, argumentative, arrogant, pessimistic, stingy, impatient, judgmental	Engaged in complicated ideas and theories or imaginary worlds. Detached from others.
Unhealthy Level To cut off all connections with the world, fend off their terrors, and sever their consciousness	The world is closing in on them and they can't defend themselves from outside perpetrators.	Retreating, delirious, sinister, resistant to help, deranged, suicidal, split off, feel damned.	*Basic fear realized: they are helpless, useless, and incapable.*

FAMOUS THINKERS
Bill Gates, Mark Zuckerberg, Meryl Streep, John Lennon, Albert Einstein, Isaac Newton, Steven King, Bobby Fisher, Howard Hughes, Tim Burton, Stephen King, Vincent van Gogh, Kurt Cobain, Sigmund Freud, Charles Darwin, Alfred Hitchcock, TV's Dr. Gregory 'House', Isaac Asimov, Friedrich Nietzsche.

THEIR MAIN PROBLEM AND HOT BUTTONS

They don't want others to waste their time. They think too much and become lost in their own world losing touch with the real world. Become angry when others question their competency, monitor or organize them, or not allowing them enough time to respond.

TO IMPROVE YOUR RELATIONSHIP AND HELP A THINKER

1. Get close by sharing their interest with them, but don't intrude. 2. Let them know how important they are in your life. 3. They like to take many seconds to respond to a question so allow. 4. Respect their need for privacy and don't take it as rejection. 5. Instead of demanding, invite them to move from talk to action.

RECOMMENDATIONS FOR GROWTH

1. Relax, exercise, and meditate. 2. Take advice from someone you trust. 3. Develop empathy and compassion. 4. Take action and get out of your head & into your heart. 5. Take up a physical practice to ground your body 6. Allow yourself to feel emotions as they are happening. 6. Learn to let yourself be seen; who you are and what you do. 7. Join a group that encourages self-disclosure, e.g. Gestalt. 8. Notice secrecy = separation.

CAREERS

They are scientists, in technical fields, inventors, the arts, e.g. music, architecture, painting, etc. They have strong analytical skills and are excellent at problem solving. Research and development, libraries, night shift at computer lab, long-range planners, or university professors are typical occupations. They have problems with jobs that require competition or confrontation or fast-paced interpersonal jobs like customer service, clerk, airline hostess.

WINGS OF THE THINKER

4 Wing: "The Iconoclast"

They are the more creative, innovative in their field, and drawn to the arts. They possess emotional depth, but not necessarily romantic. They are drawn to trivia and dark subjects. They are likely to be directors, musicians, artists, or writers. Since 4's lack identity and 5's, confidence to act, they have difficulty connecting with others and staying grounded. They are visionary and find beauty in a mathematical formula. They can seek solace in alcohol, drugs, or sexual escapades.

6 Wing: "The Problem-Solver"

They are the data collectors, true analysts and cataloguers. They enjoy philosophy, and technical subjects. They are inventive and skilled at repair work. They are practical and more business oriented than relationship oriented. They can be argumentative and defensive while being suspicious or paranoid of others. They draw meaningful conclusions from the facts and make excellent planners and forecasters. They have a good sense of humor and lovable qualities.

DEFENSE MECHANISM / ADDICTION / MENTAL DISORDERS

Compartmentalization/Disassociation / Knowledge / Avoidant, Schizoid, and Schizotypal personality disorders.

MOTTO / SIGNALS THEY SEND

Knowledge is power / They are an emotional blank screen. They have superiority and arrogance. You feel you've intruded upon them.

TO MAKE INNER CHANGES FOR HEALTHIER BEHAVIOR, REPEAT OUT LOUD

I now release:

- all fearfulness of the world around me
- isolating myself by rejecting others
- desiring to antagonize others and ruin their peace of mind
- feeling I'm a misfit in life
- the agitation and restlessness of my mind
- feeling that I always need to know more before I do anything
- all feelings of powerlessness/hopelessness
- believing that no one can be depended on
- fearing others will exploit me
- postponing my own emotional needs
- neglecting my health and appearance

I now affirm:

- that I'm secure and grounded in the reality of my life
- the value of my inventiveness and sense of humor
- that I find security in being compassionate toward others
- that my life and struggles are meaningful and rewarding
- that I reach out to others as an equal
- I'm ready to participate in the world
- I support others whole-heartedly
- faith in the future and in human being

Type 6: THE LOYALIST

(alias: the skeptic, guardian, devil's advocate, trooper)

HEALTHY

They are likable, form strong bonds with people, create stability, cooperative, spirited, self-reliant, serene, open- minded imaginative thinkers, creative, friendly, playful, loyal to others, highly organized, courageous, and excellent prioritizers. They often put themselves "on the line" on behalf of the down-trodden and unfairly treated people. They are community builders with a great troubleshooter mentality, cooperative spirit, and they form strong alliances.

AVERAGE

They can over-exert themselves and complain about stress even though they create it. Being indecisive, they look to alliances and authorities for security. To resist having more demands made on them, they react passive-aggressively and have suspicion about other's motives. They give contradictory "mixed signals," are defensive, and divide people into friends/enemies. They often complain, and want to know where everyone stands on gossip.

UNHEALTHY

This is the most complicated type. They are a mass of contradictions (self-reliant-dependent, supportive-back-stabbing) and both sides of the contradictions are correct. They become insecure, sarcastic, rebellious, feel inferior, dependent, unpredictable, and mean-spirited when others threaten their security. They lash out and act irrational.

AS CHILDREN

They often had a critical, damaging parent and weren't encouraged to trust their abilities, which created self-doubt. Wanting to be safe from a threatening environment, they turned to scanning for clues to potential threats and doubting the obvious. They became connected to the protective figure (who gave guidelines and discipline) be it, a supportive or destructive person. If it was supportive, they sought to please this person in childhood and a similar person in this role in their adult lives. If destructive, they internalized the relationship always at odds with those who they believed had power over them. They walk through life fearing they'll "be in trouble" and adopt a defensive, rebellious attitude to protect themselves from the cruel protective figure they project onto many of their relationships. Received messages of "don't be important, be careful, it'll get you, don't succeed."

VALUES

Identifies with the underdog, loyalty, duty, responsibility, persistence, welfare of others.

DESIRE →	FEAR →	RESPONSE →	RESULT
Healthy Level *To find security and support to belong.*	*Being unable to survive on their own and having no support*	Courageous, decisive, grounded, dependable, trustworthy, thrifty, responsible, self-trusting.	True courage relying on self. In touch with their inner authority without self-doubt.
Average Level To resist having more demands put upon them. To prove their worth	Losing the support of their allies and authorities and that their actions have harmed their security	Passive-aggressive, indecisive, complaining, cynical, belligerent, mean-spirited, stubborn	Overextended, losing support of others and become a highly anxious, closed off rebel
Unhealthy Level To remove all threats to their security by attacking	Others will destroy what little security they have left and be punished	Irrational, belligerent, hateful, obsessive, suicidal, tormented	*Basic fear realized: they aren't able to survive on their own; abandoned*

FAMOUS LOYALISTS

Tom Hanks, Ellen DeGeneres, Meg Ryan, David Letterman, George Bush Sr, Chris Rock, Marilyn Monroe, Jay Leno, Julia Roberts, Bruce Springsteen, John Goodman, Richard Nixon, Sally Field, Princess Diana, RFK, Malcolm X, Jay Edgar Hoover, Archie Bunker, Rush Limbaugh, Bono, George Costanza (Seinfeld).

THEIR MAIN PROBLEM AND HOT BUTTONS

They usually only act on important decisions when they have the support of others or of an authority figure. They are compliant to the superego which alters their own values to fit others and causes a loss of self-identity and integrity.

TO IMPROVE YOUR RELATIONSHIP AND HELP A LOYALIST

1. Remain strong and stable when they become reactive. 2. Help them be decisive by giving them responsibility to make small decisions. 3. Give them the commonality with you so they can feel a part of the group. 4. Tell them you aren't going to walk away in their life. 5. If you see them sabotaging themselves, ask if they would like to use you as a sounding board for help. 6. Tell them what you are thinking and how you feel. Help them trust the future by seeing alternatives. 7. Be consistent/trustworthy in your actions.

RECOMMENDATIONS FOR GROWTH

1. Explore your anxiety, learn from it, and use it to your advantage. 2. Don't become defensive and negative, and learn to effectively communicate and assert your needs and beliefs. 3. Speak up to authority and risk criticism without becoming antagonistic. 4. Be cautious of growth methods that are intellectually based and balance them with the physical. 5. Ask yourself 'Am I imagining this? Is it a true intuition or a projection?' 6. Notice when you give power away, and practice becoming your own authority. 7. Learn to notice/trust your gut reactions.

CAREERS

They work best in environments where there are defined problems and clear lines of authority as opposed to behind the scenes of wheeling and dealing. Examples: university classrooms, auditing, investigative work, attorneys, chief financial officers, planning departments, actors, receptionists, the military, and compliance officers. They are excellent at troubleshooting, overcoming obstacles, and being persistent. They may be overcautious.

WINGS OF THE LOYALIST

5 Wing: "The Defender"

They are the problem-solver, communicator, independent, good spokespersons for disadvantaged groups, for the underdog, and political causes. They are serious and see the world as dangerous. They may enjoy careers in politics, education, medicine, or engineering. They can become aggressive at perceived threats and hatch plots over others.

7 Wing: "The Buddy"

They are funny, more sociable, less serious, makes sacrifices, more extraverted and eager to be liked by others. They monitor others or provoke them to see how they'll react. They must get advice from others before making an important decision. They may overindulge--substance or food abuse. Their anxieties about key relationships are displaced onto helpless "third parties" being afraid to confront the real sources of discontent in their lives.

DEFENSE MECHANISM / ADDICTION / MENTAL DISORDERS

Projection / Security / Paranoid Schizophrenia, Anxiety, Dependent and Passive-aggressive personality dis.

MOTTO / SIGNALS THEY SEND

Question authority / They put people under the gun. Others feel cross-examined and their intentions are made to feel dubious.

TO MAKE INNER CHANGES FOR HEALTHIER BEHAVIOR, REPEAT OUT LOUD

I now release:

- my fear of being abandoned and alone
- over-reacting and exaggerating my problems
- feeling insecure and unsure of myself
- looking to others to make me feel secure
- being evasive and defensive with those who need me
- my self-defeating and self-punishing tendencies
- taking out my fears and anxieties on others
- all pessimism and complaining
- blaming others for my problems and mistakes
- being suspicious and thinking the worst of others

I now affirm:

- that I am independent and capable
- that I have faith in myself, my talents, and my future
- that I can keep my own identity in relationships
- that I can meet difficulties with calm/confidence
- that I find true authority within me
- that I act courageously in all circumstances

Type 7: THE ENTHUSIAST

(alias: the sensualist, gourmet, optimist, entertainer)

HEALTHY

They are enthusiastic, excitable, most extraverted, spontaneous, do many things well, practical, accomplished, versatile, funny, entertaining, spiritual, you want one at a party, enormous energy, highly creative, multi-talented, resilient after failure, has gratitude, and tells jokes. They become awed at the simple wonders in life.

AVERAGE

They often amuse themselves with new experiences. They become over-extended, distracted, and put no limits on themselves. Their routine might be to go have a drink after work, then go to dinner, then to the theater, and end the night with a nightcap. They are unable to fully be present. They have the feeling—"the grass is always greener on the other side," especially in conversation. They acquire new knowledge/experiences through the news and keep up with new trends. They are often distracted, uninhibited, fear being bored, thus, they keep in perpetual motion never feeling that they have enough.

UNHEALTHY

They become demanding, self-centered, addictive, impulsive, erratic mood swings, can't stay with one thing, and have imbalances in thinking--usually in past or future. They want experiences but are superficial and dabble rather than master something. They become offensive/abusive while going after what they want. They act out impulses rather than dealing with anxiety. They often give up on themselves and life leading to despair, self-destructive overdoses, and suicide.

AS CHILDREN

The were disconnected to the nurturing figure (cared for them, gave affection), and lost the safe, consistent source of nurturance at some stage. They naturally need extra contact. When the nurturing figure failed to deliver, they tried to compensate by getting comfort for themselves. They felt they lacked whatever they needed to be happy--being poor, bored, attention-starved etc. They were the most busy and popular in class, liked to try things twice, once, to see what it was like, and twice, to see if they liked it the first time. They learned to shut off their feelings and idealized the past in order to survive emotional traumas. They received messages of "don't be you, don't grow up."

VALUES

Happiness, accomplishments, pleasure, material possessions, being amused, wide choice of experiences.

DESIRE →	FEAR →	RESPONSE →	RESULT
Healthy Level To be happy, fulfilled, and have their needs met.	*Being deprived of freedom, happiness, and pleasure.*	Receptive, grateful, savoring, responsive, positive, bold, eager	Can experience joy in the ordinary, keep their optimism during setbacks.
Average Level To increase stimulation and gratification.	The world can't give them what they want. That their actions are the cause of their pain.	Attention-grabbing, greedy, insensitive, demanding, exaggerating, scattered.	Insatiable desire for stimulations and pleasure, they become aggressive, greedy, and self-centered.
Unhealthy Level To avoid pain/anxiety and feel something at any cost	A loss of ability to enjoy pleasure/happiness and have ruined their lives.	Reckless, cruel, pushy, obsessive, punitive, trapped, erratic.	*Basic fear realized: they are deprived of what they need to be happy.*

FAMOUS ENTHUSIASTS

John F. Kennedy, Regis Philbin, Robin Williams, Jim Carrey, Miley Cyrus, Katy Perry, Elton John, Britney Spears, Dr. Ruth Westheimer, Howard Stern, Mozart, Mike Myers, Mick Jagger, Simon Cowell, Charlie Sheen, Leonard Bernstein, Mel Brooks, Scarlet O'Hara, Geraldo Rivera, Liberace, Leonardo DiCaprio.

THEIR MAIN PROBLEM AND HOT BUTTONS

1. They do not like limited and restrictive choices and options. 2. People who are negative and pessimistic. 3. If you don't react to them--then they'll try even harder to provoke you. They refuse to trust life and be happy with the journey.

TO IMPROVE YOUR RELATIONSHIP AND HELP AN ENTHUSIAST

1. Relax and enjoy the show they give. 2. Set boundaries with them and set firm limits because they will otherwise stay their routine. 3. Help them recognize what they are missing by focusing on pleasure alone. 4. Create an environment in which it is safe for them to explore and express pain. 5. Help them to stay in the present by asking them how they feel 6. Point out when they are 'racing' or running away from something.

RECOMMENDATIONS FOR GROWTH

1. Let go and observe your impulses to 'fix' problems so that everyone can feel good. 2. Focus on giving not getting--material possessions won't satisfy you. 3. Take time to be grateful. 4. Don't pursue happiness and satisfaction--be present and smell the flowers. 5. Take up meditation practice and be in the present. 6. Say no to more options and yes to fewer more valuable options. 7. Use your anger toward others as a signal to listen to them as opposed to avoiding them. 8. Practice doing, and completing, one thing at a time.

CAREERS

Many sevens have several careers at once or jobs where they travel a lot. They enjoy careers that offer variety, problem solve, and interact with people such as show business, public relations, advertising, travel, nightclubs, photography, teaching, and nursing. They like challenges, think quick in emergencies, but dislike repetitive work such as in accounting or assembly lines. They are theoreticians, futurists, and multitask people. They are able to synthesize points of similarity between different fields of interest; university teaching, politics, lobbying, media production, public relations, fun fields of work for the eternally young such as health and fitness centers.

WINGS OF THE ENTHUSIAST

6 Wing: "The Entertainer"

They are highly productive, playful, silly, may have some dark experiences but retain their innocence. They believe in life's goodness, have a positive outlook, inspired sense of humor, nervous, fidgety, problems with follow through, love to fall in love, always looking for a relationship, and have a quick mind. They have high expectations for stimulation and will pout/sulk if not provided. They have contrasting traits: gracious/sassy, vulnerable/resilient, adult/ childlike.

8 Wing: "The Realist"

They are daring, driving, thinks strategically, worldly, practical, witty, accumulates many material possessions, blunt, pushes people out of way because their needs are more important, and feels "I'm worth it." They are more goal oriented and ambitious than any other type. They are realists who are stimulated by confrontations and "living on the edge."

DEFENSE MECHANISM / ADDICTION / MENTAL DISORDERS

Rationalization / Idealism / Narcissistic, Histrionic, and/or Manic-depressive personality disorders

MOTTO / SIGNALS THEY SEND

Everything will change by tomorrow. / They make exaggerated promises and claims resulting in no follow-through.

TO MAKE INNER CHANGES FOR HEALTHIER BEHAVIOR, REPEAT OUT LOUD

<u>I now release:</u>

- feeling that I will be overwhelmed by anxiety
- running away from the consequences of my actions
- sacrificing my health/happiness for instant gratification
- overextending myself with more than what I can do well
- wanting every moment to be exciting/dramatic
- insulting or abusing others to vent my frustrations
- believing that external things will make me happy
- fearing that there will not be enough for me

<u>I now affirm:</u>

- that I am happiest when I am calm and centered
- that there will be enough for me for whatever I need
- that I'm resilient/patient in face of setbacks
- that I care deeply about people and committed to their happiness
- that I can say no without feeling deprived
- that I find satisfaction in ordinary things

Type 8: THE CHALLENGER

(alias: the boss, leader, general, confronter)

HEALTHY

They are self-confident, strong, and assertive, heroic, uses self-restraint, resourceful, have a can-do attitude, decisive, confident, big hearted, defines self as "I carry others with my strength," turns the hopeless into the successful, and sees possibilities in people because they've done it too. Will sacrifice or put themselves into serious jeopardy to achieve their vision and have a lasting influence. They can achieve true heroism on the job or achieve historical greatness.

AVERAGE

They use bottom-line thinking, proud, dominate the environment, must control situations, have a lust for power, will bluff with kindness while strategizing for leverage, confrontational, and seldom back down. They hide their soft side so much that they lose touch with themselves. They are egotistical, financially independent, refuse to "back down" in conflicts. They feel they must push and pressure everyone into "shaping up" and follow their agenda. They are proud fighters.

UNHEALTHY

They use threats to get obedience from others. They become ruthless, dictatorial, immoral, and potentially violent. They can become predatory, a social outcast, a renegade, outlaw, and/or con artist. They can be vengeful, barbaric, and have sociopathic tendencies to a point where they may end up killing or murdering those who don't conform to their will.

AS CHILDREN

They learned to be tough and independent learning the best defense is a good offense. They often assumed adult responsibility by earning money to raise younger children, They felt betrayed by others which toughened their emotional side and they vowed to not let down their guard again. They were ambivalent and not strongly connected to the nurturing parent figure and, thus, took on a complementary patriarchal role (the little protector that others turn to for strength) in order to gain a sense of value, affection, and support from others. This formed their identity. They began to repress their fears/vulnerabilities to be strong enough to meet life challenges, which made it hard for them to get close to others. If abuse was given in childhood, they learned they couldn't rely on anyone and would not put their destiny in "somebody else's hands." They received messages of "don't be you, don't feel what you feel."

VALUES

Strength, power, assertiveness, having influence, wealth, control.

DESIRE →	FEAR →	RESPONSE →	RESULT
Healthy Level To always be in control of their environment, life, and destiny.	*Being harmed or controlled by others. Fear becoming weak and losing their strength.*	Courageous, selfless, gentle, compassionate, assertive, honorable, protective, decisive	Become selfless heroes who create the greatest good for greatest number of people. Protector
Average Level Convince/pressure others to do what they want in line with their agenda.	Of losing control of their environment and others are turning against them.	Combative, oppressive, defiant, extreme, boastful, bossy, egocentric.	Uses power to confront or pressure others and drives them away. Egos are too fragile to share the glory.
Unhealthy Level To be in control or invincible at any cost rather than surrendering.	Retaliation from others and their resources cannot hold out any longer.	Scheming, terrorizes others, immoral, vengeful, murderous, cruel, monstrous.	*Will sacrifice anyone to survive. Basic fear realized: they are harmed and controlled by others.*

FAMOUS CHALLENGERS

Martin Luther King, Donald Trump, Barbara Walters, Frank Sinatra, Roseanne, Alec Baldwin, "Don Vito

Corleone," Dr. Phill McGraw, Tony Soprano, Matt Damon, Mike Wallace, Betty Davis, "Darth Vader," FDR.

THEIR MAIN PROBLEM AND HOT BUTTONS
They feel, "I'm fighting for my life and others will take advantage of me if I let them." They can have a sexual lust and lust for power and desire to possess and control. Telling them what they can't do is upsetting. They want to become so powerful that everyone else would have to depend on them. They are uncomfortable with others if they can't act from this role. They create a contest of wills and bullies others to intimidate because they don't believe people are on their side.

TO IMPROVE YOUR RELATIONSHIP AND HELP A CHALLENGER
1. Be as independent as you can, don't need them or angle for something. 2. Find common values with them. There can only be one king or queen who rules. 3. Don't expect them to mellow. 4. Get to the point- not fancy or subtle. 5. Match their energy and nonverbal language with a strong voice, look into their eyes, and then lower your voice - and eventually they should follow. 6. Don't appear wimpy, indecisive, or indirect. They admire good craftsmanship even when they've been had. 7. Let them know they're hurtful

RECOMMENDATIONS FOR GROWTH
1. Review consequences before taking action too quickly. 2. Trust that most, not all, people will be loyal to you if you've been fair with them. 3. Take up a meditation practice. 4. Check out your impact with friends; are you being a pest? 5. Think of harm/good you can do to others. 6. Notice your tendency to blame others and watch how you bring on your own enemies. 6. Review insights about yourself to prevent denial.

CAREER
They are enterprising, self-starters, own businesses, have big plans and promises. They seek administrative positions or positions of power. Many are lawyers, business executives, military commanders, CEO's, union leaders, sports figures, teachers, and in the helping and health professions. They work best in a competitive environment with a clear chain of command for redress of grievances as well as in shared power positions. Their motto is "My way or the highway." If they're a boss, they won't tell you if you're doing well, but will drill you if you are not.

THE WINGS OF THE CHALLENGER
7 WING: "THE MAVERICK"
They are charismatic, bully others, independent, entrepreneurs, like large scale projects, take big risks, tell stories, exaggerate, easily feel betrayed, feel okay about making an enemy, and aggressive. They have a "cut to the chase," no-nonsense quality about them. They are the most materialistic, independent and outgoing personality of all. They throw money around.
9 WING: "THE BEAR"
Strong-willed but mild-mannered, crave power, planner, not passionate, fond of children and pets, don't like taking orders, like getting involved in politics and public affairs, have dual nature--can be warm at home and aggressive at work. They seem friendly while secretly sizing up people. They are both belligerent & kind.

DEFENSE MECHANISM / ADDICTION / MENTAL DISORDERS
Denial / Arrogant justice / Sociopath and Antisocial personality disorders.

MOTTO / SIGNALS THEY SEND
Never let them see you sweat / Straightforward, uncaring, blunt, controlling, intimidating, and punitive.

TO MAKE INNER CHANGES FOR HEALTHIER BEHAVIOR, REPEAT OUT LOUD
I now release:
- all anger, rage, and violence from my life.
- my fear of ever being vulnerable or weak
- believing that I do not need others
- feeling that I must look only after myself
- attempting to control everything in my life
- being verbally or physically abusive to others
- denying my need for affection
- my fear that others will control me
- feeling that I must never be afraid
- allowing my pride/ego to ruin my relationships

I now affirm:
- that I believe in others and care about their welfare
- that I am honorable and therefore worthy of respect
- that I'm most fulfilled by championing others
- that I love others and ask for their love in return
- that there is an authority greater than myself
- that I can be gentle without being afraid
- that I have tender feelings and good impulses
- that I'm big hearted and let others share the glory

Type 9: THE PEACEMAKER

(alias: the mediator, negotiator, conflict avoider, reconciler)

HEALTHY

They are accepting, emotionally stable, good natured, optimistic, self-conscious, trusting, supportive, reassuring, inclusive of others, independent, awakens to self, and uses kind, sweet words to others. They can listen to others non-judgmentally, good-natured, optimistic, and have a calming influence - harmonizing people together.

AVERAGE

They are too willing to keep the peace, wants things smooth and easy, gets complacent, simplifies problems, stubborn, too much eating, drinking, television, etc., passive, minimizes upsets, unwilling to change, neglectful, takes abuse for long periods and then blows up with anger-then worries that things won't ever be the same. They are imaginative and creative. They tune out reality and seem oblivious to the obvious. They become passive-aggressive and stubborn to resist attempts by others to engage them. They cling to fantasies, appease others to get them off their back, look for quick magical solutions, wait for their ship to come in romantically, and minimizes problems to appease others.

UNHEALTHY

They can get depressed, repress feelings, ineffectual, undeveloped and cut off from reality. They are the most withdrawn of all the types. The tune the negative out so nothing upsetting can get to them. They become depressed and listless and abandon themselves turning into shattered shells. They become dangerously irresponsible. Multiple personalities are possible.

AS CHILDREN

They either were close to parents or lived in a dysfunctional family and coped by disassociating from traumatic events. They never learned to become themselves and had difficulty in becoming independent from parents-- the prospect of separation between parents is terrifying to their inner stability. They have an idealized vision of reality.. They are often overlooked. They have an Idealized identification with parents = blocked out conflict = struggling to balance their rosy beliefs of parents with the pain of reality. They stay in the background. They received messages of "don't be (exist), don't bother me now, Don't."

VALUES

Emotional well-being, acceptance, harmony with others, traditional values, social/emotional stability.

DESIRE →	FEAR →	RESPONSE →	RESULT
Healthy Level *To have inner stability, peace of mind, and harmony in their environment.*	*Having conflict and losing their peace of mind.*	Easygoing, receptive, optimistic, humble, supportive, reconciling, forgiving, confrontative	Fulfillment and happy because they are present to themselves, more alive, and alert to self
Average Level To downplay the importance of problems in their world and keep things undisturbed.	Moving out of their comfort zone to deal with their problems	Defensive, puttering, ignoring, stubborn, indifferent, apathetic, "peace at any price."	Tunes out reality becoming oblivious and indifferent. Becomes resigned and waits for the magical solution.
Unhealthy Level To block out of their awareness anything that could affect them so as to preserve their illusions.	Acknowledging reality and their own role in their problems. That what has happened can't be undone.	Irresponsible, addictive "doormats," stonewalling, emotionless, numb, self-punishing, vacant	*Basic fear realized: they have become desolate, separated from others, and lost peace of mind.*

FAMOUS PEACEMAKERS

Whoopi Goldberg, Ronald Reagan, TV's "Marge Simpson," Walter Cronkite, Abraham Lincoln, "Edith Bunker", Rose Kennedy, Walt Disney, Norman Rockwell, Carl Jung, Walt Disney, Kevin Costner, Ringo Starr, Ron Howard, Janet Jackson, Gerald Ford, Hugh Downs, Jimmy Stewart, Lisa Kudrow, JFK.

THEIR MAIN PROBLEM AND HOT BUTTONS

They are reluctant in self-remembering, slow to respond to world around them, neglect the real person they're with which creates false hopes and comfortable illusions. They say "I'm nobody special"—being modest and reinforcing the desire to be in background for peace and little disruptions. Being ignored or bringing up any pain in the past irritates them.

RECOMMENDATIONS FOR GROWTH

1. Be independent so you can be there for others. 2. Wake up out of your routine. 3. Don't avoid conflicts-assert yourself tactfully and positively. 4. Join a group that encourages the expression of your gut feelings...anger.
5. Don't agree/disagree with others when you feel otherwise 6. Practice taking a position and stating it.

TO IMPROVE YOUR RELATIONSHIP HELP A PEACEMAKER

1. Do what you do and let them join in 2. Don't nag them or they'll tune you out completely or appease you.
3. Gently point out what they are denying 4. Watch their behavior, not words, give reassurance/encouragement 3. Since they deny their anger, encourage their negative feelings, say "it seemed you were mad too just now."

CAREERS

They make excellent mediators/diplomats and often found in helping, civil service, military or big-picture planning jobs (e.g. V.P. of administration), office manager, and multiple input jobs. They have problems with fast-paced jobs.

WINGS OF THE PEACEMAKER

8 Wing: "The Sensualist"
They are powerful and yet, gentle. They like rituals, action oriented, casual in nature, likes to tell jokes/stories. Enjoys jobs in consulting, sales, negotiating, and human resources. They are easy-going, yet, can have bad tempers and be stubborn.
1 Wing: "The Dreamer"
Can synthesize different schools of thought i.e. politics, philosophy and religion. They are creative and attracted to the arts, music, sports medicine, and academia. They enjoy careers in counseling, teaching, and ministering. They can become indignant and restrain anger instead of letting it out. They are sarcastic and moralizes behavior, cultures, and lifestyles.

DEFENSE MECHANISM / ADDICTION / MENTAL DISORDERS

Narcotization or Distraction / Indecision or Inaction / Passive-aggressive and Dependent personality dis.

MOTTO / SIGNALS THEY SEND

Don't rock the boat / They are unflappable. People feel unimportant because of their sloth

TO MAKE INNER CHANGES FOR HEALTHIER BEHAVIOR, REPEAT OUT LOUD

I now release:
- trimming away from whatever is unpleasant or difficult
- all dependency and fear of being on my own
- neglecting myself and my own legitimate needs
- feeling threatened by significant changes in my life
- going along with others to keep the peace
- refusing to see my own aggressiveness
- all wishful thinking and giving up too soon
- seeking quick, easy, solutions to my problems
- all inattentiveness and forgetfulness
- living through others and not developing myself

I now affirm:
- that I am confident, strong, and independent
- that I develop my mind and think things through
- that I am steadfast and dependable in difficult times
- that I am excited about my future
- that I actively embrace all that life brings
- that I'm awake and alert to the world around me
- that I am proud of myself and my abilities
- that I look deeply into myself without fear
- that I am a powerful healing source in my world

Strategy 1.7

Discover your purpose in life by summarizing your responses from the past six lessons and writing a personal life mission statement.

Your vision will become clear only when you can look into your own heart. Who looks outside, dreams; who looks inside, awakes
Carl Jung

Finding Your Mission in Life

When we become clear on our identity and who we are, we make better choices in our lives. Subsequently, we are better able to find our purpose or mission in life. A sense of identity usually evolves gradually as a result of hundreds of daily decisions: take a particular course in college, use drugs, become sexually active, date a particular person, become politically involved, and so forth. If we open ourselves up to self-knowledge, develop values, and experience the world, we start to see how we want to lead our lives. So our life mission unfolds over time.

What is a Mission?

A mission is an extension of a person's highest values. All goals you set for yourself should come from a Personal Life Mission Statement that you write for yourself; much like a mission statement that most businesses and institutions write for themselves and operate under. They do this so that their goals and objectives meet and support the values and wishes of the mission statement. This is how we should live our lives, yet most don't. So your mission is a solid expression of who you are and how you want to live your life. The mission prioritizes your values and goals and is the major criterion by which decisions can be evaluated. Your mission is to find the right direction and go down the right road in life that will bring you meaning, fulfillment, and happiness. Why? Victor Frankl drawing on his experiences in the death camp at Auschwitz, asserted that inmates who had a vision of some goal or purpose in life, had a much greater chance of surviving than those who had no sense of mission.

Many of us don't have a mission statement that guides us in life, and we therefore say 'yes' to projects that aren't related to our life mission statement. For example, if your mission statement is to only climb the corporate ladder at work and you're asked to work on four separate projects in one week, you could do the following. Instead of saying 'yes' under pressure to all four projects, say 'No' to two of the projects, consult on a committee on the third, and say yes to the fourth.

A similar scenario that shows the power of a mission statement is this one. Maybe a lateral transfer is appropriate in your position in the company so you can use your talents more productively and have less responsibility because it fits the values of your mission statement. Those values might be spending more time with family as opposed to seeking money, power, and status through your job.

Here's another scenario. If part of your mission statement is to spend one entire day during the weekend with your family, and you're invited to a baby shower on the family day, most people would succumb to the social pressure and cancel the family day. One who "sticks to their guns" and can say 'no' to the baby shower because it's family day is the one who truly achieves life balance and lives a life of character and dignity.

Myths about Missions

- You will be the only one on earth to have your particular mission. Wrong! Some parts of our mission are shared by others who have a similar mission.

- The whole world will see your mission and be affected by it. Learn instead that as the stone does not always know what ripples it has caused in the pond, so neither we nor
- those who watch our life will always know what we have achieved by our mission.
- It must be a big, grand mission that affects millions of people. There is a saying, "If you positively changed just one person's life for the better, you have done well."
- Your mission will never change. Don't think you have to get it right today. Just get it started.

How Do You Discover Your Mission?

The last six strategies of this chapter should have helped you to accomplish this purpose. You will have the opportunity to summarize your responses in this lesson. Here are some other tips to discovering your mission.

- Believe that you have a mission. Optimists are more successful than pessimists.
- Use the Mission Summary Box in this lesson to discover what brings meaning to your life.
- Identify patterns and overlapping pieces of information in your responses to the exercises and choose your top three items from the Mission Summary Box on the following pages.
- Write three results or goals you want to achieve that reflect those three items.
- Use an inner ritual to reflect upon how to put those items into action. An inner ritual is when you pause and go inside yourself (meditation, prayer, journal writing, being in nature, etc.).
- Ask yourself, "How will the world be a better place because of your mission."
- Prioritize, in order, the quality and quantity of time you wish to spend in your relationships with other people that make up the Top Seven Life Centers. Start with yourself first (and/or divine being), then your spouse (if you have one), your children, your friends and extended family, your co-workers and neighbors, your community, and, finally, the larger society/rest of the world. See below.

The Top Seven Life Centers

There are seven life centers to live your life from. If one lives life out of a center that is out of order, life becomes unbalanced leading to unhappiness and problems. They are:
1) You/The Divine Life Center. 2) Spouse Life Center. 3) Children Life Center. 4) Friends/Extended Family Life Center. 5) Co-workers and neighbors Life Center. 6) Community Life Center. 7) World Life Center. The idea is to put more attention and fulfill the first life center (your/divine life center) before spending time and energy on the rest of the life centers. When you fully know yourself, you are in the best position to then put attention on the second life center, the Spouse Life Center. If your spouse and you put time into each other, you can then have a better chance at being successful parents to children. Think about people you know who had a great relationship with their kids, or their friends, but their marriage was a mess. Spouse comes before children because when children perceive that their parents aren't in sync and are always fighting or not communicating, children learn that the world is unpredictable and inconsistent. They learn to pick up on unhealthy emotions such as shame, aggressiveness, guilt, passive-aggressive behaviors, etc., and they don't learn how to give, receive, and model the most important thing--love. Yet, when love within a marriage is present, then that naturally filters down to the children; the one thing a child needs are parents who dedicate their lives to each other instead of only to them. Keep it in order. Think of famous people who have achieved great things, yet, ended up lonely with no one to depend on and share their lives with. John Lennon fought for world causes but virtually ignored his son Julian as he grew up. If you learn how to communicate well with your kids, then you have a better chance of communicating with friends, family, community, and you will have an informed view on what's best for the future of the society.
Not communicating inside out (world-first, self-last) is like trying to teach a parenting class without ever having children. You wouldn't have a foundation of knowledge and experience. There are

many people who work for these great societal causes but their priorities have gone out of whack and they have many contradictions within themselves. For example, there are animal rights activists who believe animals are just as valuable as children and say they would have a hard time deciding whether to save a dog's life before a child's life if they could only choose one in a life-threatening drowning situation. Can you see how not being in touch with yourself and humanity can lead one astray to faulty thinking and behaving? It's because they're communicating outside-in instead of inside-out. If you place all of your energy on outside things like your career, money, and society, you'll miss out on the sacred things like enjoying meaningful relationships that truly provide long-term meaning and happiness.

Exercise 1

To become clear on where you've been and where you want to go in life, complete the following lifeline exercise. Include important dates and important people you met. Include moves, marriage, graduations, jobs, awards, broken hearts, first car, and so forth. Mark high points in your life above the line and low points below the line. *Then for the remaining years, write down what you hope to accomplish.* See the sample below to help you. *You could also record your lifeline as a poem, song, puzzle, collage, drawing of a tree branching out, or enhance it using clip art or computer graphics.*

* Will own my own clothing business

* Graduated from college

* Leadership Award in 9th grade.

* Got married

* Will retire and travel

---

0 5 10 15 20 25 30 35 40 45 50 55 60 65
Age

* Moved away to a new state (lost friends)

* Got divorced

* Broke up with boyfriend in 10th grade.

---

0 5 10 15 20 25 30 35 40 45 50 55 60 65
Age

Exercise 2 Below, transcribe the key factors you recorded in the past six lessons.

Mission Summary Box

Strategy 1.1 *(Self-awareness)* ▪ Personal Qualities ▪ Abilities ▪ Preferences ▪ Accomplishments	
Strategy 1.2 *(Values)* ▪ Personal ▪ Global ▪ Job ▪ Cultural ▪ Religious	
Strategy 1.3 *(Family Background)* ▪ Family Messages ▪ Birth Order Influences	
Strategy 1.4 *(Motivation)* ▪ Internal Motivators ▪ External Motivators	
Strategy 1.5 *(Job Skills)* ▪ Key Interests ▪ Career Personality e.g. Creater ▪ Occupations ▪ Majors	
Strategy 1.6 *(Enneagram Personality: Helper)* ▪ Personal Qualities ▪ Fears/Behaviors	

Mission Summary Box

Exercise 3 (The Mission Statement)

Below, write down a life philosophy or mission statement that incorporates your values, goals, roles, and the principles you want to live by. This mission statement should be a solid expression of who you are and how you want to live your life. Start with the end in mind by focusing on the future; what you want to be, who you want to be, what you want to do, and the values upon which being and doing are based. You could begin by writing, in order, how, what, where, when, who, and why you want to focus your time and energy with the Top 7 Life Centers mentioned on the previous pages. Then use the Mission Summary Box to further clarify your mission statement.

Examples of a Personal Mission Statement:

I will first take care of myself through the guidance of my God. I will prioritize time for me using self-care activities such as reading, talking with friends, journal writing, playing golf, and meditation. I will balance these activities with spending time with my spouse. Our relationship is a priority and if it is strong, our children will be strong. Thus, I will not spend more time with my children than with my spouse. My children are dear to me and I will sacrifice everything else for their health and well-being. If I am forced to obtain a job that requires me to work 60 hours a week, I would sell the house and get another job with less hours because it would take time away from myself, spouse, and children. My career will be dedicated toward helping others achieve their full potential. I may do this through my talents in music, social service, and/or writing. I will not allow my fear of not getting others' approval prevent me from being myself in pressure situations. I value the rights and freedoms our democratic country stands for and will defend them in all areas of my life.

My mission is to be a force for positive change and inspire others through being a model of service to others. I will seek to balance career and family as best I can. My home will be a place where my family and friends can find happiness, comfort, and joy. I will teach my children to love, learn, laugh, eat well, and develop their unique talents. I will continue to grow by stimulating my mind with new learning in the social sciences. I will not allow my fear of being ridiculed to prevent me from sharing my innermost thoughts with the ones I love. I value experiencing pleasure often as long as it doesn't hurt others or myself. Life is full of fun, pleasure, despair, struggle, responsibilities, hate, and love. I will love others more often and open myself to receiving love as well.

To help, think of it this way!

What do you want to be and do in the future? → Your Mission

↓

How do you plan to achieve the mission? → Your goals and the roles you will play

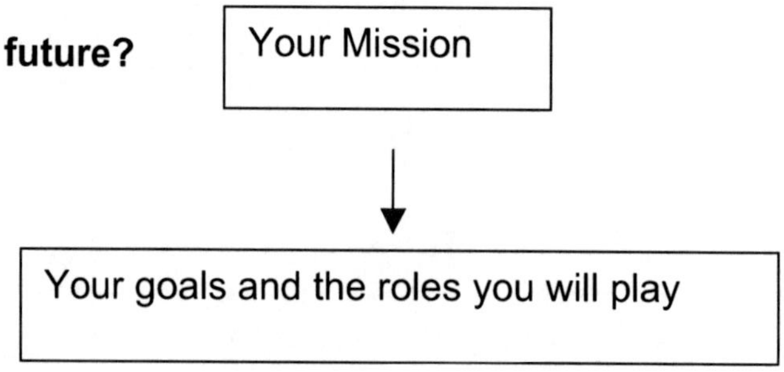

See the example on the following page.

My mission is to live with integrity, dignity, and to make a difference in the lives of others. The following goals will fulfill this mission: One, I will be charitable by seeking out ways I can sacrifice my time, talents, and resources toward helping others. Two, I will inspire others by loving them and encouraging them to be their best. Three, I will obtain a job in social services. The following roles take priority in achieving my mission: As a husband, my wife is the most important person in my life and I will spend more time with her than anyone. As a father, I will help my children become who they are inside instead of manipulating them into something they are not. As a scholar, I will research better ways to think and behave and to always have an open mind. As a brother, I will support my siblings in their endeavors and always show love.

Your turn! Write below or on a separate sheet of paper.

CHAPTER 2

Self-Understanding

Using your **Heart** to **Understand,** enlighten, and guide you toward your life's purpose.

Purpose: To allow your "True-Self" to steer you and your "life" in a direction you are best suited for.

Rewards: Meaning, Insight, On-Target, Motivation, Right Decision-Making

Obstacles: Ego, Self-Doubt, Others' Approval, Pride, Conformity

Consequence: Emptiness, Confusion, Feeling Lost, Off-Target, Bad Decisions

Symbol: **Compass**

Related Web Sites: **http://www.queendom.com**
http://www.selfgrowth.com

Self-Understanding

What lies behind us and what lies before us are tiny matters compared to what lies within us.

Oliver Wendell Holmes

Many celebrities in our culture achieve tremendous success because they take the time to understand their target audience. Yet many of these same celebrities also succeed at achieving high rates of suicide, depression, and addiction because they fail to take the time to understand their true Self and their inner values, priorities, and desires. Consider people like Whitney Houston, Amy Winehouse, Heath Ledger, Charlie Sheen, Anna Nicole Smith, Chris Farley, Elvis Presley, Curt Kobain, River Phoenix, John Belushi, and a whole host of celebrities who commit suicide, bring embarrassment to themselves, or trot through the revolving door of drug rehabilitation centers. They spend so much time mastering their communication with the "outside world," that they fail to master the ability to communicate with their "inside world." It is this key factor that causes them to suffer and go astray. We, like the celebrities, fall into the same traps without the fame and media attention.

This chapter is dedicated toward understanding the Self and the Thinking Mind that we all share as human beings. The Thinking Mind Model on the next page illustrates what occurs in the mind beneath our behaviors and can steer us toward positive change. When we take the time to understand each mental system that includes our judgments, emotions, beliefs, expectations, attitudes, and behaviors, we empower ourselves to reach our full potential. Once we do this, we can have, be, and do what we want in our lives. For example, imagine buying a $2,000 computer and bringing it home. The computer manual is lying next to the computer, but you say to yourself, "Ah, I will read it another day." In this way, you are getting about 20% out of your computer's potential when you could be getting close to 100%. Likewise, many of us do not take the time to read the <u>manual to our own mind</u>. It is commonly thought that we use up to 10% of our brain, but if we took the time to understand the contents of our beliefs, emotions, attitudes etc., we would truly begin to reach our full potential and advance our lives. This self-knowledge and understanding will allow you to bring insight into your challenges, meaning into your life, motivation into your goals, and intelligence into your decisions.

Each of us has a core personality, a true Self that would stay the same even if we were to grow- up in a different country. This is the part of us that would stay the same. Yet the pressures in life can take us away from our selves, leaving us to make decisions that can destroy our lives and cause us undo suffering. Therefore, this chapter aims at helping you access the essence of who you really are (the heart) and guides you into focusing on that part of you that knows you better than you know yourself. This will allow you to improve your ability to understand how you mentally operate and navigate through your thoughts, values, beliefs, and attitudes on a day-to-day basis. This will offer you the skills needed to make better decisions and reach your full potential so you can live, thrive, and produce like never before.

As you learn more about yourself when you complete the exercises between Chapters 2 - 4, think about how these new insights will help you to revise your Personal Life Mission Statement. You will have the chance to revise your statement in Chapter 5.

THE THINKING MIND MODEL

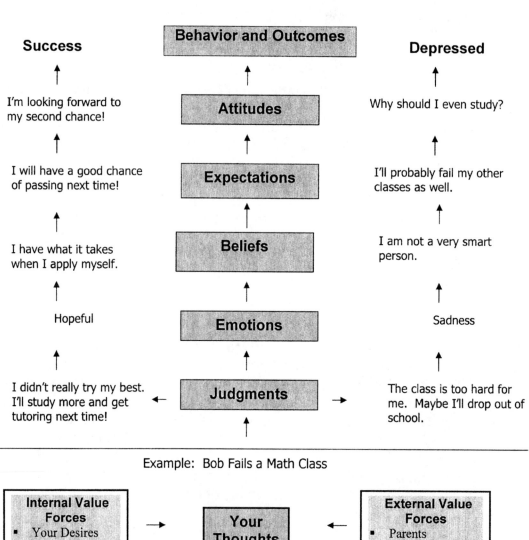

Success	Behavior and Outcomes	Depressed
↑	↑	↑
I'm looking forward to my second chance!	**Attitudes**	Why should I even study?
↑	↑	↑
I will have a good chance of passing next time!	**Expectations**	I'll probably fail my other classes as well.
↑	↑	↑
I have what it takes when I apply myself.	**Beliefs**	I am not a very smart person.
↑	↑	↑
Hopeful	**Emotions**	Sadness
↑	↑	↑
I didn't really try my best. I'll study more and get tutoring next time! ←	**Judgments**	→ The class is too hard for me. Maybe I'll drop out of school.
	↑	

Example: Bob Fails a Math Class

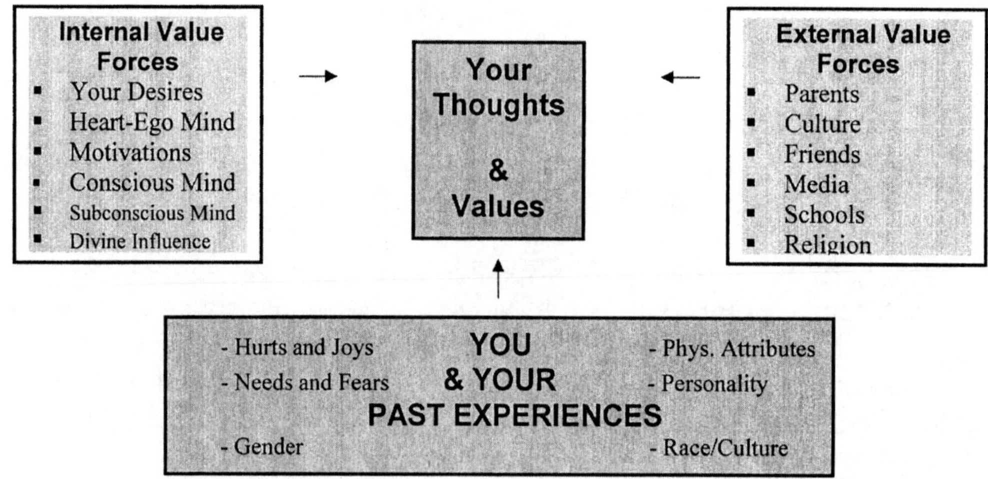

Explaining The Thinking Mind Model

Below the line: Chapter 1

The boxes below the line illustrate what was covered in Chapter One.

The lower box (You and Your Past Experiences) illustrates how you are the combination of your mental, physical, cultural, and psychological influences that make you uniquely, you. Your past experiences (your wounds, joys, how you were parented, your encounters with others) coupled with your own personality, gender, and so on influence the middle box; your thoughts and values.

The lower right box (External Value Forces) also influences your thoughts and values and what is and isn't important and valuable in life. For example, the American culture emphasizes the value of being thin.

The lower left box (Internal Values Forces) also influences your thoughts and values and what is valuable/invaluable, right/wrong, good/bad, decent/indecent. Other internal influences are the Heart and Ego Mind, the Conscious Mind, the Subconscious Mind, and Divine influence (if you have that as a value as over 90% of Americans do), which will all be explained in Strategy 2.1 of this chapter.

The lower middle box (thoughts and values) are the strongest forces within you. They will determine and color how you perceive the world as you do in your own unique way. Your thoughts will largely explain why you behave as you do and get the outcomes you get in your life.

The bad news (if you had negative programming) is about 95% of everyone's mental programming is set by the age of twenty. The good news is that you can change your thoughts in a more positive and realistic manner to undo some of the negative programming and ultimately change your behavior and life outcomes.

Above the line: Chapter 2

The boxes above the line illustrate what will be covered in Chapter Two. Now let's take a look at how each mental system (judgments, emotions, beliefs, expectations, attitudes) affects the other and results in your behavior and your success or failure in things. *Our judgments, emotions, beliefs, expectations, and attitudes are mental systems; the way we choose to describe an experience or a piece of reality and make conclusions about that experience/reality.* You can use your thoughts to change the judgments you make about yourself as well as the judgments you make about people, events, and everything that happens in life.

Example: Bob Fails a Math Class

As you follow the arrows on the opposite page (The Thinking Mind Model), your thoughts determine the judgments you make about yourself and the judgments you make about events. In the example, Bob can choose to view the event of failing his math class in a positive or negative manner. He can either make the judgment that he didn't try his best and will study more next time or he can judge the event as negative and maybe drop out of school. He has the power to choose his thoughts that influence his judgments.

If Bob judges the event of failing his math class as negative, that judgment determines (affects) his emotions (sadness), which determines his negative beliefs about himself, which determines his expectations about failing future classes, which determines his defeatist attitude toward school, which determines his behavior and outcome; depressed.

If Bob judges the event as positive and will study more and get tutoring, then that will determine his emotion of being hopeful, which will determine more positive beliefs, expectations and attitudes about completing a future class and his behavior and outcome would be to either enroll in the next class, get a tutor, and have a higher chance of success.

In addition to events, the model applies to how you feel about yourself. If Sue views herself as unworthy because she is fifteen pounds overweight, she could look at the Thinking Mind Model and see that her External Value Forces that shaped her opinion of herself came from an image and weight obsessed American Culture and the Media. She would then want to create her own value (like you did in Strategy 1.2), and she may value that being a little overweight is fine and that being healthy is what matters. This new value would empower more positive thoughts. She could use these thoughts to now judge that she is worthy but will eat wiser and exercise. This would create more positive emotions, beliefs about herself, and positive expectations and attitudes about her making both internal and external changes to create success in her behavior and outcomes.

This chapter will focus the importance of empowering each mental system. Empowering one doesn't work because you can make healthy judgments but still fight unhealthy beliefs about yourself. We need to empower each mental system to obtain inner wholeness, personal success, and Self-Understanding.

Strategy 2.1

Empower Your Thoughts Using Your 3 Minds: The Heart-Mind, The Conscious Mind, and the Sub-Conscious Mind.

Definition: The Heart Mind - An inner guide that puts us in touch with our true-self, our life purpose, and provides insight into how to best steer our life. It is the source of our emotions, personality, and deepest desires and goes beyond the intellect. It collects all our sorrows and joys and puts us in touch with the sacred. The Heart has an intelligence that seems to know us better than we know ourselves. Without it we might never weave our way through the maze of illusion, doubt, and fear we have collected as we've traveled through life's events.

The ancestor to every behavior is a thought.
Ralph Waldo Emerson

Can You Speak from the Heart?

By the time we reach adulthood, we often lose the ability to be in touch with our heart; our true self. This is because we had been busy trying to impress those we were attracted to, lying to get people to like us, or manipulating people to get what we want. Also, we were taught to suppress our feelings and control our emotions. By adulthood, speaking from the heart can become difficult because we are often not in touch with how we feel and when we are, it is hard to communicate that feeling in a genuine and sincere manner. By getting to know what is in your heart and doing the meditation exercises at the end of this strategy you will notice the following benefits.

Benefits	Obstacles
You come off authentic, real, and genuine.	Trying to impress others
You defeat doubt, fear, and need for approval.	Being fake to get your way
You make decisions that reflect your true values	Trying to avoid pain
You develop trust and respect from others	Trying to exert control over others
You generate love, compassion, self-confidence, and express your true-self.	Lying to others to get what you want.

We hear about the Heart in song lyrics, religion, and relationships! Ask yourself if you have said in the past:

"It just wasn't in my Heart",
"What does your Heart or gut say"
"It'll do your Heart good"
"From the bottom of my Heart"
"It came straight from the Heart"
"My Heart was set on..."
"I had a change of Heart"
"In my Heart of Hearts"
"To my Heart's content"
"With all of my Heart"
"Take Heart"
"I Set my Heart on..."
"Cross my Heart"
"I followed my Heart"
"I knew in my Heart"

Notice how each of these phrases reflect something intelligent within us (the Heart) that seems to know us better than we know ourselves. If you were to ask people what it was that helped them to make the smart decision to a) find their life goal or career b) choose their soulmate, or c) choose their friends, they would likely tell you that they felt something in their Heart that told them to do so. How many times in your life could you have used a "magic" decision maker like the Heart? Instead, you ignored the Heart and chose the wrong person, career, path, home, etc.

Where is the Heart?

INNER RITUAL

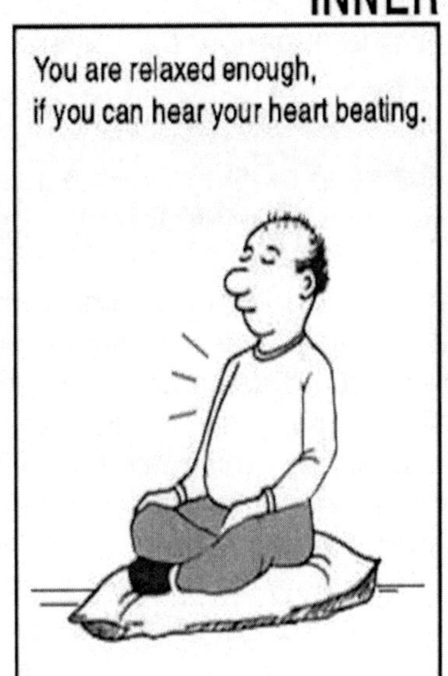

You are relaxed enough,
if you can hear your heart beating.

You are too relaxed,
if you can hear yourself snoring.
Z
Z
Z
Z

There are transmitters in the Heart that communicate directly to the brain. The Heart thinks but does not know that it thinks like the brain does. In Joseph Pearce's book, "Evolution's End," he documents that actions in the physical Heart precede the actions of both body and brain. In other words, our brain sends a running report of some environmental situation to the Heart, and the Heart, through neurotransmitters, advises the brain to make a proper response. Pearce mentions that intellect involves the brain while intelligence involves the Heart. I am capitalizing the word Heart because the human Heart is a lot more than the physical Heart. However, the physical Heart has incredible precision, complexity and perfection. It performs continuously for 24 hours a day, nonstop for up to 120 years. It is a masterpiece of strength and endurance because it beats 100,000 times a day, 2 1/2 billion times in a lifetime, pumping 6 quarts of blood through 96,000 miles of blood vessels every minute. This equals 25,000 quarts a day or 1/2 billion quarts in a lifetime. It cannot be fully duplicated. Its tissue is thinner than tissue paper, and yet pound for pound, it is stronger than steel. It oxygenates every cell and organ in the body. Whether we feel things in the physical Heart or not is not important. What is important is that **there is something deep within each of us that we can access during times of stress, indecision, and confusion.** Listen to it! Yet, 70% of people are in the wrong career (based on a survey that indicated 70% of workers were unhappy with their job) and 50% of marriages fail. We don't always make the best decisions for ourselves.

What is the Self and Where is it?

Notice the self is not an organ or a place in the brain or body that one can point to. Some believe the location is distinct in the physical body and others believe it is an individual spiritlike essence. Some psychologists say the self is that mental activity (conscious and unconscious) which determines how one thinks, feels, and behaves. Some philosophers say the self is "a bundle of perceptions," which the Buddists would say, inteferes with pure experience where one can harmoniously unify with the flow of life and have no need for the concept of an identity or a self. Nonetheless, many serious thinkers agree that one's self must be fully developed before it can be transcended. Near the onset of puberty, each developing self begins to discover its own feelings, beliefs, and thoughts. Through the years, a consistency and self-system develop which cut the umbilical cord from its parental/societal authority and goes on internal power. If one's conditioning was validating, loving, and accepting, then one is more likely to accept all that one is regardless of personality flaws, bad habits, and character defects. In this example, one with a clear sense of self knows one's likes and dislikes, has a sense of right and wrong, and is honest with oneself and others displaying authenticity and ability to be genuine. If rejected, one's life is not shattered, the integrity of the self remains intact, and the self-worth is not seriously affected. This is similar to Maslow's description of self-actualized individuals. When the self is in this empowered state, many religions encourage the transcendence of the self where again one can harmoniously unify with life and not have a need for a self. The Heart exercises in this lesson will help you to connect with this self and experience it beyond the confines of the intellect. Note the different parts of the self below.

The Self-Image - The combination of all the messages, voices, and experiences that have happened to you over the course of your life that form the picture of who you believe you are. It is the way you see or think about yourself. We all have a self-image on a low/high scale about how good of a spouse, husband, wife, father, mother, son or daughter, cook, worker, etc. that we are. Are you sure you see yourself accurately? The trick mirrors at the circus don't accurately reflect who you really are. Your self-image could be completely different compared to what others think of you or how you really are, positive or negative. Some people have an inflated self-image and others have a low self-image because they minimize their strengths. Your interpretation of your life experiences and events and the messages you accepted as gospel helped to paint the picture you have of yourself. The self-image attaches meaning to experiences and colors our perceptions so we can interpret the events in our lives. Most of us live our lives from the self-image, which consults with the ego, instead of living our lives from the "Heart".

The Ego - The ego is the selfish part of you that is interested only in self-gain. The ego is the result of social programming which has persuaded us that we are separate, distinct entities from everything and everyone. It is much more comfortable in the intellect, always judging and never wanting to submit to anything internal, emotional, or spiritual. When we react to life's urgencies and intensities with defensiveness, insecurity, anxiety, or fear, these overreactions are the ego's ways of taking care of itself when it feels threatened. It has its own set of beliefs that are perceived to be best for you but really, they aren't. It is very fragile and feels it has to control everything or else it will die! The ego believes its worth is what they do, what they have, and what others think of them and can't think in terms of one's inner worth and qualities. Switching attention from the ego to the heart will empower you to be your true self.

Differences Between The Heart and The Ego

Notice that there are always only two choices that you can listen to and follow before acting or deciding upon a decision. They are the "Heart" and the ego. The model below lists a parallel of **values** between both the "Heart" and the ego. We either consciously or subconsciously choose one of the two mindsets that create thoughts and pieces of logic in our mind. If you choose the ego mindset, you will program a false-self and low self-image because it is devastated by negative setbacks and relies solely on outside approval from others. If you choose the "Heart's" mindset, you will achieve a high self-image that is based on your own approval rather than approval from other people, which is always conditional. Your true-self is the "*you*" that can be found at your absolute core. It is all of your strengths and values that are uniquely yours and need expression, versus what you have been programmed to believe that you are supposed to be and do. It is the part of you that remains when life's pain and experiences have been stripped away. If you are empowering a false-self to fulfill a role or others expectations instead of your true-self, your energy and health will be drained. Your Heart can bring you back to your true-self where warmth, energy, and health are regained. The Heart-Ego Values Model on the next page will help you to understand the Heart's internal focus and ego's external focus.

The Heart-Ego Values Model

Heart Values (has soft voice)	**Ego Values** (has obnoxious voice)
Intrinsic *(inside oriented)*	Extrinsic *(outside oriented)*
Seeks truth (gives benefit of doubt to others)	Seeks power (only open to info. that supports beliefs)
Motivation is meaning & purpose	Motivation is self-gratification (taking care of #1)
Conscience is decision maker	Approval from group/others is decision maker
Includes others who are different	Excludes others who are different
Contains its own energy	Has to rob energy from others (like bullies)
Promotes goodness and service	Promotes selfishness (give me, give me)
Carefully & compassionately judges others	Prejudges, misjudges and discriminates others
Access is through non-thought	Access is through thought
Fulfillment through self-congruency	Fulfillment by approval and praise of others
Spiritual	Material ("buy me this, buy me that")
Liberated from the outside world	Slave to the influences of the outside world
Emphasizes personal values	Emphasizes societal or social values
Learns from bad experiences	Crippled by bad experiences (I'm a loser)
Thankful	Takes people and things for granted
Trusts	Controls and manipulates
Forgives	Holds grudges (you hurt me-I'll never forgive you)
Humble (I apologize and can learn from that)	Proud (I'll never admit I'm wrong)
Knows you better than you know yourself	Knows you less
True self	False self

The Heart as a Spiritual Messenger

Many people grow up with a certain portrait of God or similar entity, depending on their religion (if we grew up with one). People report that the "Heart" can be thought of as acting like the messenger (communication/command center) between you and one of the following entities: One's Higher Power, God, the Life Force, the Great Spirit, Mother Earth, or anything believed to be more divine and powerful than themselves. Thus, the heart can speak to you in profound ways. Many people with highly strong addictions, disease, and disorders have been cured. They attribute their recovery and health to these entities. The 12-step Anonymous Programs which have helped millions to recover from alcoholism, overeating, gambling, co-dependency, etc., have a higher success rate for recovery than any other type of therapy. The success of their participants is due to the support of a group community as well as a belief in a "Higher Power."

The Magic Pill is Within

Listening to our internal world rather than to our external world will guide us to greater **Self-Understanding**. It's fascinating that most cultures who have never come in contact with each other, teach their young a story similar to the *Adam and Eve* story of the Bible. What does that tell you? Perhaps there is something similar in human nature and the human experience that is within us all. The story mentions how Adam and Eve chose to eat from the tree of knowledge (outside) so that they could become like gods. They were tricked into believing that the answer is "out there" and separate from themselves. Today, when we need advice, don't we look toward the "tree of experts" to tell us how to proceed? This list includes the doctors, therapists, teachers, scientists, priests, politicians, popculture heroes, friends, parents, media, culture, Oprah (just kidding), and so on. Yet, when we seek the data to make an intelligent decision, we find that most of our answers are within ourselves. Human beings have been looking outside of themselves, searching for the "magic pill" or "magic bullet" or piece of knowledge that will bring happiness and fulfillment. I am not suggesting that you do not look outside yourselves for knowledge but rather to look both outside and inside yourself for your life's answers.

Empower your 3 Minds

In ancient times, people believed that psychological problems and behavior such as stress, depression, and happiness were caused by one's soul or by evil or good spirits. Today, most psychologists believe that behavior, and one's potential are caused by only a person's genetic makeup, socialization, and one's desire to control one's behavior, while psychologists often deny the spiritual side of existence.

A more comprehensive picture of powerful forces that can shape our thinking, behavior, and one's potential are presented below with explanations, metaphors, and a chart. The chart illustrates how today's most popular institutions deal with shaping behavior and what they leave out. These institutions teach wonderful teachings but often leave out at least one of the Three Minds that is within each human being. These different minds affect one's behavior and potential as well as one's inner and outer life circumstances and experiences.

1. The Heart/Superconscious Mind: This all knowing mind provides insight, creativity, inspiration, and inner and outer fulfillment and can be accessed through meditation, dreams, journaling, prayer, intuition, and several other means. Artists, musicians, or anyone who has *created* something awesome usually assert that they tapped into this higher mind. Artists like Stevie Nicks and Lindsey Buckingham of Fleetwood Mac, Juian Lennon, David Crosby, Branford Marsalis, Sinead O'Connor, Jeff Lynne of ELO and the Traveling Wilbury's, George Harrison of the Beatles, Ron Wood of the Rolling Stones, and so many other artists emphasize that true inspiration comes when they can relax their mind, get their ego out of the way, and tap into this Superconscious Mind (Boyd, 1992). Also people who have addictions that cause dysfunction, pain, disease, and death attribute the conquering of their addiction to letting go of their willpower (the conscious mind) to allow something higher than themselves to give them the power to take back control in their lives. To deny this mind is to deny the millions of people that attribute their creativity and healing to this power.

2. The Reasoning/Conscious Mind: This mind is the President of the Personality or the Captain of the Ship. It is "you" consciously perceiving (viewing events through your senses), making decisions and directing thoughts and actions into behavior through willpower, discipline, discernment, concentration, and reasoning. This conscious mind controls the mental processes of which we are aware and alert. It can be accessed for positive works in one's life by the use of affirmations, visualizations, goal-setting, problem-solving methods, and other therapeutic-like techniques. It can also be used for selfish purposes of gaining power and control of others.

3. The Non-Reasoning/Subconscious Mind: This mind can be understood as the "habit mind." It stores all of our habits (both positive and negative), memories, thoughts, feelings, desires and instincts, whether we know it stores it or not. It can follow the orders of the Reasoning/Conscious Mind whether the orders are rational or irrational. If you tell it that "you are stupid, unworthy, and a loser," then it will oblige and create thoughts and beliefs and convince you that you are that. So be careful what you tell it. People can unintentionally create illness in their body by unconsciously programming the illness into their body through fear emotions like, self-hatred, revenge, quitting, victim consciousness, self-sabotage, etc. Lower reasoning will maximize and falsify one's weaknesses and minimize one's strengths leading to low self-worth. This is why our Reasoning/Conscious Mind needs to be strong to filter out negative, lower reasoning from this mind. Otherwise, the Subconscious Mind will be the President of the Personality and "Call the shots" and send one to a life of fear, anxiety, low self-esteem, worry, and depression.
However, sometimes it will communicate to you in the form of fear (butterflies in your stomach-adrenaline) to get the conscious mind to pay attention to something important like, the need to confront somebody or take action toward something being resisted by the conscious mind (you). The conscious mind then needs to honor these feelings and fears and communicate with them with the promise of addressing the issues at hand. The fear will usually begin to subside. However, if the conscious mind chooses to ignore it, curse it, suppress it, or fear it, the fear can escalate into something bigger than it should be.

Mind Metaphors

The Gardener: The Conscious Mind can be thought of as the gardener who plants the seeds (thoughts) into the garden soil, which is the Subconscious Mind. It will grow whatever kind of seed is planted, be it a weed or a beautiful flower. For example, if you think a colleague at work snubbed you, you can either plant the seed of hatred into your subconscious mind toward that person, or you can consciously decide to confront the person to find out if it was personal or had nothing to do with you. If, for example, you want to get a college degree, you can either plant into your subconscious mind that you will obtain your degree through hard work, commitment, and visualization, or you can plant doubt, worry, and fear that you probably don't have "What it takes" to be able to really obtain an actual college degree. Either way, the subconscious will help provide what you tell it. What you put your mind and attention on, grows!! So make sure it is healthy.

The Computer Programmer: The Conscious Mind can be the Computer Programmer who programs encouraging, successful, and positive thoughts into the Subconscious mind. The subconscious mind is like the software that will obey any command you give it. Just get in a habit of allowing the conscious mind to click the positive thought button, over a period of 21 days, and your subconscious mind will follow orders with far less disturbance (not thoughts of "I can't") and computer/mind crashes.

Driving a Car: When you first learn how to drive a car, you need your conscious mind to be alert to learn the skills of driving within the lanes, using your turn signal, braking with the right foot pressure, observing other cars and signs of the road. As you learn and progress through time, this learning goes on automatic and you don't have to think as much about how to drive because the Subconscious Mind stores these skills and impulses and will perform what you have been telling it.

Instantaneous Solutions: Most of us have tried, in vain, to solve a difficult problem, only to have the solution pop into our head later when we were thinking about something else? When a problem needs to be solved, we can tell the Subconscious Mind that we would like the solution within an hour. Then while you distract yourself with something else, the subconscious mind is working hard to get the solution, which usually pops into our thoughts. Make sure you write it down because it can disappear as quickly as it appears.

The chart below illustrates (the shaded area is what each institution emphasizes) how *traditional psychology* does a great job at teaching people how to use the subconscious and conscious minds but they often don't acknowledge the power of the Superconscious Mind, (blank area) which has the greatest therapeutical track record for helping those with addictions that cause disease and death.

The Alcoholics Anonymous program and other *Anonymous programs* do a great job at teaching people how to use the Superconscious Mind to help others. Yet, they argue that all power is in God and that the alcoholic has no power. The author believes it is important to consider the need for all three. One must utilize God's power or the Superconscious power, utilize one's personal power, the conscious mind, and utilize one's subconscious mind power which can be done through affirmations and creative visualization.

The *materialist* sees everything through the lens of "science" and believes that the only thing that is real is what you can verify with your five senses. Because you cannot see the subconscious and superconscious, they do not exist to the materialist.

Hypnotists, who help some people change negative behavior to more positive behaviors give too much power to the subconscious mind and think it is largely the key to behavior but they often don't value the conscious mind, and the Superconscious/God/Higher Self.

Many *religious fundamentalists and New Age* groups who are very involved with God and with using the power to fight negative forces have never been taught to examine the programming that takes place in their subconscious mind through socialization. As a result, they are spiritually developed but not psychologically developed. Therefore, they end up experiencing similar problems without the beneficial power of using the three minds.

	Subconscious	Conscious	Superconscious
Traditional Psychology	X	X	
Alcohol. Anon.			X
Materialist		X	
Hypnosis	X		
Religious-Fundamentalism /New Age		X	X

Scientific Research Studies on the Benefits of Prayer and Visualization

Transpersonal psychology studies that which goes beyond the personal and beyond the physical. There is now scientific evidence on the effects of how prayer and positive visualization actually heal people. People have known this for thousands of years, but scientists, and most atheists, have usually been skeptical. This "nonlocal" healing has widespread support in most cultures. In fact, over 150 studies according to Benor (1993), have been conducted looking at these kinds of positive exchanges that seem to preclude any kind of conventional explanation. The research eliminates any direct placebo effect because of the use of a double blind test. See below.

- For example, a famous study conducted by Dr. Randy Byrd (1988), worked with patients in a coronary care unit. He had a randomly assigned prayer group pray for some of his patients. He then matched these patients with a control group of patients for whom there was no prayer. What he found was that people who were prayed for by the distant prayer group, and who, in fact, did not know that they were being prayed for, had fewer complications and left the hospital quicker than the control group who was not prayed for.
- To prove that positive visualizations can effect fungus cultures according to Monty & Monty (1981), ten subjects tried to inhibit the growth of fungus cultures in a laboratory by concentrating on them for fifteen minutes from fifteen miles away. "Of the194 culture dishes, 151 showed retarded growth" (p. 90-93).
- In a double-blind experiment involving 393 persons admitted into a coronary care unit, intercessory prayer was offered from a distance to roughly half of the subjects. Significantly fewer patients in the prayer group required ventilation, antibiotics, had cardiopulmonary arrests, developed pneumonia, or required diuretics. Subjects in the prayer group had a significantly lower "severity score" based on their hospital course following admission (Byrd, 1988).
- A more recent and comprehensive look at the literature was published in the March journal, "Research on Social Work Practice." The Arizona State University study conducted a comprehensive analysis of 17 major studies on the effects of intercessory prayer (prayer that is offered for the benefit of another person in distress). After compiling studies that showed prayer had no positive effect and others that showed prayer had positive effects, the final conclusion after averaging across all 17 studies, showed a net positive effect for prayer groups. **This is the most thorough and all-inclusive study of its kind on this subject because it is not a single work with a single conclusion (Hodge, 2007).**

If you doubt this, look up the research in the references at the end of this book. It makes you wonder if, in the future, when a doctor doesn't prescribe prayer for his/her patient, could the doctor be sued? "Nonlocal" events have repeatedly been demonstrated experimentally within quantum physics, our most impressive science, for over two decades Herbert (1987). If prayer/intentions/thoughts can influence the physiology of a distant person, it requires that we be more thoughtful and responsible, not only for our actions, but for the ways in which we think about and interact with other people. It is recommended that you go to that "nonlocal" spiritual part of you, the "Heart," to connect with its intelligence for your life's answers. See the exercises on the next page. Meditation and other relaxation techniques (yoga, guided imagery, self-hypnosis) are excellent vehicles that can take you to the Heart. **These techniques helped college students attain significantly higher GPAs in a key study (Hall, 1999). Other dramatic results from meditation programs include a 40 to 45 percent reduction in medical symptoms and psychological distress (Salzberg & Kabat-Zinn, 1997).** Employing a technique regularly for only 15 minutes can produce incredible results, including optimism, increased energy, centeredness, happiness, and reduction in pain. Try the exercises on the next page to start.
In the movie, "What the bleep do we know," they interview the brightest scholars about quantum physics and how the science of the future will study and tap into thae spiritual essence unseen.

Exercise 1

The Insight Meditation

1. Find a quiet spot, sit, and close your eyes. Now cover your ears with your hands (or wear ear plugs) and take slow deep breaths for about 3 minutes while listening to your breathing. Ask the "Heart" these separate questions. (Spend I minute on each question).
2. Write your answers below.

a) What part of my life should I be spending more time and energy on?________________

____

____

b) How should I go about making it happen?________________

____

____

c) What could I do to make my life more simple and quiet?________________

____

____

d) What I want most in life is________________

____

____

Exercise 2

The Love Send Exercise

1. Close your eyes while sitting in a somewhat quiet spot (home, car, office, etc.).
2. Think of loved ones you want to send love to for 1-2 minutes.
3. For the next 3-4 minutes, as you exhale, send peace and love to each person you visualize.
   Imagine filling them up with the joy and happiness they need.
4. Breathe in their pain (dark and heavy) and breathe out your happiness to them (light, clear and radiant).
5. Know that this exercise cannot hurt you, but will develop your compassion and heal you of resentments and anger.

Exercise 3

The Sacred Home Meditation

1. Collect some sacred objects that will bring you closer to your "Heart". Example: photographs of loved ones, a special quote, flowers, a candle, something from nature, religious symbols, mementos, etc.
2. Close your eyes and hold the sacred object to your Heart as you feel the sensations that arise in your body. If there's grief or pain, breathe it into your Heart.

3. Allow an image to arise. Example: place-mountain; person-best friend; or time in your life-your younger days or special event in which you felt absolutely and completely safe. Allow that image to enter your Heart to find a permanent home. Embrace the safety and access it during times of anxiety. Draw the image of safety and place it in a location you see often.

Strategy 2.2

Empower your Judgment system.

Definition: Judgments - Decisions and assumptions made about ourselves, others, events, and things. We judge things based on information taken from our memory of experiences and we either judge them as right or wrong, good or bad and/or valuable or invaluable.

A habit is something you can do without thinking, which is why most of us have so many of them.
Frank A. Clark

We are Judgment Machines

What faulty judgments lie in you today? Do you ever ask yourself, "Why am I so critical about myself and others?" To increase **Self-Understanding** in this area, observe and bring awareness to all the subconscious decisions you've made about yourself in the past. The judgment system is where all of your programming takes place. For example, the messages your parents gave you determined how you judged yourself growing up. As adults, those judgments and neurotic thinking patterns still play havoc with our minds. Some of the most successful people falsely condemn themselves as adults because of the negative programming they received as a child. For example, rape victims sometimes feel it is their fault; some men and women are taught to feel that masturbation is a sin; and top leaders in their fields such as Howard Cosell, Richard Lewis, and David Letterman often criticize their success to a point where they can't enjoy it. Growing up, we experience insults, criticisms, and judgments such as, "you can't," "you're stupid", or "you will never amount to anything." Some of these comments may have come from our parents. Likewise, we usually do the same thing by judging others and our selves. So, we judge everything. We learn to judge our pains, our joys, our abilities, our intellect, our appearance, our worthiness, our imperfections, and so on. *We judge ourselves for what we should be and rarely accept our selves just as we are. Our judgments often aim* at *maximizing our weaknesses and minimizing our strengths.* It is analogous to listening to only one instrument in an orchestra. In this way, you miss the whole symphony. So, when we attempt, but are unable to reach our idea of perfection based on messages from parents, God, and our selves, we judge our selves too critically.

Empower the Heart to Make Healthy Judgments

While the Heart relates to our emotional brain (limbic system), the judgment system relates to our thinking brain (neocortex). The thinking brain can empower healthy thought or unhealthy thought, which is related to the ego. If our ego is more developed than our Heart, we will then give more power and attention to those desires (selfishness, exerting control) and thoughts that come from the ego. However, we need to develop our Heart since our culture and, most likely, our parents, have over-developed our ego. Therefore, if we more fully develop our judgment system, we can then make better decisions about our lives that reflect our true selves. Like a Christmas tree, you'd rather get your nutrients from the ground (the Heart) instead of from a bowl of water in an artificial living room environment (the ego).

Watch your judgments, they become your words. Watch your words, they become your actions. Watch your actions, they become your habits. Watch your habits, they become your character. Watch your character, it becomes your destiny.

How Faulty Judgments Ruin Lives

A woman named Tonya was abused, sexually, by her father when she was five years old. She judged herself mercilessly because she felt like it was her fault. She thought she could have protected herself somehow and maybe would have been able to stop him. She would say to her therapist, "Nothing you ever tell me will ever convince me that I did not do something wrong." Then she was asked an important question. “If your daughter came home and told you that a big man fondled her and hurt her, would you punish her and yell at her for letting it happen? Would you tell her that it was her fault?” Tonya said, "No, of course not. How could she, so young and innocent, be responsible for such an act? I would hold and protect her and fight for her!" In that moment, she felt a rush of sadness and mercy in her Heart and cried for her children and for herself for all the judgments that she carried with her for so long. So one’s judgments do not always know the truth. Tonya’s judging mind, often the parental voice, always condemned her inability to love herself when, in fact, it was her tremendous Heart that allowed her to love her children and thereby herself. This helped her to break free of her judgments that caused her to feel guilty for falsely thinking she must have “led him on.” I brought this up because we often falsely accuse our selves of things that prevent us from emotionally growing.

Use Critical Judgment Skills

Learn to think and judge critically (not negatively), to detect fact from fiction and truth from lie. A newscaster exclaimed, “Junk food can lower your risk of getting heart disease.” After this statement, he reported that there was a flavor enhancer in junk food that can contribute to lowering heart disease. We need to bring a microscope to these sneaky news items that hog the airwaves. Junk food, regardless of the little fact that it can do some good, is mostly unhealthy for you. Another news item proclaimed that 20% of all women are battered more on Superbowl Sunday than any other day of the year. But, when looking more closely at the statement, you will see that the claim isn’t completely accurate. When administering the survey, researchers asked if the spouse was ever treated unfairly on Superbowl Sunday. The question that would have revealed the accurate statistic would have been: Have you ever been treated more unfairly on Superbowl Sunday than other days in the year? Learning from the syllogism below can help us determine if our judgments are valid or invalid. For example:

All dogs are animals.
All animals are blue.
Therefore, all dogs are blue.
OR
God is Love
Love is Blind
Stevie Wonder is blind
Therefore Stevie Wonder is God

If the conclusion logically follows from the premises, like it does from this dog example, one would think that it is valid. However, if one of the premises is not true, then the whole argument is incorrect. Bringing this critical thinking process to all that you do will help you determine what is true and what isn’t..

Judgments cause the conditions and effects in our life. If we want our life to be different in the future, we must change our judgments in the present. We are taught black and white and right and wrong thinking in our society. When critically judging and thinking, identify and eliminate absolute qualifier words such as always, never, absolutely, only, every single time, can't, etc. When critically thinking, ask if there are two or more answers instead of just one right or one wrong answer. Example: Murderers should get the death penalty. But your judgment could include a statement that isn't black or white, such as: While first degree murderers ought to be put to death, second degree murderers should get life in prison. Also, create a 'devil's advocate' in your mind. This will allow you to see both sides of a situation more clearly.

Some moral relativists believe we should never make judgments. There is a difference between being judgmental (too critical of others) and making good judgments. We need to expecially make judgments about good and evil. Can you imagine not judging a murderer, or child rapist, or child kidnapper? To do so could put ourselves in danger and justice would never occur. Just use the judgment questionnaire below to ensure your judgments are based on truth.

Faulty Judgments Can Build Walls Around Your Heart

When others hurt us, we make conscious and unconscious judgments to build emotional walls around our Heart in the hope of eliminating pain from our life. However, if no pain is allowed to touch the Heart, no love or joy will either. Therefore, be careful what you judge to be best for you. It may take years before you undo the damage. When the ego builds defense mechanisms (see Self-Observation) it suppresses the hurt and pain, creating an image that the pain has disappeared. However, the tension and pain do not disappear, but rather, remain like an electrical storm that reverberates tension throughout the biological system. That is why there are many people that lead, seemingly, rational adult lives but, internally, continue to live stormy emotional lives. They fail to embrace the pain and open up their "Hearts" to the discomfort so that they can grieve the hurtful events and move on.

The 8 Judgment Questionnaire: How To Make Accurate Judgments

Our fears and insecurities get in the way of our trying to make accurate judgments.
For example, you may have judged yourself as "lazy" because you actually were in the past. Since then, you may have become productive but you still judge yourself as lazy. To help you make accurate judgments about yourself and others, try proving your self-statement wrong or invalid by challenging the validity of the self-statement using the following cross-examining techniques. Ask:

1. Is the information I have based on fact?

2. Are there cases or times when these statements are not true?

3. Are you being excessively hard on yourself, considering the circumstances?

4. Are you over-generalizing because of a few minor events?

5. How do you react when you believe that judgment/thought? What happens?

6. Who would you be without the judgment/thought/belief?

7. Assume the opposite statement is true and restate the statement and see what you notice. When we assume the opposite of our judgment, we may find that it actually holds more truth than the negative judgment/thoughts that we were holding. This is because we tend to be too critical of ourselves. For example, I am a loser becomes, I am a winner who is learning.

Another example is, "He is unloving to me," becomes "He is loving to me" (to the best of his ability) or "I am unloving to him," or "I am unloving to me," "I can't go on without him," becomes, “I can live without him since I was doing okay before we met.” Opposite statements show us unseen aspects of ourselves. When it’s a judgment about an object, use the word thinking. “My body is unhealthy,” becomes “My thinking is unhealthy.”

8. Adjust your statement by using words such as “likely,” “usually,” and “sometimes” instead of words like “always” and “never.”

EXAMPLE
Emotion: Frustration *Situation:* Not getting good grades in first semester of college.

Current Judgment: "I'll never be able to graduate from college. I am so stupid if I can't even succeed at this." The 8 Judgment Questionnaire could help one answer the current judgment as follows:

Answers to the 8 Judgment Questionnaire.
1. There are no facts to back up that I am stupid and will not graduate from college.
2. "There were areas in my life like my 10th grade spanish class when I had a bad first semester but did better the second semester. I remember thinking, “I’ll never be able to succeed.” So, I often feel defeated when I first start something.
3. "Yes, I am new at this, and I need to go easier on myself and learn from my mistakes instead of expecting them not to occur."
4. "There are people who are willing to testify on my behalf that I am not stupid and can be successful in school. This is only one semester and I did okay in my English class.
5. I get depressed and I don’t study and do my homework.
6. I’d be a lighter, happier person who’d be content with doing his best and the results that followed.
7. "I am smart enough and will graduate from college."
8. "I *sometimes* feel stupid when it comes to learning something new at first, but it isn't *likely* that I'll drop out of school with my dedication."

Other Questions that can help if you still feel stuck include the following:

Does it serve my purpose/goals?

Could I live with this decision?

Would I be fulfilled and proud of myself for a long time?

Would it be meaningful to me?

Will it help me improve myself?

Is it logical, valid, and sound?

Am I jumping to conclusions?

Am I exaggerating?

What if the worst happens—so what?

What other interpretations are possible?

Am I focusing on the negative and ignoring the positive?

Am I assuming that something is going to happen because I’m afraid it will?

Exercise 1

Observing Your Negative Voice Exercise

Take note, watch, listen, and be aware of the times when you judge or criticize yourself for anything at all. For example: being late, how you look, how you feel, or how you perform. The purpose is not to eliminate the negative voices but to be aware of and give less power to them. Record the voices here.

____

____

____

____

____

Exercise 2

Ask yourself the following questions when making an important judgment about an event that stirs an emotion, belief, expectation, attitude, or behavior. You can also ask yourself the following questions when making an important external decision about a career, education, family, or even a first impression when you first meet someone.

Your Judgment______________________________________

Would I be proud of myself?______________________________

Does it serve my purpose/goals?___________________________

Could I live with this decision? ___________________________

Is the information I have based on fact? ____________________

Would I be fulfilled for a long time?_______________________

Would it be meaningful to me?____________________________

Will it help me improve myself?___________________________

Is it logical, valid, and sound? ____________________________

If two or more of these questions were a "NO," then the decision may be considered unhealthy and undesirable. Write below whether it was healthy or unhealthy and why it was so.

Occasionally, the conversations that we have with our selves do have some truth to them. Most often, however, they are inaccurate. Instead of avoiding or suppressing unwanted voices/conversations, bring them out into the open where you can critically evaluate them and determine their appropriateness. They are similar to Space Invaders-- the conversations keep reappearing, so just keep shooting them down. Eventually, you will replace your old conversations with healthier conversations. Over time, the healthier ones will become louder and more natural. You must practice these daily, monthly, or sometimes yearly in order to make a significant change.

Exercise 3

A. Use the 8 Judgment Questionnaire to challenge a negative judgment you have toward yourself or someone else.

State the Negative Judgment. ______________________________

____

1. Is the information I have based on fact?______________________________
2. Are there cases or times when these statements are not true?______________________________

____

3. Are you being excessively hard on yourself, considering the circumstances?______________

____

4. Are you over-generalizing because of a few minor events?______________________________

____

5. How do you react when you believe that judgment/thought? What happens?______________

____

6. Who would you be without the judgment/thought/belief?______________________________

____

7. Assume the opposite statement is true and restate the statement and see what you notice.

____

8. Adjust your statement by using words such as "likely," "usually," and "sometimes" instead of words like "always" and "never." ______________________________

____

Final Judgment______________________________

____

B. Write down two techniques that you feel would be the best plan of action to help you cope with the negative judgments. Use the following techniques for your appropriate situation.

A. Create an opposite chain reaction. Example: If you're trying to lose weight, and the internal conversation says to eat something sweet, then go and exercise at that moment. Or when you're depressed, go to a movie, gym, or visit a friend.

B. Get support from others. Example: If you want to stop being critical of others or beating yourself up, ask them to signal you at the moment of your weakness.

C. Ignore the conversations. Example: If you want to stop eating bad foods and you're watching a commercial for those foods, turn the channel or ignore it and do something else. Don't give it any power.

D. Practice a preventative technique. Example: If you get anxious thoughts, go play golf, write in a journal, go fishing, start painting, etc. (Orman, 1991).

____

____

Strategy 2.3

Empower your Emotional system.

Definition: Emotions - Feelings caused by the judgments we make about our selves, others, and events. They are the messengers of the Heart, ego, and the self-image. They are powered by judgment and cemented with belief.

Anyone can become angry - that is easy. But, to be angry with the right person, to the right degree, at the right time, for the right purpose, and in the right way - this is not easy.
Aristotle

The Magic of Our Emotions

If you think about any emotion you have had, you will find that it came from something deeper. When you look to the Thinking Mind Model on page 74, you will see that emotions come from our judgments, and our judgments come from our Heart or our ego mind that we develop over the years through our socialization. Emotions are the electricity that charges us. They connect our body to our soul. They write plays that bring audiences to tears, give birth to great art, can move one to Nazism or to a Mother Theresa. Think about the strong force that exists between a mother's love for her child. She gives of herself through pure unconditional love. Our emotions give us life and distinguish us from the animals. For instance, dogs can't anticipate tomorrow; cats can't regret sorrow; animals have sex, but people make love. Emotions are the juice of life. Without them, there is no poetry, music, art, or awe.
First, we need to allow ourselves to feel whatever we need to feel. Many people don't allow themselves this option, and, therefore, they end up suppressing their emotions instead of confronting them. We need to determine if an emotion came from either the ego or the "Heart." Since our emotions determine both our beliefs and behaviors (see the Thinking Mind Model on page 74), we need to be careful to discern whether we should obey the dictates of our emotions or not. How do we know when to act on our emotions and when not to?

Times When We Should and Should Not Obey Our Emotions

First, determine if the feeling you have is coming from the Heart or the ego. How do we know the difference? To find out, turn inside your mind and body when you are feeling a strong emotion. When it comes from the Heart, there is usually no feeling of constriction in your body. When an emotion tells you to do something, first ask yourself the following questions: Do I feel rushed? Do I feel an impulse to act? Do I feel like lashing out? If you answer 'yes' to any of these questions, it may be coming from the ego so take 10 deep breaths and decide to give yourself some more time to think it out. We have been taught to avoid feeling bad. Examples include: "Strong men don't cry," or "cheer up," or "be strong" or " have a drink, and forget about it" or "you little baby", and so on. We need to relearn the importance of honoring our feelings even if it means feeling bad for a while. Feeling bad for a while is different than feeling suicidal or getting into a long-term depression. Allow some time to grieve when experiencing sad events such as leaving a loved one, losing a loved one, being treated badly by a friend, or getting a bad grade. However, we are not meant to stay in this place of sadness. Once we have experienced our feelings, we need to release the emotion using a favorite technique and then move on. Hurt emotions can confuse us as to which course of action we should take. For example, if you felt that an acquaintance named Sue was impolite to you, your emotions might be saying one of two things, 1) "I'm hurt so don't be nice to her." (Notice that's an ego thought) or 2) "First impressions have been wrong in the past, so I will give her the benefit of the doubt and be tolerant." (Notice that's a Heart thought). Revisit the Heart-Ego Values Model on page 83 to become more clear between the two.

Often, there are times when we should not obey our emotions, especially when we feel fear around performing something. At that time, giving more power to courage (attitude) would often be desirable. For example, you are running a race and your emotion is telling you, "I'm too tired, just quit." Most of the time, it would be wiser to "stick it out," depending on your personality and how well you know yourself. Other times, the emotion may come from a faulty judgment - something you know intellectually is true, but don't feel is true. For example, if one is in an abusive relationship, his/her emotions may say, "Stay with him/her, regardless of the abuse. At least he/she loves me." Underneath the emotions may be the judgment that whispers "no one will love me if I leave (faulty judgment) and then I'll really be depressed." Yet, beneath that judgment is the Heart that whispers, "Get away from that person who disrespects and degrades your character and spirit." That is why it is so important to become clear on what your Heart tells you. It is your guidance system. If you are still unsure whether you are using faulty judgments, keep trying the Heart exercises as well as seeking out someone you trust and/or a professional.

Healing Our Emotional Wounds

In Exercise 3, you will be writing down the key wounds you have acquired in your life up until today. They were likely a result from painful events, times, or moments in your life. There is perhaps nothing more helpful to loving relationships than doing this exercise. In fact, most marriages would not end in divorce if people were able to identify their wounds and communicate to their spouse how their spouse can communicate in a way that helps heal their wounds. Most fights in relationships escalate and get more intense because of our childhood wounds that get triggered. For example, Julie grew up with a father who always told her what to do. Everything was a lesson and she was never encouraged to think for herself and control her life. Therefore, her wound was not having a sense of control or having a voice to speak her opinions. The message was "I am not worthy." In her marriage, when her husband makes a decision without asking her, or uses the remote control to change the channel, she feels those powerless feelings of not having a voice like she did with her father and not having control. When she lashes back at her husband, the husband is surprised because he did these things politely. So by identifying the wound, she can communicate to her husband to consult her when making decisions and ask for her opinions. Each person in a relationship brings their own emotional wounds to it that causes the struggles in marriages.

So write what your wounds are and across, write the messages and decisions you made about your self as a result. Like Julie in the example, the decision was, "I am not worthy. " Then ask how could you communicate your needs to other people in your life so that your wounds won't be triggered as much and you can start to do some healing. This alone will bring much more happiness and much less misery to your life.

Why EQ is More Important Than IQ

EQ or Emotional Intelligence measures one's ability to be aware and manage one's emotions, impulse control, persistence, zeal, motivation, empathy and social savvy. In Daniel Goleman's (1995), book, "Emotional Intelligence: Why it can matter more than IQ," he asks:

1. Are you capable of using your feelings to make good decisions?
2. Can you release your anger without doing harm and calm yourself when feeling anxious?
3. Are you generally aware of your emotional state and can you name it? (No, not California)
4. Can you keep yourself going, even when circumstances seem to be against you?
5. Are you hopeful despite setbacks and failure?
6. Are you adept at reading or empathizing with others' emotions and responding appropriately?

7. Can you negotiate emotions in your relationships with family, friends, and peers?
The more times you answer 'yes', the healthier your emotional EQ.

Our EQ has gone down, as a nation, while our IQ this century has gone up. Low EQ leads to crime, suicide, teen pregnancy, etc. Several studies have shown EQ, rather than IQ, is a better indicator of achievement and being employed. Some facts about EQ include:

- ***Studies show that chronically hostile people (low EQ) are twice as likely to get a major disease and seven times more likely to die by age 50.***
- ***Until the age of 16, people reinforce certain neural pathways in their brains that set the patterns for emotional behavior.***
- ***Studies suggest an increase in children's EQ when parents encourage them to handle frustrations, control emotions, develop rapport with others, develop empathy, cooperate with others, and negotiate agreements with others.***
- ***Researchers have found that babies developed a sense of emotional connectedness when their mothers reciprocated the babies' mood. For example, cooing back at a baby who squeals excitedly. By contrast, when mothers intentionally over or under-responded to their babies' signals, the babies immediately became distressed.Also, studies have found academically successful students who have grade point averages above 3.0 are those who have higher EQ scores using the Bar-On assessment form Parker & Duffy (2005). It has reaching implications for better career development, wellness, and leadership potential.***
- ***Arnold and Terry Denny at the University of Illinois studied 81 valedictorians. 10 years after graduation, only 25% were in the top tier of their job and many were doing poorly.***

The beginnings of an emotion usually occur before a person is consciously aware of the feeling itself. For example, when people who fear spiders are shown pictures of spiders, sensors on their skin will detect sweat breaking out though they say they do not feel any fear. So there are two levels of emotions, conscious and unconscious. Emotions that simmer below consciousness or awareness have a strong impact on how we perceive and react to events even though we have no idea they are at work. If someone insults you, but you brush it off as "no big deal," and then snap at an innocent person for no good reason, it is likely due to this simmering of emotion going on. They can increase their emotional intelligence by bringing emotions into their awareness as soon as they feel something. First, **identify** and process emotion in a journal throughout the day. This can help one to record events and feelings and thereby bring emotions into one's awareness. Second, **assess** what situations trigger the worry-anxiety cycle in you. Only here, can the emotion be felt, evaluated, and responded to in hopefully a confrontational but respectful manner. Investigate what was said or done and why. Often, we find good reasons why people made us upset. It could be because, they had emergencies, personal pressures, or we took something personal that wasn't personal. When one has rage, it is important to go walk it off and distract oneself with something pleasant, like watching a TV comedy, going out in nature, exercising, watching a movie, etc., and then confront the problem later. Ultimately, **release** the emotion for good. Research shows that shopping and eating are distractions that don't work because you can do them while continuing the angry train of thought. And venting and outbursts end up making one feel more angry, not less, and in the long run puts one at risk for heart disease. Follow the stress reductions exercises in Chapter three for more help.

How Men and Women Experience Emotions Differently

Men generally have a hard time **getting into** an uncomfortable emotion like sadness. Women generally have a hard time **getting out** of an emotion. Of course there are plenty of exceptions. Yet, men as boys were often taught, "thou shalt not feel," unless it was anger which is more accepted for men in our society. They were told, "Don't cry. It doesn't hurt," when actually, it did hurt. Although boys/men have been socialized not to cry, they pay the price for such repression. As adults, men often dismiss hurt feelings and can be totally unaware that they are feeling them. This can destroy relationships, fuel rage, and lead to health problems as men get more ulcers, heart attacks, and are more abusive toward alcohol. However, men can generally let go of irritations that pervade most relationships. Women are generally better at identifying emotional issues but can benefit from learning to let go of them. Girls were taught that crying is acceptable, but anger was often not.

Exercise 1

The Childhood Messages Recall

Write below, the *messages* you received growing up by identifying the healthy and unhealthy **emotions you experienced** that were both encouraged and discouraged by your parents in your childhood. Examples include:
Healthy/encouraged – ***optimism:*** I was taught that there's always a bright side to things.
Healthy/discouraged – ***being silly:*** Any type of playfulness was ridiculed.
Unhealthy/encouraged – ***control:*** I must always be in control. This message didn't allow me to express my feelings in a safe environment because expression of feelings was considered bad.
Unhealthy/discouraged – ***Anger, weakness, or sadness:*** It was not safe to express these emotions because ridicule, teasing, and excessive worry would have followed.

The healthy emotions **encouraged** by my caretakers/parents were:____________________

____

____

The healthy emotions **discouraged** by my caretakers/parents were____________________

____

____

The unhealthy emotions **encouraged** by my caretakers/parents were:__________________

____

____

The unhealthy emotions **discouraged** by my caretakers/parents were:__________________

____

____

Exercise 2

Getting Through An Emotion Method

A. Identify a conflict you've had with somebody that caused strong emotions like anger in you.

Describe the event____

____

B. Use the statements below for each of the six items to process an emotion effectively

1. **Anger** – express only your anger/rage and don't stop until it's all out
2. **Hurt** – express your hurt underneath the anger that you feel
3. **Fear** – express what you fear in a worse case scenario and what that means to you

4. **Regret** – express any regret if you didn't act in a pro-active way as opposed to a reactive way.
5. **Request/Intention –** State your request for a change in their behavior followed with your intention.
6. **Love/Appreciation** – express your appreciation and love for the person you are affected by.

1. **Anger** = I am angry that you… I hate it when… I can't believe you…

2. **Hurt** = It hurts me when… I'm disappointed that… It makes me feel sad when…

3. **Fear** = I'm afraid that… My biggest fear is… It scares and frightens me when…

4. **Regret** = I didn't mean to...... I know I could have......

5. **Request/Intention =** I am requesting..... Could I ask you..... Next time I will.......

6. **Love/Appreciation** = I like it when…… I want us to…… I love/forgive you for….. I request…..

Exercise 3

A. List 3 emotional wounds (painful events, moments, trauma, etc.) from your childhood. What message did you receive and what decision did you make about yourself. Practice writing a few below and transfer them to the next page.

Emotional Wounds	**Messages/Decisions Made About Myself**
Example: I felt unlovable because my parents gave more attention to my other brothers and sisters.	*I am unworthy and unlovable / I don't deserve the best. I will settle for second best (in job, health, marriage partner).*
1.	
2.	
3.	

B. Pick an emotional issue like hurt, fear, anger, etc., that you have about someone or a past event or pick a pain in your body that you would like to be pain-free on. Write it below.

I need relief/healing from____

Then, on page 333, in the Appendix, write an affirmation statement by filling in the lines in the sample relating to the above issue you would like relief and healing from. Write the full statement below.

Even though____

____

____

____

____

____

Write the Reminder phrase here____

____

Then go to page 330 and tap on the acu-points on your body using the Basic Recipe. Don't tap on any emotional traumas that could upset you. It is highly recommended you conduct that with a professional therapist.

Doing the four steps in the Basic Recipe on page 329 is one round of EFT. Before starting, rate your pain or emotional issue on a scale of 0 to 10; 10 being the worst you would feel. If you closed your eyes and got into the issue, what number could you get your issue up to? Then tap one round (steps 1-4) of EFT and rate yourself again and see if the number is lower afterward. Then, in round two, use the word "remaining" in the setup and reminder phrase and rate yourself again afterward. Then tap one more round; round three and rate yourself again.

Before round one, I rate the number:_______________________________________

After round one, I rate the number:____

After round two, I rate the number:____

After round three, I rate the number:______________________________________

This is one of the most effective techniques to eliminate or relieve anything negative in your life. To see the research on EFT, go to tappingintowellness.com

I feel the following after the results:______________________________________

____

Strategy 2.4

Empower your Belief system.

Definition: Belief - A group of judgments powered by emotion, supporting something we believe to be true. It is the root of the attitude. Our beliefs create the window of how we view the world.

The Power of Beliefs on Performance

Beliefs are one of the main subjects in all the major religions including the Koran, the Bible, the Torah and many others. They all knew the power of belief. Modern science has proven the power of the placebo effect. When a patient is given a pill that is reported to relieve pain, his/her mind expects the pill to numb the pain, and more often than not, it does. Yet, the pill given was a sugar pill that has no effect on the body. So, when you tell the mind to perform something, it generally can.

In 1954, nobody had ever broken the four-minute mile. It was not thought to be possible for the human body to move that fast. Yet, in 1954, Roger Bannister broke the four-minute mile by running it in three minutes and 52 seconds. Here is the amazing fact. Within two years, 37 people around the world broke the four-minute mile. There is one reason why they did. It's because they were all really, really fast. All kidding aside, the reason so many people broke this record was because **they believed they could.** They said to themselves that this was no longer an impossible feat. Suddenly, their minds were open to the possibility of breaking the record. Their minds created a physiological change in the nervous system of the body and stretched it to perform the impossible. That is the power of belief.

As a community college counselor and instructor, I met a woman who came to me after her first semester of college with 'D' and 'F' grades. I asked her what her grades in high school were, and she mentioned she was a 'B' student. I explained that college isn't that much more difficult than high school. With that she replied, "Well, what do you expect, I'm not very smart." I said, "Why do you think that?" She replied, "Because I only have a 95 IQ. I took that SAT test, and that's what I scored." After, confirming her score, I told her, "The SAT is not an intelligence test; it is an aptitude test that predicts how well you are likely to perform in college. Further, you scored in the 95th percentile, meaning, you scored in the TOP 5% of people who take this test, in the nation. You are a genius!"

There are two points here that are amazing. One, if we follow the Heart-Mind Model, we will notice that she made a judgment that she was not smart due to the test score. This caused emotions of sadness and hopelessness, which affirmed a belief of, "I won't succeed very well in school." In turn, this created an expectation to "just get by," and an attitude of, "I can't do anything about it" which all caused her behavior of minimal effort toward studying. Two, she ended up being a straight A student from then on. Why? Because she believed she was smart, which created a physiological effect in the mind, brain, and body to perform.

"What your mind can conceive and believe, it can achieve" ....Napolean Hill.

In 1972, Bruce Jenner was training for the 1976 Olympic Decathlon. To believe that he could be the winner, he took the newspaper article from the 1972 Decathlon winner and cut out the man's picture and inserted a picture of himself, Bruce Jenner. Then, each time the 1972 winner's name was mentioned in the article, Bruce Jenner replaced it with his own name. In addition, he changed all of the dates from 1972 to 1976. Bruce Jenner then read the article every night before he went to bed and, again, every morning when he woke up for the next four years. As you may recall, Bruce Jenner went on to win the most prestigious award in the Olympics. He became the 1976 World Olympic Decathlon winner. That's the power of belief.

Years ago, the actor Jim Carrey, was broke after doing standup comedy for years. He then crafted a 10 million dollar check and vowed to make that much money in five years. To do this, he focused on this check and his desire and belief to make that money. Within a few years, Jim

Carrey went on to become worth over 100 million dollars. Yet, he also practiced his art of making funny faces, six hours a day. So belief with discipline is a magical, winning combination.
In Dr. Schuller's book, "Power Thinking," he tells a story about a gentleman, named George Dantzig. In 1935, at UC Berkeley, this man took a final exam in math. He was told that the person who scored the highest test score would be awarded a professorship. This was highly appealing considering it was during the time of the depression. During the exam, he left to go to the restroom while the instructor wrote two math problems on the board that had never been solved. Later, since he was the last student in the classroom working on his problems, he asked if he could take the test home and return it on Monday. He worked on the problems all weekend, not knowing that these problems had never been solved. When he brought his test to the instructor on Monday, his instructor told him the two problems on the board were not test questions like he thought. He checked his work backward and forwards and discovered George had actually solved the two unsolvable problems when, even at that time, Albert Einstein could not do it. But, because George believed he could, he performed the impossible.

The Sources of Our Beliefs

Most of our beliefs that prevent our effectiveness are not based on reality at all, but rather they are based on messages taken in from a variety of sources such as parents, peers, and teachers. We accept these messages as the truth, and we live in a manner consistent with them. People should be able to choose their beliefs as long as: a) they are willing to be responsible for the consequences and b) they treat everyone else decently. Yet, most of us were pressured, conditioned, seduced, and brainwashed into adopting certain beliefs as children. This was a time when we had inadequate reasoning skills, knowledge, and few choices. These beliefs were then reiterated, reinforced, and rewarded directly and indirectly. **Therefore, it is crucial that you conduct an inventory of your beliefs in all areas of your life so you can determine which beliefs are truly healthy and accurate and which beliefs are false.**
Each person needs to determine which beliefs are true for him or her. The beliefs that work for one person may not work for another person from a different background, race, culture, generation, etc. Below are examples of healthy (heart) beliefs and unhealthy (ego) beliefs reported by several students.

Reported Heart Beliefs	Reported Ego Beliefs
• Some things aren't meant to be. • You can learn from any situation. • What you sow, you must reap. • Hard work eventually pays off. • You are fortunate to have what you have. • What you give comes back to you. • Every obstacle is an opportunity. • Mistakes/failures are good feedback. • Only you are responsible for changing your condition. • You already have the answers inside your "heart"...they are not outside of you. • By directing attention and action to self-improvement, you will eventually be happier, more liberated, and more successful than 99% of the population. • You have a mission and a purpose on earth in this lifetime.	• Everybody must like me in order for me to feel good about myself. • I must always be competent, adequate, and achieving. • When I'm seriously frustrated, treated unfairly, or rejected, I must view the event as awful and devastating. • Others' opinions of me matter more than my own. • There's never enough time. • There are no good men left. • My relationships will never work. • I'm not good enough. • Women don't hold those titles. • If it's not one thing, it's another. • You should be seen and not heard. • You're so smart. If only you'd apply yourself. • Money doesn't grow on trees

Examples of Subconscious Beliefs in Action

Subconscious beliefs are beliefs that we are not consciously aware of. I overeat:

- To keep men away from me so that I can be safe.
- To distract me from the pressures of the day.

- To medicate the emotional pain I feel if I give it attention.

By directing attention and awareness to our beliefs, we can take the necessary steps to address the real, underlying problems in our lives and thereby fix the secondary problem....the belief that overeating was the main problem.

Destructive Parental/Societal Messages that Sabotage Success

If you experience fear of commitment, responsibility, growing up, or change, your core fear is the fear of success. If most of your anxiety comes from the fear of rejection, confrontation, or not measuring up, then your core fear is the fear of failure. We can acquire these two main fears through parental and societal messages. Yet, we often don't realize that we have them and accepted these beliefs long ago.

Common Negative Beliefs That Cause Fear

Fear of Success "I won't do it because.....	**Fear of Failure** "I won't do it because.....
▪ "If I succeed at this, they'll expect everything I do to be a success and I won't measure up." ▪ "With success comes more responsibility and pressure." ▪ "The more successful you are, the more people dislike you." ▪ "It's lonely at the top." ▪ "The minute I achieve success, I'll probably blow it." ▪ "Once I get what I want, I won't be motivated to do anything."	▪ "I don't want to feel like a loser." ▪ "They" are out to get me." ▪ "If I don't finish, then I won't have to fail." ▪ "I work better under pressure." ▪ "Anything worth doing is worth doing perfectly." ▪ "All the great ideas are already invented." ▪ "I have nothing valuable to offer." ▪ Excuse: "I would do it if I had..........."

Realize that everyone fears failure. Even highly successful people fear failure but are able to accept their fear and go on anyway. Thinking of failure as valuable feedback for the next time will eliminate some of the fear of failure. Remember, failure is an event, not a destiny.

One of the foremost motivational speaker's, Earl Nightingale, tells the story of a trip he took to the Great Barrer Reef. He noticed that the coral growing on the sheltered side of the reef, where the sea was peaceful and quiet, looked pale and lifeless. The coral that was constantly beaten by the powerful waves, however, looked healthy and vibrant. Earl asked the guide why this was so. "It is very simple,"came the reply. "The coral on the lagoon side dies rapidly with no challenge for growth and survival, while the coral facing the open sea thrives and multiplies(produces) because it is challenged and tested every day." So it is with all living things on earth. If we never challenge ourselves and endure the struggles that are part of any goal path, we never have the opportunity to live, thrive, produce, and succeed. So, we can strengthen ourselves by learning from our failures.

Society has a huge impact on our belief system. The movie, Titanic, was watched by more people than any other film ever made at its time. Its depiction of wealthy and poor people helped create negative belief systems of wealthy people. They were boring, rude, wicked, greedy people who would shoot each other to save their own lives. Another negative message that could impact others was that poor people knew how to have a good time and poverty and free living was the answer to Kate's problems. These belief systems are powerful motivators that will actually cause you to repel success. Holding on to these beliefs cause us to sabotage our success.
Self-sabotage is a disparity between what you say you want and what your actions show. So, when your mind detects fear caused by a negative belief, it will do anything to keep you safe

and will prevent you from achieving your goal. The fear then overcomes your desire for your goal. Examples include:

- You get sick the day before your big date.
- You show up drunk the day before your promotion.
- You choose people who are unable to make commitments.
- You misplace an important file.
- You show up late for work or important meetings.
- You procrastinate often and miss deadlines or have to rush and submit poor quality work.
- You don't respond to opportunity around you or you aren't even aware of it.

By exposing and confronting your fear, you break through its control over you. Your everyday habits are broadcasting your belief system, your fears, and your unmet needs loud and clear.
Change your beliefs and you change your behaviors.
Change your behaviors and you change your results.
Change your results and you change your life.

Change Negative Beliefs to Empowering Beliefs: Do Exercises 1 – 3.

Exercise 1

The 6-Step Belief Changer

A. Identify a **self-belief** you want to change or eliminate.
B. Follow the 6 step method for changing a belief.

1. Be confident that the new belief is possible by you. Not probable, just possible. Write it below.

____

2. Believe that you deserve this new belief. Write it below.

____

3. Your new belief must not contradict other beliefs. Write below any contradictory beliefs.

____

____

4. Believe that you <u>can</u> review and recite Exercises 2 and 3 everyday despite the obstacles.
6. Believe you are likely to and <u>will</u> review and recite Exercises 2 and 3 everyday.
6. Complete Exercises 2 and 3

Exercise 2

The Ultimate Reframe Exercise (One of the most powerful exercises you'll perform)

1. Identify and write about a person who is a hero of yours that has accomplished in his/her life what you would like to accomplish in your own life.
2. Find that person, or someone who has the attributes that you admire, in a newspaper, book, magazine, etc. For example, Bruce Jenner, a psychologist, a peaceful person, a millionaire, or whomever.
3. In this article, substitute your information (your name, picture, date, etc.) with theirs and commit to reading it every morning and every night until your goal is achieved. Just like Bruce Jenner who substituted his name, the year, and his picture, you too can perform the same strategy. Meditate everyday while visualizing yourself in that role.

Exercise 3

The Belief Changer (this is used successfully with cancer patients)

1. Identify your unhealthy/undesirable emotion or self-belief

2. Obtain a 4x6 card and draw a line down the middle from top to the bottom.

3. In the left-hand column, list three reasons why you think this unhealthy belief is true.

4. Evaluate each belief with the following questions:
   a. Is the belief based on the true facts?
   b. Does your belief serve your best interests?
   c. Does your belief help you advance/protect your health and how you feel?
   d. Does your belief help you reach your goals and give you what you want in life?

If you answered no to one or more of the above questions, then it's likely to be an unhealthy belief.

5. Write out three healthier beliefs in the right-hand column directly across each of the three reasons in the left-hand column. Use the judgment questionnaire if you get stuck.

6. Keep this 4x6 card with you in your wallet or purse, and when you feel that undesirable belief or emotion, pull out the list and read it twice.

7. Then for three minutes visualize the healthier belief already coming true in your life.

Visualization enables you to see, with your mind, what we cannot see with our eyes. Practice Below.

Example:

Unhealthy Belief: I'm lonely and nobody cares.	**Challenge to Create a Healthy Self-Belief:**
1. Nobody wants to be my friend.	1. I haven't actually given people much of a chance. If others can see my good qualities, good for them. If not, they're not good prospects for a friendship anyway.
2. I don't have many friends.	2. I can make a more realistic effort to make friends with others instead of expecting them to come to me.
3. No one shows interest in me.	3. If I show interest more, maybe they will too or if I stop trying so hard, maybe people will want to be friends.

The self-belief you want to change:______________________________

____

Unhealthy Self-Belief:	**Create a Healthy Self-Belief**
1. ________________	1. ________________
________________	________________
________________	________________
________________	________________
________________	________________
2. ________________	2. ________________
________________	________________
________________	________________
________________	________________
________________	________________
3. ________________	3. ________________
________________	________________
________________	________________
________________	________________
________________	________________

Strategy 2.5

Empower your Expectation system.

Definition: Expectation - an event we believe will occur in the future.

Look at a man the way he is and he only becomes worse. But, look at him as if he were what he could be and he becomes what he should be.
Goethe

The Consequences of Unrealistic Expectations

Not only do we need to have healthy expectations about our future but we also need to eliminate our unhealthy expectations. For example, it is self-defeating and unrealistic not to expect obstacles or roadblocks to occur during our day. Furthermore, we often commit the following thought distortions that get us into trouble.

- We expect others to be like us, be nice to us, never leave us, always be there for us, etc.
- We expect life to be fair, not have any suffering, to be happy most of the time.
- We expect our goals to be easy, causing frustration. We expect perfection, causing anxiety.
- We expect the worst. We end up maximizing the negative events and minimizing the positive. Since life is unpredictable, our expectations are frequently out of synch with reality. We must change our expectations to make them empowering and real.

How We Acquired Our Expectations

There are three expectations that shape our lives. They are:
1) *Our Parents'* expectations of us became the most powerful influence growing up. What expectations did your parents have of you and of each other? What roles did you parents play? Did your parents expect you to do well in school or did they always tell you that "you will never amount to anything" or "you'll never make it"?
2) *Others'* expectations of us influenced us. They include our peers, family, relatives, teachers, society/culture, religious figures, etc. Do you mostly get positive feedback or negative feedback from these people?
3) *Our own* expectations of ourselves are a mixture of our own doing and the above people in our lives. Instead of trying to change the opinions of those people, work only on improving your expectations for the future. Your expectations could include completing college, getting a good job, marrying a quality person, making a difference in this world, making a high income, etc.

Jesus, in the Christian Bible, encouraged people to have *faith* which is another word for positive expectation. He even told his disciples that if they, themselves, didn't have faith, then no miracle could ever occur in their lives. He knew how powerful faith and positive expectations were and how healing it was to the body and the "heart."

Check Your Own Expectations

Do you have expectations of getting a mediocre job, settling for an unfulfilling partner, or just getting by? Identify if your current expectations are more success-oriented or doubt-oriented. Have positive but realistic expectations. Expect obstacles to occur in everything you do (not Murphy's Law). When we expect obstacles, they won't overwhelm us when they happen as opposed to not expecting them because we have armed our selves against them. When there are negative people in our lives, some times it helps to prepare our selves by expecting them to have their usual negative behavior. For example, if you have a mother- in-law that is controlling, the next time you see her, expect that she will be controlling, insensitive, and selfish. Then you can say to yourself, "Ah, there she goes again--like clock work."

He who expects nothing has everything.
Confucius

In other words, if you don't expect surprises or expect people to return favors, then when it does occur, it is a true gift and you will feel like you "have everything."

The Difference Between an Expectation, Belief, and Emotion

If you are unsure if you are experiencing an expectation, belief, or emotion, ask yourself the following questions. Ask, Is what I'm experiencing a feeling that I feel like anger, sadness, and so on? If so, that is an emotion. Ask, Is this something that is being done to me? That is not an emotion unless you feel something as a result. Ask, is what I'm experiencing somehtng that I believe is true. If so, that is a belief. Ask, is what I 'm experiencing something I believe will occur in the future? If so, that is an expectation.

Exercise 1

Expectation Visualization Technique

Choose one event you have a negative expectation about. It could be a test that you're going to take in college, or a sale you need to make, or a speech you need to give, or a confrontation with somebody, or just getting things done on your to-do-list. Now, take a moment, close your eyes and visualize this the success of this event becoming reality with the expectation that it's already starting to happen. See yourself in this picture, like a movie doing the things you need to do with confidence. Brighten the picture and fine-tune it like you would on your television set. This exercise should take about five minutes. Do the same every morning as much as possible.

The event I have a negative expectation about is ____________________________

____

____

Exercise 2

The Expectation Affirmation Strategy

Write down an accompanying affirmation that will match the event with the visualization. For example, "I have completed my to-do-list." Notice that the affirmation is both positive and present. "I will complete my to-do-list," or "I am working toward completing my to-do-list," are not affirmations because they are future based. An affirmation starts from the end of the goal as if it's already happened. Repeat your affirmation as often as possible (sometimes up to 200 times in a day).

My affirmation is ____

____

____

Make sure that it is both positive and in the present tense.

Exercise 3

The Brainstorming Expectation Method

A. Identify which mental or physical obstacle is preventing you from positively expecting your future event to be a success. Examples include money, children, spouse, job, low self-esteem, etc.
B. Believe that it can happen ... even though you might not feel or know it yet. C.
C. Brainstorm motivating answers using the sentence completion lines below. You will find that your answers will help you to start believing that your expectation will come true.

Example: If your negative expectation is, I'm afraid I won't graduate from college, you may write, "My expectation might be possible…"

If: "…I make a commitment to study hard despite the obstacles to finish college…"

With: "...the help of teachers, counselors, tutors, study groups, and supportive people."

When: "I'm able to receive financial assistance/aid..."

After: "…I get the kids in school and day care worked out..."

However: "…I need to talk it over with my spouse and see what time frame is best for us."

Write down your expectation.____
____

My expectation might be possible:

If____
____
____

With____
____
____

When____
____
____

After____
____
____

However____
____
____

These powerful sentence completions will give you the reasons to believe that your expectation will come true because it speaks to your brain. Your expectations will dramatically increase.

Strategy 2.6

Empower your Attitudinal system.

Definition: Attitude – a cluster of beliefs that drives a person to lean toward or away from certain people, issues, objects, or situations. Example: You may have an attitude about the U.S. involvement in the Iraq war. You may respond to the decision by telling others how you feel about the justice of it. An example of a belief is, "I am not good at math." An attitude is, "I hate solving math problems."

Life is like a grindstone. It can polish you or pulverize you depending on how you position yourself.
Les Brown

Attitude is Everything

Attitude is more important than the past, than education, than money, than circumstances, than failures, than successes, than what other people think or say or do. It is more important than appearance, giftedness, or skill. It will make or break a company, church, or home. The remarkable thing is, we have a choice every day regarding the attitude we will embrace for that day. We cannot change our past. We cannot change the fact that people will act in a certain way…We cannot change the inevitable. The only thing we can do is play on the one string we have, and that is our attitude. I am convinced that life is 10% what happens to me and 90% how to react to it. And so it is with you, you are in charge of your Attitudes."
Charles Swindoll

It is your attitude toward life, which will determine life's attitude toward you.

If you even think you're beaten, you are. If you even think you dare not, you won't.
If you even think you'll lose, you lost. In the world, we find success begins with a person's will.
It's all in the state of mind. If you think you're outclassed, you are.
You've got to think high to rise. You've got to be sure of yourself, before you ever win a prize.
Life's battles don't always go to the stronger woman or man. But soon or late, the person who wins, is the person who thinks he can.
Anonymous

Tying in the Thinking Mind Model

Again, refer to The Thinking Mind Model at the beginning of the chapter. What reactions or attitudes do you have to the following phrases: The Tea Party, Barack Obama, George W. Bush, The War in Iraq, Illegal Aliens, AIDS, The O.J. Simpson Trial, Bill Clinton, abortion, gun control, and capital punishment? Your attitude towards AIDS might be that you judge it to be dangerous and you don't want to die. You may have the emotion of fear of contracting AIDS, which could give you the belief that you could get it if you maintained your sexual practices. This is likely to give you the expectation that you'd die if you got AIDS, which could give you the attitude that it's the last thing you want in this life. This attitude could enable you to change your behavior of your sexual practices to either abstinence or safer sex. Attitudes can change when one of the following occur: we are open enough to see the conflict between our attitude and our behavior, when others persuade us, or when we discover that a new attitude is more advantageous.

Internal/External Locus of Control

Have a stronger internal locus of control. Locus of control means that you attribute the outcomes of your behavior toward something within you or outside you. There are two loci of control, internal and external. **You can change your life significantly by adopting an internal locus of control.**

Internal Control---the belief that events are due to our own efforts and behavior.
External Control---the belief that fate, luck, or chance caused the events in our lives. It can be caused by inconsistent parental discipline that makes the child's world unpredictable. Low socio-economic status tends to be indicator.
Below is a comparison of the different attitudes that internals and externals hold:

INTERNALS	**EXTERNALS**
- resist manipulators	- comply or conform to others
- not easily persuaded	- easily persuaded
- self-responsible	- rely and blame others
- resistant to social influence	- influenced by social agents

Below is a list of how they coped during stress:

INTERNALS	**EXTERNALS**
- got professional help	- hoped a miracle would happen
- made a plan of action and followed it	- wished it would go away
- took things one step at a time	- blamed themselves
- clarified value systems	- tried to make themselves feel better by eating, drinking.

Optimism vs. Pessimism

In referring to what the future holds, optimists have positive thoughts and pessimists have negative thoughts. Optimists see setbacks as opportunities, experience defeat as temporary, and believe most of life is under their personal control (internal locus of control). Pessimists see setbacks and defeats as final and beyond their control (external locus of control). Compared with optimists, pessimists learn less, have less fun, and often lapse into self-pity, depression and helplessness. They quit and give up easily. Optimists often have better health, better family lives, and better social relationships. They often make more money, seek win/win solutions, and inspire others to reach beyond the normal. They focus on the things they can control. Pessimists, on the other hand, tend to dwell on things they are unlikely to control like war, terrorism, crime in the streets, and negative people in their lives. **In a study of college students, optimists enjoyed the highest overall quality of life satisfaction while pessimists were dissatisfied and used more alcohol in an attempt to cope (Harju & Bolen, 1998).**

A study in 2011 found that optimistic cardiac patients were more likely to survive after surgery and years beyond than those who were neutral or not optimistic. The study analyzed 2818 patients and controlled for age, sex, disease severity, demographics, depressive symptoms, comorbidities, and social support (Barefoot, et all 2011).

Attitude is Most Valued in the Job Market

Employers were asked what they considered to be most important when hiring a new worker. Among the list of qualities (i.e., previous work experience, industry credentials, years of completed schooling, score on interview tests, recommendations, size of the bribe, and so on) attitude and communication skills were ranked the highest. Source: National Employer Survey by the National Center on the Educational Quality of the Workforce.

Become a Thermostat

Become more of a thermostat instead of a thermometer. A thermometer reacts to its environment and a thermostat controls its environment. Don't let others' negative attitudes influence you. Set Attitude on a positive setting. Quote: "If you are constantly being mistreated, you are cooperating with the treatment."...Robert Anthony

Follow the Six Positive Attitudes of High Performers

1. Have an innovative attitude so that you are upbeat, optimistic, and enthusiastic.
2. Have a mindful attitude so that you are focused on lasting values and self-integrity.
3. Have a flexible attitude so that you are open to growth, new ideas, and situations.
4. Have a responsible attitude so that you take an active role in controlling your own life.
5. Have a supportive attitude so that you encourage, listen, and empathize with others.
6. Have a balanced attitude so that you have a balanced perspective about your strengths/weaknesses.

Exercise 1

The Gratitude List

Only a few hundred years ago, kings and queens "had it made." They always had enough to eat and had several feasts a year with spices from around the world. After a meal, they could order entertainment with the snap of a finger. If they wanted music, a clap of the hands would bring forth dozens of songs. If they wanted variety or drama, they could watch the actors of the court. Horses were always ready if they wanted transportation. Their clothes were always dry, warm, and clean and they got new clothes at least once a year. Their house was a castle because is was clean, dry, had warm fireplaces, and were safe from nature and intruders. They lived a royal life and they didn't have it nearly as good as most people in the United States today.

Write down a list of 20 things you are grateful for on a 4x6 card (use front and back). Put this folded card in your purse or wallet and review it every morning to gain perspective and to be able to greet the day with thankfulness and appreciation. Practice below.

____

____

____

Exercise 2

Attitude Adjuster

Rehearse an attitude adjuster with a friend. We all have negative people in our lives and when we can stand up for our selves and get them to think twice about their attitude, we improve our own character. Have a friend imitate a typical phrase that a negative person in your life is likely to say to you in the future or has said to you in the past. Then you respond with a kind but killer response. For example:

Friend – "You're wasting your time by going back to school."
You – "You are the first person in my life that has given me that message. Most of my true friends have been encouraging me, and I know it is the best thing for me."

By practicing these situations before hand, you'll find yourself automatically saying these effective statements to the right people at the right time. Remember to respond positively without judgment or resentment. Ask yourself:

1. Who do I need to set a boundary with or who takes advantage of me?

___

___

2. What do they say that "gets under my skin"?

___

___

3. What could you say back?

___

___

___

Exercise 3

The Attitude Reframer

The ability to look at a negative event in a more positive light is the ability to reframe the event. It's the idea of seeing it with a different pair of lenses on. It will allow you to gain insight, learn from the negative event, and respond to it in a healthier way. By obtaining this valuable skill, you will no longer quit when things get rough, no longer get bitter when things don't go your way, and no longer stay down when the dark cloud seems to be above you. See the examples below.

Examples of Attitude Reframers

1. Negative Attitude: "I'll never be able to go to and finish college."
   Reframe Statement: "Doing something new is always frightening to me at first. I don't have to get straight A's."
2. Negative Attitude: "This is a beautiful dress, and I look awful in it."
   Reframe Statement: "This is a beautiful dress – for somebody. It's not right for me. I'll keep looking until I find one that looks good on me."
3. Negative Attitude: "I just lost an important business client. I'll never find another one."
   Reframe Statement: "I found this client which proves I can find another."

Step 1: Write the circumstances in your life that cause you to have a negative attitude in all of the following areas: your job, at home, about life, about yourself. Examples include:

Job:	Sylvia, my boss, is controlling and condescending to me.
At Home:	My spouse is unsupportive and is a jealous person.
About Life:	I know racism will always be around to make my life harder.
Yourself:	I'm not smart enough to go to and finish college.

Step 2: Gain a higher perspective that reveals the truth about these circumstances by writing a reframe statement that will produce the behavior you will implement tomorrow. See

the Judgment questions in Strategy 2.2. See the examples below.

Life Circumstance – "I know racism will always be around to make my life harder."
Reframe Statement - "I still live in probably, the best country in the world even though it's far from flawless."
Self Circumstance – "I'm not smart enough to go to and finish college."
Reframe Statement – "I usually minimize my strengths and maximize my weaknesses when starting something new."
Now write your own Reframers below in response to your own circumstances.

Job Circumstance____
____
____

Reframe Statement____
____
____

Home Circumstance____
____
____

Reframe Statement____
____
____

Life Circumstance____
____
____

Reframe Statement____
____
____

Self Circumstance____
____
____

Reframe Statement____
____
____

Strategy 2.7

Empower your Behavioral system by scheduling balanced and pleasureable activities into your day.

Definition: Behavior - A decision or judgment made which is charged by emotion, belief, expectation, and attitude to act or not act on something.

There are three kinds of people in this world: those who make things happen, those who watch things happen, and those who don't know what the hell just happened. Take Action!
Mary Kay Ash

To be happy, one should have
1) something to live for
2) something to live on
3) someone to live with
When 1 is missing---life is a challenge
When 2 are missing---life is a drama
When 3 are missing---life is a tragedy
Simpson Norwood

The Pleasure Principle

Many of us could plow through this book, but without the component of pleasure something would be missing. If you take your life too seriously, you'd miss out on the dance of life. We are supposed to find humor in things, pleasure our bodies, and create fun in every aspect of our lives.

Often, we spend too much time doing dirty laundry, paying unpaid bills, doing housework, etc., when we could spend just 15 minutes a day attending to our selves. Yet, most people don't even do that. This is the path to pleasure and life balance. Without time to nurture our selves, we become off balanced, too serious, too tense, and uneasy, leading us into a life of dread, dullness, and misery.

Bringing Balance Back into Your Life

Unless you live in a stress-free, toxic-free, and a work and family dysfunctional-free world, it is crucial that you learn how to repel today's societal, social, and psychological toxicity. This toxicity eventually creeps into our relationships, our environment, and within our selves. If we ignore our bodies, minds, and our health, the stressful world outside of us will, more than likely, "eat us alive." It has for millions of people who have suffered from all kinds of health problems such as stress/anxiety disorders, depression, being overweight, feeling lonely/confused/empty. It's easy to forget that health, meaning, and happiness lie in a place that is far more intelligent and wise than anything the outside world can provide to us. Is it any surprise that one of the two fastest growing businesses is the pharmaceutical industry who sells pills for anxiety and depression, namely, VIAGRA and PROZAC. This means that the men are aroused and the women are depressed. Seriously though, I know people who, because they perform an inner ritual each day, are able to put up with the most horrific, malicious supervisors at work and still maintain their sanity and health. They can maintain their sanity because they perform a few little inner rituals during their day that allow them to have that teflon coating to protect them.

Imagine being able to feel vibrant, peaceful, focused, and confident throughout your day, regardless of stressful events that try to trip you up. Most people are out of balance and, therefore, unhappy because they either over-extend themselves with projects and activities or they excel in one life area like work. Unfortunately, they neglect the other areas of life, causing an imbalance in their relationships and their health. I will specifically describe how to prevent this imbalance so it will not occur with you. It starts with spending 15 minutes each day in the four life areas below.

The Four Areas of Life Balance

How can you achieve life balance so that you can live, thrive, and produce like you never have before? There are four life areas that are crucial to our well-being and our ability to feel balance for an entire day, week, month, etc. If we could spend a minimal 15 minutes a day in each life area, we would surely achieve balance. The life areas are the *Spiritual, Physical, Aspirational* (your goals, what you aspire to) and the *Social.* See Exercise 1. It is necessary to understand why we ought to spend focused time in each life area. I know so many people who thrive in the Spiritual area of life. They have a great relationship with the Divine, and they have peace of mind despite life challenges. But what good is it if they are lacking in the Physical area of life, where they are often sick, drained of energy, and easily stressed out? At the same time, I know people who thrive in the Physical area of life. They are in great shape, eat well, and have plenty of energy. Yet, they are lacking in the Aspirational area of life, where they don't have motivation to improve their life plan or accomplish their goals. Then there are those who thrive in the Aspirational area of life. They accomplish all their goals, they have a great career, and almost every thing they touch is a success. But, again, what good is it if they are lacking in the Social life area, where they are constantly at odds with their spouse, their kids hate them, and their friends don't call? Finally, I know people who thrive in the Social life area. They have great relationships with others and they are active in their community. These people have a wonderful social life, but they are lacking in the Spiritual life area, where they neglect their own needs, feel an emptiness inside, and lose their sense of self and life purpose. Therefore, we need to thrive in all life areas to be balanced. Below I describe the importance of each life area.

The Spiritual

- Why should you go inside yourself and enhance your spiritual health and life? As a counselor,
  educator, and speaker, I can tell you that many clients have told me that it was their spiritual life that helped them move from confusion to clarity, from stagnation to passion, from emptiness to fulfillment, from anxiety to peace of mind, from problem to insight and solution. Why do we, so desperately, need to thrive in our spiritual lives? When we connect with our spiritual life source, our desire, which I mentioned earlier, will come from a healthy place that knows what is best for us. Yet, many of us have been "cut off" from our LIFE SOURCE since birth. The life source is that which gives us love, guidance, and strength to grow. As a child, this is our parents. As we age, our life source can become a spiritual source. In Pearce's book he explains that in most people's lives, ***a separation*** occurs between individuals and their life source in five different ways:

1) We were, more than likely, separated from our mother seconds after birth and afterwards removed from the mother to an unfamiliar nursery. This is the time in our lives when we are most desperate, vulnerable, powerless, and needing love.
2) At age two to three years old, our ego emerges and separates us again from connection to the world around us giving us an identity; a name, a proud achievement, a power struggle with a parent and so forth.
3) Daycare, when used exclusively, further separates children and infants from their life source, and most powerful influence; their parents.
4) Television is now perhaps the biggest cause of separation between child and parent, between spouse and spouse, and further separates us from our selves. Television, movies, videos, and computer games have become the substitute parent.
5) When we become adults, our work and busy lives separate us again from our spiritual center and our selves. Connecting with this spiritual center is necessary to heal the traumatic wounds we experienced from the above life separations.

So, we need to *practice* reconnection for 15 minutes a day. Some people don't want to *practice*; they just want to meet the stressors as they come and move on. You don't go on a golf course without going on the driving range or putting green first and practicing your swing. You don't just walk onto the tennis court and start the game without warming up and practicing your swing. Why? Because we will make too many mistakes. When people get stressed, they make too many mistakes. This is seen in the increased numbers of the following: health claims from accidents and injuries, divorce rates, body weight, substance and alcohol abuse, and depression rates. This is a waste because these things can be prevented. We need to *practice* growing in these four areas of life each day. One way of growing spiritually is by *practicing* the "heart" exercises each morning before your day begins. Also, as we grow spiritually, we must realize that it is just as important to avoid the pitfalls that sabotage our spiritual and psychological growth and throws us off balance. The following are potent spiritual principles that point to these pitfalls.

Traditional Pitfalls

* *Giving your personal power away to people, dark forces, and the negative ego.*
* *Becoming an extremist and not being moderate in all things*
* *Becoming too serious and not having enough joy, happiness, and fun in your life*
* *Letting your sex drive run you instead of mastering it*
* *Giving up and quitting amidst great adversity*

* *Getting caught up in the dogma of traditional religion*
* *Getting caught up in the attractions and fascinations of the material world*
* *Needing to control others*
* *Comparing yourself with other people instead of comparing self with self*
* *Trying to win and be "right" instead of striving for love*

Modern Pitfalls
* *Stopping your spiritual practices when you get involved in a relationship*
* *Being too attached to things/people or being too unattached. Strive for involved detachment*
* *Being too preoccupied with self and not being concerned about being of service to others*
* *Self-promoting your "good spiritual work" instead of just being humble*

Tricky Pitfalls
* *Loving others but not loving yourself*
* *Focusing on God/divine being but not nurturing and parenting the "child" within you*
* *Being deeply into spiritual life but ignoring the psychological area that needs mastering*
* *The glamour and holding of power over others once you become successful*
* *Expecting God or a Divine Being to solve all your problems*
* *Putting your relationship with your kids before your self and God*
* *Being a martyr on your spiritual path*
* *Taking responsibility for other people and being the savior type*

The Physical

- There is no better way to get energy and feel great than to exercise, eat well, and manage your stress. You can be 10 times more successful when you feel terrific for most of your day. Most people feel sluggish after they eat. They feel exhausted at work and when they come home from work. For these people, their energy does not serve them in finding their treasure of living, thriving, and producing like never before. So, spend 15 minutes a day moving your body.

The Aspirational

- When we see famous people on television, like actors, musicians, movie stars, comedians, and sports figures, we assume they are just naturally talented and that they don't have to work hard for their success. Nothing could be further from the truth. We never see the hard work that they do, how they practice for three to eight hours a day, or the hundreds of rejections they encounter on their way to the top. All we hear and see is their success on the big screen or television. That is, we see the treasure others found and achieved but with no road map on how they got there. So, spending time in the aspirational life area and using self-discipline techniques are the key factors to our success. These skills give us the power to prioritize and accomplish the things in our life that are most important.
- Perhaps your biggest challenge, and most important life goal, will be to develop your intellectual brain so that it fits your "heart's" mission statement. With excessive TV watching, bad health choices, and marital mistakes, we have to stop dumbing down our intelligence by reducing the attention and power we give to advertisers. Advertisements are specifically designed campaigns to stimulate our sexual desires and food appetites. What is actually being stimulated is our first reptilian brain—our <u>dumbest brain!</u> It's difficult to resist these enticing temptations when you can hardly drive a block on any American road without seeing at least 2 fast-food burger drive-ins like McDonalds or Jack in the Box. In addition, there are three billboards attracting you with the mouth-watering picture of sex selling cigarettes, candy bars and our favorite alcoholic beverage. The

more we give in to these enticements, the more our reptilian brain, our dumbest brain, develops and takes control of our most intelligent brain. This part of us takes control and steers our life down a meaningless road with no treasure to be found.

- We also need to reduce the attention and power that we give to emotional stimulations around us. This includes the overuse of viewing movies, soap operas, and junk news that you see at
the checkout stand. These stimulations develop our second brain—the emotional limbic system. To avoid pain and the real issues in their lives, most people escape to the fantasy emotional dramas like the movies, sports teams, and so on. With such distractions as these, moderation is the key, but when you escape your inner issues, the business you need to take care of, then there are two negative repercussions. One, that which you escape from will come back tenfold in a more negative way. Just think of those with drinking problems, eating problems, relationship problems, personality problems, and on and on. Two, that which you escape to develops your second weakest brain and, like the reptilian brain, it will take control of our most intelligent brain, which is just like a five-year-old taking control of the parental duties of a six-person family. Not a good scene although there are weak parents out there where this is actually the case.
- Our third brain, the neocortex, is the brain that we need to give more attention and power to. Reading, researching, and learning valuable skills and life principles develop our most intelligent third brain, and this is the one that should be the commander of the other two brains. Most people, however, make life decisions based on the dictates of the first reptilian brain, which causes one to overeat, have an unwanted pregnancy, and so on. Others base their life decisions on the dictates of the second limbic system brain, which causes slave-like dependency on others (men or women). This dependency causes immature, insecure personalities and weak characters because these people act out of their feelings only, instead of acting from both feeling and intelligent thought, which needs to be the necessary combination. If this is not done, these people usually have very unhealthy relationships.

The Reptilian brain is ego based; give me give me, give me.
The Limbic system brain in self-image based; like me, like me, like me.
The Neocortex brain should be" heart" based, following the dictates of a superior intelligence. Unfortunately, most people's neocortex is ego based. You know, the person that tries to sound intelligent and makes you feel stupid just so he/she can feel important.

By developing your aspirational life, you will automatically be developing your third brain. So, spend at least 15 minutes a day planning your goals.

The Social

- We, as a society, have become a group of distant, uninvolved, "Don't say hello to strangers," type of people…I do it sometimes, too! If you need outer motivation to be sociable, know that networking with others is the single, most effective way to increase business and opportunity for yourself. Many people make the mistake of only networking with those they think will offer an advantage to them. Opportunities come when you sow your seeds. Sow your seeds wherever you can….this is not condoning philandering.
- What would you guess is the leading cause of death? It is loneliness. According to Dr. Dean Ornish's book, "Love and Survival," love, connection, and community have a stronger effect on our health and well-being than lifestyle, surgery, diet, drugs, and even genetics.
- In Rosita, Pennsylvania, it was found that a long-living community had zero heart disease. The American Medical Association and the American Heart Association went there to see what they could find. They expected jogging, fiber-eating meditators. Instead, they found obese, sedentary, meat-eating smokers. What was it that this community had that made

them live into their 90's? They had community. When somebody was sick, the whole neighborhood made it a priority to help out. Those types of communities are almost unheard of in today's society.

Therefore, spend 15 minutes a day intimately connecting with someone. So............

You don't need *Money* to spend 15 minutes a day to thrive in the Spiritual life area.
You don't need a *Gym* to spend 15 minutes a day to thrive in the Physical life area.
You don't need a *Motivational Guru* to spend 15 minutes a day to thrive in the Aspirational life area.
You don't need a *900 number* to spend 15 minutes a day to thrive in the Social life area.

Exercise 1

Choose the 15-minute tasks you will perform for each life area and write down when you plan to perform them. Examples below.

Spiritual	15 min.	Time in silence going inward: prayer or meditation – while in the restroom, while car is warming up, in the office	**Listen To It**
Aspirational	15 min.	Planning goals, working on daily planner – in car, at work, in bed. Bring planner wherever you go. You should have family goals, financial goals, career goals, educational goals, and self-improvement goals,	**Plan It**
Physical	15 min.	Aerobic exercise, stretching or lifting weights – in office, at home, listening to music, in front of TV.	**Move It**
Social	15 min.	Intimate communication face-to-face with others – friends, family/relatives, co-workers, spouse, boy/girlfriend.	**Share It**

Now write below what activities you will complete as they relate to each life area.

Spiritual____

____

Physical ____

____

Aspirational ______________________________________

____

Social ____

____

Exercise 2

Determine how you will schedule the following two-hour blocks into your week. Schedule it now into your daily planner.

Each Week (On top of doing 15 minutes each day)

Physical	2 hours	Recreational- sports, hiking, walking, etc. (watching TV doesn'tcount).
Social	2 hours	Intimate and close conversations with more than one person.
Spiritual	2 hours	Ritual activity- church, being in nature, meditating.
Aspirational	2 hours	Implement your goals, plan, create something

How will you spend 2 hours a week in each area? Write below.

Spiritual____

____

Physical____

____

Aspirational____

____

Social____

____

Exercise 3

Make a list of additional activities you would like to become involved in and schedule once every month for the next 12 months. These should be bigger payoffs than your daily pleasurable activities. Slowly, balance will begin to creep back into your life. Doing this is a way of watering the plant to your own self and to your life. Without pleasurable activities, a part of us wilts and dies.

Examples include listening to a symphony, listening to your favorite music, thoroughly enjoying a good meal, taking an early morning walk , telling or enjoying a good story, sitting by a rushing stream, encouraging or telling someone you appreciate them, writing a poem, taking a friend to lunch, watching clouds, making a new acquaintance, going to a sports event, going to the beach, lake, or mountains.

Determine how you will spend your vacation time and/or pleasurable activities every month, year, and decade.

Each month: 1 day of vacation (recreational – getting away)
Each year: 1 week of vacation (plus the 12 days from the 1 month above)
Each decade: 1 month of vacation (not doing any work, i.e., housework)

Each Month____

____

Each Year____

____

Each Decade____

____

For the next month, complete the Power Hour Card below.

The Power Hour Card will help make you accountable in achieving balance in the four life areas. Write both a daily and monthly reward for hitting your target goal. You write your target goal at the beginning of the month, and your monthly total is the actual number you completed at the end of the month. You can make a copy below onto a 4x6 card and carry it with you to monitor your progress.

Spend 15 minutes (minimum) a day in each life area. Circle the date (number) after you've completed that area for the day. This is your daily POWER HOUR CARD!

Life Area		Target Goal	Monthly Total
Spiritual	1 2 3 4 5 6 7 8 9 10 11 12 13 14 15 16 17 18 19 20 21 22 23 24 25 26 27 28 29 30 31	____	____
Physical	1 2 3 4 5 6 7 8 9 10 11 12 13 14 15 16 17 18 19 20 21 22 23 24 25 26 27 28 29 30 31	____	____
Goal	1 2 3 4 5 6 7 8 9 10 11 12 13 14 15 16 17 18 19 20 21 22 23 24 25 26 27 28 29 30 31	____	____
Social	1 2 3 4 5 6 7 8 9 10 11 12 13 14 15 16 17 18 19 20 21 22 23 24 25 26 27 28 29 30 31	____	____

Daily Reward:

Monthly Reward:

Chapter Insight & Commitment

After completing this chapter, I learned the following about my heart, judgments, emotions, beliefs, expectations, attitude, and behavior:
Example: I realized that I have a hidden belief that I don't deserve good things to happen to me. This causes me to not try as hard, quit early on, and thereby, fail at many things I attempt.

I can take active steps to help me achieve my future goals and become more of the person I am or strive to be by:
Example: I realize that I do deserve success and am entitled to it. When I feel this negative urge in the future, I will surround myself with people that support and encourage me. I will remind myself of my worth and seek counseling so I can achieve my goal of graduating from college in two years.

CHAPTER 3

Self-Observation

Using your **Eyes** to **Observe** and convert self-defeating thoughts and behaviors into self-empowering thoughts and behaviors.

Purpose: To achieve self-confidence by strengthening and maintaining positive
thoughts and behaviors like the retainer on crooked teeth.

Rewards: Personal Efficiency, Healthy Mind, Forward Progress

Obstacles: Outside Stimulations, Laziness, Negative Childhood Messages

Consequence: Non-growth, Self-sabotage, Stagnation

Symbol: Mirror

Related Web Sites: **http://www.habitsmart.com/index.html**
http://queendom.com/coping.html

Self-Observation

Once you are able to understand the "inner workings" of your mind and make the positive changes in your mental systems (thoughts and behaviors), you then need a tool for ensuring that these mental systems can withstand the pressures of life.

Often, without knowing it, we think and do things as a result of this pressure around us. We end up consciously and subconsciously making poor decisions because we were not in our "right mind" (the Ego). For example, most people at some point in their lives are pressured to conform to the belief systems of their parents, their supervisor, their friends, their cultural background, and/or the society they grew up in. We learn that if we do not adopt these beliefs and follow their lead, there will be dire consequences. These consequences often consist of alienation, loneliness, ridicule, not belonging, disapproval, reprimands, and sometimes punishments of the worst kind. The end result is a tremendous amount of stress and anxiety in the mind and body that can wreak havoc with a barrage of dis-ease like symptoms. Managing this stress and anxiety, as well as grief and the death of loved one's becomes a crucial life skill to master. The consequence of not managing them is depression and a whole host of mental disorders which will be discussed in this chapter.

As children, we learned to conform and cope with the above consequences by choosing defense mechanisms to protect us. In other words, we learned to suppress our feelings, deny, distort, rationalize, engage in lying, and participate in a whole list of self-protecting behaviors. Though these defense mechanisms did help to protect us in childhood, they often remained with us into adulthood due to comfort and familiarity. However, relying on such coping techniques creates very limited life experiences. Adults pay a higher price as a result of this. Defense mechanisms "drug" our awareness of our feelings. For example, when people hurt us, we may become numb, hindering our ability to learn from our failures and set boundaries with those who take advantage of us.

Therefore, we need to use self-observation to bring these "decisions to defend" into our awareness so that we can self-correct them as they happen. This monitoring of thought and behavior, as we will discuss in this chapter, allows us to work through and resolve the most important key issues over time. We then become the strong person we always wanted to be and who, by nature, we truly are inside. Your ability to perform this self-observation and self-correction will improve in Chapter Four when you develop love, appreciation, and compassion for yourself.

Strategy 3.1

Manage stress and anxiety by becoming objective to your thoughts using centering and stress reduction practices.

Effects of Stress

What would happen to you if you had just finished entering a twenty-page paper into your word processor and before you had a chance to print out the report, the electrical power in your dorm failed and you lost the entire paper? Or, how would you respond if you forgot to pay your phone bill and the telephone company disconnected your phone while you were waiting for a call from the bank to see if your car loan had been approved? You might define these circumstances as major sources of stress. Stress is the body's normal reaction to any danger or pressure. But remember that an event is not stressful. It is your perception and interpretation of the event that causes the stress. Remember, the judgment comes first, then the emotion, then the belief and so on. Stress is prevalent most at home and particularly on the job. Causes of job stress in a survey were linked to excessive workload, unreasonable deadlines, and overcrowded conditions. According to Girion (2001), nearly 1/3 of 1,305 workers who responded to a telephone survey on desk rage (attacks on trash cans, keyboards, and co-workers) admitted to yelling at someone in the office. Work stress had driven 23% of the respondents to tears, and 34% blamed their jobs for a loss of sleep. In fact, at least half of all Americans report difficulty falling asleep, frequent awakenings during the night, and poor quality of sleep. As a result, according to the National Sleep Foundation, we sleep about 25% less than our grandparents. Lack of sleep prevents you from managing stress and thereby will cause more stress during your day.

Rising Stress and Anxiety in the 21st Century

The number one mental health problem in the United States are anxiety disorders according to the National Institute of Mental Health. Up to 40 million people have suffered from panic attacks, phobias, or other anxiety disorders in the past year, which makes up around 25% of the adult population. These disorders are a serious problem for the entire society because they interfere with a patient's work, schooling, and family life. Anxiety disorders also contribute to the high rates of alcohol and substance abuse.

Why has stress and anxiety been so widespread and increasing each year for more than a decade? Today, people living in Western society are currently experiencing more stress than they have at any previous time in history, which has caused so many anxiety disorders. While it can be argued that human beings have always had to deal with stressful conditions such as wars, plagues, famines, economic depressions, and so on, there are four reasons for suggesting the overall stress level is higher now that ever.

First, our social order and environment have changed more in the last 40 years than they have in the last 400 years. The increased pace of modern society and the technological change of computers, cell phones, the Internet, and constant stimulations have deprived people of adequate time to adjust to these changes. Second, to make it worse, today more than ever, there is a lack of a consistent set of values and standards traditionally received through religion or society that has left people feeling confused, empty and they are left to fend for themselves. Faced with a barrage of inconsistent world views and values presented by the media such as TV, the movies, commercials, and pop music, people are having to learn to cope with the responsibility of creating their own meaning and moral code. All of this makes it very hard to establish one's identity and develop a sense of stability or consistency in one's life. Third, the terrorist attacks on September 11th, 2001 have heightened fears about biological, chemical, and weapons of mass destruction upon the United States from terrorists. Fourth, the mass media is constantly shoveling bad news and fear mongering upon the public because it gets ratings. The evening news is filled with violence, murder, child molesters, natural disasters, robberies, and so forth. If that's not bad enough, they imply that it can happen to you any day. For example, shark attacks in the southeastern part of the United States in June and July of 2005 dominated the news. Though the news made it seem it was dangerous to go to the beach, only one person a year gets killed from a shark. Therefore, what seems like a dangerous society is always overblown by the news coverage and probably overblown by our nervous systems. I don't believe our nervous systems were wired to digest the tragedy of six billion people in daily news reports. Watching the news can make you want to take ex-lax, advil, and mylanta simultaneously. It is truly a proctologist view of society and in my view, bad for the mind. As a result, depression, anxiety disorders, addictive behaviors, and depression continue to rise.

The Difference Between Fear, Anxiety, Phobia, and Anxiety Disorders

When you are afraid, your ***fear*** is usually directed toward some concrete, external object, person, or situation. The fear is very possible to happen. Examples include: not meeting a deadline, failing an exam, being unable to pay your bills, or being rejected by somebody you want to please. However, when one experiences ***anxiety***, the focus of anxiety is more internal and a response to a vague, distant, unrecognized danger that you can't necessarily specify. Examples include: you feel "something bad is going to happen" or you feel that you might "lose control" of yourself during some situation. *Situational anxiety* is different from everyday fear because it tends to be out of proportion or unrealistic. Examples include more simple things like having anxiety about driving on the freeways or seeing the dentist. Situational anxiety can become ***phobic*** when you actually start to avoid the situation. For example, you stop driving on the freeway or going to the dentist.

Anxiety is experienced by virtually everybody to some degree and is part of living in today's society. It is appropriate and reasonable to react with some anxiety when experiencing personal challenges, failing at something, or worrying about the bills to pay. However, ***anxiety disorders*** come about when anxiety is 1) highly intense (like panic attacks), and 2) lasts longer than normal (it persists for months instead of going away after the stressful situation has passed), and 3) can lead to phobias that interfere with one's life.

There are various anxiety disorders defined by the DSM-IV (a diagnostic manual which some of the following information comes from and is used by psychiatrists). They are panic disorder, phobias, generalized anxiety disorder, obsessive-compulsive disorder, post-traumatic stress disorder, substance-induced anxiety disorder, acute stress disorder, and anxiety disorder due to a medical condition,. In all of these cases there are mild, moderate, and severe levels of anxiety. In other words, not all people with anxiety disorders experience the same intensity as another with the same disorder.

Panic disorder is characterized by sudden episodes of intense fear that occur "out of nowhere" without any apparent cause. They can last from anywhere between a few minutes to a few hours. The following symptoms occur: shortness of breath, chest pain, fears of going crazy or of dying (having a heart attack), dizziness, faintness, shaking, sweating, nausea, numbness or tingling, hot and cold flashes, and/or feeling spacey (lost sense of self, time-space is off, as if you're "not all there" often called depersonalization or unreality). About 2% of the U.S. population suffers from panic disorder while 5% (one in every twenty), suffer from panic attacks from agoraphobia described below.

Agoraphobia involves the fear of having a panic attack while going to crowded public places such as grocery stores, department stores, restaurants, enclosed places like elevators, and a hairdresser's chair. Also, public transportation such as trains, subways, planes, buses, being at home alone, driving on the freeway, being far away from home or from a "safe person" (usually your spouse, partner, parent, etc.), or high places are other typical places one can be phobic. It is estimated that 5%, or one in twenty people, in the U.S. have this disorder.

Social phobias include avoiding certain places because you fear embarrassment or humiliation. Examples of situations include: a school setting, dating, eating in front of others, using public restrooms, parties and social functions, and giving a talk in front of people. It is estimated that 2 – 5% of people in the U.S. have this disorder.

Generalized anxiety disorder is characterized by chronic anxiety that lasts during and longer than six months but is not accompanied by panic attacks, obsessions, or phobias. The anxiety and worry must focus on two or more stressful life circumstances like one's health, school performance, finances, relationships, etc. The intensity and frequency of the worry are always out of proportion to the actual feared events happening. This disorder affects about 4 % of the U.S. population.

In Obsessive-compulsive disorder, behaviors of things needing to be neat, tidy, and orderly are carried to such an extreme that they disrupt and significantly interfere with several areas of the person's life. Common obsessions and behaviors include thoughts of hurting loved ones, overly checking the locks on the doors, repeatedly washing hands and other things, counting, and fear of coming in contact with a toxic substance. Recent studies show that the disorder affects up to 3% of the U. S. population. Causes are unknown but a low neurotransmitter substance in the brain known as serotonin is associated with this disorder. Medications that increase serotonin improve the symptoms. The obsessions and compulsions often begin in childhood or adolescence.

Post-Traumatic Stress disorder occurs from a traumatic event in the person's past that produce feelings of fear, terror, and helplessness in his/her present life. It was first identified during World War I when soldiers were observed suffering from chronic anxiety, nightmares, and flashbacks for weeks, months, or years following combat. It was known then as Shell Shock.

Substance-induced anxiety disorder can occur as a result of taking a substance such as a drug (like hallucinogens, amphetamines), medications (prescriptions or cough medicines), or toxin that produces panic attacks or generalized anxiety. An allergic reaction to any of the above can cause this disorder if there was no previous history of anxiety disorder.

Self-Diagnosis Questionnaire (Bourne, 2000)

Circle yes or no

1. Do you have sudden anxiety attacks that "come out of nowhere" but do not have phobias? Yes No 2. Have you had at least one such attack in the last month? Yes No

3. If you had an anxiety attack in the last month, did you worry about having another one and what that might mean to your physical or mental health? Yes No

4. In your worst experience with anxiety did you have more than three of the symptoms mentioned above under panic disorder? (Shortness of breath, dizziness, fear of going crazy, etc.) Yes No

*If you answered yes to all four, it is likely you've met the conditions for **panic disorder.** If you answered yes to three or less, and had fewer than four of the symptoms for panic disorder, then you are experiencing limited symptom attacks and not full-blown panic disorder.*

5. Does fear of having panic attacks cause you to avoid going to certain situations? Yes No
*If you answered yes, it is likely you are dealing with **agoraphobia.***

6. If you answered no to number 5 above, but still have phobias, do you avoid certain situations because you're afraid of being embarrassed or criticized by other people? Yes No
*If you answered yes to number 6, it is likely you are dealing with **social phobia.***

7. If you answered no to number 5 and 6 above, but still have phobias, do you fear and avoid any one or more of the following when you have to face them: insects or animals, heights, darkness, illness such as heart attacks or cancer, injections, blood, thunder or lightning, doctors, airplanes, etc. Yes No
If you answered yes to number 7, it is likely you are dealing with ***a specific phobia.***

8. Do you feel anxious most of the time but do not have panic attacks, phobias, and do not have obsessions or compulsions? Yes No

9. Have you been prone to excessive worry for at least the last six months? Yes No

10. Has your anxiety and worry been associated with at least three of the following six symptoms? Restlessness, feeling on edge, difficulty concentrating or mind going blank, being easily fatigued, irritability, muscle tension, sleep disturbances (difficulty falling or staying asleep or unsatisfying sleep).

If you answered yes to numbers 8 – 10, you are likely dealing with ***generalized anxiety disorder.*** *If you answer yes to number 8 but no to numbers 9-10, you're likely dealing with an anxiety condition not severe enough to qualify as generalized anxiety disorder.*

11. Do you have recurring intrusive thoughts such as being contaminated with a toxic substance, fearing you forgot to lock your door or turn off an appliance, or hurting a close relative, or an unpleasant fantasy? You notice that these thoughts are irrational but you can't stop them from coming into your mind. Yes No
12. Do you perform ritualistic actions such as washing your hands, checking on things, or counting to relieve anxiety you feel or to relieve anxiety over irrational fears that enter your mind, etc. Yes No

If you answered yes to number 11 but no to number 12, you are probably dealing with obsessive-compulsive disorder, but have obsessions only. If you answered yes to number 11 and yes to number 12, you are probably dealing with ***obsessive-compulsive disorder,*** *with both obsessions and compulsions.*

13. Have you had a traumatic experience/event in the past that today causes the following symptoms that have lasted more than one month: repetitive, distressing thoughts about the event, nightmares related to the event, flashbacks so intense that you feel or act as though the trauma were occurring all over again, have a phobia related to the trauma (like phobia about driving after having been in a car accident), emotional numbness, feelings of detachment and spaciness, sleeping problems, and losing interest in activities that once gave you pleasure. Yes No

If you answered yes to number 13, you are probably suffering with ***post-traumatic stress disorder.*** *If the symptoms have been less than one month, it is called acute stress disorder.*

If you have these symptoms you still might not have an Anxiety Disorder.
If you suspect you may have an Anxiety Disorder, have it diagnosed by a doctor or psychiatrist. They will rule it out by making sure your anxiety is not caused by some other condition. They will have you take tests for hyper or hypothyroidism, hypoglycemia, cardiovascular conditions like mitral valve prolapse and others, premenstrual syndrome (PMS), inner ear disturbances, deficiencies of calcium magnesium, potassium, niacin, and vitamin B12, neurological conditions, withdrawal from alcohol, caffeine, tranquilizers, sedatives, and environmental toxins such as mercury, hydrocarbons, food additives, pesticides, etc. Once these are cleared up, anxiety often subsides.

Causes of Anxiety Disorders

If you fit any of the above definitions for anxiety, you are probably asking yourself, "Why do I have panic attacks?" or "Why can't I shake this phobia or obsession or compulsion?" "Why does adrenaline shoot into my stomach for no apparent reason?" "What caused this to happen in the first place?" The symptoms often seem irrational and unable to be explained.

Experts in the field verify that there are several factors that cause anxiety disorders. Be careful of thinking that there is only one cause, which, if removed, would eliminate the problem. These "single-cause" theories greatly oversimplify the disorders because most have both a biological and psychological cause involved as well as other factors I will mention. Some doctors might give you the biological fallacy and tell you that the anxiety disorder is entirely biological and that your neurotransmitters (allows nerve cells in your brain to transmit and communicate) are deficient. But, if you suffer from anxiety, ask what caused the neurotransmitters to become more deficient to a point where it now disturbs your life? Could it have been chronic stress over a period of months or years that made you vulnerable? Could it have been the suppressed anger that sets up a disturbance in brain serotonin levels that contributes to obsessive-compulsive disorder as well as depression? Some therapists or friends might tell you the psychological fallacy. That is, that social phobia or generalized anxiety disorder is caused by having parents who neglected, abandoned, or abused you resulting in a sense of insecurity or shame that causes our phobia or anxiety. Family background does contribute to these disorders but to see it as the only cause oversimplifies the issue. After all, not all children who grow up in a dysfunctional family develop anxiety disorders. Therefore, some people are predisposed or set-up from birth or childhood to develop anxiety later on. Some also acquire disorders from stressful life events. Still other causes that keep anxiety going once they have developed, include psychological factors described below.
The major causes are:

1. **Heredity** – According to Bourne (2000) the following statistics are true. About 20% of children growing up with one agoraphobic parent become agoraphobic themselves while the general population is only 5%. With identical twins, where one person has the disorder, the other twin is on average 60%, likely to also have the disorder. It is 20% for fraternal twins. A general personality type is usually inherited that predisposes you to be overly anxious. But, there is usually "more to the picture."

2. **Childhood Circumstances** – Anxiety disorders become more possible to occur to children when they become adults when parents 1) suppress their child's self-assertiveness, 2) overly criticize and set excessively high standards for their children, 3) communicate an overly cautious and dangerous view of the world, 4) neglect, reject, abandon through divorce or death, 5) physical or sexually abuse the child. In fact, growing up with alcoholic parents contributes to anxiety disorders. Adult children of alcoholics grow up with the following characteristics: obsession with control, difficulty trusting others, avoidance of feelings, over responsibility, all-or-nothing thinking, and excessive eagerness to please at the expense of their own needs. Therefore, they try to find safety to deal with their insecurity, which can often develop into agoraphobia.

3. **Biological Causes** – These refer to physiological imbalances in the body or brain that create anxiety disorders. The causes of these imbalances could be from the result of any or all of the following reasons: hereditary vulnerability, cumulative stress over the years, and unhealthy psychological beliefs and behaviors. In a panic attack, an oversensitive "fear system" in parts of the brain stimulate your pituitary gland and your nervous system sets off several different rapid and intense bodily reactions. It causes the adrenal glands to release large amounts of adrenaline that creates dread, terror, sweating, chest pain, stomach acid, etc. While the physiology of panic is well understood, the mechanisms in the brain that cause it are less understood. However, brain researchers believe that there is a deficiency of a neurotransmitter called GABA that tones

down brain activity. That is why anti-anxiety medication and herbs work. They increase the activity of this one, of many, neurotransmitters. It is important to realize that the adrenaline release during panic gets reabsorbed by the liver and kidneys within a few minutes. So, if you can "ride it out" (the body symptoms) without fighting them like telling yourself how horrible they are, and breathe properly from the stomach, they will tend to subside faster.

4. Triggering Life Event Stressors – The most common life stressors that trigger panic attacks or anxiety conditions are:
- A significant personal loss like a death, divorce, or separation of an important person. Other losses include loss of employment, loss of health through illness, or loss due to a major financial reversal.
- A significant life change event like getting married, having a baby, changing jobs, or moving away to go to college or the military.
- Drugs. Excessive caffeine in coffee can cause a full-blown panic attack as well as cocaine, amphetamines, PCP, LSD, high doses of marijuana, and withdrawal from narcotics or tranquilizers.

5. Conditioning – Phobias come about by a traumatizing event or by one's over-reaction to an event. For example, if you got into an elevator and it got stuck, you might have overreacted and said to yourself, "What if I never get out of here?" Your mind then forms a strong association between being in an elevator and experiencing anxiety. When you start avoiding elevators, you become phobic. The key to overcoming phobias is exposing yourself to them in a safe environment with support. In post-traumatic stress disorder, an array of symptoms re-creates the original trauma and it is the mind's attempt to gain control of the original event and to neutralize the emotional charge it carries.

6. Unhealthy Psychological Factors – These factors that involve ways of thinking, feeling, and coping tend to keep the anxiety going and thriving. The good news is that you can usually manage these with practice and strong desire to overcome them. Most of these factors are presented in the chapters in this book. The most common factors that stimulate anxiety are: not confronting your fears, nervous self-talk like using "What if" statements -- 'What if I have a heart attack," mistaken beliefs like "I am powerless," "I am I'm a failure," "I'm unimportant," and "The world is dangerous." Denied or suppressed feelings that are avoided too often cause deeper lying fears to resurface as well as muscle tension so learning to relax the muscles helps (see Exercise 3). Others include: a lack of how to nurture and love yourself, poor nutrition and food allergy anxiety triggers like coffee, tea, cola, wheat, dairy products, medications, food additives, and sugar, a Type A personality with a high stress lifestyle, and a lack of meaning and purpose. When one discovers something larger than self-gratification, a sense of life purpose arises that eliminates the confinement one feels from not reaching their potential. Confinement is a strong breeding ground for anxiety, phobias, and panic attacks.

How to Manage Stress, Anxiety, Phobias, and Anxiety Disorders

The good news is patients do have some power over their reactions to anxiety and several practices are successful in managing them. Some therapists still use a single-gauged approach to treating anxiety and anxiety disorders. Some therapists solely treat it as a psychiatric condition that can only be cured with medication. Others treat only childhood adjustment problems. Others treat only behavior problems and habits of thinking and behaving. Can you imagine a full recovery on just medication while the person does nothing about their thinking, behavior, eating patterns, and social relationships? Only part of the person is being addressed. The recent trend has been to steer away from single-gauged solutions that have proven to temporarily relieve the problem. This anxiety only seems to return again. Lasting recovery becomes successful when a more comprehensive approach is taken that incorporates healing the physical, emotional, behavioral, cognitive, social, spiritual, and "whole" self areas.

1. Healing Physically

Breathing techniques help to correct shallow breathing and chest pain that contributes to anxiety. One of the best techniques I've learned comes from Dr. Andrew Weil and he describes this technique as similar to taking an anti-anxiety medication only healthier and with no side effects.

It is called the 4-7-8 Breathing Method. Put your tongue on the roof of your mouth next to your front teeth. Next, breathe in 4 counts through the nose, hold it for 7 counts, and breathe out slowly for 8 counts. Repeat this three or four times for a week and increase it carefully.

The Progressive Muscle Relaxation Technique in Exercise 3 will help you heal anxiety because when your muscles are relaxed, your mind becomes relaxed.

Meditation has proven to help one feel calmer in general, often making it unnecessary to rely on tranquilizers.

Regular Exercise is one of the single most effective strategies for reducing muscle tension, stress, and anxiety. Research completely backs this up. See Strategy 4.6.

Taking rests or "cat naps" in the mid afternoon will decrease anxiety and combat fatigue while boosting your immune system and overall health.

Getting enough sleep cannot be overstated. It will determine your irritability, mood, energy level, and health status more than almost anything else. Try to get at least seven to eight hours of sleep at night, preferably starting at 10pm.

2. Healing Emotionally

Often feelings of panic are merely a "front" for buried feelings of anger, grief, or desperation. Many people with anxiety disorders grew up in families that discouraged the effective expression of feelings. As adults, they have a hard time identifying what they feel, much less express those feelings. See Strategy 8.2 on how to express feelings appropriately. Also seek professional help through a therapist to assist you through this. Through the years we have learned habitual ways of thinking, believing, and reacting and these patterns are tied to fear and hope. The emotions of anger, pride, jealousy, and worry interfere with our emotional intelligence. We fear change (what we had) and hope that our future desires will make us feel complete. Therefore, we get addicted to being caught up in the past and the future. We should be focused more on the present, moment to moment where stress thoughts lose their power. When one can focus on the present, like in meditation, our basic nature shines through.

3. Healing Behaviorally

When we are feeling panic or anxiety, our tendency is to "will" our way out of it and resist it. Learning to observe and "go with it" will help the anxiety subside faster. Also, avoidance of what you fear will just make the fear grow stronger. Learning to confront the fear in a safe environment with support is a major step toward healing. Other behavioral methods include: talking to another person, repeating affirmations (make them positive and use the present tense), and visualization.

Visualization is an important solution. Make sure you are relaxed and perhaps do some breathing exercises before. Visualize each step you need to take to achieve peace of mind and success. For example, if you need to give a speech, visualize walking to the podium until you can do that without anxiety. Then move to the next image until finally the audience is applauding you.

Distraction is perhaps one of the best ways of curing anxiety disorders. Life experiences result in the permanent imprinting of the stressful experiences in the emotional circuits in part of the brain called the amygdala. The adrenaline level in the blood is higher and as time goes by, the body becomes accustomed to higher blood adrenaline levels. The road rage, money worries, fighting kids, job pressures, and credit card bills of modern life increase levels of adrenaline in the blood. The body is in a constant state of stress. When you dwell on things all day, make distraction your new habit. Have you ever been doing something fun and not felt anxious? But as soon as you stop the activity, you feel anxious again. This is because you are using your instinctual behavior to carry out those tasks? In these states of mind, you are conscious of your anxiety all the time. So when you remove the consciousness by distraction (concentrating on something else), this becomes your new conscious state of mind. This in turn changes your subconscious state of mind and your anxiety level drops in the amygdala in the brain over time. So rewiring the brain and the neural pathways requires you to change your thinking (remember the thinking mind model), and divert it to something fun like music, photography, dancing, yoga, or any fun hobby.

Diversion tactics to prevent panic attacks when you feel one coming on include the following:

First, *tell yourself that panic attacks cannot kill you.* They are only sensations even though they feel horrible. If you are afraid of giving a speech, tell yourself, "I may be afraid, but I'm going to enjoy giving this speech today." Use any of these methods to stop the anxiety from going further: *Breath into a paper bag.* It rebalances the deficit of carbon dioxide in the blood that is experienced when hyperventilating. Take a long breath out and place a paper bag over your nose and mouth. Long breaths in and long slow breaths out are most effective. You can also try holding your breath for 5-10 seconds and slowly letting it out. Then breathe normally, 3 seconds in and 3 seconds out. *Also try, splashing your face with cold water.* This produces the dive reflex and causes your brain to send messages to your body to slow down. *Count down from 100 as fast as you can. Do math problems or anything that occupies your mind. Listen to your favorite music loudly and sing along to it. Watch a funny video on TV and laugh out loud. Don't look at yourself in the mirror. Gently slap your cheeks and dance around-confuse your thoughts to distract them. Do not sit down. Keep moving by dancing or walking.*

4. Healing Cognitively

Self-talk has a major effect on your state of anxiety. People with anxiety are known to engage in "what-if" thinking, which is imagining the worst possible outcome in advance of facing the fear. Beneath negative self-talk are mistaken beliefs about oneself, others, and the world that produce anxiety.

When you find yourself dwelling on something and you want to let it go, ask yourself the following questions. 1. Would I be willing to hold onto this forever? Once you answer no, ask the next question. 2. Could I allow myself to let this go? In other words, do you have the capability to let you? If you answer yes, then go to number three. 3. Would I allow myself to let this go? In other words, are you willing to let this go? If yes, then ask the next question. 4. When? And give an answer like, now! Repeat this as often as necessary until you let it go. In the meantime, distract yourself with something fun. Also see Strategy 2.2 and 2.6 for learning how to judge (The Judging Questionnaire) and reframe events.

5. Healing Socially

Much of anxiety that people experience arises from challenges in their personal relationships. Being able to set limits and boundaries with others, saying no when we mean it, standing up for your rights, and learning to be assertive allows relationships to flow with more ease and less conflict. See chapter 8. With anxiety disorders, it is actually worse to talk about your anxiety to others all the time. Give yourself a small time limit and get on with life.

6. Healing Spiritually

Finding a broad purpose in one's life that provides true meaning decreases anxiety in a major way. This often involves taking up a new career or vocation that fulfills one's true talents and interests. Anxiety could be a message to push you to explore and actualize an untapped potential in your life that you are missing. Try the meditation, relaxation, and Heart exercises from the last chapter and this chapter.

7. Healing Energetically

Though these therapies have been around in native cultures for thousands of years, energy healing with modernized versions of it came to the western world a few decades ago. Methods such as Emotional Freedom Technique (EFT), TFT (Thought Field Therapy), TAT (Tapas Acupressure Technique), Advanced Integrative Therapy, chakra healing, human biofields, and others have had incredible results in treating those suffering from emotional challenges anxiety, depression, phobias, personality disorders, and trauma. The umbrella title for these therapies is called "Energy Psychology." See energypsych.org for more information and research. See Appendix A in the back of the book to learn how to use EFT.

8. Medications and Herbs

Check with your doctor to find which medication is right for you if you choose this path. Forty years ago, very little was around to help people deal with anxiety and depression. Medications today have considerably helped those who have not been able to cope using other natural methods. The pros and cons of medication are unique and variable to each individual case. Anti-anxiety drugs like Xanax, Klonopin and Ativan and anti-depressants such as Prozac, Zoloft, Paxil, Celexa help many people raise their low mood levels to a point where they can start functioning better. Also, doing the other seven healing methods mentioned above will help bring more success. Anti-anxieties (benzodiazepines) are highly addictive and after several weeks one can experience terrible side effects while trying to come off of them. Drill your doctor about these effects and get more than one opinion. Those people whose bodies don't react well to prescription drugs might try, with their doctor's recommendation, herbs like Kava and Valerian Root for anxiety and St. John's Wort, Sam-e, and amino acids for depression.

The Six Core Fears

Most stressful thoughts have a knot of fear tied to them. In fact, all negative emotions like anger, hurt, guilt, shame, and worry all stem from the paralyzing emotion of fear. It is recommended to use self-observation or centering techniques from this chapter and book to determine what kind of fear is trying to scare you and pull you off center. There are six core fears that people experience. As you read them, identify which of the six fears you experience more often.

1. **The fear of rejection, ridicule, or shame**
2. **The fear of loss of control**
3. **The fear of death, injury, or pain**
4. **The fear of abandonment, isolation, or being alone**
5. **The fear of confinement**
6. **The fear of something strange or unknown**

1. Fear of rejection, ridicule, or shame: Especially if you grew up with parents who were overly critical or punitive, you are likely to experience this fear as an adult when you are in the presence of someone who is critical or verbally abusive. You may find yourself agreeing when you don't really agree, or you may try to be accepted and get approval so that you can prevent this fear from bubbling up in your body and mind.

2. Fear of loss of control: Any bad experience, event, or person that interferes with your orderly and predictable life can cause this fear. This is especially true when a parent suddenly dies, being in an accident, suffering a serious illness, or living through a natural disaster. These events can leave you with an increased feeling of vulnerability about losing control again in the future. If someone tried to sabotage your reputation in the past, any slight insult from someone else could trigger this fear of "no control" once again.

3. Fear of death, injury, or pain: Many people can develop phobias if a loved one passes on. For example, they can easily fear that almost any minor ailment they have could be cancer or something terminal. Traumatic events can predispose you toward being fearful about any situation that could potentially lead to a similar unpleasant experience.

4. Fear of abandonment, isolation, and being alone: Often during childhood, having to experience the loss of a parent or close relative can lead to this chronic fear. One may also experience feelings of abandonment if their parent's were neglectful, abusive, or unavailable. This forces a person to "go it alone" at an early age. Later, feelings of the fear of isolation and loneliness can develop.

5. Fear of confinement: This fear can arise in adulthood as a result of a dysfunctional childhood. The child may have experienced parents who were either physically or sexually abusive, or alcoholic. The child's fear of being unable to get away was felt more intensely. In adulthood, fear of being trapped by your job, marriage, or with the kids, can also produce this fear of confinement.

6. Fear of something strange or unknown: Strange body sensations or fear of strangers could trigger this fear. If one was overly preached to in avoiding the dangers of strangers when they were a child could cause this fear in adulthood. It can also arise in response to a new or unusual situation, especially when you are far from home. Also, such fears arise from a "prewired" part of the brain that both humans and other mammals have. This fear will often show when one is suddenly confronted with an unfamiliar person or other animal.

How can we best deal with these fears that can grip us in adulthood? Over thirty years of research on psychotherapy has repeatedly demonstrated that desensitization and real-life exposure can help those suffering along with the new energy psychology methods for getting over fears and phobias.

The 5 Step Fear Buster is the recommended remedy.

<u>Step one</u> is to recall the first actual experience or event that triggered the fear in the past. For example, if you had someone close to you die while you were growing up, this is the first event that triggered your fear of abandonment. You can put a feeling word to it as well like, "I'm feeling frightened or sad."

<u>Step two</u> is to be aware of the fear when it comes up and express and to release the feelings of the fear whether it is in the form of sadness, guilt, shame, or anger. Try to re-experience and work through any possible unresolved emotions that might be left over from the past. If it is an intense fear or phobia, it is recommended you do this with a professional therapist that you feel safe with and can trust. You can either talk it out (see strategy 8.2 Boundary Request Model), write it out (journaling), cry it out (music can help), and/or rage it out (on an inanimate object like a pillow, couch, yelling in the car, chopping wood, hitting a baseball bat against the bed, etc.).

<u>Step three</u> is to relate back to your inner child who experienced the trauma or fear. Give compassion and validation to the child who has had to endure this into adulthood. Let the child know you are going to be there for him or her from now on so that those feelings don't have to be experienced alone anymore. If it is an intense fear or phobia, it is recommended you do this with a professional therapist that you feel safe with and trust.

<u>Step four</u> is to use the Belief Changer that was illustrated in Chapter Two to change beliefs you have around your fear. By doing so, you will develop an entirely new and more positive attitude toward what you previously avoided. You can use it now to empower yourself to confront any triggers you may have in the future related to the past event. For example, if you developed a fear of being trapped because a parent used to hold you down and hit you, you can reach the point where you develop alternative positive beliefs: "The past is gone and I'm free to feel safe in circumstances that are physically confining.

<u>Step five</u> asks you to expose yourself to the situation slowly, in a safe environment that caused the fear. This is called ***desensitization.*** For example, in the scenario of the *Confinement* example above, you could follow up your commitment with action by continually exposing yourself to physically confining situations you used to avoid. Another example includes: if you have a fear of public speaking, expose yourself by learning to speak in front of three to ten people at first,

then move to twenty or thirty, and up from there. You will be more successful in overcoming the fear by breaking down the big goal into smaller goals.

The above approaches have been recommended for people who are survivors of physical and sexual childhood abuse and of course they work the same for less intense fears. When working with a therapist, the work of this process in "talk therapy" can take up to a year or longer depending on two factors: one, the intensity of the trauma and two, the ability of the person.

Another method that can accelerate the elimination of fears is hypnosis. Traumatized children repress or dissociate their feelings in connection with the trauma, and then, later in life, develop symptoms of anxiety, emotional numbness, and phobias. Not until the traumatic incident is recalled and the original feelings are fully expressed, can such individuals entirely let go of what happened and be free to go on with their lives.

One other method that can help one confront fears is Eye-Movement Desensitization and Reprocessing (EMDR). Eye movements induced by the procedure are similar to those of REM sleep which functions to complete "unfinished business" (past experiences that were not thought out and processed to satisfaction). Unprocessed traumatic material often turns into anxiety, nightmares, emotional numbness, depression, obsessive and compulsive thoughts and behaviors, self-criticism, and phobias. EMDR is practiced by over 4,000 therapists and is well researched in helping rape victims and Vietnam Vets with overcoming trauma and Post Traumatic Stress Disorder.

Emotional Freedom Technique (EFT) has been found by this author to be even more powerful in eliminating trauma, anxiety, and pain. See Appendix A on page 329 to learn how to use it yourself. Also visit the main EFT website ***emofree.com*** or **eftuniverse.com** and the author's website ***tappingintowellness.com.***

Exercise 1

Take the following Stress Assessment to see if you have a stress-prone personality.

Score as follows: 1. Never 2. Sometimes 3. Frequently 4. Always

1. Do you try to do as much as possible in the least amount of time? ______
2. Do you become impatient with delays or interruptions? ______
3. Do you always have to win at games to enjoy yourself? ______
4. Do you find yourself speeding up to beat red lights when driving? ______
5. Are you unlikely to ask for or indicate you need help with a problem? ______
6. Do you constantly seek the respect and admiration of others? ______
7. Are you overly critical of the way others do their work? ______
8. Do you have the habit of looking at your watch or clock often? ______
9. Do you constantly strive to better your position and achievements? ______
10. Do you spread yourself too thin in terms of your time? ______
11. Do you have the habit of doing more than one thing at a time? ______
12. Do you frequently get angry or irritable? ______
13. Do you have little time for hobbies or time by yourself? ______
14. Do you have a tendency to talk quickly or hasten conversations? ______
15. Do you consider yourself hard-driving? ______
16. Do your relatives or friends consider you hard-driving? ______
17. Do you have a tendency to get involved with multiple projects? ______
18. Do you have a lot of deadlines in your work? ______
19. Do you feel vaguely guilty if you relax or do nothing during leisure? ______
20. Do you take on too many responsibilities? ______

Total________

- Scores between 20 and 30 show that your life lacks stimulation and that you may be nonproductive. Being under-stressed can be as stressful as being over-stressed!
- Between 30 and 50 designates a good balance in your ability to handle stress. Yet, if you are close to 50, learn some stress prevention techniques.
- If you totaled between 51 and 60, your stress level is reaching burnout and you are bordering on being excessively stressed and may start to see health problems.
- If you exceeded 60, watch out. You may be a candidate for a heart attack. The exercises below will help. Perform them as often as possible throughout the week.

Exercise 2

The exercises below are powerful on many levels. First, they help you to become objective to your thoughts so that you can respond intelligently to them. Second, they enable you to concentrate entirely on one thing without distraction from competing thoughts. This is valuable because all of us, while reading a book, taking notes, or talking in conversation, have daydreamed for seconds to minutes while our attention was supposed to be on the subject at hand. How many of us have read a paragraph or a page in a book and when finished, we asked ourselves, "What in the heck did I just read?" That is because our mind is not always focused on the present moment. It daydreams to the past or to the future, which robs us of our learning experience. Third, by these relaxation exercises, you will be able to become clear on thoughts and emotions that you have put out of your mind for weeks, months, or years. Many of these thoughts and emotions are often key issues that need our attention in order for us to grow and move forward in numerous areas of our lives. By being able to observe past painful events in a safe, meditative state of mind instead of being consumed by them in a less stable state of mind, we develop the ability to face, and not run from, our problems. This is the key to our growth and happiness. Thousands of my clients, including myself, have enjoyed using this simple, easy, free, but powerful technique. Even during busy days, I find time to meditate while the car is warming up in the morning, in my office (with the door shut, of course), under a tree, or for those really busy days, in the bathroom.

Insistent thoughts become annoying and distract us from being focused, centered, and goal-oriented. The more we control our own thoughts and inner voices instead of them controlling us (for example, trying to go to sleep but the mind keeps racing), the more we become the "conductor to our own symphony." So it becomes vital to practice living in the present moment. This one skill is perhaps the most important skill to master because it gives you the ability to respond to stress appropriately, view situations from a different angle, and enjoy life more fully. All sources of stress and anxiety are either a thought we create from the past or a thought we create about the future. Keeping our thoughts in the present allows us to experience life more fully, with more focus, more relaxation, more joy, and less anxiousness. The following relaxation exercises with help you to sharpen this skill. Practice it several times a week and you will notice an incredible difference in how you will be able to respond to stress more positively.

Tom's Meditation Exercise

Sit in a quiet spot, close your eyes, and hold your hands 18 inches apart with your elbows pointing down. I like to light a candle in front of me because it throws more light on the eyes in a darker room making it a more sacred environment. Don't think of anything except that space between your hands. When a thought does arrive, notice it, don't give it any power, and return to visualizing the space between your hands. Do this for 15 minutes. During the 15 minutes slowly move your hands closer together without forcing them. You will find that, as they move closer, your hands will experience a magnetic energy. Just play with the energy and let it remind you of the present moment. If you want to boost the experience, put earplugs in your ears and listen to yourself breathe as you meditate.

As you learn to get into the meditation zone, ask the "Heart" any question for which you would like an answer. For example, how should I deal with my child's bad behavior? How can I better understand my spouse and avoid our fighting? How can I get more peace of mind? Then, in the silence of the moment, let the answers come to you over the next few minutes. If it doesn't happen the first few times, keep it up and it will come. It is like lifting weights. You won't see muscle the first time but you will eventually.

Beach Scene Visualization

You can have a friend read this visualization to you or you can speak it into a tape recorder. If these two options are not possible, merely remember the main images in the following paragraph. Find a comfortable chair or couch to sit on. Close your eyes and take 10 slow breaths. Then take a minute and count slowly from 1 to 10 and let your body completely relax. Let your mind float away on a voyage and take in the following scene after you reach 10.

You are walking on a sandy beach. It's mid August and it's very hot outside at five o'clock in the afternoon. The sun is getting low on the horizon but it is blazing yellow. The sky is a brilliant blue. Feel the heat from the sun against your face; feel the warmth of its rays against your skin. You are barefoot. Feel the hot, dry sand beneath your feet. You start to walk closer to the water as you feel the sand become cooler between your toes. You can hear the beating of the waves against the sand. Hear the loud, high cries of the seagulls circling overhead. You continue walking. Smell the salty, moist air as it blows upon your face. You can feel the cold water come up to your shins as it rushes past you. It feels invigorating as you completely take in this scene. You then start to walk down the beach. As you look up toward the sand, you see a mound of white sand covered with pink rose petals and bright yellow buttercups. You then start to jog toward the flowers. Once you are upon the flowers, they engulf your whole body and as you jump onto flowers. You feel completely relaxed and blissful. The sea is like a mirror of silver, reflecting the sun's rays, a mass of pure, white light. The sun is beginning to set. The sky is turning violet, red, gold, scarlet, and amber. You feel delighted that you can return to this place anytime you like as you soak it all in. Gently, you feel yourself carried upward and outward into space, feeling at one with the universe.

You then bring yourself out of the imagery state by telling yourself that when you count to 5, you will open your eyes, completely relaxed, alert and totally refreshed. You can best memorize this scene, or any experience you've had in life, by recalling how the five senses (see, hear, smell, taste, and feel) perceive the experience. Also, by practicing this technique one to three times a day, you are likely to join the many people who use it to relieve headaches, backaches, mental fears, phobias, and other unwanted conditions.

The Neuro-linguistic Peace of Mind Exercise

To experience peace of mind, sit in a comfortable chair and close your eyes. Now, sit the way you would sit if you felt total peace of mind. Wait one minute and experience the sensation. Then, breathe the way you would breathe if you felt total peace of mind. Wait one minute and experience the sensation. Then feel the way you would feel if you felt total peace of mind. Wait one minute and experience the sensation. Then look the way you would look (the expression on your face) if you felt total peace of mind. Wait another minute and experience the sensation. Now, slowly open your eyes and feel total peace of mind.

Exercise 3

1. What are the major stressors in your life today? What steps can you take to reduce your stress?

____
____
____
____
____
____

2. What personality characteristics do you have that either help or hinder you in dealing with stressful situations? Do you blow things up more than they should be? Do you take things too personally?

____
____
____
____
____
____

3. Write below how you are coping with stress? What stress reduction methods help you? Is it exercise, deep breathing, talking to a friend? Are you treating yourself and others right? Then start writing a daily journal with this theme in mind.

____
____
____
____
____
____

4. How do you manage your time? Are you spending your time the way you want to? Are you feeling rushed often? Are you balancing activities that you need to do with ones you enjoy? Could you plan your day better? What could you do to manage your time better?

____
____
____
____
____
____

5. How does stress affect your body? Do you get headaches, muscular aches, constipation, have trouble sleeping, or experience appetite changes? What could you do to rest or take care of your body during the day?

____
____
____
____
____
____

Strategy 3.2

Bring your awareness to the specific moment right before you give your power away to people, emotions, substances, and/or habits.

Take Away The Power

Often, without knowing it, we give our power and attention to people, emotions, substances, and habits, which, in turn, leave us powerless. It is as if we carry a power plug in our hands, and throughout the day we estimate that if we insert this plug into people and things, we can pull power from them and make our selves feel better. Of course, it never lasts and leaves us in a weaker state. This is the exact reverse order of natural law and achieving balance. We are to obtain our power from within. When you give power to drugs, alcohol, lying, and other people, the energy and strength gets sucked out of you like a vacuum. For example, many people often give too much attention and power to people who say unkind, unfair, and dishonest things to them. Think of your own experiences. Remember thinking about it over and over for days. Did it keep you awake at night? Did the resentment of what the person did to you build up? Instead of suppressing your anger, learn to observe your impatience and see the value in overlooking and making allowances at the very moment the demeaning person offends you. Give the mind a break, go inside your "Heart", and let your "Heart" do the thinking. This is not easy at first, but it is necessary for you to regain your power back instead of giving it to others. When you do play into their game, they can feed off it as a bully does. So instead of being judgmental and resentful, be glad when people are rude or unkind, for here is your opportunity to be patient and so through patience give up judgment. If there were no danger, you could not possess courage. If there were no demeaning people out there, you could not develop understanding. Unthinking people are giving you the opportunity to rise above your problem and free you from these types of people and situations. They don't know this, of course. But observe and discern their words instead of judging them. Take resentment out of everything. Do it because you yearn for understanding and want to see truth and good prevail. Besides, you advance your own ability to forgive and you'll find that things that have always gotten you upset and flustered in the past will be the very things that bring you happiness and laughter because you'll start to see the folly of those people you'll learn how to respond properly. However, I am not saying that you shouldn't confront others. We need to confront others who have said something inappropriate to us. But we can do it with firmness, patience, kindness. And there are those times when silence can speak louder than words.

Be aware of the today's spell-casters. Back in the medieval days, witches, wizards, and warlocks put curses or "power thoughts," capable of penetrating and controlling the unconscious of an individual. Potions were often used as carriers of these thoughts as does too much alcohol. Parents can unknowingly put a spell on their children telling them they are stupid, evil, or not smart enough. Advertisers are professional spell-casters luring you to buy their products using actors, sex, emotion, and flat out lies. Politicians often cast their spells by agreeing to opposing opinions and spinning the truth so they can fulfill their own personal agendas. To break the spell, we must first become aware of anything that takes us out of our "Present" mind.

The exercises in this lesson, as well as the other lessons in this chapter on centering practices, will help you achieve this task. Below are some examples of what/who we give our power away to.

- People: approval--authority figures, peers, boss, parent, etc.
- Emotions: resentment, worry, fear, etc. Practice forgiving on the spot.
- Substances: alcohol, food, smoking, drugs, etc.
- Habits: gambling, lying, sex/pornography, work, chores.

Exercise 1

Make a promise to jot down the event and time of when you give your power away. Write this down below for the next three days. Do it right after the event occurs. Example: 10:22 am at work – said 'yes' to an extra project when I really didn't have the time.

Exercise 2

Review your list and write down any patterns that you notice.

Exercise 3

The Power Reclaimer

1. Make a list of all people who intimidate you or whom you give your power to. Now choose one of these people and write down where it takes place and with whom.
EXAMPLE: My boss, Judy- when I ask her for a day off, she makes me feel guilty.

2. Identify the behaviors that you do (e.g. agreeing when you really disagree, not saying no, etc.)
EXAMPLE: My voice gets soft. I feel guilty for asking and I agree when I secretly disagree.

3. Write down why you think this controls you.
EXAMPLE: My boss, Judy reminds me of my Dad when he'd make me feel guilty.

4. Write down a strategy that will help you prepare and arm yourself for your future meetings (e.g. being silent, saying no, asking for help). Make an intention not to repeat the behavior. Promise it to yourself and someone else and consider any failures as intelligent feedback.
EXAMPLE: With both kindness and firmness, "Judy, I hope my dedication and commitment to this company is enough for you to trust me when I say that it is personal and necessary for me to have this day off."

5. Write down how you will manage your emotions (e.g. screaming, talking, writing, meditating, or talking to a supportive friend/partner).
EXAMPLE: Vent with the intention of it being therapeutic. Do this without resentment. "I can't stand when he degrades me like that and it makes me so much rage toward him."

Strategy 3.3

Identify and correct your common thinking errors and thought distortions to strengthen your perceptions, judgments, and self-observations.

The test of a first-rate intelligence is the ability to hold two opposed ideas in the mind at the same time, and still retain the ability to function.
F. Scott Fitzgerald

Common Thinking Errors

As a result of negative childhood or life experiences, most of us have some negative programming and strong fears that tear down our self-esteem. It is this low self-esteem or our feeling of inadequacy and insecurity that activates many of our day-to-day thinking errors and distorted reasoning patterns. These thinking errors and the negative messages we tell ourselves contribute to neurosis, high anxiety, depression, and emotional instability. Below is a list of common thinking errors. As you identify the thinking errors that you often use, apply them to beliefs you currently have about yourself. The exercises afterward will help you to confront these thinking styles as well as inner messages so you can more accurately see the truth about yourself and the world around you. Circle the ones you use the most.

1. ARBITRARY INFERENCE - Conclusions are made in the absence of supporting and substantiating evidence. For example, a man whose wife arrives home a half-hour late from work concludes, "She must be having an affair."

2. SELECTIVE ABSTRACTION - Information is taken out of context; certain details are highlighted while other important information is ignored. For example, a woman whose husband fails to answer her greeting the first thing in the morning concludes, "He must be angry at me again."

3. OVERGENERALIZATION - An isolated incident or two is allowed to serve as a representation of similar situations everywhere, related or unrelated. For example, after being turned down for an initial date, a young man concludes, "All women are alike; I'll always be rejected."

4. MAGNIFICATION AND MINIMIZATION - A case or circumstance is perceived in greater or lesser light than is appropriate. For example, an angry husband "blows his top" upon discovering that the checkbook is unreconciled and states to his wife, "We're financially doomed." (magnification)

5. PERSONALIZATION - External events are attributed to one's self when insufficient evidence exists to render a conclusion. For example, a woman finds her husband re-ironing an already pressed shirt and assumes, "He is dissatisfied with me."

6. POLARIZED THINKING - Experiences are codified as being all or nothing, a complete success or a total failure. For example, a husband asks his wife her opinion of his construction job in their recreation room. The wife questions the height of the ceiling and the husband blurts out, "You don't think I can do anything right!"

7. LABELING AND MISLABELING - Imperfections and mistakes made in the past are allowed to define one's self. For example, subsequent to continual mistakes in meal preparation, a partner states, "I am worthless", as opposed to recognizing the errors as being human.

8. TUNNEL VISION - Sometimes partners see only what they want to see or what fits their current state of mind. A woman who tells her husband that she only talked to her ex-boyfriend at the party and the long-time jealous husband says, "I know you're still in love with him.
9. CATASTROPHIZING - You expect disaster. You notice or hear about a problem and start "what if's:" What if tragedy strikes? What if it happens to me?"

10. FALLACY OF FAIRNESS - You feel resentful because you think you know what's fair but other people won't agree with you.

11. BLAMING - You hold other people responsible for your pain, or take the other track and blame yourself for every problem you encounter.

12. SHOULDS - You have a list of ironclad rules about how you and other people should act. People who break the rules anger you, and you feel guilty if you violate the rules.

13. EMOTIONAL REASONING - You believe that what you feel must be true--automatically. If you feel stupid and boring, then you must be stupid and boring.

14. HEAVEN'S REWARD FALLACY - You expect all your sacrifice and self-denial to pay off, as if there were someone keeping score. You feel bitter when the reward doesn't come.

I'm Hearing Voices

We receive thousands of thoughts a day from our mind. Some thoughts are positive about our selves, and some negative thoughts border on self-abuse. The negative voices and/or messages may say: "I'll never get a job/mate," "You'll never amount to anything," "It won't happen to me," "I'm so stupid," and so forth. Absolute phrases such as "every single time," "you never," and "I always" can trigger negative emotions such as anger, worry, frustration, sadness, fear, guilt, and shame. Therefore, messages from others can often repeat themselves in our mind when these people are not even in our presence or they could even be dead. These voices are powerful and often have identities of mother, father, and/or sibling in them. There is usually an element of truth in them, but mostly they are false and need to be challenged. Choose conversations that you know are unhealthy and probably false, yet you may often feel they are true. For example, you may feel you are unattractive, but this is open to others' interpretation.

Exercise 1, 2, and 3

The Critical Thinking Assignment

1. Write down three of the most common thinking errors, written in this section, that you use most often.

____

____

____

2. Next to each of the three thought distortions, write the actual thoughts, behavior, and circumstances that accompany the distortion. For example: <u>MINIMIZATION</u>
Thought: Even though Joe insulted me in front of everybody, it's no big deal.
Behavior: Giving Joe the silent treatment and avoiding him.
Circumstance: When I do something wrong at work, Joe usually let's everyone know.

3. Continue by writing, for each thought distortion, an affirmation (make it positive and present), an intention (what you want to change), and a verbal statement (what you could or intend to say to somebody). For example:

Affirmation: "I act on any disrespectful comment toward me." Make sure it is stated in the *positive*. "I will not" is not positive. Make sure it is stated in the *present*. "I will" is future based, not present.
Intention Statement: "I intend to stand up for myself whenever anybody is disrespectful to me.
Verbal Statement: I will think of an event that is likely to happen in the future where somebody, like Joe, will likely insult me. I will have a planned, yet, confident verbal comeback such as: "Joe, this is the last time I will let you dishonor me in public," or "Joe, it seems that every time we get together, you insult me, and I don't like it. I'm requesting that you put a stop to that for good." If Joe refuses to stop, sometimes you may have to resort to more extreme tactics if you can't avoid Joe altogether. Examples: "Joe, should we talk about all the times you screw up," or "Joe, you sure are critical; you must have had a very negative critical parent," or "Joe, I'd hate to have you as a parent. I feel sorry for your kids." Only use this as a last resort and if it fits your personality style. Use it with caution!

Thought Distortion #1 ______________________________

Thought: ______________________________

____

Behavior: ______________________________

____

Circumstance: ______________________________

____

Affirmation: ______________________________

____

Intention Statement: ______________________________

____

Verbal Statement: ______________________________

____

Thought Distortion # 2 ______________________________

____

Thought: ______________________________

____

Behavior: ______________________________

____

Circumstance: ______________________________

____

Affirmation: ______________________________

____

Intention Statement: ______________________________

____

Verbal Statement: ______________________________

____

Exercise 3: The Energetic Alignment Method

Practice thinking emotionally positive. Thousands of successful people owe their success to the following method. Go through steps when you see your reminders on the mirror, dashboard, etc.

Thoughts are physical particles that have magnetic, vibrational pull….Albert Einstein

Use your thoughts to help you to be, do, or have what you want in life. Pick a main goal of something you have a burning desire for. Let's say Bill is a good college student and his main goal is to become a university professor. Then make it believable. Working backward from that goal, Bill would need to obtain at least a Master's Degree to teach. And before that, Bill would need to obtain a Bachelor's Degree. So if the Bachelor's Degree sounds more believable to him, then that would be his sub-goal.

1. My main goal is:____

My sub-goal is:____

2. **Feel It.** Find a way to "Feel Good Now" before the next steps. If you struggle with feeling good, then do something to "feel better" than you do now. The following activities can help you feel better: music, exercise, read something positive, smile, think of all the things you're thankful for, dance, sing, work with your hands such as cooking, gardening, etc., hugs, massage, laugh at a comedy sitcom, etc. When we feel good, the methods below work more effect effectively.

To "feel good now" I will:____

3. **Affirm It.** When you are feeling good, create an affirmation that corresponds with your sub-goal. Use an affirmation that is similar to the EFT affirmation you learned from the previous chapter. Just tap your karate chop point while saying the affirmation with feeling as many times a day as you can.

My affirmation is:____

4. **Visualize It.** Create a positive, emotional visualization. When you visualize, picture yourself in color with the goal achieved. Bill could visualize his college degree handed to him while speaking to university students. Use your senses like sight, sounds, smell, etc. Create the positive emotions you would feel when you visualize it such as excitability, happiness, joy, and so on. Do it often each day for at least 1 - 2 minutes.
My visualization is:____

5. **Become It.** Use the Bruce Jenner technique using someone who's created this goal. Bill could cut out a picture of a university professor and supplant it with his picture. If you can't find one, take a photo of yourself doing the goal. Put it in places like your car, bathroom mirror, etc. Focus on it daily.

The picture I will use will be:____

6. **Touch It.** Get close to or touch your goal. In the university professor example, Bill could find an empty class at a university and go inside to the head of the class and start speaking as if he were a university professor. Getting the feel and believability that it will happen is crucial to your success.

I will get close/touch my goal by:____

7. **Flip It.** When you find yourself thinking negative thoughts about whether you can achieve the goal, flip the thought to a positive thought using other affirmations such as, "I allow it," "Everything always works out," "it's all good," "I feel so lucky," "I don't know how it will happen, but it will."
The positive phrases I will use when I think negative will be:____________________________
____

Strategy 3.4

Notice and learn from the times when you are resistant to something.

What you Resist, Persists

When you resist an idea, an emotion, or an action, the mind works in the following way. It tucks it away in the short-run, but over time, it comes back with more power and energy. It's as if you shake a Coke bottle with the expectation that nothing will happen. Pretty soon, it's going to burst open and come streaming out because of the carbonation. It is the same with resistance. What you resist, persists. Examples of resistance in action include: change, resisting the confrontation you need to have with an insulting person, looking for a new job, resisting the feelings of emotional pain, guilt, or shame, and so on. It can also cause physical ailments like headaches, anxiety, and depression.

By becoming aware of your resistance, you can learn clues and gain valuable information about your motivation for doing something or not doing something. Once we know what motivates us, we can then be more productive and achieve goals at our own pace without anxiety and pressure. Once we know what we're resisting and why, we can then more often take the right course of action, which will lower the dread and anxiety in the long-run. It is similar to the metaphor of walking into the cold ocean at the beach. Some resist and take 25-minutes to inch their way in. Instead of the 25-minute torture, they could ease themselves in over a couple minutes. Many of us are resistant to change because we are afraid of failure, being uncomfortable, success, and so on. Yet by learning to appreciate our resistance and learn from it, it can become a teacher for us instead of a tyrant.

Exercise 1

Identify and write down a list of things that you are resisting. Choose one now to work on.

____

____

____

____

____

Exercise 2

Answer the following questions to the resistance item that you choose.

1. How is your resistance making life easier?
2. What are you afraid you won't have any more of if you give in to it?
3. What benefit could emerge if you give in to the resistance?
4. Is it the right time in your life to do this?
5. If you do give in to your resistance, ask a close friend/partner to help you accept it.

____

____

____

____

Exercise 3

1. Find a quiet place to sit and close your eyes. Now, focus on breathing for two minutes.
2. Then tighten all your muscles in your body and recall the thing you are resisting. Feel the discomfort of the resistance for 20 seconds.
3. Then relax all of your muscles and visualize doing the thing you are resisting. If you decide it's not time yet in your life to do the thing you are resisting, make peace with it and see how it's okay, for now, that you don't do it. Know, however, that we cannot fully grow in this area without taking care of the issue. Use this exercise as a reference point for future resistance issues in your life. Examples of things that are not recommended to resist for a long period of time include confronting people who are abusive to you or who disrespect you on a regular basis. It is quite possible that you may be pushing yourself too hard and need more time to relax. In this case, you may feel the need to rest before dealing with your resistance. Write your experiences below.

Also, try saying "Yes" to whatever you are resisting. Say "Yes" to it over and over again throughout the day. You can also say "I love you," to it as you say "Yes." It should start to fade away as the object is the release that which is disturbing you.

Next, as a symbol of "tuning in," sit down in a quiet place before going to work, if you work. Take three deep breaths and cover both ears with the palms of your hands and press in so you can hear yourself breathe. Or, you can buy earplugs and do the same. Get to know this inner world that has existed in you every day. Notice the tone of the hum that you hear and make this your sacred sanctuary. Do the exercise for five to ten minutes.

Finally, write down which set of circumstances distract you and make you go off target away from your true self and your goals. Examples: Eating so as not to feel emotional pain, talking too much so as not to seem uninteresting to others, excessive television so as not to work on projects, study or spend quality time with friends and family or being too busy so as to avoid being alone with yourself, or approval from others so as to feel good about yourself.

Strategy 3.5

Learn to Cope with the Grieving Process, Death, and Challenging Life Events.

How Do You View Death?

Hopefully, by now, you have learned the importance of managing your fears. The Enneagram in Chapter one discussed how giving into our fears limits our ability to fully become our true selves and enjoy life. Do you fear death? Often, how you view death determines whether you will live life in fear or live life to the fullest. If not thinking of our own death isn't bad enough, thinking of a loved one's death can be even more excruciating. Have you ever asked yourself the following questions?

Do you prevent yourself from getting too close to others because of the possibility of losing those you love? In what ways do you think your fears about death and dying might be affecting the choices you make now? What fears do you experience when you think about your own death? Do you worry about what will happen after death? Are you anxious about the way you will die? Do you worry most about your loved ones who will be left behind? Do you dislike funerals because they make you dwell on a painful subject or remind you of something unpleasant? Do you fear you won't be able to accomplish all that you want before you die?

Death Can Spur Opportunity!

Although the topic in this strategy might seem morbid or depressing, an honest understanding and acceptance of death and loss can allow you to build a rich and meaningful life. If we accept that we have only a limited time in which to live, we can make choices that will make the most of the time we have. Even young people need to think about death because it can come when one least expects it, whether it is an automobile accident, AIDS, a drowning, or some act of violence. The pressure of time helps to force one to choose how one will spend one's remaining days, especially for the terminally ill. Irvin Yalom (1980) found that cancer patients in group therapy had the capacity to view their crisis as an opportunity to spur change in their lives. They often:

- Rearranged their life's priorities and dumped the little trivial matters
- Developed a deeper communication with loved ones than before the crisis
- Developed a deeper communication with God or higher power
- Felt a sense of liberation and living in the present because they could choose to do those things they put off all their lives
- Found pleasure in taking more risks in life than "playing it safe" and grasping for security as usual.

So, why wait for a terminal illness to occur in your body. You can do these things now. Siegel (1993) writes about the reality of living fully. If we are, then dying isn't as much of a problem. If you want to live forever, then love someone. One of his patients told him, "Death is not the worst thing. Life without love is far worse." Knowing that loved ones will be around at the time of our death as opposed to dying lonely brings peace. In addition, unresolved grief is considered a key factor in the onset of a variety of physical illnesses. Siegel (1988) cites numerous examples of people who developed cancer after a significant loss through death or divorce. Finally, cultural and religious beliefs are powerful influences that can help us cope with how we view our own death or a loved one.

The Grieving Process and the Five Stages of Grief

The grieving process is the inner experience of a person who loses of a loved one through death. The experience differs between cultures. In America, one is encouraged to break one's emotional ties with the deceased relatively quickly and return to their regular routines. In contrast with Japan, the bereaved are encouraged to maintain emotional ties to their dead loved ones by having altars dedicated to family members. Family members routinely talk to the deceased and offer them food.

Dr. Elisabeth Kubler-Ross, a pioneer in the contemporary study of death and dying, wrote the landmark books, On Death and Dying (1969) and Death: The Final Stage of Growth (1975). She discusses in these books the psychological aspects of death, the experience of dying, and the emotional stages that occur. Thanks to her efforts, many people have become aware of the almost universal need the dying have to talk about their impending death and to complete their business with the important people in their lives. She reveals society's ignorance of the dying process. In addition, she exposes how the needs of dying people as well as the fears of those around them can rob the dying person of the opportunity to fully find peace. A greater understanding of the psychological stages of dying can help us to come to an acceptance of death and be more helpful and present to those who are dying. According to Kubler-Ross's research on cancer patients, there are five stages of dying. These stages will be examined below as they relate to Robert, a 40-year old cancer patient.

Stage One: Denial

When Robert was told he had six months to live because of the cancer, he was shocked and refused to believe that the diagnosis was correct. Even after getting several medical opinions, he still refused to accept that he was dying. Therefore, he was in denial; a disbelief about a probable truth. His wife also denied his illness and was unwilling to talk to him about it. She also thought it would make him more depressed.

Loved ones can help the dying by: facing the fact that the person is dying. Don't force the person to talk about it but you can be available and sensitive to the dying person when they stop denying their death and show a need to be listened to.

Loved ones can help themselves by: realizing that the numbness and strange feelings they've been feeling will soon wear away and real grieving will begin. Some people stay away from the grave for a while, leave the deceased's room unchanged, keep pictures in view indefinitely, and gradually, move to acceptance over time.

Stage Two: Anger

As Robert began to accept the diagnosis, his denial was replaced by anger. He was angry that he wouldn't be able to get to see his children grow to their mature years. He felt it was unfair that he got the disease. He directed his anger toward the doctors who "didn't know what they were doing" and to the nurses who were "cold and distant." The dying person can become nasty, demanding, difficult, and hostile while they direct their anger toward hospital staff, their family, friends, or God.

Loved ones can help the dying by: not taking what the dying person says, personally. They have reason to be angry so know that withdrawing support or taking offense can set them back. Allow the person to fully express the pent-up rage inside so they can come to terms with their death.

Loved ones can help themselves by: enlisting a friend to listen and to help them cope with how difficult the dying person may be behaving. Even after the person has died, allow people to offer help with funeral preparation, making telephone calls, hosting out-of-town relatives, and housekeeping chores. Accept help from funeral directors, pastors, etc. Try to see the funeral experience as a supportive event as friends and family come to honor the deceased. You can express your anger by screaming into and pounding a pillow, beating a mattress with a bat, hard exercise, journal writing, and talking about it with a professional or good friend. You can allow yourself a daily 20-minute period of "anger time." You could have a pillow fight with someone and vent the anger that way until you start crying or laughing.

Stage Three: Bargaining

Robert decided that if God hadn't responded to his angry pleas to heal them, he may respond if Robert asked more nicely. He kept asking the doctors how he could get more time and postpone death because he still wanted to move into his dream home and watch his daughter graduate. He tried several different treatments from alternative to conventional. There is a deep sense of yearning at this stage to be well again.

Stage Four: Depression

When Robert realized that there was no possibility of remission. denial turned into depression. He felt bad about becoming more weak and thin after the chemotherapy treatments and feared the unknown. He felt guilty because he was demanding so much attention and time due to the treatment, which was depleting the family income. A hopeless feeling surrounded him and mornings were the worst just to pull himself out of bed.

Loved ones can help the dying by: letting the dying person talk about their feelings and make final plans. It may not help to try to cheer them up. They are about to lose everyone they love, and only the freedom to grieve these losses will allow them to find peace in a final acceptance of their death.

Loved ones can help themselves by: Taking care of themselves as well. They need to find someone who will listen to them without judging the rambling and repetitive talk that is common and normal. Distracting themselves into activity like sports, music, etc., is very helpful but without running away from the circumstance. ***Guilt*** often sets in because they might feel that they should have been more responsible about the dying/deceased person's health when they were well, and lots of "if only's" creep in. Guilt is normal. Face it and then get rid of it. Accept your fallibility and get professional counseling if needed. A clergyman may be able to help you deal with guilt on a spiritual level. In cases of intense, prolonged grief, physicians prescribe an antidepressant drug. See this as a temporary measure but it will only mask reality. Get professional help and join a grieving support group. Most people recover slowly but surely. Down times can take months or years but healing does come as you work on it.

Stage Five: Acceptance

Kubler-Ross found that when patients had enough time and support to work through the previous stages (e.g. expressing anger, mourning), most of them reached a stage at which they were neither depressed nor angry and could accept their death. Robert accepted his death but it wasn't a happy stage. It's just that the pain was gone, the struggle was over, and there was some peace. Some people don't reach the acceptance stage nor do they want to. Sometimes the inner limitations of the patient and/or the inability of the loved ones to provide a comfortable environment for the patient to express their anger and grief, can maintain the patient's anger and depression at the time of passing. The patient who is "now" ready to die will usually want someone warm, caring, and accepting at this time and verbal communication may be totally unnecessary.

Remember, that these stages don't always go in order, and Kubler-Ross states that it is a mistake to use these stages as the standard by which to judge whether a dying person's behavior is normal or right. Whether you are the patient or the loved one, nobody escapes grief. The key is expression. Everyone is different. Those who are dying move back and forth in the stages and from mood to mood. People grieve at different rates of time. The stages are meant to add understanding and summarize what many patients experience during this time. Delayed grief can occur when people suppress the emotions of the death of a loved one and years later get depressed or react to an acquaintance's death with extreme depression. They feared that the pain would consume them if they allowed themselves to completely feel it so they shut it off. Unfortunately, the price involves shutting off closeness, intimacy, and joy. People can go years to a lifetime if they don't allow themselves the proper time for them to grieve. The Hospice Movement best demonstrates the trend toward more time and direct involvement with family members and allowing the patients to be mobile between home and medical care. Patients report less general anxiety and fewer bodily symptoms than those being given traditional care.

Kubler-Ross's work has been questioned of late. Her findings were almost entirely based on American cancer patients and people who die from other circumstances may have different experiences. Also, cultural differences, age, sex, race, and personality are other factors to consider.

Still, her work is the most exhaustive to date. Some recent findings have challenged the traditional view of grieving, which holds that distress and proper grieving is an inevitable response to loss. Some individuals are able to handle loss without significant distress. However, bereaved persons, on average, have scores that are higher on depression, lower on life satisfaction, and are at greater risk for illness than are the nonbereaved.

Helping Children Cope

How do you tell a child that someone he or she loved has died? It's hard, but being straightforward is the best rule. Distortions of reality can do lasting harm. For example, the deceased has "gone to sleep" may lead to a fear of going to sleep, and "God took her" may lead to a hatred of God for being cruel. Also, "death in a hospital" may lead to a fear of hospitals unless the child is reassured there is no correlation. Give your love and support while expressing that love does not mean the loss of others including the loss of love with you. Young children often think that anything "bad" that happens in their little world is somehow their fault, so reassure that they are in no way to be blamed and that they will be "taken care of."

Also, let the child participate in the family sorrow and grief. It may be distressing to see father cry, but it's far more distressing to see "business as usual." Be careful to not say "you are the man of the house, now," or "be brave," because putting up a false front only adds more grief for the child. Give as much attention to the child that cries as to the one that doesn't cry.

Silence between children, parents, siblings, spouses, and friends about the deceased makes things worse. It is vital that people talk about the deceased especially in a marriage. Otherwise people often feel like nobody cares. Even though the motive is to protect you from the pain of remembering, the pain of loneliness and isolation is worse.

Challenging Life Events

The five stages of grief have application to coping with challenging life events as well as to a death. Events like divorce, separation from children, breaking up with a boyfriend or girlfriend, children leaving home, losing a job, and facing unemployment cause many people to go through a similar questioning and struggling. To illustrate, if Jill goes through a divorce, she may be in ***denial*** about how the marriage wasn't that bad and, "Why is this happening to me," or "Why is he doing this to me?"

Reaching stage two, Jill may feel, "I gave so much to this relationship and now I'm being deserted." She may feel cheated about how the divorce has caused so much injustice. Jill would want to express her ***anger*** like the dying person so that it doesn't get bottled up inside and turned against herself causing depression, a kind of self-punishment. The ***bargaining*** stage may take the form of feelings like, "Maybe the separation will give him time to see we are supposed to be together." This sometimes happens, but often does not. ***Depression*** may be strong when they realize that the divorce will stick. They may ask themselves, "I wonder where I went wrong," as they experience self-doubt, emptiness, and the loss they feel. If people allow themselves to mourn their losses, grief work usually leads to a stage of acceptance. New possibilities open up, resentments are forgotten, and a new life can be established. When any type of loss occurs, whether it is a death, a loss of job, divorce, etc., keep these feelings and stages in mind.

Are You Dead Psychologically and Socially?

I believe it is important to broaden the definition of death and dying to being "dead" or dormant in such areas as: the roles we play, not giving our body pleasure, not being playful, and being dead to our feelings, our relationships, and intellectual and spiritual parts of ourselves. As we pursue one area of life, be it parenting, job, or whatever, we tend to neglect other areas of ourselves. Think how you may give too much attention or not enough attention to your role as a student, parent, son or daughter, employee, and so on. What roles do you neglect? Does your dominant role e.g. mother/father/student deaden you to other joys that are a part of life? Do drugs and your diet deaden your body and energy? Do you pleasure your body enough? Can you be silly, spontaneous, fun, and playful? Can you let yourself cry? Can you feel pleasure and laugh a lot? Can you show your fear to others? Do you give yourself or your partner enough space to grow? Are you growing your mind and learning about new things instead of the usual? Are you finding or pursuing peace, meaning, value, and happiness in life? Or, is it the same old routine? Are you ready to change your culturally conditioned life patterns into states of consciousness that allow for self-empowerment and helping others to become empowered? Don't let your age, sex, race, class, or anything else limit your future growth as a human being. Find out what hidden gifts you have inside. Leo Buscaglia says, people come into the world as gifts to others but sometimes fail to even open up the ribbon and wrapping paper to discover their gift. The exercises will help you help yourself to become alive in these other areas.

Creative Coping

Some people are never able to accept the death of a child or a spouse. They may get stuck by suppressing their feelings and not working through their pain over the loss. Like being on novocaine. they can begin to function on "Automatic pilot" feeling numb and being unable to express a wide range of emotions. But once the novocaine wears off, like it always does, the pain seems to intensify. It's important to know that, as they begin grief work, it often gets worse before they feel better.

Can you cry to get the tears and grief out? Often men have a hard time with this. To help, take time to grieve by looking at mementos, playing nostalgic music, looking at pictures, and/or reading old letters. Crying helps others to see your love and is a healthy model for children. If parents experience the loss of a child, guilt can ruin the relationship, especially if one feels the other had some responsibility. Do not accuse. Seek counseling from a psychologist, pastor, or other counselor.

Turn Grief into Artistic Expression

Here are some examples of turning grief into expressing yourself artistically.
When Bill's wife died, he didn't want to talk to anyone about her death. Being a **teacher** and educating students was the only thing that gave him joy. He followed his friend's suggestion and committed to making reference to his wife or their relationship in some of his lessons. He set a goal to weave their experiences into the lesson plan once a month. By processing his grief this way, he was able to work through his loss, through his teaching, his greatest strength.

Parents can also use the same strategy to talk to their kids about the loss. Lisa's life had been centered around ***dancing*** for years with her sister, Gloria. When Gloria was killed in an automobile accident, Lisa was devastated and seriously questioned how she could ever dance again. Lisa's therapist suggested that Lisa not only continue dancing, but that she make her dances an expression of her love and grief for Gloria. When her dances were to express joy, she would dance the joy she felt with Gloria and the joy she saw in Gloria. When her dances were to express sadness, she would dance the grief she felt in losing her sister. When her dances were to express love, she would actually imagine herself dancing with or before Gloria. Lisa's therapist was helping her grieve by using her strength: her talent and ability to dance.

When Karen's mother passed away, she channeled her grief into painting. The first painting was entitled "Sadness and Depression." The painting involved a mixture of finger painting, brush strokes, and flinging paint on a canvas. Colors were chosen to express the title. A week later she entitled the second painting, "Happiness." The third painting a week later was entitled, "Hopefulness." A week later, she discarded the first painting and let go of some of the feelings that went with it. She felt painting was a great outlet for her to express her grief and get out the emotions.

Faith, Prayers, and Personal Growth

Researchers in death and dying have discovered that *faith* is a powerful aid in coping with bereavement/loss of a loved one. If you have spiritual roots, you are likely to pass more easily through the process of grief and may even avoid some phases altogether. The experience of love and assurance is sometimes delayed until months of anguish have passed and the bereaved believe this is God's gift to everyone who earnestly seeks him. Also, they mention how they feel the *prayers* of those that are praying for them to heal from their loss. I love this prayer: Help me to embrace my wounds, not despise them. Teach me how to learn from my grief. Remind me that I possess the power to turn my curses into blessings, my sadness into strength, and my pain into compassion. Amen.

Religious, spiritual, and nonspiritual individuals can conduct guided imagery to obtain insight about how to face death or how to deal with the loss of a loved one. *Christians* can close their eyes and see Jesus in all his power and vulnerability as he asks, "What can I do for you?" One could say, "Please tell me how you felt as you faced death?" Imagine his words, his tone of voice, his facial expressions, etc., as you get your insight. *Jews* can imagine Moses and ask the same questions. *Buddhists* can imagine Gautama in his youth and then the Buddha. *Muslims* can imagine Muhammad and so on. A *naturalist* can imagine a great oak tree that towers before the individual with its deep strong roots, and branches reaching out in all directions. One could ask, "Please tell me how you weather the winter?" Imagine how this oak tree would describe its winter condition. One could imagine a great medicine man in the rainforests and ask him questions regarding one's purpose in life.

You can see this as a time for *personal growth* as well. Many survivors become more involved in their loved one's work and will take over their business, listening to their favorite music, creating a memorial fund or foundation, recalling humorous times with them, assisting other bereaved people or volunteering. It is far better to become a force for good and stay active than to waste your life in unproductive sorrow.

Ceremonies and Rituals

Most cultures have rituals designed to help people with the grieving process. The funeral practices of the Irish, the Jewish, the Russians and others specifically trigger and release painful feelings. Many cultures have a formal mourning period of usually a year and the bereaved have direct involvement in the ceremonies. In the American culture, those who suffer are typically "protected" from any direct involvement in the burial and praised for not displaying overt signs of grief. The funeral ritual does more than acknowledge the death of someone loved. It helps provide the grieving person with the support of caring people. More importantly, the funeral is an avenue and space for the person to mourn. If others tell you that rituals such as these are silly or unnecessary, don't listen.

The Ancient Stone Ceremony

A participant or a group of people would go to a place where there are many stones. A six-foot wide circle would be drawn in the dirt and someone would invoke the deceased to come into the circle while some time was spent feeling the person's presence. A stone would be placed on the south edge of the circle while people, or one person, faced the stone. They would then bring to mind the childhood of the person who had died and childlike qualities of that person. Afterward, someone would touch the stone and verbalize appreciation for the child in the person. The same would be done by placing a stone on the west side of the circle and bringing to mind the brave and courageous qualities of the person who died. The north stone would bring to mind the skills and talents of the person who died. The east stone would bring to mind the vision and dreams of the person who died. Then someone would thank the person who died for all the contributions the person made to the community and the world. The stones would then be returned to their original places, the circle erased, and a meditation upon two realities occurs. The first reality is that we cannot change time or place. The second is that no thing or no person is completely confined to a particular time or place. One can carry that person with oneself now, in memory, and in everything one witnesses and experiences.

The Altar of Remembrance

Designate a place (coffee table, end table, top of a dresser) in your home that includes items of the loved one. For example, a cloth made from some of the person's clothing, photographs of the person, a ring, watch, or other piece of jewelry, a favorite book, kitchen utensil, a flower or plant, a candle to burn on the loved one's birthday, anniversaries, etc.

The Letting Go Ritual

The bereaved person selects an object (clothing, picture, possession) that symbolizes the deceased. Then the object is taken to a special place the deceased and bereaved enjoyed together. A hole is dug in the ground or a fire pit for a ritualistic burial or burning of the object. A short meditation is offered before the object is buried or burned. Afterward, the bereaved mediates upon letting the object and the deceased go. The same could be done as one drops an object into a quiet river.

Use Affirmations

You can buy little books in the bookstore to help with saying affirmations. For example, I like the following: May my mind think of peace. May my lungs breathe in comfort. May my heart beat with strength. May my blood flow with courage. Peace, comfort, strength, courage: May they be mine. May I get them. May I give them. May I live them.

Last Thoughts

If you have lost a loved one, here are some suggestions to prevent depression from lasting too long. Accept the grief and take time to cry. Talk about it with a friend, family member, support group, or a professional. Keep busy doing purposeful work that occupies the mind but avoid frantic activity. Take care of yourself, as grief can be a threat to your health. Eat well and exercise regularly. Postpone major decisions. Record your thoughts in a journal. Accept your understanding of death even though you may not get an acceptable answer. You can always work up to another level of understanding later. Associate with old friends and talk about the subject of loss. Take advantage of your religious affiliation and the scripture you have faith in.

Remember your rights. You have the right to talk about your grief and experience it your own unique way. You have the right to feel a wide variety of emotions including guilt, fear, and relief. You have the right to experience grief "attacks" that can come out of nowhere. This is normal. Remember, no matter how deep your sorrow, you are not alone. Others have been there and will help share your load if you will let them. Don't deny them the opportunity.

Exercise 1

Below, write down which times during each day you feel alive and the times when you feel "dead." Reflect on the roles you play, your psychological and spiritual life, leisure time, social relationships, etc. *Do you notice any patterns? What can you do to feel more alive?*

____

____

____

____

____

____

____

____

Exercise 2

A. Reflect and write about how the death of those you love might affect you. *As you think of each person, how would your life today be different if they were not in it? What changes could you start to make in each of those relationships?*

____

____

____

____

____

B. In Stephen Levine's Book, "A Year to Live," (1997), he encourages us to live this current year as if it was the last. He mentions how often people have remorse on their death beds because they neglected a relationship and/or their spiritual life, and wished they had one more year to live. Many say they would have changed their work situation or quit. Many on their death beds speak of interests like learning that new musical instrument, taking up painting or computer art, taking long walks in nature, going back to church or some meditation practice. *If you knew you were going to die within a year, in what way would you live your life differently? What might you stop doing? What might you start doing that you're not doing or experiencing now?*

____

____

____

____

____

____

Exercise 3

Write **three** eulogies for yourself. Make each eulogy **one paragraph (minimum 5 sentences).**

1. Write one that you think actually sums up your life, e.g. Bill was an insecure but funny man....
2. Write one that you fear could be written about you.
3. Write one that you hope could be written about you. Write them as if you had died today. If you want, seal them, and revisit them in a year to find out if your hopes and fears have changed.

Strategy 3.6

Become aware of your personal weaknesses and issues and resolve to improve them. Identify and cope with depression.

Seek Personal Growth

Do you have any of the following issues? Are you overly critical, feel unworthy, stupid, inadequate, shameful or guilty, dishonest, depressed, anxious, arrogant, overly stressed, controlling, or a perfectionist? If so, these characteristics are hurting you now and will in the long run prevent you from getting what you want out of life. Make a commitment now to work on these every day and follow the goal-setting model to provide you direction and keep you on track. Look at your dynamics, such as patterns in relationships, attraction to parent figures, birth order, how you were punished as a child, projection of emotions onto loved ones, and other similar tendencies. You can purchase plenty of books on these subjects in bookstores under the Psychology or the Self Improvement section.

What is Depression?

Depression is a common and sometimes serious disorder of mood that causes you to feel sad or hopeless for an extended period of time. More than just a bout of "the blues" or temporary feelings of grief or low energy, depression can prevent enjoyment of your work, health, your life, and the people you care about. It can be mild to intense and attack the mind and body at the same time. It may be associated with an imbalance of chemicals (neurotransmitters) in the brain that carry communications between nerve cells which control mood and basic bodily functions such as appetite, energy, and sleep. Depression may carry a stigma for some people who think it is a weakness or character flaw. It is none of these and a depressed person can't just "snap out of it." Depression affects each person differently in its symptoms, how long it lasts, and what treatment works best. It often shows up as something else, such as fatigue, insomnia, stomach and digestive problems, backaches, headaches, weight change, and/or trouble concentrating. In children and teens, if left untreated, it can greatly affect the quality of life for the young person and his or her family.

Causes of Depression?

Depression can be triggered by other medical illnesses, medications, nutritional deficiencies, certain personality traits, and genetic factors. Although causes of depression are not always entirely understood, researchers know it is linked to an imbalance in brain chemistry and neurotransmitter activity. Once the imbalance is corrected, symptoms of depression generally improve. There are usually several factors between the psychological and biological areas that cause depression.

Biological or genetic factors influence the likelihood of developing major depression or bipolar mood disorder. Twin studies showed that 67% of identical twin children who had depressed parents ended up with depression. It was only 15% for fraternal twins. Therefore, genetic factors and heredity can create a predisposition to mood disorders and environmental life factors determine whether this predisposition is converted into an actual disorder.

Psychological factors such as the thoughts and beliefs of how people draw conclusions about events, others' behavior, and their own behavior play a role in determining one's mental health. For example, if you failed a biology test, what do you usually attribute the cause to? People who attribute the cause to internal, unchangeable, and global factors are more prone to depression than people who attribute them to things that they can change. For instance, Bill thinks he failed the class because he is not intelligent (internal and unchangeable) and, as a result, believes he is not a very worthy person (global). Some studies found that depressed people who *ruminate* about their depression remain depressed longer than those who try to distract themselves (Nolen-Hoeksema, Morrow, & Fredrickson, 1993). Their study found that women are more likely to ruminate than men and this may be the primary reason why depression is more common in women. Rumination occurs when the person repetitively focuses their attention on their depressing feelings, thinking constantly about how sad, lethargic, and unmotivated they are, which makes it worse. Ironically, depressed individuals self-evaluate themselves more realistically than non-depressed individuals. The exercises in this chapter will help to interpret events accurately.

Social factors influence whether one becomes healthy or depressed. Studies show that individuals with poor or inadequate social skills are correlated with those same people having depression. They lack the risk-taking ability to meet new people and the social finesse to acquire good friends, good jobs, and desirable spouses. When they suffer with depression they are often irritable, pessimistic, complain a lot, and aren't enjoyable companions. Therefore, they further alienate themselves because of social rejection and lack of support. I recommend Dale Carnegie's book, How to Win Friends and Influence People.

Stressful life events can trigger depression such as divorce, loss of a loved one, loss of job, loss of health, or any kind of loss. Some theorists believe that stress leads to disruptions of biological rhythms and sleep loss, which lead to neurochemical changes that cause mood disorders. Of course, many people endure great stress without getting depressed. Everybody has a different threshold of stress they can or can't manage. That is why this book is dedicated to helping you cope with life stressors, reframe challenging life events and personal beliefs, and tap your inner strengths so you can live, thrive, and produce.

Types of Depression

Dysthymia is a milder, chronic form of depression that lasts two years or more. People with dysthymia function fairly well on a daily basis, but their work and relationships suffer over time.

Bipolar depression is the depressive phase of the manic-depressive illness (bipolar disorder), in which there are both extreme highs (mania) and extreme lows of mood. The symptoms are similar to major depression listed on the following page. During the mania phase, the person may feel insomnia, overconfidence, racing thoughts, reckless behavior, increased energy, and appetite changes. It is often disguised by substance abuse and can be triggered by a death or loss of a loved one, job, or physical ability. It usually gets triggered between the ages of 20 and 40. Bipolar and major depression are the psychiatric diagnoses most commonly associated with suicide.

Seasonal Affective Disorder is a type of depression that follows seasonal rhythms, with symptoms occurring in the winter months and lessening in spring and summer.

Postpartum depression can occur in women the first few months of giving birth.

***Major depression* or unipolar depression** is the common type of depression. It is possible for a person to have only one episode of it, but it's more common for episodes to repeat several times and be long lasting during the person's life. It is characterized by at least five of the key symptoms listed on the following page.

Symptoms of Depression

Depression is more than just the normal, temporary feelings of sadness sand hopelessness associated with difficult life events. The symptoms are often subtle at first and over time become more intense. The symptoms include:

- persistent sad, empty, depressed mood
- loss of interest or inability to enjoy pleasure in ordinary activities
- changes in appetite or weight
- inability to sleep or oversleeping
- restlessness, sluggishness and/or decreased energy or fatigue
- difficulty concentrating or making decisions
- feelings of guilt, hopelessness, or worthlessness
- thoughts of death or suicide
- slowed thoughts and speech
- complaints that have no physical cause

All of these symptoms can interfere with your quality of life. Even if you don't have major depression, if you have experienced a few of these symptoms for at least two weeks, you may have a less severe form of depression that still requires treatment.

Treatment for Depression

The good news is that more than 80% of people with depression improve with treatment within several months, although it may be necessary to try multiple forms of treatment until the right ones are found. For a majority of persons, the combination of psychotherapy or professional counseling and medication is the most effective treatment.

Psychotherapy has multiple purposes It is beneficial in helping the person develop new ways of thinking, changing distorted beliefs, improving relations with other people, or resolving current or unresolved conflicts from childhood. Resources for counseling include: community mental health centers, general and mental hospitals and clinics, spiritual leaders, family service agencies, schools and employers, and self-help groups such as alcoholics Anonymous.

Antidepressant Medications may take several weeks to be effective.

Electroconvulsive Therapy (ECT) is actually a relatively safe and effective form of treatment for individuals with severe depression. This is beneficial to those who cannot tolerate medication.

Light therapy is often helpful for depressed people, which expose them to bright artificial light. Light lamps can be purchased online.

The herb St. John's wort can be effective for those sensitive to medication.

Self-help groups can provide a supportive environment for individuals with depression as well as for their family and friends. A therapist or family health professional can diagnose you. Since depression is often overlooked, tell your doctor or therapist if you suspect you have depression. Don't just leave treatment options to one person to decide for you. You should know your body better than anyone. You and your health professional can decide on the best treatment.

Exercise can lift certain mood chemicals and contribute to a feeling of well-being, self-discipline, and positive self-esteem while reducing stress and raising energy levels.

Schedule fun activities into your schedule. Bring pleasure and relaxation back into your life.

Think positive by changing negative thoughts and beliefs into positive ones. See chapter two as well as the information on optimism vs. pessimism. You can learn to be an optimist.

Distract yourself. When you feel the depression coming on, go do something else like taking a walk, listening to music, taking photographs, etc.

Reach out and give to others (unless you are a helper type and that is part of the problem). Spend time with positive, supportive people. Focusing attention away from yourself is often helpful.

Unbelievable Statistics (researched at St. Mary Medical Center)

- About 20 million Americans each year develop some form of depression.
- Women experience depression twice as often as men. Women attempt suicide four times more often than men yet men are more than four times more successful in killing themselves.
- Depression costs over $50 billion annually in the United States alone in lost productivity, worker absenteeism, medical expenses, and disability.
- By the year 2020, major depression will be the second most burdensome illness in the world in terms of lost years of healthy life.
- Depression has been linked with increases in risk, severity, and mortality of cancer and heart disease. Heart attack survivors with depression have 3-4 times greater risk of dying within six months. Seniors are at greater risk for Alzheimer's dementia, Parkinson's disease, and stroke.
- One in eight adolescents have clinical depression but usually don't show outward signs of being sad. They spend a lot of time alone and talk of death or suicide.
- About two-thirds of people who complete suicide have a depressive disorder at the time of their deaths.
- 70% of persons who commit suicide communicate their intentions. Take the talk of suicide seriously.

Suicide

It is estimated that there are over 250,000 suicide attempts in the United States each year; roughly one in eight of these attempts are successful (Weiten & Lloyd 1997). This makes suicide the ninth leading cause of death in the United States, accounting for about 30,000 deaths annually. Many suicides are disguised as accidents, either by the suicidal person or by the survivors who try to cover up afterward. So the number is probably bigger. Married people commit suicide less often than divorced, bereaved, or single people. In regard to race, suicide rates are higher among white Americans than African Americans. Suicide rates have tripled among adolescents and young adults in the last several decades. Groups at high risk are those people who have interpersonal problems (spouse, boyfriend/girlfriend breakups) and loneliness as well as those who have serious physical illnesses like AIDS. Suicides are highest for people with mood disorders. Also, alcohol and drug disorders are correlated with an elevated incidence of suicide.

There are four typical myths about suicide. *The first myth is that people who talk about suicide don't actually commit suicide.* Many people who kill themselves have a history of earlier threats. *The second myth is that suicide usually takes place with little or no warning.* About 80% of suicide attempts are preceded by some kind of warning that ranges from clear threats to vague statements. To determine how high the risk is when somebody threatens suicide, find out if they have a plan, a timeframe, and the means (like a gun) to carry it out. *The third myth is that people who attempt suicide are fully intent on dying.* Actually only about 3 to 5% of those who attempt suicide definitely want to die. Most want to send out a very dramatic distress signal and arrange their suicide so that a rescue is quite likely. That is probably why only one in eight suicide attempts end in death. *The fourth myth is that people who are suicidal remain so forever.* Many people who become suicidal do so for a limited period of time. If they manage to ride through their crisis period, thoughts of suicide may disappear entirely. Apparently, time heals many wounds-if it is given the opportunity.

If you know someone or if you are considering suicide, find empathy and social support from friends, family, church, or community support. Most individuals have people in their lives that can support them. Yet, many individuals thinking of suicide will tell you that they don't because they are no longer talking to some family members. They are amazed to find that the people they least expect to help, usually do. Most mental health professionals have at least some experience in dealing with suicidal crises. Many cities have suicide prevention centers with 24-hour hotlines. It is important to try to get a suicidal person to seek professional assistance as soon as possible.

Exercise 1

Identify the one issue you need to work on from the following list: overly critical, dishonest, depressed, anxious, arrogant, overly stressed, controlling, a perfectionist, feel unworthy, low self-esteem, inadequate, shameful or guilty. Buy or borrow from the library two books on this subject and become an expert on this topic. Apply the material you learn instead of just intellectualizing the information. Most people read these books and the material, but they never get past their intellect and into their "Heart".

Write down the times you are most likely to feel this way. Follow steps two through five in Strategy 3.2 on giving your power away. Note: If the process becomes too intense or too painful over a period of time, seek help from a therapist, psychologist, priest, rabbi, or religious/spiritual figure who is trained in your problematic area.

____

____

____

____

____

____

____

____

Exercise 2

Ask yourself if you ever try to escape depression and loneliness? Circle the following statements that you think apply to you. I bury myself in work. I drink or take drugs excessively. I schedule every moment so that I'll have very little time to think about myself. I constantly seek to be with others. I avoid my troubles by watching television or listening to music. I eat compulsively. I sleep excessively. I become overly concerned with helping others. I seek constant stimulation.

Write below how you might change the patterns you use from above so you can cope with whatever you are escaping from. Hints include: reading books on the subject, talking to someone who knows, support groups, enlisting a personal friend/advocate to help you, etc.

____

____

____

____

____

____

____

Exercise 3

1. When you consider the physical, social (relationships), spiritual, psychological, intellectual, emotional, leisure (fun), and financial, areas of life, write down which area you think is helping to cause any depression or unhappiness in your life? What answers did you right down to Strategy 2.7's exercise on life balance that may address this issue?

____

2. Does your job express what you truly want to be doing? If no, how can you begin to discover and do work that would be more fulfilling?

3. Do you have creative outlets? If not, what creative activities could you start to develop?

4. What would you like to accomplish in your life by the age of 70 in order to feel your life has been productive and meaningful?

5. Is there anything you deeply value and yet feel you haven't fully experienced or realized in your life? For example, happy family life, friendship, intimacy, good health, peace of mind, serving others, material success, career achievement, personal growth, spiritual awareness, social cause, special talent, etc. What changes do you need to make or what risks do you need to take to live these values?

6. What are you willing to commit to and start fulfilling during the next month, year, and three years to eliminate any obstacles to the above questions?

Strategy 3.7

Become aware of, and slowly eliminate, your defense mechanisms.

Definition: Defense Mechanism - a mental maneuver that one consciously or unconsciously chooses to use to distort or falsify the truth of one's experience in order to protect oneself from feeling painful emotions such as anxiety, shame, or guilt. It is usually used during conversations with others.

Open Up The Defenses

When something painful or unacceptable is encountered, we will often distort our perceptions to protect ourselves. If we distort often, then the distortion, or defense mechanism (D.M.), becomes automatic, often without our even knowing that we are distorting something. In the same way, when we learn a new skill or task, like learning to play a new sport, play the piano, type, or drive a car, we are conscious of learning the details at first. Then, once we repeat it over and over again and get better at it (like driving), the detailed parts of the task move out of consciousness and we are mindlessly, like a machine, in a trance without intelligent thought. We use defense mechanisms in a similar unconscious way. Neurotic individuals tend to use them much more frequently. Neurosis is defined as an emotional disorder in which feelings of anxiety, obsessive thoughts, compulsive acts and physical complaints without objective evidence, dominate the personality. The key to our growth is to wake up and identify the exact time and place we use our defense mechanisms.

A defense mechanism is like a shock absorber on a car. It absorbs much of the sudden energy of the initial jolt and then releases it much more slowly and much less perceptively over time. Defense mechanisms aim at protecting us by building walls around our selves. The goal then is to slowly eliminate the walls through awareness so that even a shock absorber isn't necessary. The defense mechanism sedates, or drugs, our awareness of the disappointments and threats we encounter in our lives. We then are unable to learn from our failures and shortcomings. So we must understand and correct these distortions so as to cultivate our higher nature. The defense mechanisms' aim is noble, to protect us from suffering. It is intelligent and motivated to exist and that's why it's hard to eliminate.

Useless suffering is caused when our deep feelings, desires, and talents are shamed and invalidated during the course of parental conditioning and enculturation (reinforcement to fit societal norms, e.g. ridicule, insults, spanking, guilt, etc.). Though it is thought to help things in the short-run, the cost to the individual is high in the long run. The invalidation of our feelings plus the tension and anxiety in everyday life alienates us from our selves, which leads to suffering, disorders, and neurosis. We've lived so long with our D.M. in place and we are so comfortable with them that we can't see how they limit our life experiences of enjoyment and growing. For instance, if you've watched the TV show "Seinfeld," you'll notice that all the main characters are highly anxious people. They all fear disapproval and harsh judgment from others and from society's standards, which, in turn, causes them to express just about every D.M. on the next page. What awaits us, when we eliminate these defense mechanisms, is true freedom from doubt, fear, shame, guilt, and other destructive emotions as well as a greater sense of well-being and true liberation.

Strategies For Removing Defense Mechanisms

The following strategies on the next page can help direct more awareness to hidden defense mechanisms.

Reading: Reading all the personal growth materials you can on your dominant defense mechanism.

Writing: Journal writing about your feelings and actions during the day as well as your progress.

Talking: Talking to a close friend, therapist, spouse, boy/girlfriend.
Meditating: Finding quiet time to be fully present and bringing that with you wherever you go.
Praying: Consulting, asking, and communicating to your spiritual advisor.
Screaming: Into a pillow, in a car, silent scream.

The following is an incomplete list of defense mechanisms.

DEFENSE MECHANISMS

1. LYING

One lies for either self-gain or for sparing oneself from ridicule, rejection, or punishment. One estimates that lying will be to one's advantage. Phrases like "Everybody does it" or "It doesn't mean anything" are often used when deep down we know we haven't lived up to our higher selves. Habitual liars can even believe their own lies and use such phrases as "I swear I didn't do it." It ends up causing more anxiety in our lives and weakens our character.

2. RATIONALIZATION

Occurs when a person justifies something that is perceived as wrong/bad. Failures and inadequacies are a threat to the ego. The ego then rationalizes, "I could have won the race today, but the track was wet." This statement has an element of the truth, but it denies the larger truth that someone else was faster. "He beats me, but he really loves me anyway," or "I got fired, but the boss was a jerk."

3. IDENTIFICATION

Occurs when we only see the part of us that we want to see because the truth would be too painful. A mean-spirited person only identifies with the good part of him or herself, and states, "I'm always a nice person." Or, an insecure man joins a fraternity to boost his self-esteem because he feels inadequate. Many will identify with rock-star heroes, movie stars, or famous athletes to bolster their self-esteem.

4. DISTRACTION

Occurs when one distracts oneself from an unacceptable truth. Example: Someone says, "Consumer Reports says the expensive car you just bought has bad maintenance ratings." Instead of considering the truth of the statement, the person chooses to resist the truth through distraction. He/she may begin discussing how well the car runs, its sporty look, and turns the conversation to proposing a movie for the night. The person keeps his/herself busy so as to avoid the truth or any real feelings.

5. COMPARTMENTALIZATION/DISASSOCIATION

Occurs when a person compartmentalizes, he/she disowns a feeling or desire by creating a separate self who does not have this feeling or desire. A person who is for the death penalty states, "It is an inhuman act." This act of creating a separate self (with different feelings/desires) makes it so that the two selves never associate. This often creates a person with many contradictory opinions.

6. REGRESSION

When adult defense mechanisms haven't worked for us, we may regress to a personality we had at an earlier childhood age. When an adult doesn't get their way, he/she states, "It's not my fault, it's your fault," and begins to have a temper tantrum. Immature patterns of behavior emerge such as bragging.

7. OVERCOMPENSATION

Occurs when a person covers up felt weaknesses by making up for frustration in one area and over- gratifying herself in another. For example, a dangerously overweight woman goes on eating binges when she feels neglected by her husband. Instead of dealing with the feeling, she estimates the eating binges will gratify the feeling of emptiness she feels around her husband.

8. REPRESSION

The person forces the unacceptable feeling out of awareness to a point where he/she doesn't even know it has been done. It is usually a threatening memory or event that is driven into the unconscious and is involuntary. It could be a simple reprimand or as serious as a rape. It can surface in dreams or come out in the form of 'slips of the tongue', etc. It's as if there is a mental sign that whispers to the person, "WARNING, this material must always be kept from consciousness." So, repression is the blocking of the unacceptable, whether the unacceptable is an event or a desire of some sort. For instance, when a person who doesn't get along with his mother is asked, "How do you get along with your mother?" He answers, "Just fine. I love her," but he turns pale. Negative feelings about the mother are so unacceptable to him that they are blocked from his awareness.

9. DENIAL

The person doesn't acknowledge the validity of the desire but does acknowledge its presence. Denial opposes force with force. Example: The alcoholic expresses, "I may like to drink, but I'm not an alcoholic." Or, a smoker concludes that the evidence linking cigarette use to health problems is scientifically worthless. Recommendation: Accept your mistakes, weaknesses, and all your thoughts and feelings. Remember, when you resist, you give it power to exist. If you find yourself feeling extra strong reactions of rejection, you may be denying something.

10. SUPPRESSION

The person is aware of the unacceptable desire and validates it (sees the truth in it) but intentionally tries to keep it from expressing itself. Example: "I know I'm an alcoholic, so I'm going to go on the wagon." Another example includes a homosexual who intentionally doesn't date members of the same sex so that the unacceptable does not express itself. A common experience in suppression occurs when an introvert is conditioned to be an extrovert. Have you ever suppressed getting angry in public or resisted standing up for somebody due to losing others' approval?

11. PROJECTION

The person attributes one's own perceived negative attributes onto someone else. Example: Blaming an instructor for a bad grade or saying to somebody, "You envy me," when actually, you envy the person. Or, a person cheats on their spouse and blames the spouse for cheating.

12. DISPLACEMENT

The person diverts emotions and acts out on a less threatening object or person. Example: After somebody makes you mad, you kick the dog, punch the wall, or yell at your child. Bullies are famous for using displacement because somebody else is usually abusing them, which they act out on others.

13. REACTION FORMATION

The person does the opposite of what he/she preaches, feels or believes. It is the hypocrite. Example: A preacher who preaches against adultery when he's fighting off his own impulses and then involves himself with a prostitute. Or, a person who feels envious or anger at somebody, tells their friend how wonderful that person is. The person is usually not aware of it.

14. INTELLECTUALIZATION

The person is afraid to confront the issue by talking esoterically around the subject and doesn't deal with true feelings. (Phares, 1988). Example: When asked how he feels, he replies, "Other people might feel sad and that's the thing about our society ...." but he never brings up how he feels. It's possible to intellectualize this material and not make changes in your life.

Exercise 1

Identify the <u>three</u> defense mechanisms from the previous pages that you believe you use the most in your life. If you're not sure, monitor yourself throughout the day. Be able to name and identify the defense mechanism you use at the exact time it happens. When you find yourself using a defense mechanism, don't beat yourself up. Simply notice it, take 10 deep breaths, and center yourself by recalling the silent peace experienced in the meditation exercise. You will then be able to let go of any urge you have to control or manipulate your feelings. It might help to write down in a journal your actions and feelings of events throughout the day.

____

____

Exercise 2 & 3

For each of the 3 defense mechanisms, write a few sentences that answer each of the following questions.

1. What is the defense mechanism and the <u>circumstances</u> that normally take place when you use it?
2. Why do you think you use the defense mechanism?
3. How is the defense mechanism serving you in the short run?
4. What are you trying to protect?
5. How would life be easier if you didn't use the defense mechanism and found a healthier way of responding?
6. What is a healthier way of responding to your circumstance and how will you put it into action?

EXAMPLE: (Possible answers to the above questions include:)

1. DENIAL - You might say to yourself, "I don't care if Mark doesn't like me." If you actually do care, then the defense mechanism used would be DENIAL.
2. Because I don't want to feel the hurt/pain of not being liked by somebody I like.
3. I don't have to feel the pain, which allows me to supposedly get on with my life.
4. My ego, self-worth, and self-esteem so I don't have to feel bad about myself.
5. I wouldn't have to keep telling myself over and over again that I don't care about Mark when I really do.
6. I can admit that it hurts and realize that everybody can't like me. I can write or talk about it with somebody while keeping myself busy doing more productive things. See next page.

Defense Mechanism #1:

1.

Defense Mechanism # 2:

1.

Defense Mechanism #3:

1.

Chapter Insight & Commitment

After completing this chapter, I learned the following about my power, thoughts, voices, resistance, reactions to stress, and defense mechanisms:

Example: I have observed that I give to much of my power away to people at work like Sue and Jerry. I want their approval and am afraid they will isolate me at work. I find myself "kissing up" to them and I don't feel like myself when I do that.

I can take active steps to help me achieve my future goals and become more of the person I am or strive to be by:

Example: I will commit to challenging self-defeating thoughts that enter my mind throughout the day by remembering that I have earned many friendships, trust others will see my strengths, and challenge people who try to isolate me. This will help me achieve my goal of becoming a business manager because it will give me the communication skills needed to move up in the business.

CHAPTER 4

Self-Compassion

Using your **Arms** to have **Compassion** and love for the wounded part of you and for others.

Purpose: To develop lifelong love and appreciation for yourself enabling you to do the same to others.

Rewards: Self-worth, Self-Esteem, Happiness, Fulfillment, Joy

Obstacles: Negative Experiences/Upbringing, Overly Self-critical, Cruel People

Consequence: Depression, Numbness, Self-Alienation

Symbol: Blanket

Related Web Site: www.queendom.com/test/index.html

Self-Compassion

When we can clearly and accurately observe the truth of our behaviors, we can then begin to judge and view ourselves more clearly. This clarity is a prerequisite for feeling good about ourselves because many of us learned to minimize our strengths and maximize and distort our weaknesses. This mindset produces low self-esteem. Low self-esteem in a recent study of college students revealed higher levels of depression, stress, and loneliness (Salmedla-Aro & Nurmi, 1996). Qualities such as innovation, personal responsibility, self-management, and self-direction are all by-products of high self-esteem (Branden, 1992).

There are scores of people who are financially successful. They have a successful job and wonderful relationships. It is stunning that these same people are often miserable, sad, or depressed, despite their success. This is because they do not value themselves. They have low self-worth and self-esteem and judge themselves unfairly. What is most needed is the ability to have compassion for that part of our selves which has been wounded by criticisms. These criticisms not only come from outside influences but also from the person you would least likely expect to hurt you-- yourself. This wounded part of our self needs to be found, "held," apologized to, comforted, and assured that every effort will be taken to protect and empower that Self so that it can come out from hiding. Once this happens, a new Self emerges and slowly takes the helm to steer your life in the direction it is meant to take. Along the way, you feel empowered to be yourself despite the outside influences and disapproval from those who pressure you to conform to their ways.

In this chapter, you will learn how to cultivate effective self-compassion skills and complete required exercises that enhance self-esteem, self-respect, and self-worth. You will learn effective ways of mastering a skill. This is directly related to feeling good about yourself. Included in this chapter is information on how to acquire help from others who can support and encourage you to be who you are. When your supportive circle of people is not available, you will learn how to attain additional help and motivation from outside resources that will nourish you along the way. You will not only develop compassion for yourself but, equally as important, you will also learn to develop compassion for others. There are so many people who have experienced similar pressures, invalidations, and criticisms from the culture in which we all live. This development of compassion for yourself and others will propel you to reach higher levels of happiness, security, fulfillment, and energy that seem to escape most people. This will be one of the most significant acquired skills that will serve you throughout your lifetime.

Strategy 4.1

Convert low self-worth into high self-compassion.

When Low Self-Worth is Born

By the time we're adults, we often work against ourselves and sabotage our success and self-esteem more than others do. No one but you can develop compassion for yourself. Many of us are deeply wounded because of the primary messages we received growing up and often still receive as an adult. Each individual needs to take the time to acknowledge his/her own struggles in life. It is affirming to honor yourself, accept your faults, and have compassion for the part of you that has worked hard to get through life. This chapter aims at accomplishing this act of self-love. The two most powerful sets of messages that affect our self-identity, self-esteem, and self-worth are parental messages and cultural/societal messages.

Parental Messages

Parental messages are powerful because parents often, without knowing it, give love to their children conditionally. Parents usually have good parenting intentions and do not mean to hurt their children. Yet, in their quest to get their children to obey, many parents withdraw their love and attention and use an arsenal of weapons to isolate, ridicule, abuse, deny, invalidate, and shame their children. Unless, the parents often respond back with apologies and messages of care and love, the child who does not have the intelligence to outwit the parents, can do nothing but conform to and accept the messages that he/she is powerless, unworthy, stupid, invisible, inferior, and weak. Perhaps the role you played in your family or your gender was not valued and, therefore, you were alienated from becoming whom you really are deep inside. ***Once we believe we are inferior, the mind then seeks out only that information to justify this inferiority.*** For instance, the adult with low self-worth who receives 20 compliments and only one criticism about the speech he/she gave will give more value and attention to that one little negative criticism, hence negating all the other positive messages. These imprinting messages can take a lifetime to manage for some, but with attention and intention to work through them, they can be managed successfully in our adult life. These messages that the child blindly accepted as truth are always false, and so the task of the adult is to not only negate them on an intellectual level but to negate them on the deeper emotional level where adults feel them most.

The Seven Parental Circumstances that Cause Low-Self-Esteem.

1. **Parental rejection -** When a parent rejects a child, the child feels like they are unwanted and will often doubt their right to exist. This leads to the child growing up feeling insecure, worthless, lonely, and of course, rejected. Whether the parents are preoccupied with themselves, their work, or other concerns, this damages the child's self-esteem and they will often neglect their own needs.

2. **Parental overindulgence** – This is also known as "Spoiling the child." Children need boundaries, limits, and correction to learn to be safe, develop, and grow. Yet, when a parent gives the child everything they want and they don't learn to postpone their pleasures, the child grows up bored, unable to achieve goals or discipline themselves, and unable to take responsibility for their lives. They expect the world to stop for them and they become very self-absorbed. Like not teaching a child to learn in school, this spoiled child becomes ignorant of others and drowns in the sea of life.

3. **Parental Over protectiveness** - These parents usually have good intentions but their children never learn to trust the world outside of their immediate family and risk independence. Again, insecurity and low self-esteem creep in because the parent's limit their life experiences and they don't develop the self-confidence needed to expand their personal development and succeed in the world of other people.

4. **Overly critical parents** – These parents set impossibly high standards of behavior for their kids. The kids who are now adults feel either guilty for not being good enough, or suffer from perfectionism to compensate for feeling inferior inside. This perfectionism and self-criticism causes a tremendous amount of anxiety and often produces anxiety attacks into adulthood.

5. **Parental abuse** is one of the worst circumstances that children experience. Whether its physical, verbal, or sexual abuse, it leaves the child who grows into an adult with a mix of feelings from lack of trust of others, rage, and inadequacy. Adults who experienced this type of violence in their childhood are likely to either become violent toward others or themselves through rape or abuse, or they will turn their rage into seeing their identity as a victim and be consumed with self-loathing. Intimacy into adulthood becomes a major obstacle in their relationships. Support groups are one of the best ways to deal with these traumas in adulthood.

6. **Parental alcoholism or drug abuse** – This circumstance creates a chaotic, unreliable family atmosphere. As a result, the child never learns to trust and find inner security. They end up denying their own feelings and pain and become "Out of touch" with themselves and their identity. This opens the door for others to take advantage of them because they don't have a good sense of boundaries to set with others. Again, support groups are one of the best ways to deal with these traumas in adulthood.

7 **Major childhood loss -** Whether it is the death of parent or divorce, the child usually ends up feeling abandoned. When the child grows into an adult, they often are devastated by other significant losses in their life and become over-dependent on another person, on substances, or work to cover the pain they feel.

Most people grew up with parts of these elements in their childhood to some extent. Yet, when it reaches moderate to extreme levels, a child develops neurosis that sets them up for anxiety, depression, and low self-worth as adults. Negative self-talk becomes common in the adult who struggles with their self-esteem. When we finally realize that we are not responsible for our childhood past, we can then begin to realize **how foolish for us to punish ourselves in the present, because someone else hurt us in the long ago past.**

Cultural/Societal Messages

Cultural/Societal messages are powerful because, like parental messages, they can also isolate, ridicule, abuse, polarize, distort, deny, invalidate, discriminate, shame, and coerce people into believing that they are inferior beings. Examples of these messages include:

- Don't affirm your cultural heritage.
- Don't be different.
- Don't be separate.
- You're not like us.
- You are flawed.
- You are inferior,
- You are a criminal/animal.

These messages are communicated through the media (movies, advertisements, television sitcoms, etc.), teachers in our schools, peer groups, and so on. They distort the truth about people's culture, religion, race, and backgrounds.
Therefore, these negative parental and cultural/societal messages often contribute toward a feeling of self-hatred. However, it is not enough to work only on empowering ourselves by attacking the parental or cultural messages alone. We must also deal with the new messages that we have designed for ourselves. Cultural messages can often be more difficult to eliminate for "people of color" because they constantly receive these direct and indirect messages in daily life from members of the "majority" culture. Imagine having to live with your abuser every day of your life. It makes it much harder to work through the pain, rage, anger, hurt, and fear associated with these messages. Again, that is why we must surround ourselves with healthy people as much as possible. There will always be those people in our lives that will discriminate, invalidate, and belittle us (some more than others). Therefore, we must create a circle of positive people around us while we are working to redefine our self-concept and convert our self-hatred into self-compassion.

There are so many people who have experienced similar pressures, invalidations, and criticisms from the culture in which we all live. This development of compassion for yourself and others will propel you to reach higher levels of happiness, security, fulfillment, and energy that seem to escape most people. This will be one of the most significant acquired skills that will serve you throughout your lifetime.

It is important to mention that it is vital that you don't spend time "feeling sorry for yourself" and seeing yourself as a victim. A victim identifies oneself as if their victimhood is there whole personality. That approach of becoming self-absorbed takes you further to the depths of low self-worth. It is like living in quick sand. You will not get better. I recommend self-compassion without victimhood. Also, to get "out of yourself," do something for somebody else or give some type of service that is needed in the community. That kind of focus will actually help you to keep a healthy balance of attention to self and society.

Converting To Self-Compassion

So, the first step is to cross-examine and negate the negative parental and cultural messages we have received. To accomplish this, find a support group and/or friends that you can safely talk with about your feelings associated with these negative messages. It is essential to get in touch with that "child" inside of you that has been hurt by the outside world. Learn to have compassion for this little boy or girl who has been trying his/her best to get by but has received unfair treatment for many years. Instead, of running from the pain, embrace that hurtful part of you, cry with him or her and tell him/her that you are now taking action so that the pain will be dealt with. The 12-step program is more successful for treating addictive behaviors because it uses the 2-step punch. First, meetings are set up so that people can process their painful experiences with others who have similar experiences. Second, the person must believe in a spiritual divine being that is more powerful than him/herself. The understanding is that this higher power will assist the person toward reclaiming his/her spiritual, emotional and physical health. This is why it is so important to connect with your spiritual core which is the essence of your "true-self". This is the part of you that would remain the same regardless of which culture or planet you grew up on. This spiritual core is stronger and deeper than any parental or cultural message we have encountered.

Millions of people would tell you that miracles can happen if you can believe in something that is greater than yourself and can communicate with your spiritual core inside of you. To get in touch with this spiritual core, refer back to the "heart" exercises in Strategy 2.1. We are the artists. We can change the picture that has been painted for us. Know that it does take some hard work and constant effort over a period of time. At times it may seem like you may not be making much progress, but stick with it. You are "growing roots," and although there may not be visible evidence of growth at first, trust that it will show itself as you continue to grow.

The 7 Steps to Building High Self-Esteem

This chapter has many strategies for building self-esteem and they are not just theory. These strategies come from many areas I've chosen to be the best of the healing arts and social sciences and they have helped millions empower their lives. Below you will find three strategies that you can practice. Find quiet time by yourself to allow yourself to direction your attention inside. Make sure you are not interrupted during this time.

Step 1 – Communicate with your Inner Child

Step one is to get in touch or cultivate a relationship with that "Inner child" inside of you that has been hurt by your parenting or the society. Now this might sound a little "touchy feely, " but you might be surprised at how much happier and fun life can be when you learn to do this. You'll basically learn how to parent your inner child. It's been said, "It's never too late to have a happy childhood." Know that it does take some hard work and constant effort over a period of time. At times it may seem like you may not be making much progress, but stick with it. You are "Growing roots," and although there may not be visible evidence of growth at first, trust that it will show itself as you continue to grow.

To cultivate a relationship with your inner child, or what Carl Jung referred to as the divine child, it is important to first identify some characteristics of the inner child. The inner child is the part of you which feels like the little boy or girl inside you and feels your deepest emotional needs for trust, love, affection, and security. While being alive, creative, enthusiastic, and playful, it is also the part of you that still carries the pain of your childhood that can include feelings of anger, fear, loneliness, insecurity, shame, or guilt. The inner child can also be manipulative, rebellious, obedient, and selfish.

He or she usually wants to play all day and not work. And he or she wants attention. The key is to allow the child to express him or herself, instead of suppressing and scolding his or her desires. When you are working on your hundreds of tasks during the day, the inner child is usually telling you to relax, forget this work stuff and go have fun. Many people ignore or deny this need in themselves and become workaholics or stressed out because they don't listen to his or her inner voice inside. By allowing your child to express him or herself, you will feel happier, more creative, more peaceful, and more yourself. How do we allow the inner child to be expressed?

Visualization: Heal Mother and Father Wounds Within

First, you can use visualization to re-experience your inner child in your growing years. The way you do this is, turn out lights, maybe light a candle in your house, and put on some soft, New Age music in the background. And imagine drifting back through the years of the 1990's, 80's 70's, 60's and so on. Start to see that little child while you are at your old house where you grew up between the ages of four to ten. What does it look like? What is there? Who lives in the house? Involve the senses like the smells in the house, conversations you hear, what is seen, what is felt through touch, and so on. Then, as that little child, imagine you are in your mother's arms. Is it joyful? Then take that in. Imagine her asking you why you are sad? Is it because she didn't give you enough attention? Did she hurt you or neglect you in some way. *Tell your mother what kind of love you needed back then.*

Then, imagine you are in your father's arms. Is it joyful? Imagine him asking you why you are sad. Is it because he didn't give you enough attention? Did he hurt you in some way? *Tell your father what kind of love you needed from him.* Then, tell both your parents how you feel about them as this young child and that you longed to be with them, that you wanted their love, and so on.

Know that this is an intense exercise that is likely to bring on some tears if not weeping. The point of the visualization is not to blame your parents for what you didn't get growing up. Your parents most likely did the best they could with their available personal resources, which may have been quite limited as a result of the limitations they experienced with their parents. The point is to ***release*** the emotions and rebuild your current emotional mindset and stability. Old patterns that are based on fear and anger will tend to interfere with your current relationships until you can identify and release them. Once you can acknowledge and eventually forgive your parents for what they were unable to give you, you can then start the journey and joy of caring for yourself. If possible, you can do this work with a parent on the conditions that they are still alive, they would be supportive, and/or you can handle it without being disrespectful. If not, seek professional help from a therapist or other professional.

Write a Letter to Your Inner Child

There are three ways to help you achieve this. One, get a photograph of yourself when you were young. Look at the photo before writing. Two, use the following subject material. Write about how you feel about your child. How would you like to get to know him or her better? And, what would you like to learn from him or her? Three, nurture your child by communicating to the child using the three ego personalities or inner voices. Their names are the parent, adult, and child.

The **parent** is the part inside you that represents the messages and voices you hear in your mind that sound like a parent who uses lots of "shoulds" and "You ought to's." It usually creates the negative self-talk that occurs. The positive parent personality in you is nurturing and loving and the negative one is critical and demanding.

The **child** inside you, like I've mentioned, holds all the strong feelings and hurts, is sensitive, and wants to play most of the time.

The **adult**, is the objective voice that is rational, works with the truth and the facts, and is the peacemaker between the parent and the child. You can promise that you, as the adult, will listen more to the needs of the inner child instead of ignoring him or her. You can tell the inner parent that things don't always have to go right or that you don't have to be perfect at everything but you appreciate their concern.

So for example, it's 8pm and your inner parent is screaming at you to get your homework done. The inner *parent* says if you don't get it done, you're going to fail your class and then maybe drop out of school. Your *child* voice, says, you are always pressuring me, forget homework, you've been working all day, take the rest of the night off for god's sake. The *adult* being the peacemaker and rational voice, says, alright, *parent* we are going to allow the child to have some fun, by watching her favorite TV show, eating an ice cream and taking a hot bath. Afterward, I promise to do my homework so both of you are satisfied. Do these inner voices sound familiar? They should! Every time you write this, you develop the ability to think all of this right on the spot so that you can manage anxiety better and achieve peace of mind. The assignment in Exercise 3 of keeping an insight journal for the next twenty-one days by recording the inner messages of the parent, adult, and child allows you to identify and unlock suppressed anger, hurt, and fear that prevent happiness.

Step 2 – Schedule Self-care Activities To Meet Your Psychological Needs

If you recall Maslow's hierarchy of needs, after the physiological and safety needs were met, the psychological needs or the belonging, esteem and self-actualization needs emerge. That is where many of us are stuck. As I list some needs, ask yourself two questions. "In what areas do I come up short?" And, "how can I get those needs met." Let's start.

Is your need for friendship satisfied? If not, you can start taking the initiative by starting conversations, joining clubs, groups, etc., and setting up fun gatherings. Next, is your need for "being listened to," satisfied? You can often have people in your life that talk and talk but never listen to you and your thoughts. Next, is your need for respect and validation being met? Learning to make requests and set boundaries for others brings that to you. Next, is your need for physical touching and being touched be satisfied? Do you get enough hugs, pat on the backs, and so forth during your day? How about your spiritual need to connect with the Divine or higher power? Are you taking time and putting attention there like you experienced in the Heart meditation. Is your need for creative expression being met? You might have a job in which the routine details are all you attend to and you are not really using your talents. Ask yourself, how you can get this need met when you are not working. Next, is your sense of freedom and independence being met? It is important to get away by yourself or with a different crowd to bring more balance into your life. Are you making room and satisfying your need for fun and play? Maybe scheduling into your day and week, more movies, dancing, dinners, walks on the beach, getting a massage, walking in the park, playing your favorite music and dancing to it, sleeping under the stars outside, taking a scenic drive, buying new clothes, reading an inspirational book, writing a letter to an old friend, or listening to a positive, motivation tape. Some of these should help to satisfy this need for you. Next, are you satisfying the need of making a contribution or serving others? By satisfying this list, you are serving yourself to better be able to serve others in your community and the society. Are there hospitals, shelters, social service agencies you can volunteer your time for an hour or so? We automatically start polishing our heart and become happier when we serve others and ourselves in combination. Are you setting goals, like fulfilling this needs list, and achieving them? This vastly increases self-esteem. Is your need for sexual expression or intimacy being fulfilled? We start to feel cold, distant, and alienated when these needs are not met and may turn to unhealthy forms of attachments to satisfy them. And last, is your need for trust and loyalty being satisfied? It is important to find good friends that you can trust and be intimate with. Spend less time with people who aren't able to be that way with you and more time with those who can. This can mean spending less time with your best friend because your best friend might not fit that description.

Satisfying this list of needs will automatically build self-esteem, because like watering a plant, you are putting time and attention on feeding yourself instead of ignoring your needs just to get by in life. Make these self-care activities your next goal in life.

Step 3 – Write a Support Letter to Yourself

Writing a letter to yourself by using the six-step method of getting into an emotion that you learned from Strategy 2.3 will help you to heal self-criticism. Remember, write about what angered you first, then hurt, then fear, then regret, intention, and love and appreciation.

For example, the **anger part** could proceed, "You are such a loser. You complain about not feeling well, and never having to time to have fun in your life, when you are the one that schedules your day. You're such a victim and I'm sick of hearing it. You have to be Miss. Super achiever, and exhaust yourself by over-doing things. I'm fed up with your excuses so start acting a like a grown woman.

The **hurt part** could proceed.....It hurts me to see you beat yourself up this way. It hurts that you drive yourself so hard to please others while you try to be your best. It makes me feel sad to watch you put yourself down and compare yourself to other people. It hurts to see you treat yourself with so much criticism when I know you need so much love.

The **fear part** could proceed....I'm afraid you will always beat yourself up and make yourself sick if you keep working this hard being overextended. I'm scared that your insecurities will run your life and ruin it. I fear that you will never realize the wonderful person you are and how much you have done for yourself and your family.

The **regret part** could proceed.....I'm sorry I don't tell you more how wonderful you really are. You've achieved a lot and I never acknowledge your progress. I'm sorry I compare you to other people and make you feel you aren't good enough the way you are. I'm sorry for not scheduling more time for play and just keep pushing you toward the next goal. Please forgive me for not loving you enough.

The **intention part** could proceed....I want to start scheduling more fun time for you. I want you to start asking people for what you need instead of always pretending you are so strong. I promise to remind you when you get overworked, that you need a rest and you don't have anything to prove to anyone.

The **love part** could proceed....I am so proud of all the wonderful things you do to help other people. You deserve the best and to be loved. I believe in you and am so proud that you have come so far and worked so hard. Thank you for writing this letter and I will always love and support you.

If you are writing to your inner child, you can write with your opposite writing hand. You will start to feel like that little child and the memory of learning to write brings you closer to that time. Since, I'm right handed, I write with my left hand. Write more than one letter. Make it a habit to write at least one a month. If you journal write, you could do it then. This is a powerful tool.

The other four of seven steps to building self-esteem are contained in the strategies in this chapter. By building self-esteem, you generate self-love by caring for yourself. You then will be in a better place and have greater ability to love others around you. What is more important than this? Dr. Serokin, Harvard sociologist, wrote, "Love is the single most powerful force for influencing and changing behaviors." In my view, most scientists and doctors ignore love. Nobody wants to teach it. Novelists mistreat it. And Hollywood perverts it. Anthony Walsh in his book called, Human nature and love says, "Love is the most beautiful, powerful, meaningful experience of humanity. Love insulates the child, comforts the aging, cures the sick, raises the fallen, comforts the tormented, inspires the composer, the painter, the artist, and the poet."

The 4 Mental Archetypes

- The 4 mental archetypes (mindsets we all share) will make you confront your powerlessness, fears, and obstacles to self-empowerment.
- Ask which one is controlling or influencing you in any moment.
- Develop rapport with it to identify when they are "controlling the show" so you can withdraw its authority on you and instead, empower yourself.

1. The Victim – This archetype/mindset blames everyone and everything for their circumstances.

- Fears aloneness
- It believes the illusion that everybody has authority over his or her lives and they have none.
- It is controlled by fear of not enough money.

- Fear of change = fear of aloneness
- It attracts other victims and share an energetic bond
- When taken advantaged of and they learn from it, they may say, "I will never be taken advantaged of again."
- MONEY: Sees money as the force others have to control them. Debt is their false god. They give too much fear and power to it. Visualize chipping away at the block of debt. Then, visualize melting the debt. Ask how does the debt serve you? Then say "Thanks for the role, now goodbye."

2. **The Prostitute** – This archetype/mindset negotiates (sell it to others) their power (physically, their opinions, their thoughts and emotions).

- It sells one's honor, integrity, energy and time to get approval, a paycheck, or money.
- The core of self-esteem is that you can't be bought. Earthly pleasures aren't higher than spiritual pleasures.
- It asks, "Can you be bought?" so you don't have to feel vulnerable. It's not usually the body but it is the prostituting of your power, intuition, dignity, and your inner authority.
- MONEY: The wife who knew her husband had a continual affair with her friend says to herself, "I must get pregnant so I can be guaranteed financial security. She sells her Heart for safety/security. She ended up having cancer of her uterus, the place where she prostituted herself (Caroline Myss 1996).
- The man who says, "I must stay in the marriage for the children." under bad circumstances.

3. **The Saboteur –** This archetype/mindset tells you how and why you will fail before it tells you how you can succeed.

- It will find your weakest link (approval) and pulls out the fear of yesterday to not act. Therefore they will miss opportunities.
- It says if you fail or are successful…what ever will you do?
- Ask yourself how many times and different ways do you tell yourself you will fail or "it" won't happen for you." It works hand in hand with the Victim.

4. **The Child-** This archetype/mindset looks to the external world for validation.

- It shakes with fear that he/she will be harmed or abandoned.
- It holds the hope that one can mend the parent relationship. Ex) Anne Frank "I still believe mankind is good." That's her child voice talking.
- MONEY: When the child is in charge, the person doesn't save or manage money well. Money, with the child, is the engine, not the caboose on one's life path.
- LIFEPATH: Age 38-45 is a passage point where one can become unhappy with their direction in life and time is the most practical commodity. If the child has too strong of a voice, they will not change directions to improve their condition. They'll say, "I'm not ready yet (school), or "I don't know enough." They're afraid to live and afraid to die.

Example: An opportunity arises like, a job promotion, being a leader of a group, or something similar.
The Child says, "I'm scared because of things that have happened in the past."
The Victim says, "The same old thing reminds me of Jim and you know how that turned out."
The Prostitute says, "You could have a blast if you make a lot of money."
The Saboteur says, "You can't handle all that responsibility; whatever will you do? And then doesn't act.

Self Messages from The Four Stress Sub-personalities

Insistent thoughts become annoying and distract us from being focused, centered, and goal-oriented. The more we control our own thoughts and voices instead of them controlling us (for example, trying to go to sleep but the mind keeps racing), the more we become the "conductor to our own symphony." If we don't get control, little sub-personalities emerge that dominate our whole personality. They are the Worrier, the Perfectionist, the Critic, and the Victim.

The Worrier – The worrier produces anxiety within themselves by imagining the worst-case scenario. When they imagine confronting their fear, they think of disaster and catastrophe because they overestimate the odds of something bad happening. Their favorite saying is the "What if" question. What if I'm alone and there's nobody to call, or what if, I'm so weak I start crying?, or what if they see me shaking? Again, use the questions in Strategy 2.2 of the self-understanding chapter if you identify the worrier in you. Some questions include: What is the evidence for this? Is this always true? What are the odds? Am I looking at the whole picture? Also, use the Heart meditations.

The Perfectionist - This type promotes chronic stress and burnout because they believe that their efforts are never good enough and that they should be working harder and have things under control. They are intolerant of mistakes or setbacks and their self-worth is dependent on externals outcomes like achievement, money, and acceptance by others and so on. Their favorite saying is I should always be.....and then fill in the blank – whether it's unselfish, the best, pleasant and nice and so on. Again, ask the questions I mentioned before to empower yourself if you identify the perfectionist in you.

The Critic - The critic inside the person is constantly judging and evaluating their behavior emphasizing weaknesses and flaws. It will criticize the person for not performing at their best, or it will compare them with others while usually seeing others coming out more favorably. It ignores the positive qualities of the person. Their favorite saying is, "What a disappointment you are" or "That was stupid." The inner voice could be personified by the voice of the person's mother or father. This type promotes low self-esteem more than any other type. Again, ask the questions I mentioned before to empower yourself if you identify the critic in you.

The Victim - The victim usually feels helpless or hopeless. This personality produces more depression than any of the four sub-personalities. It convinces the person that they are not making progress, or a certain condition is incurable, or the road is too hard and long to try. They feel deprived, defective, and unworthy while complaining and regretting things they often have control of. Their favorite expression is "I can't and I'll never be able to..." and then fill in the blank. Again, ask the questions I mentioned before to empower yourself if you identify the victim in you.

Therefore it becomes vital to practice living in the present. This one skill is perhaps the most important skill to master because it gives you the ability to respond to stress appropriately, view situations from a different angle, and enjoy life more fully . All sources of stress and anxiety are either a thought in the past or a thought in the future. The more present we are, the more joyful and less anxious we become. Practice the exercises at the end of this strategy.

We Are Not Our Thoughts

Your "true-self" is not just represented by your thoughts. When you say or do things that you later regret, it is self-defeating to scold yourself and think your thoughts and actions are what only represent who you are. We can always change and grow. In other words, kick the act, not the actor. Human weaknesses and faults are part of everyone's being. You are unique and have a rare combination of talents and characteristics that are unlike anyone else in the universe. You are different but not "less than" others. *It will be important to work on becoming free of any need to prove yourself to others.*

Exercise 1

A. No matter how bad or unworthy you think you are, realize that each of us is born with certain gifts. Parts of you have not been encouraged and nurtured from childhood. Therefore, give yourself a break and permission to feel the sadness, anger, etc., before beating yourself up. Have compassion for that part of you.

- Below, identify what you "beat yourself up" for. *Example: "I'm so stupid because I always let people talk me into doing things I don't want to do," or "I'll never get an 'A' paper, because I'm too dumb."*
- Also, write down what unhealthy and healthy messages you received in childhood from both your parents and society.

B. Below, write down which of the four mental archetypes (victim, prostitute, saboteur, child) dominates your personality more than the others. Write down the circumstances, the things or people that trigger this archetype in you, and possible solutions for getting control of it.

C. Below, write down which of the four stress sub-personalities (worrier, perfectionist, critic, victim) dominates your personality more than the others. Write down the circumstances, the things or people that trigger this archetype in you, and possible solutions for getting control of it.

Exercise 2

Find a quiet place to sit or lie down and perform the "Healing mother and father wounds" Visualization from the material on the previous pages. It is helpful to play slow, soft, "new age" type music in the background as you. Afterward, get a photograph of yourself when you were young. Look at the photo before writing. Write about how you feel about your child. Write how you would like to get to know him or her better. And, what you would like to learn from him or her. Care for your child by communicating to the child using the three ego personalities or inner voices which are the parent, adult, and child. It is powerful to write with your opposite hand as you will feel like a child when you first began to write years ago. Write this in a journal book or on your computer.

Exercise 3 (The Insight Journal)

As you learned there are 3 ego personalities inside each human being-- the parent, adult, and child. Each individual constantly shifts from one ego personality to another throughout the day. What ego state are you in right now? The idea is to bring more awareness to the ego states you are in from moment to moment. When you can identify them, you can more easily balance your thoughts and control your mind. This occurs when you give more attention and power to the adult voice and when appropriate honoring the wishes of the parent and child voice. The adult needs to be in control of the show instead of the other two.

The Parent part of the personality inside you represents the messages and voices you hear in your mind that sound like a parent's voice. These statements usually contain "shoulds" and "oughts" and other rules for living. A positive ego Parent state is the nurturing parent voice, and a negative one is the critical/demanding parent voice.
The Adult ego state is the objective part of our personality and gathers information about what is going on. It is not emotional but works with the facts. Its thinking is analytical and it acts rationally. It is the peacemaker between the parent and the child.
The Child ego state consists of feelings, impulses, and spontaneous acts. It is manipulative, rebellious or obedient, egocentric, and creative. It usually wants to play all day and not work. And it wants attention.

A. Write down how your inner **parent** (the critical voice) talks to your inner **child** (the one who feels hurt/pain/ignored the most) and vice versa.
Hint: What self-care activities from the psychological needs could the **adult** recommend to the **parent**.

*For example, the parent might say to the child**,** "You're so stupid for trying," or "I told you that you'd screw up again. You'll never make it." Then the child might say, for example, "You are constantly putting me down, so just leave me alone," or "I can't make any mistakes without you criticizing me, and I'm sick of it." Finally, give a voice to the **adult** (the rational, mature voice). As the adult**,** tell the child how sorry you are that he/she has had to endure a lot of pain and that the adult will try to help the parent be more understanding. Also, promise that you, as the adult, will listen more to the needs of the child instead of ignoring him or her. Tell the parent that things don't always have to be right or that he/she doesn't always have to be successful (e.g., be on time, give a top performance) and yet you do appreciate that he/she does want the best for you* (Bradshaw, 1990).
Some common parental messages that often go unsaid include:

"Don't make mistakes,"	"Don't be important,"	"Don't be a child,"
"Don't succeed,"	"Don't be yourself"	"Don't belong,"
"Don't talk,"	"Don't trust,"	"Don't feel."
"Don't say no"	"Don't exist"	"Don't be intimate"

B. Keep a journal for the next 21 days and record the inner messages from the parent, adult, and child each day of the 21 days. Describe the circumstances involved as you give a voice to all three of these ego states. Your pain is a part of you. At the end of the 21 days, write a ½-page summary on the experience and what you learned.

Strategy 4.2

Surround yourself daily with positive, supportive, and encouraging people.

Keep away from people who try to belittle your ambition. Small people always do that, but the really great ones make you feel that you, too, can become great.
Mark Twain

The critics know the way, but they can't drive the car.
Kenneth Tynan

The Importance of Supportive Friends

Think of the special people in your life who validate, compliment, and try to instill confidence in you. These people are usually genuine and happy and enjoy helping you. It is important that you are open to their gentle criticism. Ask them to give you feedback on areas of you that they feel could contribute to your personal growth. It's fine if there is only one person in your life with whom you feel close enough to do this. If there are no people in your life like this, then entrust a school/college counselor or other professional to help you in this endeavor. Most people become jealous of others' success and will try to bring them down if they see them succeeding. That is why we need positive people in our lives-- so that we can move beyond these obstacles. Slowly eliminate as many negative and discouraging people, as possible, out of your life.

The Consequences of Unsupportive Friends

You probably have known some people who were bright, strong-minded, independent, and "well-parented." Before long, however, they began to mingle with the wrong crowd. Almost every time, the negative crowd converts this "strong" person. The negative influence is like a virus that takes over a human body. This independent person usually estimates that he/she is strong enough to be his/her own person and to withstand peer pressure. This is not always the case. In fact, these people usually take on the negative values of the crowd they surround themselves with over a very short period of time. My wife and I avoid this problem by not spending time with people who do not support and respect our values and our marriage. If you had the choice, would you surround yourself with sick, coughing, sneezing, bed-ridden people on a day-to-day basis and estimate that you are strong enough to withstand the germs? This parallel is quite similar. One deals with physical health, the other emotional health.

Exercise 1

Make a list of the positive people in your life that you can entrust.

____

____

____

____

____

____

____

____

Exercise 2

Write down different ways you can bring new positive people into your life. For example: making an effort to join a club/group at church, college, community, or getting closer with a friend or relative you believe might be a positive and encouraging force in your life.

Exercise 3

Make a commitment to call these people and schedule time together. Make sure that part of the time spent is around your area of personal growth. Also, ask yourself if you are with a boy/girlfriend or spouse that always seems to be discouraging to you or acting selfish. Make requests to these people and give them ultimatums if they don't honor your requests. For example: "Going to a party sounds good, Joe, but I need you to understand that I have to study tonight. Can you respect that?" If they don't, tell them that you question their friendship if their needs always seem to come before yours. So, spend less time with discouraging, selfish people and more time with encouraging, selfless people.

Who will you call and when?

Strategy 4.3
Read, listen, and watch personal growth material.

Food For The Mind

Don't just say to yourself, "I wish I had self-esteem and felt good about myself." Do something about it every day. Read books, listen to tapes, and watch videos about how to learn and get the most out of yourself. This type of material provides the nourishment needed for the health of our emotional and mental chemistry in the same way food nourishes our body chemistry.

Peak performers are those people who hire motivational coaches to help them exceed their limitations and comfort zones. Since many of us cannot afford to hire these personal coaches, the next best thing is to listen and view the material presented by these motivational coaches who have expertise in your subject area. It doesn't make a lot of sense to tackle some of these issues on your own when there is a wealth of resources, experts, and programs available to you at your fingertips. Take advantage of it and know that "nobody grows on their own" without getting help.

Exercise 1
Write down which type of personal growth material you want to view or listen to.

____
____
____

Exercise 2
Buy, rent, or check out from the library different books, cassette tapes, and/or videos. Listen and view these learning tools throughout your week. Listen to them on your way to work, while running errands or while exercising. Perhaps the biggest supplier of personal growth cassette tapes and videos is Nightingale-Conant Corp. **Call for a free catalog at 1-800-525-9000.**

Exercise 3
Tonight, for 30 minutes, read some personal growth material. Write below what you learned.

____
____
____
____
____
____
____
____
____
____
____
____
____
____

Strategy 4.4
Practice getting approval from yourself instead of from others.

If you are being mistreated, you are cooperating with the treatment.
Robert Anthony

Be yourself, everyone else is taken.
Oscar Wilde

Approval: Losing Connection To Our Self

We usually compromise our own values in order to get approval from others. When we do so, we become a lost soul and lose touch with who we really are and what we really care about. The approval- seeking person becomes like a programmed robot who only acts in response to its master, the people they rely on to praise them and approve of who they are. Because many of us did not get the approval we so desperately needed during childhood to develop our identity and ego structures, we spend our adult energy searching for this approval from others. Realize that not everyone will like you, nor would you want them to, considering all of the strange, unhealthy, and cruel people in society. This is why it is so important to surround yourself with positive people as mentioned in Strategy 4.2.

Re-think being a people pleaser. People-pleasers often take care of others at the expense of themselves and go to great lengths to avoid conflict. Depression and physical ailments can start to set in. Treat yourself as nicely as you treat others.

Resist Comparisons To Others

We often don't see our uniqueness, beauty, and special qualities because we compare ourselves to others. Don't compare yourself, in any way, to other people (grades, sports, decor, personality). Would you fault the rose because it is not an orchid? Are trees unworthy compared to birds because birds can fly and trees cannot? This comparative thinking is detrimental to self-esteem because it constantly looks for something or someone that is perceived as being better. When we do this, we compromise our character and self-respect. You will automatically exceed others' qualities when you focus on being the best you can be, beating your own record, and staying on your purpose in life.

Examples of Approval Seekers

There are famous people who, because they feared disapproval from others, have sabotaged their own mission and successes. For example:

- Lyndon Johnson didn't stop the Vietnam War even when he and his staff admitted we couldn't win. He was afraid his friends in Congress and the American people would see him as the man who 'lost the first U.S. war.' He feared that the label of losing the war would overshadow his contributions of his Great Society social programs.
- The Milgram Study, in the early 1960's, proved that approval from authority figures was so powerful in our country that most people were willing in the study to administer an intense painful shock to a person for getting wrong answers because the scientist told them to do so.
- When we master both inner and outer communication, we become whole human beings. However, think of celebrities who have <u>only</u> been able to master their outer communication.

- Jimi Hendrix	- Whitney Houston	- River Phoenix	- Michael Jackson
- Curt Cobain	- Amy Winehouse	- John Belushi	- Elvis Presley
- Anna Nicole Smith	- Chris Farley	- Heath Ledger	- O. J. Simpson

It can have disastrous results!

Bring Lightness Into Your Life

Be able occasionally to laugh at yourself. When we take ourselves too seriously, it gives more power to our ego, which craves self-protection and does not allow us to be ourselves and grow. By taking things more lightly, you will develop humility and others will automatically like to be around you. It also gives other people the comfort to accept their flaws and be themselves more easily in your presence. It often helps to rehearse the affirmation, "Smile, laugh, and lighten up on yourself."

Think of one thing that you do that you are bad at or unsuccessful at and tell at least one person. Work it into a conversation. For example: "You think that's bad? You know my memory. I can't remember a person's name if my life depended on it. It's definitely not one of my strengths." Or "My memory 'sucks' so much that I forget a person's name 5 seconds after he tells me." Don't abuse or shame yourself in the process but, instead, say to yourself, "It's not that important. It's just who I am and where I'm at now at this stage in my life."

The Proper Way To Cope

We go to great lengths to change our external world by plastic surgery, getting approval, weight loss, make-up, saying the right thing, money, fame, and attention when these things don't last. It is only in the changing of our internal world that we'll get everlasting change, integrity that meets every challenge and provides the greatest joy. To distract ourselves from dealing with inner pain, we often seek excessive outside excitement such as sports events, clothes, shopping, concerts, electronic toys, television, computers programs, and the like. We must become entertained by the silence of the "heart" and direct our attention inward. Only then can we have a truly successful outer world experience.

Exercise 1

Practice letting go of approval by challenging yourself to experience others' judgments. Begin with small steps. For example, doing something outrageous like wearing clothes that clash, acting childlike or playful, etc. I used to practice this exercise by walking to the market *with my bathrobe on* early in the morning. Then I would close my eyes and almost feel other people looking and judging me for my attire. It was soon after that their judgment had no effect on me whatsoever. It is one of the most liberating experiences I've ever had.

Small behaviors I could start are: ______________________________

Exercise 2

Keep an Actions and Feelings Journal and write in it about the times during the day when you feel the need to get approval. Write how you felt about each circumstance. This exercise will help you to monitor your thoughts around this issue and will assist you in slowly eliminating this type of dependency. Start with your first entry below.

____
____
____
____
____
____

Exercise 3

A. Make a list of the more difficult situations that will help you improve your skills of letting go of approval. Examples include: Standing up to your spouse, mother, father, in-laws, etc., when they demean, belittle, or tease you. Or, it could be standing up for your principles when the pressure to conform to the rest of the group is strong. You should feel very proud of yourself after doing this.

____
____
____
____
____
____
____

B. Look at this list every day by either putting it in your wallet/purse or placing it where you'll see it often like a bathroom mirror, refrigerator, bulletin board, etc.
Ask yourself if you are the type of person who usually makes a "mountain out of a molehill," (makes things heavier than they actually are--maximizes) or makes "molehills out of mountains" (makes things lighter than they should be--minimizes). Most people in this program probably maximize the irritants in their life. Make a list of the insignificant or unimportant things that you maximize.

____
____
____
____
____
____
____
____

C. Now visualize the thing that you maximize. See it as big, bright, clear, and make it even bigger. Now do the opposite. See it getting smaller and smaller, shrinking and melting into a little dot onto the floor. Example: Your in-laws constantly give you advice. Make it bigger by seeing them as giants pointing down at you at what you ought to do. Then, as you grow, make them shrink smaller and smaller until they are little dots on the floor as their voices get higher and higher. It becomes humorous as you are then in a place to be able to give less power to them.

Strategy 4.5

Become good (skilled), then great (an authority), then an expert in one subject area or thing that you enjoy.

Practice Makes Expert

A major contributor to high self-esteem and feeling competent is expertise in an area of interest. The expertise you choose will help you to appreciate unique abilities in yourself because you are learning it and earning it. This will give you confidence in your ability to accomplish and master other things. You are skilled in some things more than others. Example: Someone may say, "I am skilled at playing piano. I am an authority on golf. I am an expert accountant."

Business consultants assert with regard to your area you want to excel at that:
If you practice 1 hour a day for 1 year, you will be considered skilled in that area.
If you practice 1 hour a day for 3 years, you will be considered an authority in that area.
If you practice 1 hour a day for 5 years, you will be considered an expert in that area.

You can become an expert in any subject that you deem as valuable.
Below are examples of subjects that you could learn to become better at:

Music
Sports
Politics
Social problems
Nutrition
Economics
Multicultural issues

Art
Relating to people
Studying/learning
Parenting
History
Gardening
Spirituality/Religions

Exercise 1

Write down the one subject area or thing you want to work on for the next five years.

____
____
____
____

Then, write down the reasons why you want to work on this subject area.

____
____
____
____
____
____
____
____
____
____
____
____

Exercise 2

Write down the tools, books, and people you will need and be utilizing to help you become an expert in this one subject area.

Exercise 3

Write down a schedule of when and where you will practice this new skill every day. For example: I will practice the guitar every day after dinner in the family room for one hour.

When?

Where?

Strategy 4.6
Customize an exercise and nutritional health program.

It Does A Body Good

We are better able to have compassion for ourselves and others when our body feels good. When we are lethargic, sick, or have low energy levels, it prevents us from doing the emotional work mentioned in this book thus far. There is no better way to feel good physically than to exercise and eat healthy.

Consult your doctor before activating the following points on exercise and nutrition.

The Value of Exercise

Studies show that all we need is a minimum of 15-20 minutes of exercise a day. Not bad out of 24 hours! No, sex does not count! Yet most of us put exercise off because we feel that an exercise program takes hours a day to be successful. This couldn't be farther from the truth. The Seligman (1994) study revealed that huge benefits result when exercising minimally to moderately. According to Seligman (1994), when they studied people who chose moderate to maximum amounts of exercise, zero benefits and, sometimes, negative outcomes occurred. They got sick more often and injured themselves more frequently. Dr. Kenneth Cooper, founder of the Cooper Aerobics Center in Dallas, believes too much exercise stimulates an outpouring of free radicals, which are chemicals formed in the body when oxygen is burned (Press Enterprise, Feb. 13, 1996). Studies show that exercise improves our immune system, lowers risk of diseases, elevates our moods throughout the day, gives us energy, and increases our chances of being happy. See below.

In two randomized, controlled studies, David Nieman, a professor of health and exercise science at Appalachian State University in Boone, N.C., compared overweight, sedentary women who began a program of brisk walking for 45 minutes, five days a week, with matched controls who remained sedentary. He found the walkers suffered only half as many sick days from colds as the control group. More intriguing, Nieman found that the number of immune cells, some of which normally live in the spleen and lymph nodes, increased temporarily in the walkers' bloodstreams.

So many people try to stick to an exercise program. Their efforts may last for one to four weeks but then they stop. Either people a) can't find the time or b) they get bored. It is up to you to see how valuable exercise is. You must find the time to make it happen. Boredom with exercise is one of the reasons people do not stay committed to a program. The best advise for staying motivated to exercise comes from Robert Lewis Stevenson who suggests that people seek out affordable and enjoyable recreation. Don't do something that you hate and would dread doing. Find something that is convenient, that works in your schedule, and is not dreadful. For example, you could:

- Perform aerobic exercise
- Jog
- Perform yoga
- Swim
- Golf
- Dance in your living room w/ motivational music
- Lift weights
- Bicycle or stationary exercise bicycle
- Perform calisthenics
- Bowl

So if you only have 10 minutes in the morning to exercise, don't say to yourself, "Well, I blew it and I'll try to do it tomorrow." Do your 10 minutes in the morning and find 5 minutes during the

rest of the day or when you come home from work. Remember, make it affordable, enjoyable, and convenient. I exercise in my office by closing the door and performing the following regimen for 10 minutes.
a. leg lifts, sit ups, push ups, etc.
b. yoga: the plow, the cobra, and the crawl
It's a great quick pick-me-up and it gets you through the afternoon 'blahs'. You can do the same in your own living room through dance, calisthenics, and aerobic exercises.

There are three areas to build your body: Aerobic, Stretching, and Muscle Resistance Exercises.

1. AEROBIC EXERCISES - the heart's ability to pump blood through the body.
The heart can only be exercised through working out the large muscle groups. A strong physical heart enables the spiritual "heart" to be more clear and efficient.
Examples of aerobic exercises:
- rapid walking or jogging
- swimming
- aerobic dance
- bicycling
- cross country skiing
- yard work

This type of exercise will give you more energy throughout your day than anything. It also increases your metabolism, which helps you lose weight faster.

2. STRETCHING EXERCISES - helps bring blood flow and oxygen to all the muscle groups. This can be a warm up and should be done before and after cardiovascular exercises.
Examples of stretching exercises:
- stretching arms, legs, stomach, back, etc.
- yoga, which can be aerobic & stretching

3. MUSCLE RESISTANCE EXERCISES - occurs when muscles are pushed with resistance. You can either tone your muscles by working out moderately or strengthen and build your muscles through lifting weights. Examples of muscle resistance exercises include:
- push-ups
- sit-ups
- pull-ups
- lifting weights

When lifting weights, you will build strength during your last repetitions when the muscle fibers rupture and the nerve fibers register the pain. Then, within 48 hours, the fibers are made stronger. That is why you should exercise that muscle group only every other day. Weights should be heavy enough that you can only lift them 8 - 10 times before needing a rest. You can get a good workout with just buying two dumbbells and a weight bench or use some heavy cans of tomato sauce in your pantry.

By consistently exercising, your pulse rate will go down as your heart and oxygen-processing systems will become more efficient, allowing you to experience joy and energy.
It is best to start slowly and be aware of the latest research findings with **your doctor's recommendations** and your common sense. Evans (1996), recommends the following do's and don'ts.

DO's
- Follow the "neck up" rule for exercising with a cold: If symptoms are in the nose, exercise is ok.
- If you run, a good goal is 10 to 15 miles a week. More than that won't boost longevity or health, and running more than 30 miles a week may be detrimental to joints.

DON'Ts
- Don't exercise if you have symptoms below the neck such as a bad cough, a fever, or muscle aches. Muscle aches may be a sign of infection with the coxsackie virus. Exercise can cause this virus to migrate to the heart, with potentially fatal consequences. If you're coughing from bronchitis, exercise may trigger asthma.

- Don't exercise hard for more than 90 minutes at a time to avoid release of cortisol, a stress hormone and immune suppressant.

You Are What You Eat

Most people have dieted in the hopes of losing weight and gaining some control with their eating habits. However, most people fail in their attempts. There are a variety of reasons for this:
a) Emotional: Some people use food to numb themselves so they don't have to deal with the pain in their own lives. Or, they'll overeat to fill a void of emptiness they feel within their soul.
b) Willpower: Some people give up too soon because they fail a few times by splurging on that chocolate cake. They say to themselves, "Here I go, failing one more time. So I might as well quit."
c) Addiction: Most people just love the taste of food and don't want to give up their addiction like a cigarette smoker, despite the health risks.

No one can give somebody the willpower to make a change in his/her life. Some people have to hit rock bottom before they make a dramatic change. Some people have to be hospitalized. The key to making any change in life is to take small steps. The point to any diet change is to make slow change. Eating two additional pieces of fruit a day is a positive change that can set you on your way to greater success.

One of the best ways to improve your nutritional diet is to substitute healthy foods for unhealthy foods. Like developing a taste for wine, you can change your taste buds in a matter of one week. There are excellent substitutes for mayonnaise, butter, sweets, meat, cheese, chocolate, sugar, alcohol, milk, salt, aspirin, and so on that I will describe below.

Take note of the obvious success behaviors. Eliminate: smoking (see doctor or join self-help group); frequent use of medications; and large consumption of alcohol. A woman should eat no more than 25 - 40 grams of fat a day. A 200 pound man should keep his fat intake under 60 grams. Read labels and don't buy items with more than 3 grams of fat for each 100 calories. For example, most fast food burgers = 36 grams of fat, cheesecake pie = 35 grams, Cream of Mushroom Soup = 24 grams, two slices of pizza = 22 grams, 6 oz of spareribs = 48 grams, chili relleno = 36 grams, chocolate chip cookie = 10 grams.

DO's
- Eat a well-balanced diet with plenty of fruits, vegetables, and whole grains.
- Allow time for sleep and rest.

DON'T's
Don't lose weight too fast. Losing more than two pounds a week may compromise T-cells (a type of immune cell). If you exercise and starve yourself, your body may interpret this as stress and pump out cortisol (a stress hormone and immune suppressant).

Exercise 1

A. Spend 5 - 10 minutes doing some kind of aerobic exercise. This gets the blood pumping through your whole body and will give it more endurance throughout the day.
B. Then, spend 5 - 10 minutes doing some kind of stretching exercises. You can do this at home, at work, in the restroom, outside, etc. This, plus anything aerobic, including yoga, can get you through the lulls in the afternoon.
C. Finally, spend 5 - 10 minutes doing some kind of muscle resistance exercise. At the end of this day you will feel balanced and, more importantly, you will be better able to deal with tomorrow's pressures and stressors. Write below any comments of what you learned from the above exercises.

Exercise 2

A) Plan to arrange your shopping list to the following schedule. Change your diet by only eating fruit for breakfast. Studies have shown that our bodies go through an elimination cycle from 4am to 12 noon. If we give our body the chance to eliminate toxins instead of digesting a big breakfast, our bodies will cleanse themselves. Plus, you are adding more fruit to your diet and most people will notice extra energy in their morning from this type of breakfast. If you eat your fruit breakfast (I recommend a fruit smoothie in a blender), at 8am, you will probably be hungry around 10:30am. So, just eat another piece of fruit or two until 12:00 noon. Try this for a week.

B) Improper food combining can also decrease our energy drastically. Most people will notice, from a half hour to an hour after they eat lunch, that they will feel less energy for the following few hours. This is because when we combine a protein with a starch, our stomach will produce acid to break down the protein and alkaline to break down the starch food. When the acid and alkaline mix, they produce a liquid that is less potent to break down the food you just ate. So instead of it taking 3 hours to digest your food, it takes 8 hours, which takes up your body's energy reserves. Examples of improper food combining include: ham sandwich (ham=protein, bread=starch) and steak and potato (steak=protein, potato=starch). Meat, dairy, and nuts are proteins. Breads and pasta noodles are starches. Proper combining includes: steak and vegetables; bean burrito; avocado, tomato, and lettuce sandwich. Try to have your starch or protein with a vegetable or two and notice the difference in how you feel. Try it for five days and record the results below.

Day 1

Day 2

Day 3

Day 4

Day 5

Exercise 3

For the next six days, write down in your daily planner:

a. What you ate throughout the day.

b. How you felt afterward on a scale of 1 – 5 (5 being the worst). You should rate how you felt each day at least four times. It is helpful to see how you feel a few hours after you ate. If you didn't feel good, write a little note describing any pain or moodiness you feel.

EXAMPLE:

Monday

7am – milk with Wheaties Cereal and toast
8 am – 1 score
9am
10am
11am
12 noon – Ham Sandwich with potato chips
1pm – 2 score... felt a headache coming on
2pm – 4 score...headache got stronger
3pm
4pm
5pm
6pm – ate pasta with pesto sauce and a salad
7pm – 3 score...headache gone but felt moody and irritable
8pm
9pm
10pm – ate a Hershey bar
11pm – 4 score...couldn't go to sleep until 12 midnight

c. Then, write below, an interpretation and summary about anything you learned concerning how particular foods made you feel throughout the week. Also write how you intend to eat from now on.

____
____
____
____
____
____
____
____
____
____
____
____
____
____
____
____
____
____

Strategy 4.7

Complete a personalized asset list. Then obtain an encouragement letter from three people and write an encouragement letter for 3 people.

Communicating Appreciation and Love

Getting feedback from others often helps us emphasize those special parts of us that we seem to either take for granted or tend to minimize. Most people do not communicate their love verbally to others. So, chances are, there are people out there who think highly of you, yet, you probably don't know it. But this is one of the most important pieces of information you can get about yourself when it feels like nobody really cares. Some people will say how they deeply feel on their deathbeds, if they are lucky. That is so sad, pointless and unnecessary. Let people know how you feel about them now.

Exercise 1

For your personalized asset list, identify at least 7 skills, 7 qualities or characteristics, and 7 accomplishments/experiences that you are proud of. Write them below.
Example of Skills: communication, selling, clerical, repairing, managing, teaching, problem-solving,
Examples of Qualities/Characteristics: supportive to others, open-minded, responsible, sense of humor, charming, loving, adaptable, nature-oriented, even tempered, etc.
Example of Accomplishments/Experiences: in charge of a project, worked on a team for a good cause, trained others, carried out instructions, solved a problem, sold an idea, good times.

Skills: ______________________________

____

____

Qualities/Characteristics ______________________________

____

____

Accomplishments/Experiences: ______________________________

____

____

Exercise 2

Contact three people and request a Personalized Encouragement Letter to be written by them and given to you as soon as possible. The Encouragement Letter should include: their perceptions of your capabilities, potential, strengths, talents, and qualities and why you are important to them. Make sure that you pick somebody you know who is mature and supportive enough to do this exercise. Most people will be happy to do this for you. If you confront resistance, pick someone else. Also, sometimes it is better to choose someone who you perceive may not automatically and easily say great things about you. You may gain valuable insight.

Exercise 3

Because it is often better to give than to receive, choose three people that you can send a Personalized Encouragement Letter to, describing the characteristics above and the true feelings you have toward that person. Not only will you be spreading cheer, but you will also learn the skill of communicating your important thoughts and emotions. *I suggest you do this without expecting anything in return.*

Chapter Insight & Commitment

After completing this chapter, I learned the following about my self-esteem, the impact of my childhood and societal messages on my self-image, my health, and asset list:

Example: I have discovered that I learned how to be overly critical of myself through my parental conditioning. This has caused me to feel depressed at times and feel a lack of of self-confidence.

I can take active steps to help me achieve my future goals and become more of the person I am or strive to be by:

Example: I will give my parental voice a rest and empower the adult voice within me. I will start journal writing, which will help me to be more happy. This will positively affect those around me in my work environment. This will help me achieve my goal of getting a promotion at work.

CHAPTER 5

Self-Advancement

Using your **Hands** to **Advance** your goals, skills, health, and life.

Purpose: **To learn and employ strategic skills and plans to achieve desired goals.**

Rewards: **Success, Skill Proficiency, Personal Effectiveness, Being Thorough**

Obstacles: **Ignorance, Laziness, Impatience, Routine-oriented**

Consequence: **Stagnation, Being in a Rut, No Growth**

Symbol: **Treasure Map**

Related Web Sites: http://www.mindtools.com/page6.html

Self-Advancement

If you don't have a plan, you will fit into somebody else's plan.
Anthony Robbins

In Chapters 1, 2, and 3, you learned how to empower your identity and change negative thoughts and behaviors. In Chapter 4, you learned how to appreciate others as well as yourself. The first four chapters of the book were designed to help you develop the *"inner skills"* needed to live like never before. The last four chapters of the book are designed to help you develop the *"outer skills"* needed to thrive and produce like never before. In Chapter 5, you will learn an assortment of life skills with the central theme of how to choose, plan, and achieve personal goals you desire. To help you achieve these goals, you will also learn how to think creatively and problem solve on the job and at home, how to develop a budget and increase your cash flow while lowering your expenses, how to improve your decision making skills, and how to identify your dominant intelligence and learning style modalities needed for advanced learning.

It is beyond imagination that we can go through 12 years of education and not receive one day of instruction on how to do a variety of skills such as draft a goal-setting plan, make excellent decisions based on quantifiable and intuitive methods, manage a financial budget (which every adult must perform), and identify a dominant style of learning so that one can maximize his/her comprehension of any educational material. Most personal growth programs exclude this information in their programs. Yet, they are a necessity for long-term success.

After revising your Personal Life Mission Statement in Strategy 5.1, the second through fourth strategies ask you to draft a comprehensive goal-setting plan. This plan is a synthesis of advice from the top experts in goal setting over the past 100 years. This plan also includes a construction of ideas and materials, based on the advice and contributions of working professionals and college students over the past 25 years. Clients attest that this goal-setting plan has helped them achieve their goals much faster than normal because they learned the strategies that enabled them to work smarter, not harder.

Goals are achieved when the four pillars of goal setting are completed. That is, goals must be 1) believable, 2) desirable, 3) achievable, and 4) measurable. When goals are written down, we are more likely to achieve them. A billionaire was once asked what it takes to achieve a challenging goal. The billionaire replied, "If you desire the goal bad enough to sacrifice what it takes to achieve the goal, you most certainly will." Though achieving the goal may bring fulfillment into your life, it is who you become in pursuit of the goal that really matters. Infusing the goal-setting process into your life will help you to be less afraid of taking risks and you'll become more disciplined. You'll may want to help others achieve their goals, you'll be able to identify with the struggles others experience when pursuing a goal, and you'll enjoy many other benevolent outcomes. If our goals are worthy and they help others, then goal setting will be one of the most pleasurable activities you will engage in over your lifetime. However, to live a full life, you ought to have self-improvement goals (like this program), family goals, educational goals, career goals, financial goals, and community contribution goals. When choosing goals to work with in this chapter, be sure that your goals align with your Personal Mission Statement.

Strategy 5.1

Learn to optimize your Decision-Making using the 5-Step Mind & Heart-Smart Decision-Making Method. Revise your Personal Life Mission Statement.

Being Logically Decisive

We are often faced in life with two or more options when making a decision. Situations will frequently dictate which option to choose especially when we are in a hurry to decide. The decision to be made is usually work-related, home related, or just life related. Have you had to make a decision as to which college you should transfer to, which career or major you should pursue, which person you should be in a relationship with or get married to, which job you should pursue, whether you should buy that expensive computer, whether you should confront the insulting co-worker at your employment? This powerful technique below will help guarantee excellent decision making with little or no stress involved. It combines the logic of quantitative reasoning with the intelligence of heart- centered thinking.

Exercise 1

Think of an important decision you need to make that involves two or more options. Write it below

____

____

Then proceed through the following steps.

1. Data Collection and Analysis. Answer the following questions.

* Which data do I need to make this decision?_______________________

____

____

____

____

____

____

____

* Who/What can supply the data and answers for me?___________________

____

____

____

____

____

____

Exercise 2

2. The External "Mind-Smart" Decision Making Method

Once you collect the information, you can then accurately assign rating numbers using the worksheet on the next page to see which decision is more favorable. Use the example below to help you understand. Then complete the worksheet on the next two pages.

1st - List the values-- the reasons that make a decision attractive.

2nd - Weigh the values on a scale of 1 – 10 (10 being what you most want).

3rd - Assign a rating number to each decision. This number should be based on how well each of the decisions satisfies each value on the 1 – 10 scale. In the example on the next page, across from the value of more money, this person may have found out that the Counselor job pays $45,000 a year and the Program Director pays $60,000 a year. He/she might then assign a 6 rating number to the Counselor job and a 9 rating number to the Program Director job. See the next page.

4th - Multiply the weight by the rating number for each decision. Put this number under the decision.

5th - Total/Add the numbers under each decision and note the highest total under each decision.

6th - Double check to see if your values are correct. (See the next page)

Weight	**Values**	**(rating)**	*Decision 1 (Counselor)*	**(rating)**	*Decision2 (Program Director)*
8	More money	6	48	9	72
10	Close to home	6	60	8	80
7	Helping others	9	63	7	49
7	No data work	8	56	2	14
8	No admin. work	7	56	2	16
			Total 283		Total 231

Note: Make sure you don't write both "*helping others*" and "*not helping others*" under the Values category or else that value will cause an inaccurate score. Also, a value negatively stated like the above, "no data work," will give a decision with that value a higher score like the Counselor position received.

3. The Internal "Heart-Smart" Technique.

Use the meditation technique from chapter three. Ten minutes into your meditation, conjure up the problem. As you repeat this process a few times, the solution or best decision should surface in the next five minutes.

4. Discuss decision outcomes with a diversity of experts.

These experts should be people who are knowledgeable about the problem/decision to be made. Take them through the values, weights, and rating numbers to see if they are able to influence points up or down based on their perspective. Make the appropriate changes.

5. Revisit the "Heart-Smart" Technique

The "Heart-Smart" technique will now give you an even clearer picture so you can choose the best option based on both your external and internal sources used in this five-step process.

WORKSHEET

			Decision # 1		***Decision # 2***
			____________		____________
Weight	**Values**	**(rating)**		**(rating)**	
___	____________	___	____________	___	____________
___	____________	___	____________	___	____________
___	____________	___	____________	___	____________
___	____________	___	____________	___	____________
___	____________	___	____________	___	____________
___	____________	___	____________	___	____________
___	____________	___	____________	___	____________
		Total	____________	Total	____________

			Decision # 3		***Decision # 4***
			____________		____________
Weight	**Values**	**(rating)**		**(rating)**	
___	____________	___	____________	___	____________
___	____________	___	____________	___	____________
___	____________	___	____________	___	____________
___	____________	___	____________	___	____________
___	____________	___	____________	___	____________
___	____________	___	____________	___	____________
___	____________	___	____________	___	____________
		Total	____________	Total	____________

Exercise 3

Revise your personal life mission statement from Chapter One. Take into consideration, what you have learned about yourself from chapters two, three, and four. Ask yourself the following questions.

1. Do heart values influence my personal life mission statement in any way?
2. Do my past beliefs, attitudes, and behavior have an impact on my personal life mission statement in any way?
3. Do the stress events in my life have an impact on my personal life mission statement in any way?
4. Do my personal limitations (thinking errors, defense mechanisms, etc) affect my personal life mission statement in any way?
5. Does my low self-esteem have an impact on my personal life mission statement?
6. Do my personal strengths have an impact on my personal life mission statement?

Write your revised personal life mission statement below.

Use the goal setting plan in the next three strategies to write goals that will help fulfill your mission statement. You will have the opportunity to write the action steps down in a calendar so you can get started on it.

Strategy 5.2

Draft and outline a goal setting plan.

Relating Goals to Your Mission Statement

Your Personal Life Mission Statement will help you decide on exactly which goals you should pursue. Goals are the plans that fulfill what you want most (your Personal Life Mission Statement). Objectives are the mini-goals or the action steps that need to be taken in order to achieve the goal. In the example below, the goals of getting a college degree and becoming healthy are the plans Bob has chosen to fulfill the mission of empowering himself. The objectives of studying, tutoring, jogging, etc., are the action steps that need to be taken in order to achieve the goals of getting a college degree and becoming healthy.

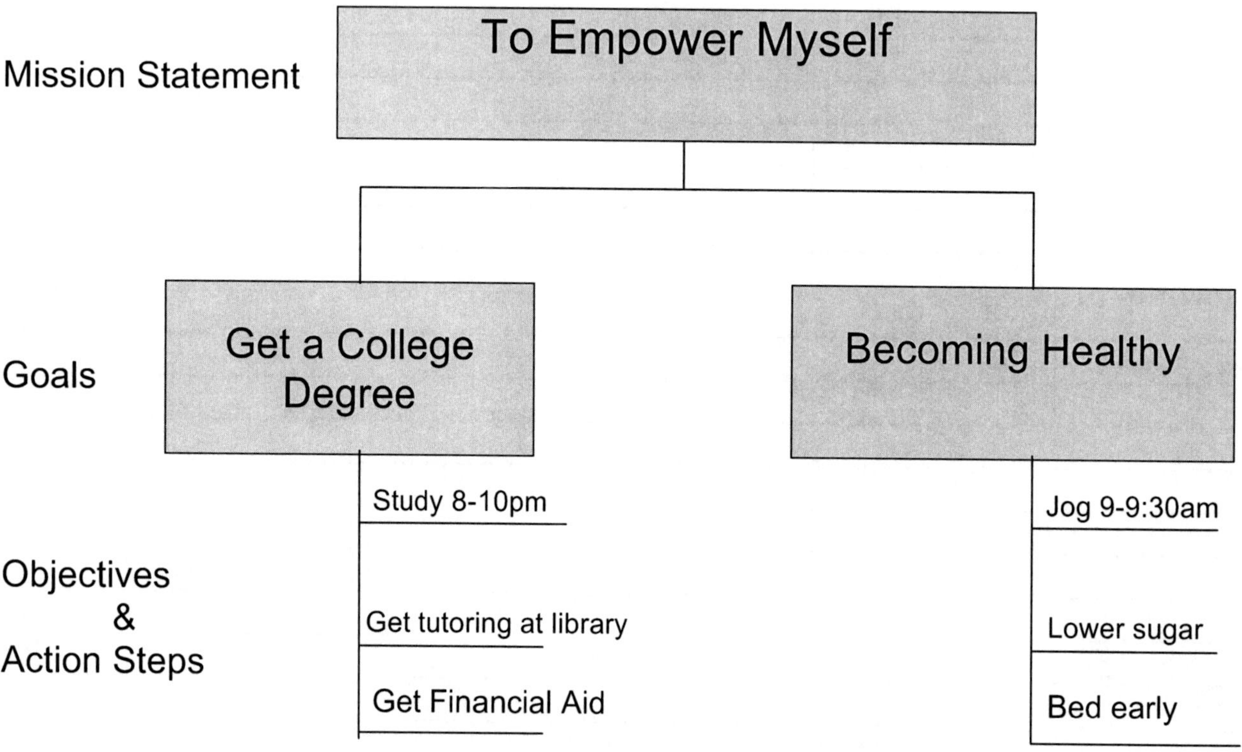

Which Goals Should You Choose?

Recall the Sea of Success at the beginning of the book. Rather than being like a ship without a rudder, drifting until you end up on the rocks, Burnout City, and so on, goals direct and chart a course showing you what to do, how to do it, and keeps you on course even though you can't immediately see the destination. So your goals arise from your mission statement and they help fulfill your mission statement.

If you are wondering what goals you should set, ask yourself, what is lacking in your life right now? What one thing could you bring into your life that would really better your life? Make that your next goal! You can look for a need that no one is fulfilling. Think about setting goals in the following ten areas: Physical goals (exercise, diet), Career goals (current job and future job), Educational or Intellectual goals (college degree, skill training), Financial goals (how much money you want to make a year), Social & Relationship goals (how you interact with your partner, friends, family, etc.), Recreation & Leisure goals (fun, relaxation, adventure, travel, concerts, etc.), Self-improvement goals (the kind of person you want to be such as optimistic, caring, patient), Material Possession goals (the things you want to have such as houses, cars, etc.), Charity goals (what you want to do for others like serving, donating money), and Spiritual goals (your relationship to a higher power such as worshiping, prayer, meditation etc.). You should be able to relate all of these types of goals to your Personal Life Mission Statement. Briefly write possible goals you could pursue in the goal areas below.

Physical Goals____

____

____

Career Goals____

____

____

Educational/Intellectual Goals____

____

____

Financial Goals____

____

____

Social/Relationship Goals____

____

____

Recreation or Leisure Goals____

____

____

Self-Improvement Goals____

____

____

Material Possession Goals____

____

____

Charity Goals____

____

____

Spiritual Goals____

____

____

How Do You Achieve Goals?

A well set goal has seven important characteristics: It is believable, etchable, specific, measurable, achievable, realistic, and time-related **(BE SMART).**

B – Believable Do you really believe you can "pull it off." If not, try using the Goal Sentence Completion Method in Exercise 3 in Strategy 2.5. This will help you to believe you can achieve it. Also recall from Strategy 2.4 how Bruce Jenner used the newspaper article to help himself believe he could win the Olympic decathlon. Use Journal Writing to vent out frustrations and acknowledge gains.

E – Etchable Are you able to etch in your mind and visualize achieving the goal? Practice visualizing yourself having achieved the goal. This will etch it into your mind. If you want to lose 15 pounds, visualize yourself, 15 pounds lighter. Or if your goal is to get a college degree, picture it in your hand.

S – Specific Instead of saying, I will lose weight by this Spring, be specific and say the exact amount you want to lose. For example, "I will lose 15 pounds by Spring." Muhammad Ali used to be specific and predict the exact round he would knock out his opponent. He was often correct.

M – Measurable If you were trying to lose weight, how would you measure it if you did? Answer: Using a scale. If we don't measure our progress, we might quit thinking we didn't make progress when we actually may have made progress. A study at Yale University found that, of the 1953 Yale graduating class, 3% of the class who completed an extensive goal-setting workshop and wrote their goals down were worth more financially than the other 97% of graduates 20 years later in 1973. They were also happier, had better family lives, and more successful in their careers.

A – Achievable Is the goal doable? Can you actually succeed at this goal, or are you dooming yourself to failure because you're trying to be something you are not such as a physicist or astronaut. You must have a burning desire to achieve the goal so you won't quit when facing obstacles.

R – Realistic Is the goal realistic in that does it fit your schedule, financial situation, values, or your other goals? Is it challenging enough?

T – Time-Related Does the goal include a time frame for evaluating whether you have achieve it? Make sure you specify a specific day of when you want the goal accomplished. For example, I want to complete my college degree by May 18th, 2008. Pick a day/time that will challenge you.

Exercises 1, 2, and 3 are listed below.

If you don't write your goals down, you'll be working for somebody else who does.
Anthony Robbins

1. Choose one specific, measurable goal and the outcomes you would love to get from attaining this goal that relates to your Personal Life Mission Statement.

Goal: ____

____

Outcomes: ____

____

2. Choose a challenging, yet realistic *Target Date of Triumph* for the completion of your goal.

- For example: If you want to lose 20 lbs, make the *Target Date of Triumph* challenging, such as three months from now, as opposed to losing 20 lbs in two years. Yet, also make it realistic. To lose 20 lbs in a week is not realistic. Write your Target Date of Triumph below. Make sure it is a specific date, e.g. May 18th, 2015.

____

____

____

3. Identify below how you will measure your progress toward your Target Date of Triumph.

- Examples include daily planners, calendars, educational plans, scales, tally marks, etc.

____

____

____

____

____

4. List the personal qualities you need to achieve your goal and the day-to-day tasks needed to produce those personal qualities. (Put tasks in your Activity List at end of Strategy 5.3's lesson).

Personal Qualities Needed (Examples below)		Tasks Needed to Produce Those Qualities
To be productive – don't procrastinate	→	**Make a daily To-Do list**
Make good use of time during the day	→	**Watch less TV in the evenings**

5. Write four reasons why you want to achieve this goal and how it will benefit your life. Clarifying your reasons will motivate you more than anything else will!

1. ___

2. ___

3. ___

4. ___

6. Write down four consequences of not achieving this goal.

1. ___

2. ___

3. ___

4. ___

7. Write down all the tasks you will need to perform in order to achieve this goal.

These tasks are your objectives, which are like mini-goals that help you achieve your larger goal. You will brainstorm others in the next strategy.

(Put these tasks in your Activity List)

1.

Strategy 5.3

Launch and take action on your goal-setting plan.

The have and have-nots can often be traced back to the dids and did-nots.
D. O. Flynn

Exercises 1, 2, and 3 are listed below.

1. **Identify the tools, people, organizations etc., you will need to help you achieve your goal. (Put them in your Activity List at end of Strategy 5.3's lesson).** Examples include:
   Tools: books, computer, organizer, etc.
   People: advisor, close friend, expert in the field
   Organizations: college, state agency, associations, etc.

2. Write three times in your life when you were successful or did well at something.
Describe the resources you used and the method used to succeed. Examples include memorizing a presentation, time with kids, learning how to type, high school graduation, etc.

How could you use these resources/methods for your goal? (Put these ideas in your Activity List)

3. List four obstacles that are most likely to distract you from achieving your goal. Across from each obstacle write down how you will manage each obstacle. (Put how you will manage these obstacles in your Activity List).

Obstacles	**How I will manage each obstacle**
Ex) Eating sweets and junk food	Bring lunch to work and adjust grocery list for healthy eating
1.____________________	____________________________
2.____________________	____________________________
3.____________________	____________________________
4.____________________	____________________________
5.____________________	____________________________
6.____________________	____________________________
7.____________________	____________________________
8.____________________	____________________________

4. Write down three people who have achieved your specific goal and the qualities and behaviors they used to achieve their goal. (Put these in your Activity List)

Picture this person giving you advice such as, "Watch what the stock market does."

Person	Qualities and behaviors they used
1.____________________	____________________________
2.____________________	____________________________
3.____________________	____________________________

What advice might they give to you? (Put in your Activity List)

5. Write down and then design your perfect environment that would bring out the best in you. Design one this week and one for the future--later in the next year. (Put these in your Activity List). Write down what you have to do or buy to make it happen. Examples include writing by the ocean or in an office, using an art pad; being around supportive people; putting motivational reminders in your bathroom, on the computer, dashboard, refrigerator, mirror, etc, that help to remind you to work toward your goal.

This week____

The future____

6. Determine four sacrifices you will need to make to achieve your goal. How do the costs affect your family, time, self, finances, and so on?

1.____

2.____

3.____

4.____

7. ACTIVITY LIST

A. **Transcribe the tasks you wrote down from the exercises in both Strategy 5.2 and 5.3's lesson. Look for the statement, "Put these in your Activity List."**

1. ____________________
2. ____________________
3. ____________________
4. ____________________
5. ____________________
6. ____________________
7. ____________________
8. ____________________
9. ____________________
10. ____________________
11. ____________________
12. ____________________
13. ____________________
14. ____________________
15. ____________________
16. ____________________
17. ____________________
18. ____________________
19. ____________________
20. ____________________

Strategy 5.4

Implement your Action Plan using the easy 4-Step Method below.

1. Prioritize and then schedule each task above to a day in your favorite daily planner *or in the calendar following this page* so that you can measure your progress to eventually hit your *Target Date of Triumph.* Put your *Target Date of Triumph* in a place in your daily planner so your eyes and mind will see it each time you open it up. This will program and etch that date into your mind, resulting in an eventual sure achievement.

2. Every day, review this goal setting plan (Strategy 5.2 – 5.3) to keep you motivated and refreshed. Read it every morning when you wake up and every night before you go to bed.

3. Affirm your goal as if it's already achieved throughout the day. Use present tense and make it positive. For example: "I weigh 130lbs.." or "I am a great teacher" or "I earn $70,000 dollars a year". Write it here ____________________

   ____

4. Do your inner ritual (heart meditation, praying, nature reflection, etc.) and during it, visualize your goal as if it's already achieved. Imagine watching a movie on the screen of your mind with you as the main character possessing your goal. Relinquish your attachment to the goal outcome by eliminating any fear you have about not obtaining your future goal. Trust that your desires, working this goal project, visualizations, and/or the universe/divine being will supply it.

MONDAY	TUESDAY	WEDNESDAY	THURSDAY	FRIDAY	SATURDAY	SUNDAY

Strategy 5.5
Learn to Problem Solve using Creative Thinking Strategies.

A problem cannot be solved with the same mind that created it.
Albert Einstein

The 10 Step Problem Solving Method

Step 1 - Approach the problem as if it were simple to solve with an easy, logical answer.

Step 2 - Use positive words and call it an issue or a challenge, not a problem.

Step 3 - Define the issue/challenge in writing and in detail.

Step 4 - List the possible causes that created the challenge.

Step 5 - Develop possible solutions using the following Creative Thinking Strategies.

- *Use verbs to manipulate the problem.* For example: problem = the computer won't print. Possible solutions = activate, replace, fix, restart, ask someone else, reselect, research, interview, ask, experience, shadow, etc.
- *Draw a map outline* by stating your problem/purpose in the middle of the map and circle it. Then, draw a picture of the problem and solutions using lines radiating from the center. Use short key words to describe it. Brainstorm ideas and put them down on the radiating lines. Don't worry if the idea seems stupid; write it anyway. Give yourself a time limit to accomplish this. This mental map inspires answers to long-standing problems and simplifies the complex. It has been used to develop the greatest advances in human history. Danish physicist Niels Bohr developed the Model of the Atom by comparing it to the solar system...The sun is like the nucleus and the planets are like the electrons that circle the nucleus. The Chinese say, "A picture is worth a thousand words."
- *Write a letter* to a friend describing the problem and possible solutions using conversational language.
- *Keep a journal to log your ideas throughout the day.* Ask yourself....What are the answers? Meanings? Results? Look for more than one right answer. You might have a good one but not a great one.
  It also helps to write a question to the problem you are trying to solve. After, rephrase the question as many times as possible.
- *Think outside of the box* by asking "What if"..... What assumptions can be dropped? Look at it backwards. Is the timing right?
  What if...(think of someone else) the Godfather, Freud, King, Einstein, Jesus was asked this question? How he or she answer it? What constraints, expertise, and assumptions would they add?
  EXAMPLE
  A City in the Netherlands had a bad city problem of littering.... The streets were filthy. They tried doubling the fee of the penalty—that didn't work. They tried doubling the littering police—that didn't work. Then someone asked WHAT IF....we paid people to put trash in the cans...an electronic meter that would pay each time it was opened. Outlandish considering that the city would have gone broke. But ask....WHAT IF we used a similar idea....reward them in another way. Each time the can was opened an electronic joke would be told and they
  changed the joke program every two weeks. That city is now one of the cleanest in Europe,
  thanks to this creative thinking.

Step 6 - Assign responsibility of who makes the final decision.

Step 7 - Make a decision based on the "Mind & Heart-Smart" Decision Maker displayed in the next day's exercise.

Step 8 - Set a deadline for making the decision.

Step 9 - Take action using the Goal Outline & Action Plan.

Step 10 - Evaluate the outcome.

Break the Rules and Be Creative

Quote: "Every act of creation is fruit of an act of destruction." ...Picasso.

Destructive thinking, like metaphors inspires answers. Examples:
Beethoven broke the rules on how a symphony is composed by trailing codas and orchestral fugues. *Einstein* broke the rules of Newtonian physics by equating mass and energy as different forms of the same phenomenon.
Almost every advance in art, cooking, music, education, design, etc., has occurred when someone challenged the rules (destructed) and tried something else.
- If the rules hadn't changed, foul balls wouldn't count as a strike, football wouldn't have a passing game, and jump balls would be required after every field goal in basketball.

WE LEARNED TO FOLLOW THE RULES! For example, we learned, don't color outside the lines. Students are rewarded for regurgitating answers they often don't fully understand.
- The order of the top row of letters on a typewriter were put there after people complained the keys stuck from stroking them too fast. This was done to slow down the typist. Yet, we still live by these rules. What old rules are you still living by? Quote: "SACRED COWS MAKE GREAT STEAKS"... Richard Nicolosi

Exercise 1

Describe a problem below that you would like to solve and the probable causes of the problem.

____
____
____
____
____
____
____

Exercise 2

Develop possible solutions using the ideas in Step 5 above.
Solution 1____
____
____

Solution 2____
____
____

Solution 3____
____

Solution 4__________

Solution 5__________

Solution 6__________

Exercise 3

What is the deadline date to solve this problem?__________

After implementing the solution for a period of time, evaluate the outcome.
Did you achieve your objective?__________

What activity/strategy worked well to achieve part of or the entire objective?__________

What activity/strategy did not work to achieve the objective?__________

What additional activity/strategy could be pursued to achieve the objective next time?__________

Strategy 5.6

Learn to become an excellent manager of your money.

Rich people plan for four generations. Poor people plan for Saturday night.
Gloria Steinem

Annual income, twenty pounds, annual expenditure, nineteen pounds; result, happiness. Annual income, twenty pounds, annual expenditure, twenty one pounds; result, misery.
Charles Dickens

Save First, Then Spend

According to a study by the Department of Health and Human Services in 1993, for every 100 people starting their careers in this country, the following situation exists at age 65...

25 will be dead
20 will have annual incomes below the poverty line and be broke.
51 will struggle with incomes at the poverty line up to $35,000 (median = $12,000)
4 will be living more comfortably with incomes over $35,000

Most people by the age of retirement are broke for one reason! They didn't plan to fail; they *failed to plan.* By smart investing and planning wisely, there is no reason to retire broke. Roadblocks that make it harder include inflation, taxes, bad investments, disability, saving to spend, and lack of discipline.

One of the most important strategies for managing your money wisely is to save and invest first, and then spend. The 55% of people who are broke, do it in reverse. They spend first, and try to save and invest what little is left. Before you invest, a guideline for economic survival is to:
a) have your savings equal to three to six months of living expenses.
b) save for major purchases such as a house, car, retirement, child's education, etc.
When these are taken care of, then, invest. See your banker or independent certified financial planner for advice about saving and investing. Avoid seeing stockbrokers for advice since they often don't have your best interest at "heart."

Money problems usually result from spending more than one can afford. The solution is simple, but not always easy--don't spend more than you have. Misuse of credit cards is the biggest reason why people go into debt. If you can't control your spending, throw them away. If you can control it, make sure that, for the majority of the time, you pay off the entire credit card balance each month. Interest on credit cards is so high it's almost "robbery."

Budget Wisely

Decrease expenses by conserving your resources and avoiding waste. Utilize the following insightful pieces of advice.

Food:
Eat healthy. This will save on medical bills. When you grocery shop, use coupons, compare price per unit: ounce and pound (by bringing your calculator). Make a food shopping trip no more than one time per week; this will save gas, time and money. Buy produce in season; double or triple standard recipes when making spaghetti sauces, chili, or stews and then freeze for later use; purchase things you have to reach for on the shelf since high priced goods are placed at eye and waist level; buy generic brands since they can save you up to 30%; stay clear of prepared

foods which can add 20% to your bill; bring your lunch to work/school--same with the kids; don't eat out-- the average family spends over 40% of their food budget eating out; and refuse to shop when you are hungry or upset--it results it poor food choices.

Housing:
Buy furniture on sale, garage sales, or second hand shops; cut down on cleaning supplies and find items that clean multiple things; make minor repairs on your home before they become major repairs; have a yard sale to raise money; increase the deductible on your home insurance; get a roommate; move to a cheaper location depending on moving costs, deposits, and safety of neighborhood; refinance your home, if advantageous, using a no-points loan; encourage children to do extra work around the house.

Clothing:
Buy following seasonal clearances for new stock: after Christmas, Easter, and July 4th; buy best material you can afford, not designer clothes; don't scrimp on shoes; for young children, shop garage sales or thrift stores and accept family/friend giveaways; buy color-coordinated clothing to mix and match; use cloth baby diapers and launder them yourself; spot-clean clothes promptly to save in future.

Transportation:
Sell any vehicle you can't afford and purchase a proven used car; carpool; walk or bike whenever possible; combine errands to save time and gas; skip the high octane gas; get small problems fixed before they become large expensive ones; shop around for repair quotes and get a written estimate; keep your tires inflated and fluids up for better gas mileage; use self-service gasoline pumps; take advantage of auto repair classes held in your community or local college; drop collision insurance when your car's value has dropped sufficiently; drop comprehensive coverage on an older car.

Phone:
Take advantage of email before you phone somebody; let family and friends call you first; research the long-distance carriers to get the cheapest rates you can find; eliminate collect calls and calling cards; put a timer next to the phone when making calls to help you keep them short; split long distance phone calls with family or friends.

When you budget your money, you'll know how much is available for all of your expenses in the categories. Keep a record of your spending in each category so that you can ensure that you don't spend more than the amount you budgeted for. Many people put money they budget for into a separate envelope, one envelope for entertainment, one for utilities, etc. For example, when the cash in the entertainment envelope gets low, you will know to watch your spending in that category. Keep track, item by item, of where the money goes every day, week, and month. Do this as a family.

Exercises 1, 2, and 3

Budget the money you have coming in (your income/resources), and the money going out (your expenses) by completing the budget planner on the next page.

Budget Planner

Estimated Expenses	**Monthly Amount**	**Yearly Amount**
Housing/Rent		
Utilities……		
Electricity		
Gas		
Telephone		
Education: tuition		
Books/Supplies		
Miscellaneous		
Food/Groceries		
Meals Out of home		
Transportation/Gas		
Car Payment		
Repairs/Parking		
Bus/Train/Air		
Auto Insurance		
Clothing		
Medical Insurance		
Prescriptions		
Insurance: life, etc.		
Childcare		
Personal Expenses:		
Laundry		
Barber/beauty		
Shopping		
Tobacco/alcohol		
Books/Magazines		
Gifts/Holidays		
Entertainment		
Sports/Movies etc.		
Interest Payments		
Miscellaneous		
Total Expenses:		

Estimated Income & Resources	**Monthly Amount**	**Yearly Amount**
Income/Job		
Financial Aid		
Loans		
Grants		
Scholarships		
Institutional Grant		
Service Programs		
Nontaxable Income		
Welfare		
Veterans Benefits		
Social Security		
Disability		
Other		
Family Contribution		
Friends		
Savings Interest		
Investments		
Other Income		
Total Income:		

Strategy 5.7

Learn to identify your dominant learning style modality and intelligence area to maximize your learning in every facet of life.

Exercise 1

Identify your learning style. Place a check on the appropriate line after each statement.

	5 Often	31 Sometimes	Seldom
1. I can follow written directions better than oral directions.	____	_____	____
2. I can remember a subject better through listening than reading.	____	_____	____
3. I need to re-read things I write down so that I can remember.	____	_____	____
4. I require explanations of diagrams, graphs, or visual directions.	____	_____	____
5. I enjoy working with tools.	____	_____	____
6. When I am learning about something, I will use graphs and charts to better understand the topic.	____	_____	____
7. I remember best by writing things down several times.	____	_____	____
8. I can understand and follow directions on maps.	____	_____	____
9. I do better at academic subjects by listening to the teacher or tapes.	____	_____	____
10. I can better understand a news article by reading about it in the newspaper than by listening to the radio.	____	_____	____
11. I find dancing pleasurable.	____	_____	____
12. I learn spelling by first writing the word with my finger either in the air or on a table.	____	_____	____
13. I would rather listen to a teacher's explanation than read about the same material in a textbook.	____	_____	____
14. I understand something better if I can hold it in my hands.	____	_____	____
15. I would rather read directions than have them read to me.	____	_____	____
16. I prefer listening to the news on the radio rather than reading about it in a newspaper.	____	_____	____
17. I would rather participate in a sport than watch it.	____	_____	____
18. I follow spoken directions better than written ones.	____	_____	____

A. Place the point value above on the line below next to its corresponding item number.

B. Next, add the values to obtain your total score under each heading. Your highest number is your dominant Learning Style Modality.

Visual	**Auditory**	**Kinesthetic**
1. __________	2. __________	
3. __________	4. __________	5. __________
6. __________		7. __________
8. __________	9. __________	
10.__________		11.__________
		12.__________
	13.__________	14.__________
15.__________	16.__________	17.__________
	18.__________	
______ **Total**	______ **Total**	______ **Total**

Interpretation of Your Learning Style

Choose the highest total from above and note your learning style below. There is no single right way to learn. Not everyone learns the same way. Early in life, we discover a dominant way to collect and process information that worked for us and made sense to us. We use all three modalities (visual, auditory, kinesthetic), but we use a dominant one more often. By identifying your dominant style, you can then adjust study sessions in college, job training programs, how you take down directions, or any kind of information you need to process in a structured manner. You can take advantage of your learning strengths and compensate for your weaknesses. It will be easier to grasp new material and choose instructors whose teaching style relates to your learning style.

Visual Processors include about 55% of the population. The television generation might have something to do with that since most of us started watching before we entered school. These people tend to be fast thinkers and use visual imagery when they communicate with others. They will use phrases such as, "I see what you mean," or "I get the picture." To take advantage of this style, it will be important for you to recreate the information you are "taking in" by drawing charts, figures, diagrams, pictures, and concept maps so you can better understand and remember the information in a structured way. Copying and recopying your notes may help you to also learn material better. Choose instructors/trainers who use the blackboard to illustrate important concepts and who distribute outlines of their teaching material. The map outline explained on page 209 will be a huge help in comprehending difficult subject material.

Auditory Processors make up less than 20% of the population. These people tend to be good listeners but may be slow to answer the other person. When communicating with others, they will say phrases like, "I hear what you're saying" or "That sounds right" or "That rings true." To take advantage of this style, it will be important for you to discuss the information with others in something like a study group. Your style is the only style that would benefit from tape recording lectures and listening to them over and over again to understand the information more completely. Asking questions in class and in tutoring sessions is suggested so that you can hear the answers and process them accurately. Also, verbally repeating and reciting new learned information out loud will further your understanding of any subject "at hand."

Kinesthetic Processors make up about 25% of the population. These people are feeling and touch oriented and focus on emotions rather than logic and reason when learning material. They usually find *doing* to be the best way of learning. They prefer to walk through a demonstration or project and learn "hands-on." When communicating with others, they will say phrases like, "That feels right," or "I get a sense of what you mean," or "I'm getting a handle on it," or "I have a gut feeling." To take advantage of this style, it will be important for you to write down information and apply it to real-life situations. It will also be important for you to gesture, get up, pace around, and act out the information while studying a subject. Using flash cards and using your hands to understand material is vital as well as working in study groups, simulations, and role-playing scenarios.

To find out more about how you learn, seek out books in the bookstore that discuss left and right brain learning. The more you can learn about you, the more you will empower yourself to live, thrive, and produce like never before.

Exercise 2

Write which learner you are and how you will adjust your study habits to fit your style of learning.

____

____

Exercise 3

To discover your dominant intelligence areas, rate each item on the scale below and write the number of your response (1-4) on the line next to the statement. Then, total each set of five questions.

1 – Rarely **2 – Sometimes** **3 – Usually** **4 - Always**

1. ____ I pace when I'm thinking/studying.
2. ____ I enjoy working with my hands.
3. ____ I prefer to learn through doing.
4. ____ I enjoy physical activities.
5. ____ When sitting, I move my legs or hands.

____ **TOTAL for Body/Kinesthetic**

1. ____ I enjoy drawing or photography.
2. ____ I prefer a drawn map over written directions.
3. ____ I use maps easily.
4. ____ I draw illustrations when explaining ideas.
5. ____ I can assemble items easily from diagrams

____ **TOTAL for Visual/Spatial**

1. ____ I have a good voice for singing to music.
2. ____ I move my fingers or feet to music.
3. ____ I have good rhythm.
4. ____ I like to express my ideas through music.
5. ____ I play a musical instrument well.

____ **TOTAL for Musical**

1. ____ I enjoy helping others.
2. ____ I like doing a project with other people.
3. ____ People come to me to help settle conflicts.
4. ____ I am good at understanding people.
5. ____ I am good at making people feel comfortable and/or validated.

____ **TOTAL for Interpersonal**

1. ____ I enjoy telling stories.
2. ____ I like to read.
3. ____ I like to write.
4. ____ I express myself clearly .
5. ____ I am good at negotiating.

____ **TOTAL for Verbal/Linguistic**

1. ____ I like and do well in math in school.
2. ____ I like and do well in science.
3. ____ I often question how things work.
4. ____ I problem solve well.
5. ____ I like planning/designing something new.

____ **TOTAL for Logical/Mathematical**

1. ____ I need quiet time to think and work alone.
2. ____ I am interested in self-improvement.
3. ____ I know what I want out of life.
4. ____ I think about issues before I want to talk.
5. ____ I understand my thoughts and feelings.

____ **TOTAL for Intrapersonal**

According to Gardner (1983), we are capable of at least seven different types of intelligence and learning and not just one or two. His theory of multiple intelligences identifies the following types:

1. Verbal/Linguistic Intelligence: (The Word Player) This intelligence, which is related to words and language (written and spoken), dominates most Western educational systems. These people like to read, write, and tell stories. They are good at memorizing names, places, dates, and trivia. They learn best by saying, hearing and seeing words. It will help to highlight texts, rewrite notes, and outline.

2. Logical/Mathematical Intelligence: (The Questioner) These scientific thinkers use inductive and deductive reasoning, numbers, and use of abstract patterns very effectively. They like to conduct experiments, solve problems, work with numbers, and explore patterns and relationships. They are good at math, logic, problem solving, and reasoning. They learn best by categorizing.

3. Visual/Spatial Intelligence: (The Visualizer) This intelligence, which relies on the sense of sight and being able to visualize an object, includes the ability to create internal mental images and pictures. These people like to draw, build, design, daydream, play with machines, and look at pictures/slides. They are good at imagining things, sensing changes, reading maps, charts, and working with puzzles. They learn best by visualizing, dreaming, and working with images.

4. Body/Kinesthetic Intelligence: (The Mover) This intelligence is related to physical movement and the knowings/wisdom of the body, including the brain's motor cortex, which controls bodily motion. These individuals like to move around, touch, talk, and use body language. They are good at sports, dance, acting, and crafts. They learn best by touching, reciting while moving, interacting with space, and processing knowledge through bodily sensation. Also, move fingers while reading the words.

5. Musical/Rhythmic Intelligence (The Music Lover) This intelligence is based on the recognition of tonal patterns, including various environmental sounds, and a sensitivity to rhythm and beats. These folks like to sing, hum tunes, listen to music, and play an instrument. They are good at picking up sounds, remembering melodies, keeping time, noticing pitches and rhythms. They learn best by associating new material to songs, melody, and rhythm movements.

6. Interpersonal Intelligence (The Socializer) This intelligence operates primarily through person-to-person relationships and communication. These people like to talk to people, join groups, and they have many friends. They are good at understanding people, leading others, communicating, manipulating, and mediating conflicts. They learn best by sharing, comparing, relating, cooperating, studying in groups and interviewing. Also, using flashcards and teaching someone else will help.

7. Intrapersonal Intelligence (The Individual) This intelligence relates to inner states of being, self-reflection, philosophizing, and awareness of spiritual realities. These individuals like to work alone and pursue their own interests. They are good at understanding themselves, focusing inward on feelings, following instincts, pursuing interests and goals, and being original. They learn best by working alone, conducting self-paced instruction, reflecting on the personal meaning

Write down what you believe your number one, two, and three top intelligences are and how you can use them more often/wisely. Also, how can you excel more in the ones you scored low in?

____

____

____

____

____

Chapter Insight & Commitment

After completing this chapter, I learned the following about my problem-solving, decision-making, pursuit of goals, money management, learning style, and dominant intelligence:

Example: I learned that when I have made decisions in the past about my choice of major and career, it was based on what my friends and parents said I should go into instead of listing the things that I value that would help me choose what is best for me. I also learned that I quit pursuing my goals when I hit the second or third obstacle.

____

____

____

____

____

____

____

____

____

____

____

____

____

I can take active steps to help me achieve my future goals and become more of the person I am or strive to be by:

Example: I will use the decision-maker when I need to make important decisions in the future. I will also follow the goal setting project this year when I try to transfer to a university so I can stay on track when I run into an obstacle like lack of money or discouraging people.

____

____

____

____

____

____

____

____

____

____

____

____

____

CHAPTER 6

Self-Integrity

Using your Spine **to** Integrate **your** values, words, and actions.

Purpose: To bring wholeness to your character.

Rewards: Wholeness, Invincible Character, Respect, Peace of Mind

Obstacles: Selfishness, Fear, Lying, Others' Approval

Consequence: "Wimpiness," Distrustfulness, Weakness of Character, Disrespectfulness, Immaturity, Bad Reputation

Symbol: Badge of Honor

Related Web Site: http://www.selfgrowth.com

Self-Integrity

It is crucial to the social order that its members are able to trust one another in order to develop successful institutions, communications, and thrive. Yet, if individuals are mostly dishonest, not responsible, disrespectful, and selfish, then trust is broken and the strength and integrity of the social structure and within the individual, crumbles. In Chapter 6, you will learn how to match your words with your behaviors to bring honor, respect, dignity, and integrity to others and yourself. The word integrity means to bring together or unite our thoughts, values, words and deeds and consistently "act them out" in each life context or situation that we experience on a day-to-day basis. This integrating allows us to be a whole person as we interact with others. Bringing integrity to the Self will help promote your trustworthiness, respect, and honesty when interacting with others, especially when moral questions are contemplated and processed. There is considerable empirical research that indicates that when people have clarity and can define and act upon their values, they become less apathetic, less flighty, less conforming, less over dissenting, more energetic, more critical in their thinking, and more likely to follow through on decisions.

By the time we arrive at adulthood, our self-integrity is not always strong. This is no surprise when you consider the number of conflicting values presented by parents, church, peer groups, Hollywood, popular magazines, high-school teachers, college professors, Presidents of the United States, spokespersons for the counterculture, and experts in the media. It is no wonder that most people are confused when confronted with an ethical dilemma at work. In such a situation, many people have no idea how to make an ethical decision or how to communicate their convictions. For example, the boss asks you to commit a small, minor offense that is illegal, but it is sure to give you a promotion with substantially higher pay. Where is your value strongest? How do we learn to relate to people whose values differ from our own? What do we do when two important values are in conflict? Unfortunately, many people make important life decisions like choosing an occupation, a spouse, or a candidate on the basis of peer pressure, mindless submission to authority, or the power of the mass media.

Simon Blackburn's Book "Being Good: A Short Introduction to Ethics," published by Oxford UP (2005), suggests that human beings are ethical animals. We grade and evaluate, compare and admire, and claim and justify. We do not just "prefer" this or that, in isolation. We prefer that our preferences are shared and standards of behavior and their consequences be abided by in society. Racists and sexists like slave owners in America, always have to tell themselves a story that justifies their savage belief system. An ethic gone wrong is an essential preliminary to the sweat-shop or the concentration camp and the death march.

In this chapter, you will learn to thoroughly think through your values, ethics, and morality. You will also cultivate an understanding, acceptance, and appreciation of other people's value systems as well. Finally, you will learn how to take full responsibility for your actions. This one quality is perhaps the most critical element in determining one's likelihood for success in life. By developing these integral skills, you will be on the road to developing an invincible characte

Strategy 6.1

Take responsibility for your moral and ethical development to strengthen your self-integrity, sharpen your critical thinking skills, and promote societal justice.

Definition of Morality – Behavior aimed at right conduct that avoids hurting others.

Definition of Ethics – High standards of honest and honorable dealing and of methods used especially pertaining to the professions or in business.

Why Be Moral or Ethical?

Since childhood, all individuals engage in a combination of lying and truth telling as well as proper and improper behavior. They do so in order to either protect their ego/pride from feeling guilt and shame or to advance their own selfish causes. Ask yourself if in the past you have cheated on your taxes, stolen from a store, gossiped about somebody without having all the facts, cheated on a test, exaggerated a story or an accomplishment, were cruel to somebody, taken a bribe, and so forth. Have you ever said to yourself, "If he can get away with it, why can't I?" Why shouldn't we be selfish and get away with anything we can? One response to that question is, what if everyone acted the same way in the society? Would society change for the better or worse? If we lived in a world where our actions had no consequences, there could be nothing wrong with anything we might do. Since this is not the case, we need to be able to govern our behavior so as not to injure others, our community, or ourselves in the long term. Otherwise, communities would rapidly fall apart without any adherence to rules or suppression of actions. Social order is crucial to the survival of any social species. This system of controlling our actions and our thoughts in order to operate in a community is what we often refer to as morality.

Sometimes, it is hard to figure out. The devastation left behind by Hurricane Katrina has raised difficult questions of ethics: When, if ever, is looting OK? Though food was looted and stolen in New Orleans, so were microwave ovens, jewelry, guns, and all kinds of merchandise not needed for survival. When is it acceptable to break the law and what happens to society when law itself breaks down? Is stealing only justified when somebody's life is on the line? We will discuss these issues in this chapter.

Kohlberg's Seven Stages of Moral Development

Lawrence Kohlberg (1981), a moral philosopher, psychologist, and director of Harvard's Center for Moral Education, developed seven stages of moral development as a result of observing how children develop a sense of right, wrong, and justice. These thought-processing stages progress consecutively from one stage to the next, depending on one's desire to advance in this area. Though different cultures and communities have different moral standards, Kohlberg's conclusions have been verified in cross-cultural studies done in Turkey, Taiwan, Yucatan, Honduras, India, United States, Canada, Britain, and Israel. The seven stages are as follows:

Stage 1 – (Ages 4 –12) They act to avoid punishment. They will obey the rules only when punishment is sensed from an authority figure. If the authority figure is absent, despite the consequences, the attitude will be, "If it feels good, do it." Intelligent and charismatic Level 1's can be the most dangerous people in the world. Adults can function at this level as evidenced by the atrocities carried out by soldiers during the Holocaust who were simply "carrying out orders" under threat of punishment. An adult who consistently operates at this level will either end up in prison or dead.

Stage 2 – (Ages 4 –12) They act to get a reward. They obey the rules only for a reward in return. They have the attitude, "You scratch my back, I'll scratch yours." They will help others but only conditionally. In school, children will band together to keep from getting in trouble, but will tell on a friend if it will help them. They can easily be bribed into doing what others want. Many businesses operate on this level with the thinking of, "I will stretch or break the law until punishment starts to arrive." Then they make some token changes to their tactics to demonstrate good faith and play by the rules but later, turn around and stretch/break more laws.

Stage 3 – (Ages 12 – adult) They act to get approval. They will obey the rules in order to win approval from others. They are conformists who get into groups (fraternities) or gangs to get approval from their peers. They often copy the trends and fashions of the majority in clothes, hair, and vocabulary. They want credit for having good intentions despite their behavior. Many companies and athletic teams operate at this level because the team comes first.

Stage 4 – (Ages 12 – adult) They act to bring order to their world. They will obey the rules because an authority established the laws and rules which are more important than one's selfish desires. They perform best when they know what is expected of them and what the limits of behavior are. It is different than stage one punishment because even though the laws punish, these people see the value of how laws help maintain a social order. They may say, "He must be right; he's the Pope, or President, or the Judge." They can slip into moral relativism often taught at colleges. This was well noted in the hippie culture of the 1960's, where there were no absolutes because everything was thought of as relative. They lived with the motto, "Just do your own thing." For example, a front-page article in the Los Angeles Times (May 25, 1992) on African American attitudes toward the four African American men who beat and almost murdered truck driver Reginald Denny was headlined: "Denny Suspects Are Thugs to Some, Heroes to Others." The article asserted that the gang members were either thugs or revolutionary soldiers who sounded the first shots of a racial insurrection and are heroes, depending on your opinion. The behavior is rationalized in the name of doing good for a group. They are unable to see universal implications of such actions which is a Stage 5 and 6 level mentality. It is important to recall that Denny's life was saved by four heroic African Americans. Yet, far more press attention was paid to the four African American thugs than to the four African American saints.

Stage 5 – (teen – adult) They act to bring a social justice to the world. They will obey the rules and laws because a community has conscientiously chosen it, not just an authority figure. This person has a strong belief in laws but will change the law for the good of the people. The U.S. Constitution was written on this level. They often have a high regard for the differences in personal values and opinions of others despite what their opinion is. They think about the needs of others as well as their own.

Stage 6 – (teen – adult) They act to bring justice to the world, despite what the law says. Thus, they will break a law for good cause: going to war, abortion, human rights, etc. They think in terms of universal principles of justice; equality of human rights and respect for the dignity of others. They are willing to die for a belief/cause other than their family. Their conscience is their guide; however, their moral system must be universally applicable and logically consistent. Kohlberg equates this level with the thinking of Abraham Lincoln and Martin Luther King, Jr.

Stage 7 – These people are unique. They are in the world but not of it. They have risen morally above the level of all other humans in thought and deed. Kohlberg lists Jesus and Mohammed at this stage.

Key Points to Kohlberg's Theory

1. Individuals usually operate from one stage most of the time
2. From a stage that an individual is at, he/she can understand behavior at all levels below but only two levels above.
3. One must progress through the stages in order.

How to Advance Through the Stages

1. Have the desire to advance your moral development.
2. Desire to solve problems in the social injustice area. As you open yourself to this idea, you will begin to see forms of injustice around you like never before. The person who is growing will look for more adequate ways of solving problems. If there were no problems, it is unlikely that we would try to advance ourselves. For example, if two sisters want the last piece of pie and the bigger sister will probably get it because she's stronger, the little sister has an incentive to seek fairness and justice. The big sister is operating at a level 2 and does not think of sharing it when asked to.
3. Think deeply and critically about social issues. Research it and develop your own views. Then get the views of others and adjust if necessary.
4. When thinking of social issues, ask yourself, "How will this affect others and the society in the long run?"
5. Expose yourself to diverse experiences and learn about different cultural beliefs. Then apply moral issues to your own experiences.

Example of What People Might Say to Themselves at Each Stage

Stage 1 – I pay taxes so I won't go to jail.
Stage 2 – I pay taxes as long as I get services in return.
Stage 3 – I pay taxes so I will be seen as a good citizen by others.
Stage 4 – I pay taxes because it's the law of the land.
Stage 5 – I pay taxes because society has legally determined that it's beneficial to others/society.
Stage 6 – I pay taxes not because it is the law, but because it is the right thing to do.

Test yourself

Case # 1: What stage would you operate on if you were a crime investigator who had been working on a murder case for months. Finally, you are assured a conviction but only if you <u>illegally</u> interrogate the defendant.
Case # 2: A man named Tony had a dying wife. The wife had an almost fatal disease. The local pharmacist owned a $20,000 drug that could save her. Tony could not raise the money in time, and he certainly did not have the cash to buy the drug. Tony, therefore, made a decision that night to break into the drug store and steal some of the medication. What would you have done?
Case # 3: What level would Sue be at if she doesn't steal because it hurts other people?

Exercise 1

Write down the circumstances and thought processes you had when you operated at a Stage 1, 2, or 3 within the last year or so.

Exercise 2

Write down the circumstances and thought processes you had when you operated at a Stage 5 or 6 within the last year or so.

Exercise 3

Write down the circumstances or the people that challenge you to operate at the lower Stages of 1 – 4. For example, Joe's father tells him that it is foolish for people to politically be in the Libertarian Party. When Joe decides not to tell his father he is a Libertarian, Joe is operating at a Stage 3 because Joe estimates that he would fall out of approval with his father.

Strategy 6.2

Grow, protect, and cultivate your sacred character by practicing honesty and maintaining a congruence between your word and your deed.

If we are strong, our character will speak for itself. If we are weak, words will be of no help.
John F. Kennedy

Acting Your Way to a Strong Character

Grow your character by realizing the more times you are honest, responsible, thoughtful, thankful, giving, encouraging, supportive, complimentary, and so on, the more your character will strengthen with power and grow. Example: The more times you do something that you don't have to do (e.g. visiting a relative, picking up a piece of trash on the sidewalk, remember somebody's birthday, tell the truth when you feel the pressure to lie, treating yourself with respect and asserting yourself) the more likely you will:
a) repeat the noble behavior with ease and desire rather than by chore and obligation and b) acquire those powerful attributes into who you are -- your character.

Practice honesty with everyone you know and, most importantly, yourself. Perhaps the biggest element that destroys Self-Integrity is not being honest with both your words and with yourself. What causes us to lie is that we're usually covering up mistakes we made which can tap into our own feelings of inadequacy and perceived weaknesses. *The experts estimate that the average person lies up to forty times a day.* Women usually lie to spare somebody's feelings. Men usually lie to promote themselves. When you feel yourself wanting to lie about something, embrace and experience the urge to lie without acting. By admitting and learning from your mistakes (lying), you will be less likely to even tell small lies, and respect for yourself and others' respect for you will dramatically increase. You have the right to make mistakes, and if other people have a hard time - then too bad (except on the condition that you are constantly making mistakes).

Character Defects

- prejudice	- procrastination	- insecurit	- perfectionist
- power hungry	- controlling	- jealousy	- intolerance
- dishonest	- argumentive	- greed	- materialistic
- helpless	- cruelty	- pride	- selfishness
- inconsiderate	- condemning	- abusive	- obsessive
- possessive	- envious	- impatience	- irresponsible

Integrate Your Words and Actions

Some people try to pressure us into doing or saying things that go against our values, beliefs, and philosophy. What often ruins self-esteem is not being congruent with your beliefs, words, and deeds. When we do something against our will, beliefs, etc., we don't respect ourselves. It tears apart our personal integrity and we become ***spineless***, more able to be manipulated by others and thereby becoming a programmed robot. Examples include: agreeing to gossip, sweet talking somebody, and so on.

Advertisers and politicians do three things to persuade you to change your beliefs/attitudes.

1) They find somebody to deliver the message: usually a credible expert, fast talker, someone who is likable, and whom the audience can identify with. They are usually attractive, famous, etc.

2) The content of the message: usually uses logic, reason, emotion, or fear.
3) Target audience: targets message to one's self-esteem, age, one's vulnerability, people who are depressed, or lonely.
Rise above these tricksters by not reacting or flinching when they try to change your beliefs, values, and critical thinking skills.

The Dangers of Not Communicating Well

Communication is not as easy as it seems. Chapter 8 will show you how to effectively communicate your thoughts and feelings. In order to communicate well, one has to educate oneself on knowing the receiver of one's communication. When countries don't communicate well, there are wars with many dead. Governments often don't educate themselves on the culture with whom they war against. When people don't communicate well, there are divorces, domestic violence, discrimination, and so on. They don't educate themselves on the other's needs, experiences, and history before communicating with them. It requires one to be open, nonjudgmental at first, and honest.

Ethics and morals need to be part of the communication process. If everyone practiced hedonism (pleasure seeking), there would be a lot more rape, murder, and more rape. Therefore, we must put controls on our animal nature and reach to our higher nature. Is it wise to grow the economy and pollute without thinking of our environment? We need to put controls on the way we grow. If one believes we are not higher than the animals consider the following. Do humans eat and "poop" at the same time like animals. Do we lick from the bowl or do we use utensils like forks and knives? We have a higher nature that we try to aspire to. Your relationships and character will grow when you are open, educate yourself about whom you have relationships, pursue your higher nature, and communicate well to yourself and others.

Exercise 1

A. Choose to do one thing today that is noble. The dictionary states "noble" means "of an exalted moral character or excellence, admirable in dignity in manner of expression or execution, of an admirable high quality, magnificent, notably superior."
B. Write below the last time that you lied about something. Was it to a mother, friend, teacher, boss, co-worker, brother, sister, boyfriend, spouse, etc? Ask yourself, could you have come up with a creative, nicer way to tell the truth? There's always a nice way to say even an ugly truth. For example: When a friend calls and wakes you up in the morning, instead of saying, "No, you didn't wake me up," (in a breathy scratchy voice) say something like, "Yes, but that's ok; could you just call after 9am in the future?" ____
____
____
____

Exercise 2

A. Imagine your character as an 8 1/2 by 11 piece of paper. Now obtain an 8 1/2 by 11 piece of paper and hold it in your hands. Think of a time when you gossiped about somebody. Now tear a corner of the piece of paper off, representing a piece of your character being destroyed. Think of a time when you spoke negatively about yourself. Tear off a bigger piece of paper. Now for every time that we practice positive behaviors, we restore our character as if we are able to glue or tape the pieces back together again. So just because you are wounded or have little self-respect doesn't mean that you can't gain this respect back. Tape the pieces together that you tore off and reverse the procedure. Then, commit to some more positive behaviors.

B. Write down an upcoming lie you might tell or maybe something that you might exaggerate (could be a real life story that happened to you). Also, write down a time when you were enticed to lie about something but instead you told the truth. How did it feel? Why did you tell the truth?

____

____

____

____

____

____

Exercise 3

A. Sit down with a supportive friend, partner, etc., and practice responding to these three scenarios.

1. Friend gives you a compliment. In return you merely say "Thank you".
2. Friend oversteps your boundaries, and you make a verbal boundary statement in return. For example, he/she might say to you, “What do you mean; you don't feel that way about spanking?” In return, you could state for example, "No actually, I do feel that there are better ways to discipline a child other than spanking." But use any example that would make you a bit uncomfortable and that would be appropriate in your life right now.
3. Friend accuses you of saying something to somebody. For example, "I can't believe you told Linda that I didn't care for her." In return, you could state something like, "It's important to me that you know that isn't exactly true--what I said was that you have a hard time when she can be a little controlling," or something to this effect.

B. Identify the following.

1. When or what circumstance will you usually lie about at work? (e.g. when you come in late).
2. Whom do you usually tell? Write down the specific person.
3. Write down why you think you do. Gain insight into when, who, why; it will be easier for you to pinpoint this area so you can improve it and move toward revealing more of the truth.

____

____

____

____

____

____

Identify two strong beliefs or values you hold dear, and communicate those beliefs or values to two people today. Don't overwhelm them; just find a way to work it into the conversation. This will help you to be strong in your convictions cementing your self-integrity. Example: If you want to talk about your value of teaching -- then start the conversation by asking, "What occupation do you believe helps our society?" After they respond, you can easily communicate your belief or value now because it flows in the conversation. Write below what you said and how it went.

____

____

____

____

____

____

Strategy 6.3

Bring honor to yourself and others by understanding and appreciating people who are different from you. This includes the disabled, the poor, men, women, multicultural groups, religious groups, the elderly, homosexuals, children, and others.

Acceptance, goodwill and respect are the cornerstones of successful communication and exchange--ones that cross all barriers of class, gender, race, and ability.
Bob Abamms-Mezoff/Diane Johns

Have You Mostly Been an Insider or Outsider?

Anyone can love and treat people they know who are just like themselves. It doesn't mean you are a good, honorable, and/or compassionate person. The Germans in the Nazi Party loved and treated people like them very kindly. So, if you are already doing that, It's NO BIG DEAL!!! Your integrity, your honor, your true love for other people is measured by not only those whom you know and love, but by how you treat strangers and those who are different from you. Your socialization or how you were taught to perceive people who are different from you is still likely determining your behavior toward those groups of people today. Before moving to the next point, which should convince you that you ought to appreciate others who are different, consider the following. Have you ever been an Outsider? Have you ever been "out of the loop," not know anybody at the party, been picked last on a sports team, not included in a group of people (colleagues, friends etc.)? Imagine feeling that kind of isolation, loneliness, and invisibility almost every day of your life. That is how many "people of color" and disadvantaged groups (the elderly, homosexuals, obese people, disabled people...) feel living in this society that gives the double message, "But you're just like us. But you really aren't." Close your eyes and try to feel some of that pain. Don't just push it away like most everyone else does. Use the "Heart" exercises from Chapter Two to help you get "in touch" with it.

Diversity: Appreciating Cultural and Religious Differences

We have always lived with people of different races and cultures. Most people living in the United States come from families who immigrated just two or three generations ago. The things we eat, the words we speak, the tools we use, the clothes we wear, the music we listen to, are a cultural tapestry woven by many different cultures. There are cultures of men and women, heterosexual and homosexual people, older and younger people, urban and rural dwellers, people with disabilities, different religions, ethnicities, and personalities. When we look at the world through the eyes of another culture, we "step inside their shoes" and our own view of the world becomes broader, more accurate, more complete, and more inclusive. Instead of judging cultures from our own knowledge base, we can instead say to others who are different than us, "This is what I know and here is my way. Now what is yours?"

The poor, the elderly, children, homosexuals, and people with disabilities are often discriminated against in most cultures. It used to be that students with disabilities faced a restricted set of choices in school. New technology with such as voice commands gives new hope to the visually and hearing impaired with regard to choosing majors and career. The term disability includes chronic illness, physical challenges, and learning disabilities. If you think you have a disability, seek out services at your college that offer permits to park a car closer to classrooms, note-taking services, lecture transcriptions, textbook reading services, sign language interpreters, tutors, TTY/TDD devices for students with hearing impairments, and assistance with taking tests.

As we become an increasingly more multicultural nation, we need to become more respectful and sensitive to people from different backgrounds. This is vital for building communication skills and team building skills that will be highly marketable in today's job market. Industry is closer to a point where now it would be considered a detriment to the company's bottom line to have an employee who holds racist, discriminating, prejudice views about disadvantaged groups who, more than likely, work at their employment. And if they don't work there, you can bet that their customer base is made up of a part of that group.

Sub-cultures are a group of people from a culture, which differentiates them from the larger culture to which they belong. Take responsibility to learn about the backgrounds of African Americans, Native Americans, Middle Easterners, Mexicans, Asians, European groups, Jewish Americans, as well as their sub-cultures and different religious groups. Become aware of the nonverbal messages that you might accidentally send that may offend a certain group. The best way is to become friends with someone from that group and learn and understand as much as you can. Look for common ground to build rapport by comparing values, interests, and so on. There is really nothing to fear but fear itself. Remember to be gentle as you ask for cultural information because it can be a very sensitive, vulnerable, and a painful subject to bring up for some people. However, if they see your "Heart" is in the right place and you are a person of good character, they will be more likely to share their experiences.

Point out discrimination whenever you see it. Some is intentional and some is unintentional because of a lack of experience and knowledge with that group. You might see people from another culture ignored in class, passed over in job hiring, or people ridiculed in class.

Contrasting Eastern and Western Values

The illustration below shows why Eastern and Western Cultural Values often clash or are at odds with each other. Yet, each contributes to the richness of the other's perspective and holds value in different contexts of life. Think how there might be times when both can serve the self and others without hurting anybody. For example, some may say collaboration is always better than competition. There are times when collaboration can yield better and more creative results than competition. Yet, competition in the marketplace has led to the most significant inventions and discoveries that have positively changed the life of almost every one on the planet. See below.

Eastern/Native Cultural Values	Topic	Western Cultural Values
Individual identities are sacrificed in interest of group or family identity.	Identity	Individual identity is not sacrificed but celebrated. Self matters.
One grows wiser with age and the elderly are wise and respected.	Age	Youth. Old age is viewed as "over the hill" and losses in health and intellect.
Present Based: Being there is more important than being on time.	Time	Future Based: Punctuality is very important.
Collaborate	Problem Solving	Compete
Be patient	Goals	Learn to be aggressive
Live in harmony with nature	Nature	Conquer nature
The Great Mystery	The unknown	Skepticism
Humility	Ego	Pride
Spiritual	Faith	Religious
Listen	Communication	Speak up

Learned Helplessness and Racism and Sexism

It is my assumption that we, not our circumstances, are in greater control of determining our well-being and our destiny. It is thought that we only use 5-10% of our human brain. Our potential is endless. The human spirit is virtually unstoppable when it wants something badly enough. However, the reader needs to understand that many individuals in our society are victimized by conditions and circumstances such as racism, incest, or a disability that was not their own doing. Though it is important that each victim of oppression or a traumatizing act be able to search deep within and grow somehow from their negative experience, e.g. Nelson Mandela, Christopher Reeve, it is just as important for both victim and non-victim to understand and acknowledge these negative events and conditions that exist in the society.

In lab experiments with animals, it has been demonstrated that they learn "learned helplessness." These animals are given repeated punishment with no opportunity to escape. Then they give the animals an opportunity for escape, but they fail to take this opportunity because they have been defeated by previous acts of punishment from the environment. If human beings are punished (subjected to continuous prejudice and societal judgment), they tend to give up and not act on their best behalf even when opportunities are provided. Therefore, the message to disadvantaged groups is to seek out people around you for validation and empathy such as self-help groups, social service agencies, and educators. The message to the nonvictim is to really understand and try to "put yourself in the other person's shoes." Empathize with them and take steps to be a part of the solution by making them feel accepted, empowered, and loved. Explore the root causes of your attitudes regarding race and people who are different. Respect the culture, customs, language, traditions, religion, music, dance, habits, food, and other expressions of a culture. Start conversations with individuals of other groups and look for things in common that you both share. Nothing creates more rapport than sharing common experiences and finding humor in the different aspects of life.

In the United States, women make up the majority of first-year students in higher education. Yet until the early nineteenth century, they were banned from colleges and universities. Today women in higher education still encounter bias and sexism. Instructors might gloss over the contributions of women, use only masculine pronouns-he, his, and him to refer to both men and women, career counselors hint that careers in math and science are not appropriate for women, people assume that middle-aged women who return to school have too many family commitments to do well in their classes, and so on. According to the Civil Rights Act of 1964, sexual harassment includes unwelcome sexual advances, requests, and verbal or physical conduct of a sexual nature when 1) submission to this conduct becomes a condition of employment, 2) women's response to such conduct is used as a basis for employment decisions, 3) this conduct interferes with work performance or creates an offensive work environment. The law also states that schools must take action to prevent sexual harassment.

Being Blind to Our Connectedness

From the moment of our first awareness as children, we develop the unshakable conviction that we're separate and disconnected from all other members on the planet. From then on, we live our lives apart from the divine, nature, and one another because we accept the evidence of our senses and appearances that everyone is disconnected. We become blind to our unity within the created order. We become blind to how we are all really the same inside despite the appearance of looking different from others. We must not believe that we are disconnected. It is this perception that causes the "it's every person for themselves" mentality, and we become obsessed with our own personal survival. The ego then kicks in with fear and tries to exert control and power over others to feel safe, secure, and immortal. To rise above that animal mentality, we must give others the benefit of the doubt when our fear-based thoughts try to tell us something that is not based on facts. Gather all the facts and judge fairly, accurately, and intelligently. Trust your ability that you will survive just fine. To bring integrity and connectedness to yourself and others, start to value diversity. *The ability to value diversity brings honor to*

yourself. Our society is becoming more and more diverse. In the year 2000, one in three of the total population in the United States was a person
of color. People need to be prepared to work with people of diverse backgrounds since the world is becoming smaller and more accessible as we communicate more easily with people in other parts of the world.

Valuing diversity is:

- sharing your thoughts, ideas, and opinions with others
- listening openly to a variety of opinions and perspectives regarding social issues
- being honest with your own biases toward others
- seeing the strength in diversity. The U.S. has won more gold medals than any other country in
  the Olympics for one reason. There is a diversity of racial talent in this country that is unlike any other country in the history of the world.

Valuing diversity is not:

- a lecture on how you should think, feel, or act
- white-male bashing.
- saying what you think others want to hear.
- giving lip service to position yourself for promotion.

Accepting and Embracing Gender Differences

One of the biggest differences lies in gender. Women usually have no idea what it's like to be a man, and men usually have no idea what is like to be a woman.

- Our brains are biochemically wired differently. The male fetus' brain is immersed with testosterone at only 8 weeks in the womb.
- Anthropologically, 10,000 years ago men gathered and hunted for food and became oriented toward achievement or conquest. They like to cut to the chase and see the big picture.
- Anthropologically, 10,000 years ago women took care of children and supported and talked with each other in the neighborhood while the men were gone. Therefore, they became more process-oriented, able to see details around the home better, and developed the emotional and supportive parts of the self.
- The roles that men and women play today come from a long history of roles that men and women have been in for thousands of years. Men have been the traditional "breadwinner" for the family, but this is changing for virtually the first time in history. Women have traditionally been the nurturing parent who stays at home and cares for the children. Thus, both men and women's identity for years have largely come from the roles that they've played out. The whole social structure for thousands of years has been constructed to ensure that these roles stay the same. To deviate from them was to bring suffering, ridicule, or death upon oneself. Below are examples of the how men and women **generally** think differently.

MEN	**WOMEN**
- Told he's lost--he hears "you failed" →	- Told she's loved--needs to know why
- Conquer-oriented, (sex-1st to 5th gear)	- Process-oriented, (sex-foreplay -1st gear to 2nd)
- Macro-oriented: reads world news, sees big picture	- Micro-oriented: remembers details…birthdays, etc.
- Needs transition time after work	- Needs to talk after work about the day
- Desires fixing and solving	- Desires comfort and validation
- Needs a project or appointment time	- Needs relaxing down time - not doing
- Minimizes problems	- Maximizes problems
- Hot buttons: chance annoyances or delays, hostility, unfair or unreasonable orders, nosey people, being manipulated make men very angry due to a feeling of powerlessness.	- Hot buttons… social slights, being let down by people they trust, not being perfect, cruel actions make women angry due to the need for self-worth, don't like feeling foolish, naïve, or criticized.

Facts and Statistics on Men and Women's Lives

Research on your own or discuss in class the facts you could add to the following points about the different ways men and women experience their gender. Note the referenced research.

Men

According to the U.S. Bureau of Health and Human Services (2009, 1991), regarding the first two points below: (see references in back of book)

- Suicide for boys is 6 times higher than that of girls to age 24. It is 1,350 times higher after age 85. As of 2009, suicide for boys was 5 times higher than girls (Farrell's Multi-partisan Commission Proposal to the White House Council on Boys and Men).
- Men die seven years earlier than women; it was only one year earlier in 1920.
- According to Cancer Facts and Figures (1991,1999), prostate cancer is equally as fatal as breast cancer while breast cancer got 660% more funding in the 1990's. Prostate cancer grew at twice the rate of breast cancer in the last eight years of the 1990's.
- According to the U.S. Dept. of Justice (2010), men are twice as likely as women to be victims of violent crimes and three times more likely to be victims of murder . Yet, magazines, talk shows, and TV specials mostly focus on the dark side of men and the victimization & light side of women.
- A husband whose wife dies is about ten times more likely to commit suicide than a wife whose husband dies according to Farrell (1993, 2000).
- When a study published by the New England Journal of Medicine revealed that wounded Vietnam combat veterans suffered more from PTSD (post traumatic stress disorder) than victims of rape and muggings, it received little publicity. In New York, only four social service organizations deal with veterans, yet, over fifty such agencies deal with women's issues all publicly funded according to Farrell (1993, 2000).
- *African American boys who drop out of high school have a 60% chance of prison time by age 35.

Women

- Often live in fear of being mugged, raped, or killed by men.
- Many get stuck with being a single parent with little support from the father.
- Get paid less for equal work (U.S. Dept. of Labor 2008).
- 91% of all rapes are against women (U.S. Bureau of Justice Statistics (1997).
- May work as many hours as their husbands but do more chores and spend more time with kids.
- According to Sapiro (1994), before the Civil War, women could not control/own property even through inheritance. The husband had a right to her wages. The husband also decided on the education and religion for the family.

Exercise 1

Complete a cultural research paper using the numbered guidelines below.

1. Conduct research in the library or on the Internet for recent studies on the following topics:
   A. Choose a Native American tribe or non-western sub-culture.
   B. Choose any topic among the following and relate it toward the above cultural group: gender roles, birth order, identity issues, rites of passage, methods used for emotional healing, how decisions are made, family expectations, or how one chooses a career/path.
   C. Write about these topics as they have occurred any time within the last 150 years.

2. The last paragraph must address how this information will affect you, your beliefs and your life.

3. Report your findings in a 2-4 page summary. It must be word-processed with a maximum of a 12 font and 1-inch margins. It must be single spaced and double spaced between paragraphs.

4. Reference summary, citing the books, journals, internet, etc. used to obtain the information.

Exercise 2

Participate in a cultural plunge. What events and activities could you participate in to increase your awareness of different cultural or religious groups? Choose one cultural group/race different from your own. Ask the following questions as well as any of your own if desired. As you interview them, dig deeper if you receive short replies. Write below.

Name of person and cultural group

What was it like growing up in your culture?

What kind of racism did you encounter if any?

How do you try to overcome this racism?

What kind of values were you taught?

What kind of advice would you give young kids who grow up in your culture?

What angers you most about society?

What pressures do you experience?

What are you proud of in your culture?

What cultural events are significant to you?

Other comments.

Exercise 3

Participate in a gender plunge. Identify and interview somebody of the opposite sex that you feel could give you information about how he/she experiences their gender (being a man or woman). Ask the following questions and write below what you learned. Dig deeper if you receive short replies.

Name of person and gender group____________________________________

What aspects do you like most about being a man/woman?____________________

What do you dislike most about being a man/woman?____________________

What angers you most about being a man/woman in this society?____________________

How often do you think about sex?____________________

How often do you think about how you look to others?____________________

What fears do you have about being a man/woman? How often do you think about those fears?

You would be considered a failure in the future if you…what and why?____________________

What do you wish men/women knew about women/men? Example: If interviewing a man ask: "what do you wish women knew about men."

What responsibility do you have as a man/woman?____________________

Other comments:____________________

Strategy 6.4

Take responsibility for only those things you can control.

Effort Linked to Results

Take responsibility to do an outstanding job in as many areas of life as you can. Use the chart below to help you understand that the effort we put in doesn't always give the results we would like. You can apply this example to relationships, your job, taking tests, or your performance in any skill.

If the quality of your effort and job was:	Your results are likely to be:
Poor	Painful ....leading to divorce, getting fired, etc.
Good	Mediocre (below average)
Excellent (90 – 92%)	Good
Outstanding (97 – 100%)	Extraordinary

When one does outstanding work, in addition to working hard, he/she puts "heart" into what he/she is doing. This person goes above and beyond the amount of effort it takes to be extraordinary.

Keep Asking, How am I Responsible?

We often expect others or institutions to take responsibility for us. However,
- Society can't give you moral character
- The University can't give you an education
- Business/industry does not owe you a job
- Therapy will not give you happiness
- Religion will not save your soul
- Doctors can't give you good health

We have to take responsibility for acquiring these things ourselves. We want benefit packages without productivity requirements, love without commitment, sex without consequences, character
without guts and taking risks, and we want self-esteem without working through the pain and issues in our lives. Affirm this 2-letter, 10-word statement-- IF IT IS TO BE, IT IS UP TO ME.

People can't make you do anything. Consider the statement, "My husband gave me a complex about my body." We can only give people permission to give us a complex about ourselves.
Learn to set boundaries with those people who disrespect you. In this example, she could say to her husband without resentment, “As long as you continue to disrespect my body, there is no way we can have sex together." You will learn to set boundaries in Week 8.

Cultivate your own garden first before digging up another's. Some of us are more interested in fixing others' lives and faults when we need to fix our own. Quit butting in!!

Many students at the college wonder why they are in the predicaments they are in. Many of these don't see how their actions got them where they are. They will drop their units, obtain a low grade- point average and then wonder why financial aid has put them on probation. A student that I counseled decided to drop a needed support service that would have given her free book money and pay for other college expenses. She terminated herself from the program because she didn't agree with the rules. But one year later, she complained to me that the system wouldn't give her the money needed for her to attend college and graduate. Does she have a right to complain when a well-known and well-run support service was willing to give it to her but she refused?

People on welfare will sometimes tell you, "I have three kids, and it's too hard for me to go to college. It's not fair that I have to work three times harder than everybody else.” If her condition was caused by irresponsibility like having unprotected sex numerous times, then she does not have a good case, and her attitude does not empower her to make changes. Not taking responsibility is perhaps the most important function that determines success or failure because with responsibility comes good attitude, perseverance, patience, and dependency on yourself.

Things you can control are your energy level, diet, free time, communication skills, spiritual life, response, attitude, tongue, friends, purpose in life, meaningful work, and family contribution.

Take responsibility for narrowness in your thinking. Examples include: prejudice, seeing all things as black or white, seeing what you want to see despite the truth. Narrow thinking keeps us focused on what exists instead of what is possible. It stifles creativity and is incapable of seeing things from different angles and perspectives. You then live a “rose colored” ignorant life, leaving yourself completely clueless to the real truth of matters. Narrowness in thinking does not seek out truth or see creative solutions since it is usually in mode of only one solution, and it doesn't allow us to see what might exist and the possibilities in yourself and others.

If others make mistakes, don't accuse. Just understand that is where they are at this time. It is not what they are doing or not doing that is the issue. It may be their fault, but it is your problem to deal with. So if you start to think the problem is “out there,” stop and just do your part of the job.

We often don't take responsibility because we fear success. We can fear success because we may have to give up pleasurable habits like watching television, loafing around, time with friends, and risking criticism from others since we would have more exposure. Also, we would have to delay gratification in other important areas like not being able to spend times with self or family because in many instances, we will be working longer and harder. So when we don't take risks and responsibility, we can more easily succumb to the three ruts of being mediocre: following conventional wisdom, conforming to group-think, and blaming others.

Exercise 1

Meditate or reflect for five minutes on the phrase: "I am responsible for….."

Write below any insights you received. Examples include improving your relationship with your spouse, mother, father, kids, etc., improving your job performance, paying the bills on time, making sure your kids don't watch too much TV, not gossiping about others, and so on. After, complete the sentence *"If I take full responsibility for my (actions, thoughts, feelings, education, me) I will………*

Example: "If I take full responsibility for my actions, I will have no one to blame and will get things done."

Exercise 2

Take your top two items that you are responsible for from the above list and

1. Write a commitment statement. For example, if you want to improve job performance, you could write:

- I commit to putting my files away instead of having the secretary do it.
- I commit to taking care of my clients even after they have bought the service/product.

Exercise 3

2. Write how you will put this into action. For example, I will put my files away everyday at 4:00 p.m. sharp.

Strategy 6.5

Don't take responsibility for things you can't control and things you shouldn't control.

What You are not Responsible For

You cannot control, traffic, discrimination, bureaucracy, and, most importantly, other people. Many people take on too much responsibility and are labeled appropriately by psychologists as rescuers. Rescuers take on other people's responsibilities to feel needed and bring harmony to relationships. Unfortunately, it robs the rescuer of power and energy, and it robs the rescuee of the same energy and power to learn from their actions or mistakes.

Some rescuers "should on themselves" and feel guilt and shame for not fixing someone like a close friend or sister because they've calculated that the person will never be fixed without their help. This can often be egotistical. We all make mistakes, even the best parents! Example: If a rescuer did something truly wrong, he might feel, "I am responsible for my child's pain; therefore, I am a bad person. Instead, what he/she could affirm is, "I am responsible for what I've done, but I can learn from it, and I can change." Irresponsible people would not want to change.

Other examples of things we cannot control are family, prejudice (you can advocate against it), genes/natural look, the world, family, disease, whether somebody hires you, traffic, the weather, etc.

Exercise 1

What areas or events in your life have you taken on too much responsibility or inappropriate responsibility? Make a list. Example: Do you take on too much responsibility in your relationship, at work, or in fixing people? Do you ever apologize for things that aren't your fault? What were the circumstances?

____

____

____

____

____

____

____

____

____

____

____

____

____

____

____

____

____

____

____

Exercise 2

Think of a specific circumstance from the previous exercise. Now visualize a new behavior dealing with the circumstance appropriately by not taking on the extra responsibility. Picture yourself tactfully saying 'no', or smiling confidently while you set a verbal boundary with somebody. During your visualization, you can even make a mini-movie out of it. Develop a cast of characters with you as the hero. This will help relieve some of the anxiety while simultaneously making your imagery become reality.

Exercise 3

Pick one circumstance and role-play with a friend/partner or empty chair. Have that person play the part of the specific person that entices you to take on extra responsibility. And start new behaviors by practicing boundary setting and request making. Describe the circumstance below and what you would say. See the example below:

Situation: "You always feel the need to fix your friends' problems."
Friend: "I'm afraid to tell my boyfriend I want to break up with him."
Old you: "Well, if you're afraid, I'll do it for you and casually let him know that's what you want."
New you: "I'm sure you are afraid, but after you do, I'm sure you'll feel it was the best thing to do."

Exercise 6.6

Set a high character standard for yourself.

What is a Character Standard?

A character standard is a set of valuable rules you make up that you compare yourself to in order to behave the way you desire. By defining our character standard, we will become clear on who we want to be and commit to behaving that way. For example, possible rules you might set for being a good friend to others might be someone who can keep a secret, someone you can count on, have a fun time with, and be totally honest with. You might develop the rule that it is not somebody who doesn't value your time or support your goals. Once this standard is defined, you can more easily identify those people who do and don't fit your standard. Would you want to have a friend who disrespects your values and goals? Yet many of us have friends like this.

You may have a work standard that you aspire to at work. It might be don't tell off- color jokes, be professional, dress nice, treat each person with respect, etc.

Some people apologize for things they are not guilty of or shouldn't feel guilty for. If you're not guilty, don't apologize because it isn't fair to yourself. For example, "I'm sorry you couldn't get a hold of me." Instead you could say, "Oh, you called at 6 p.m. I actually don't come home until 7 p.m., and I would love hearing from you next time." Don't forget if it is something that you are guilty of, open the heart, apologize sincerely, and let it go relatively fast.

Exercise 1

Write down the answer to these questions.

1. What is my character standard in a loving relationship? For example: I ought to be open, honest, treat others kindly, be healthy, respectful and accepting, etc.

____

____

____

____

____

____

____

____

____

____

____

____

____

____

____

____

____

____

____

____

____

____

Exercise 2

1. Write down the answer to the question, what is my character standard as a student and an employee at my work?

Exercise 3

Write down the answer to the question, what is my character standard as a parent?

What is my character standard as a friend?

Look at these character statements every day so you will more likely incorporate them into your life. These actions will help you rise toward your character standard!!

Strategy 6.7

Set a high character standard for others.

When Is It Their Problem?

We need to know that people are responsible for expressing their own feelings and wishes. It is not our job to guess what they are thinking. For example,

Friend Situation: You are asked by a friend to go out to a party or movie .

You reply: "I'd love to go out with you, but I need to study tonight and get caught up" You later think: Maybe I hurt her feelings when I said 'no' to going out.

A high character standard might be determined this way: If he/she was a true friend, he/she would respect your decision, while not necessarily agreeing with it. We want to be able to give this person the benefit of the doubt of being strong enough to rise to your expectation, your character standard. Let go of the worry and guilt, and empower this person to handle the high character standard you've assigned to him/her.

Most people are highly controlled by their parents. For example,

Parent Situation: You are invited last minute to go to your parents or in-laws for dinner.

You reply: We'd love to come over this weekend, yet it's important for us to catch up on our obligations. Why don't we plan another time soon, and that way it'll be in our calendar? We'll look forward to it. You later think: I hope they don't think we don't want to spend time with them; I could tell they were a little upset. A high character standard might be determined this way: a healthy parent would understand last minute and shouldn't have expected us to drop everything to come over. Besides, we did show interest about coming over soon.

If the friend doesn't respect your wishes over time, then you might want to consider the next point. He/she doesn't care about you as much as you might think; you might be better off without them as a friend because of their selfishness. Since we do not get rid of our parents, and let's say they continue to being controlling and nagging or withdraw their love, you can give them a dose of a healthy relationship. You can say to them, "Mom, when you nag/fight with us and disrespect our decisions, it makes us not want to spend time with you. I don't feel like seeing you for a while now, and I don't want that because I want us to be close." By this type of boundary setting and consequence, you will teach them to act accordingly, regardless of how they might be feeling underneath. At least you've gotten them to comply with your wishes in the same way you would do for them. But give them time. You need to be strong and not need their approval too much. Remember that they are learning a new behavior, so be patient with them.

Exercise 1

Who are the people I need to set a high character standard with? List them. Think of parents, spouse, children, boss, co-workers, friends, relatives, neighbors, etc.

____

____

____

____

____

____

____

Exercise 2

Narrow the choices in Exercise 1 to one and set a date this week to communicate your high character standard to this person. Write down what you want to say word for word.

Exercise 3

Practice with a partner/friend on the telephone how you are going to state your high character standard to this person. Have this person act as if he/she was that specific person. Also, have that person give you ideas about what you could say and how to say it. Then, perform it. Write the results of your experience below.

Chapter Insight & Commitment

After completing this chapter, I learned the following about my honesty, morality, how I treat others, my responsibilities, and character standards:
Example: I learned that I am more apt to lie when it serves my purpose like when I exaggerate a story to make me look better. I also need to take responsibility for my own character and my life instead of trying to rescue and control others.

I can take active steps to help me achieve my future goals and become more of the person I am or strive to be by:
Example: By being more honest in my dealings at home and at work, I can take full responsibility for the outcomes in my life instead of blaming others. This will help keep my reputation clean and positive which will assist my accounting business to grow.

CHAPTER 7

Self-Discipline

Using your **Mind** to Discipline your thoughts and behaviors toward correct action.

Purpose: To resist the urge to misperceive events and gratify one's self in the short-term so one can control one's destiny and benefit from long-term rewards.

Rewards: Top Performance, Inner Harmony, Balanced Emotions, Long-term Success, Deep Fulfillment, Ability to Cope, Productivity

Obstacles: Outside Temptations/Vices, Addictions, Instant Gratification, Laziness

Consequence: Suffering, Loss, Compulsiveness, Hopelessness, Unfulfillment

Symbol: Force Shield

Related Web Site: http://www.selfgrowth.com

Self-Discipline

Self-discipline is defined as the ability to resist the urge to gratify one's self in the short-run so that he/she can benefit from long-term rewards. There are tendencies and drives within human nature to become too lazy, selfish, addictive, and hedonistic. When one tries to discipline oneself, a struggle often occurs which involves fighting off these emotional and behavioral tendencies and drives to take the easy way out. Yet, when we discipline our mind and behavior, the rewards are awesome. Imagine being able to acquire any skill, discipline, or habit that you want in the world. You could achieve almost anything! Research shows that if you have the self-discipline to perform that skill or habit for at least 21 days, you can acquire it. Yet most people do not have the self-discipline to practice their skill for more than three days. One reason for this is that they do not want their skill or goal strongly enough. In other words, most people are not willing to make a commitment to it. This means that they are not willing to sacrifice and pay the price in time and energy that it takes to acquire such a goal. People do not commit to creating a new habit because they do not have the knowledge and inner strength that is needed to acquire their goal. There are two types of self-disciplines that one must be able to master in order to succeed in this area. They are the following:

MENTAL SELF-DISCIPLINE:
Mental self-discipline includes three abilities: 1) the ability to view things and events in our lives through wider, more objective lenses rather than narrow subjective lenses (Perspective), 2) the ability to become resistant toward unhealthy emotional temptations (Patience), and 3) the ability to have healthy relationships with all elements of life and resist attachment to them (Detachment). Once we have mental self-discipline, we are able to drive down any path in life we desire. Having mental discipline is like having a fine tuned automobile that can handle any bump or terrain in its path. Yet in order to be completely successful, one must master the second type of self-discipline.

BEHAVIORAL SELF-DISCIPLINE:
Behavioral self-discipline includes four abilities: 1) the ability to perform things efficiently and resist the urge to settle for less or become lazy (Performance), 2) the ability to resist the urge to over indulge in life's joys and vices (Moderation), 3) the ability to resist the urge to quit when pursuing our goals (Perseverance) and, 4) the ability to resist the urge to become more selfish as we build a life for ourselves (Goodwill).

You will increase the likelihood of achieving the goal that you decided to pursue from last chapter by using the self-discipline strategies in this chapter. Once the self-discipline exercises from this chapter are completed, you will be able to increase your productivity, possess control in your life, achieve goals and success in many of your endeavors, and improve your ability to handle difficult situations.

Strategy 7.1
Practice Inventive Perspective.

Definition: Perspective - the ability to frame an experience or event in an objective, insightful, new way that can be learned from.

Getting a Fresh Perspective on Things

Most people meet or respond to obstacles, failures, and roadblocks by quitting, stressing out, getting depressed, or believing the world is against them. What often separates the successful from the unsuccessful is the ability to see things from a different perspective. Many of us, when progressing toward our goals, wear the same old lenses. When meeting setbacks, these lenses show us no way out, and we often decide to quit. Or the old lenses may paint a picture in our minds from which we may expect things to progress more smoothly. When this expectation does not occur, any perceived roadblocks may be more devastating to us. What is needed is a new pair of lenses that allows us to view an event from a different angle. When meeting setbacks and roadblocks along the way, it will be important for you to be able to reframe bleak pictures into opportunities to learn and grow from.

Understand that your job cannot guarantee security. Rather, security lies in your skills, abilities, talents, knowledge, and power to communicate and produce. You are the "**goose** who lays the golden eggs" for your employer. It is not the egg (what you produce) that is valuable; it is the goose (the person who can produce it).

Old Perspectives Die Hard

Old perspectives, when pursuing goals, use:

- <u>Short-run thinking</u> - avoids short-term pain (needed in all pursuits), which ends up preventing long-term gain.
- <u>Personalized thinking</u> - when conflict arises with others, they dwell and fixate on how bad things are.
- <u>Negative thinking</u> - expects things in the future to fail.
- Old perspectives cause discouragement, anxiety, and quitting.

New Inventive Perspectives Live On

New inventive perspectives use:

- <u>Long-run thinking</u> - expects short-term pain, knowing greater long-term rewards will result.
- <u>Open thinking</u> - learns from situation and uses that knowledge toward goals.
- <u>Positive thinking</u> - sees multiple options and choices; applies knowledge.
- New inventive perspectives cause renewal, progress, appreciation, and motivation.

Example of negative experience: You were fired from your job.

<u>Old Perspective</u>	<u>New Perspective</u>
- Decided that you were incompetent and not a good worker.	- At least I know what I did right and wrong
- Feel your record is tarnished forever.	- I can be more knowledgeable next time.
- Outlook now is, "Settle for a mediocre job".	- I may not need to put this on my resume.
	- Use as an opportunity to get better job.

The 5 Step Inventive Perspective Method

To gain a new inventive perspective out of something undesirable, ask yourself:

a. How can I learn from this situation?

b. How can I apply this to the future?

c. Will this event be important when I look back on it 30 years from now?

d. Could this situation be pointing me in another direction or option I haven't considered?

e. What can I do to resolve it?

Exercise 1

Identify a time when you didn't use perspective and answer the five questions from above.
Example: Getting bad grades in college.
a. I need to change my study habits.
b. Research a better instructor.
c. No, because I would have already graduated and it will seem like a small event.
d. I can work hard or get tutoring, and it's showing me that I need to work smarter and harder.
e. Repeat the course for a better grade.

____
____
____
____
____
____
____
____
____

Exercise 2

Write below when and where you used perspective in the past. Which events? Examples of events include bad grade in school, missed deadline at work, traffic on the road, talked down to by retailer, events with family, friends, etc.____________________________________

____
____
____
____
____
____
____
____
____
____
____
____
____
____

Exercise 3

A. Write down two events in your life that seemed unjust or unfair to you.

B. What is your attitude toward them on a scale of 1-10, 10 being the most negative and angry?

C. Does this attitude help you achieve your goals? Yes___ No___

D. Write an attitude that is more helpful to accept and how you can learn from it.

E. What future events in your life could you apply this to?

Strategy 7.2
Practice Calm Patience.

Definition: Patience - the ability to calmly and faithfully wait for future events to occur to prevent quitting and needless anxiety.

Why Develop Patience???

Patience is another virtue that, if not acquired, causes quitting, stress and anxiety, and discouragement. Because our expectations of how things should be usually fall short of reality, we often become impatient. Frustration occurs when our expectations don't occur within the timeframe we set, e.g. waiting in a grocery line when the person in front of you has a ton of coupons.

As a community college counselor and instructor, I see thousands of students who burn themselves out because they have a graduation timeline that they cling to. When it looks like they have to postpone their goal a semester or two, they get anxious, depressed, and many times quit. I experienced this anxiety in my junior year when I realized I was not going to obtain my bachelor's degree in four years. I made a decision, despite all my friends who were on their way to obtaining their degree in four years, that I would get my degree in six years and work two to three jobs to support myself. As it turned out, I earned a higher education level than my friends, and many of them even dropped out of college. Be patient.

Be patient and evaluate all the pros and cons of big decisions such as when buying a home, buying a car, or having a baby. If you make a hasty decision, life can be very stressful when you lose money, go into debt, or when you're not emotionally and financially ready for a family.

Patience does not mean that you should not assert yourself, stand up for yourself, or take responsibility. For instance, if you have been waiting for a half hour for a table in a restaurant, a proper response would be to either tell the host or hostess how long you've been waiting (and to calmly continue to wait) or to go to another restaurant.

Throughout the generations, administrators and CEO's have failed to consult the lower chain of command when making key decisions. It is the lower chain of command that is actually more in touch with customers/clients/students. Terrible decisions with disastrous results are made because administrators are either not patient to receive the information from their employees or their egos and arrogance are so high that they think they know what is best.

Exercising patience is similar to exercising your muscles. When you exercise patience beyond your previous limits, the emotional fiber is broken, nature overcompensates, and next time the fiber is stronger. So, too, will be your patience.

The Patient Chinese Farmer with Perspective

There's a story of a Chinese farmer who used both patience and perspective to overcome traumatic events in his life. The farmer's son, who plowed the farm, broke both of his legs. People from the village came over and said, "What could be worse; you'll be ruined." He replied, "Maybe yes, maybe no." ** That same year, a bloody war broke out and the army did not draft the son to go to war. A year later, after the war, his best horse that plowed the field ran away and people from the village came over and said, "This is terrible luck. Your farm will never be the same. You'll be ruined." He replied, "Maybe yes, maybe no." **A week later the horse brought a team of stallions back to the farm.

Moral: By skipping the enticing judgment process right after a negative event, we can judge and interpret an event more accurately if we wait so that we can more fully understand why things happen to us. Often, there is a valuable lesson or insight to be learned so that our attention and energy can be redirected to something more productive.

Exercise 1

Perform the following steps when things are not going your way or when stress begins to build up. For example, when you're trying to repair something and a tool breaks, you are in a hurry to get to work, or you're trying to get chores done around the house.

A. Take six long, slow, deep breaths.

B. Slow your pace down by walking slower, moving slower, etc., because a couple of seconds in the end usually doesn't matter anyway.

C. Accept the worst and then consider the most likely scenario. For example, you may be worried about getting to work on time and how your boss may fire you (accept the worst) for being late. However, a more likely scenario is that your boss may mention your tardiness to you and request that you be more punctual.

Exercise 2

When running an errand to the bank, store, or when just driving home, find the longest line and wait patiently in that line. Notice if you feel any discomfort in your body and mind. Try to relax, knowing you are doing this to practice and increase your skills in becoming more patient so that you can meet future anxiety-ridden events with more ease and centeredness. Record your feelings and experiences below.

____

____

____

____

____

Exercise 3

Recall your experience from Exercise 2 and answer the following questions.

Describe below if you were angry at anyone as you were waiting? ______________

____

____

____

____

D. Think of a time in the past when you were "slow," made a mistake, or held up a line. Describe the situation and how you felt during the time.______________________

____

____

____

____

____

____

____

____

____

Strategy 7.3

Practice Conscious Detachment.

Definition: Detachment - the ability to resist the urge to overly need any one thing in life.

What Attachments Do You Have?

Most problems people have are due to attachments to people, objects, substances, bad habits, thoughts, ideas, etc. Our attachments to people (losing ourselves while overly-needing somebody else), destroys the relationship with that person and disables us from acting healthy toward them in an assertive and equal way.
Example: - Putting priests, teachers, or love partners on a pedestal. We can also have attachments to beliefs and ideas that narrow our thinking like being prejudice, constricting our creativity and reasoning skills, and preventing open mindedness.
Example: - A teacher who believes that Indian students aren't smart. The teacher, regardless of the achievement of the Indian student, would likely dismiss or deny the Indian student's progress and continue to hold onto his/her judgmental beliefs.

Many of us have a strong need to be liked by everybody. This, again, is an attachment problem that demands we obtain others' approval in order to feel good about ourselves.

Many of us have a strong need to drink a cup of coffee in the morning with our breakfast. This is an attachment problem with substances. We may have an attachment to watching television while eating dinner. Some attachments are harmless and others are harmful. Think of all the attachments you might have.

Exercise 1

Practice the Progressive Muscle Technique. Relax your entire body and take five deep breaths. Tighten your left foot for four seconds and feel the attachment of holding that muscle. Then let your left foot relax and feel detachment as the blood flows back into the foot. Now do the same for the right foot, left leg, right leg, stomach, buttocks, chest, hands, arms, neck, back, shoulders, jaw, and forehead.

This exercise should help you to understand attachment and detachment through the tightening and releasing of muscles in your body.

Exercise 2

Write down three things you are attached to that may be unhealthy. Relax your entire body and take five deep breaths. Think of one unhealthy attachment like coffee and go through the entire Progressive Muscle Exercise for each attachment. When you feel your attachment, clench a body part. Then, as you see yourself detach from the attachment, relax that same body part.

Visualize yourself, from week to week, becoming less and less attached to these unhealthy attachments in your life. See yourself focusing and redirecting your energies and attention to other matters. Do this for 10 minutes. Make the visualization bright, clear, and colorful.

____

____

____

____

____

____

Exercise 3

A. What/Who in life are you attached to in an unhealthy way?

B. What commitment can you make to become less attached?

C. How will you schedule it?

Strategy 7.4
Practice Balanced Performance.

Definition: Performance - the ability to successfully carry out activities in a speedy but relaxed fashion.

How To Manage Your Time and Perform at an Optimum Level

Self-esteem is directly related to performance. When we do something well, we feel special and good about ourselves. In order to become excellent in any area, we need to reach beyond our comfort zone. Whether it's completing a task or a long-term goal, the quality of our performance determines if we complete it in a timeframe we desire. In order to greatly improve our performance, we must have the desire to improve ourselves and have the desire to become a master at something. This can be achieved using two major time management skills: A) Starting and completing tasks and B) Performing efficiently during those tasks.

A. Start and Complete Tasks.

You can have all of the education, talent, and intelligence in the world, but if you fail to take action toward worthwhile goals, you will be a failure. Calvin Coolidge said: *"Nothing is more common than unsuccessful men with talent. Unrewarded genius is almost a proverb, and the world is full of educated derelicts. Persistence and determination alone are omnipotent."*

Many people who learn time management skills in college or seminars fail to incorporate them successfully into their lives because of one main reason. That is, they haven't assessed their personality style beforehand to determine which time management strategies would work best for them. To do so, take the following Type A - B Assessment summarized from Phares (1988) (p. 452).

- *Do you perceive time as passing by rather rapidly? Yes/No*
- *Do you work near maximum capacity even when there is no time deadline involved? Yes/No*
- *Do you become aggressive and hostile when frustrated? Yes/No*
- *Do you become motivated by intense desires to master your physical and social environment to maintain control? Yes/No*
- *Do you respond impatiently with people who are slow? Yes/No*
- *Do you find it hard to eat properly, get adequate sleep, and exercise? Yes/No*

If you answered 'Yes' to 4 of the 6 questions, you're probably Type A.
If not, you're probably Type B.

Most people are a blend of Type A and B elements but usually lean toward one or the other. Now that you have a good idea of what personality style you are, it is important to use the following Time Management Strategies to start and complete tasks and projects.

Type A Time Management Strategies

Type A Time Management Strategies are like Self-Care Strategies and are a necessity for the Type A personality, who is usually high strung and in a hurry to get things done. This person needs to constantly ask him/herself the question, "How can I make it easier on myself?" Or, "Should I take a break soon?" By using Self-Care Strategies, the Type A personality won't become as stressed. It is this excessive stress that actually lowers the quality of the Type A's performance. Type A's shouldn't overwhelm themselves with obligations and tasks. Though the Type A's organizational skills are probably better than most and have been a credit to his/her achievement, often this type of person can burn him/herself out. This can result in a decrease in performance and health. If you are a Type A personality and you wish to return balance to your performance, practice flexible time management. If you need to postpone something on your To-Do list, it's not the end of the world. Start to use the following Type A Time Management/Self-Care Strategies throughout your day while you begin and complete tasks.

- Before starting tasks, ask yourself, "Does the project I'm about to start contribute to balancing my life?" Do you need to spend more time on the social, spiritual, or physical area of your life?
- Build space in your daily calendar for emergencies, relaxing time, time with family/friends, break time, etc.
- Spend money wisely. If the product comes with a 500-page manual as opposed to one hour of training, invest in the one hour of training.
- Learn to slow down. Drive 10 mph. slower and out of the fast lane; shower after work to "wash away" the day's work; focus and take deep breaths before starting a task.
- Allow yourself the feeling of enjoyment from completing a task. Try to avoid the need to immediately move on to the next project.
- Spend time with loved ones (and yourself) doing such activities as journal writing, meditation, prayer, a walk out in nature, etc. Most people look back at their 20's as having been wasted in pursuit of corporate success and look back at their 30's as missing out on their children's upbringing.
- Weed out activities that deliver little reward.
- Keep a non To-Do list. List those things you will not do so you can focus on the important tasks.

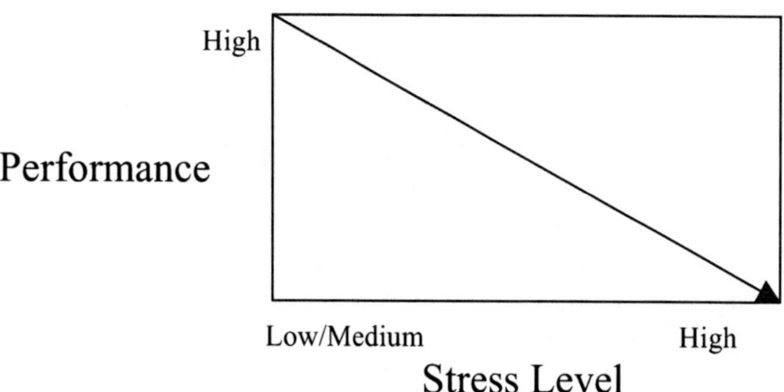

Notice from the chart above that as your stress increases, your performance drops to a lower level. As your stress lowers, your performance increases higher. That is why Type A's need to learn to be calm, cool, and collected when performing. They tend to burnout on the job and have higher incidents of heart attacks and hypertension. The most amazing performers, from athletes to war heroes to professional speakers, all perform with precision when they are cool and calm.

Type B Time Management Strategies

These strategies are like Self-challenge strategies and are a necessity for the Type B personality. The person with a Type B personality is usually relaxed and casual about things, but he/she can also be lazy and procrastinate. Start challenging yourself in all areas of your life including the occupational, personal, self-improvement, intellectual, and physical areas. Don't try to work on everything all at once. Choose one strategy for a while then another. By making just a little improvement, the Type B can perform and score at a much higher level of achievement.

Example: In baseball, if you get 2 hits out of every 10 at bats, one extra hit every 10 at bats will increase your batting average from 200 to 300. That's a difference in pay of $2,000,000 a year. The same math applies to many sales occupations in this country. Type B's usually settle for less and lounge around more often. This is why Type B's need to challenge themselves to move out of their "comfort zone" when starting and completing tasks. This person needs to take advantage of proven **Time Management Skills**. These people should constantly ask themselves, "What are the benefits of completing this task?" Or, "What's the best use of my time right now?" Or, "Am I getting things done on my to-do list?" Or, using the affirmation, "I do it now." By using Self-Challenge Strategies, the Type B personality won't procrastinate as much and will increase his/her chances of starting and completing projects. Start to use the following Time Management Strategies in your day while you start and complete tasks.

Time Management Strategies for the Type B Personality:

- Prioritize your most important tasks and complete them in that ranking order. Your most important tasks should be related to your long-term goals that you have in writing.
- Keep a daily planner and plan the day in fixed blocks of time the night before.
- Add flexibility in your schedule for emergencies, errands, paying bills, laundry, recreation, and so on.
- Take note of your best time of day. Do you perform certain tasks better in the morning, afternoon, or at night? It is different for everybody. There is no right answer. Some people (early birds) swear that morning time is their most alive and refreshing hour. Others, like me (night owls), think better, read faster, write clearer, and come alive after 11pm.
- Note what environment you work best in and then change your environment to optimize your mental and physical energy level. Do you work best in silence, with music, bright lights, outside, in nature, with earplugs, etc?
- Make good use of waiting time. Get your reading done, balance your checkbook, or go through your mail while waiting for your doctor's appointment, the bus, late friends, etc.
- Say no to people and projects that don't fit into your lifetime goals.
- Get a head start on tomorrow. Instead of being in a rush on my way to work, I will take care of needed tasks the night before, such as ironing my clothes, shaving, making my lunch, and putting needed items by the door so I don't forget them. This saves at least 20 minutes of time in the morning and I am more relaxed instead of being in a frantic mode, which sets the tone for the day.
- Allocate an appropriate time to spend on a task, depending on its importance. There are times when it is perfectly fine to complete something satisfactorily. There are other tasks we need to complete with excellence, and still others with near perfection.
- Delegate tasks to your roommates, family members, colleagues, spouse, friends, and so on, instead of trying to do it all by yourself.
- Observe how you spend your time and make adjustments. Most Americans will tell you they only spend a little time out of their day watching television when, in reality, most Americans average over three hours of T.V. a day. Source: TV-Free America.
- Instead of cramming last minute before a deadline, take big projects apart and complete small tasks over a period of time until the project is complete. When we cram, our quality of effort and health decreases.

B. Perform efficiently during the task.

1. Arrange your environment appropriately: When I work on tasks at a desk, I will play light, soothing music, which clicks my brain to the right side to relax me while increasing my thought and performance power.

2. Use a reward system: After completing a task, identify a reward you will give yourself for completing the day's tasks. An incomplete list of rewards includes watching favorite TV program/video, going out for ice cream, taking a bath, leisure reading, calling a friend, browsing the internet, going out to dinner, etc.

3. Visualize your performance beforehand. All successful performers will tell you that they visualize a successful performance before they actually perform it. For example, college students, the night before a test, can visualize themselves walking to the class the next day, sitting down at their desk with a smile and a confident look on their face while the instructor hands them the test. They can see themselves working effortlessly through the problems during the test and handing in the test to the instructor with a positive expectation of receiving a high grade. You can visualize the same for any performance.

4. Use deep breathing during the performance. When I am attempting to fix or repair something and I feel impatience and frustration building, I will focus on my breathing and make my breaths long and deep. This also helps in traffic, giving a public speech, taking a test, during an interview, etc.

The 80/20 Rule

The 80/20 Rule. Identify which of all your tasks carry most of the value. Then spend most of your time completing those tasks. Most people spend 80% of their time on activities that produce only 20% of the results that they want. The idea is to spend 80% of your time on 20% of the most valuable tasks on your To-Do list. To help you understand the 80/20 Rule....
80% of the clothes you wear come from 20% of your favorite wardrobe.
80% of the interruptions come from 20% of the people.
80% of phone calls come from 20% of the people you know.
80% of profits come from 20% of the sales.
20% more effort could result in an 80% better paper/speech, etc.

Exercise 1

High achieving people are those who work most of their time on high-value tasks. Low-achieving people are those who waste their time on low-value tasks. A to-do list works well for Type B people because it helps them stay committed and aware of the things they need to get done. Type A people may get better results taking relaxation and stress breaks throughout their day because they can become overly consumed with their to-do list as well as their mode of working.
If you are Type A - choose a relaxation method now and perform it for five minutes.
If you are Type B – write down your to-do list for today and this week.

Exercise 2

Write down which performance strategy (to-do list, relaxation, reward system, environment, other) will work best with your personality so that you can motivate yourself to start and complete projects and tasks. Research shows that it takes 21 days to start a new habit. So complete your performance strategy for at least 21 days until it becomes a part of you and your life. Write it down below.

A. The performance strategy I choose is ______________________________

____

____

____

B. What can you do to improve your performance while working/studying?____________

____

____

____

C. What can you do to improve your performance on your job? ____________________
____
____
____

Exercise 3

As mentioned above, your tasks should be related to your lifelong goals. Complete the Task Priorities Table below after viewing the example. The Ranking category in Step 4 means that 1 is the most important task to work complete onward up to the least important task. You are to put a check in the check-off category in Step 5 when you have completed the task.

Example:

Step 1
Goals:
A. Spend more time with family
B. Earn an Associate Degree in accounting
C. Increase study time

Step 2	Step 3	Step 4	Step 5
To Do Tasks	Goal Connection	Ranking	Check-Off
Read chapter 4	B, C	3	
Swim with children	A	1	
Watch TV		7	
Work with accounting study group	B,C	4	
Candlelight dinner with spouse		2	
Go shopping		6	
Review flash cards	B,C	5	

Now you try!!

Step 1
Goals:
A. ____
B. ____
C. ____

Step 2	Step 3	Step 4	Step 5
To Do Tasks	Goal Connection	Ranking	Check-Off

Strategy 7.5
Practice Committed Perseverance.

Definition: Perseverance - the ability to resist the urge to quit during difficult times.

Falling down doesn't make you a failure, staying down does!
Theodore Roosevelt

Using Self-Correction to Persevere

Don't get discouraged when pursuing your goals. An airplane, when approaching its destination, is constantly off course and has to continually correct itself. What counts is the fact that you get to your destination. As a college counselor, I see so many students who feel their whole world is shattered and ruined because something got in the way of their timeline to graduate in 4 years. I took my time and did it in six years. Going off course is part of the game. It's your responsibility to get back on course without uselessly beating yourself up. As you read about perseverance in this lesson, keep your goals in mind from the previous chapter and the mission statement you wrote.

A Lesson from the Moso Bamboo Tree

The Moso Chinese Bamboo Tree is one of the most extraordinary plants in the world. This is seen in the story about a Chinese farmer who waters his bamboo plant every week. After three months, the villagers say to him, "Why do you waste your time watering something that is not there?" The farmer disregards the villagers' words and continues to water his plant every week for three whole years. Finally, the first sprout emerges and grows 60 feet in 60 days. What was the Moso Plant doing during the three years? It was growing miles of roots deep into the ground preparing itself for its future. Often times, when we are pursuing a goal, we want to give up because we don't see evidence of growth (above ground). Be perseverant and know that if you work smart and work hard, you will grow and results will occur in due time.

Models of Committed Perseverance

When you hear names like Kerri Strug, the KFC Colonel, Helen Keller, Thomas Edison, The Beatles, etc., what do you think they have in common? They all are people who kept pursuing their goals, purpose, dreams despite the obstacles and the failed timeline in which they hoped to achieve their goals. Many of them had to fail over and over again, such as the KFC Colonel whose chicken recipe was rejected over 1000 times before it was finally given a chance. Babe Ruth failed more times than he succeeded (struck out/homeruns), but he is remembered for his successes. Obstacles, when met with poise, make us stronger. If we know ahead of time that obstacles will occur along any goal path and if we can estimate the quantity and type of the obstacles, then when the obstacles do occur, we don't feel devastated by them. Instead, we usually feel armed and ready. We may say to ourselves, "Oh, there are those typical obstacles; time for Plan B" and we adjust our timeframe. When obstacles show themselves to us, we often think, "The universe, or God, is against me. It is out of my control," and we give up. Stick with it. **Most people achieve their greatest achievement right after their biggest disappointment. So keep taking risks and when you fall down, don't stay down; get back up and keep going.**

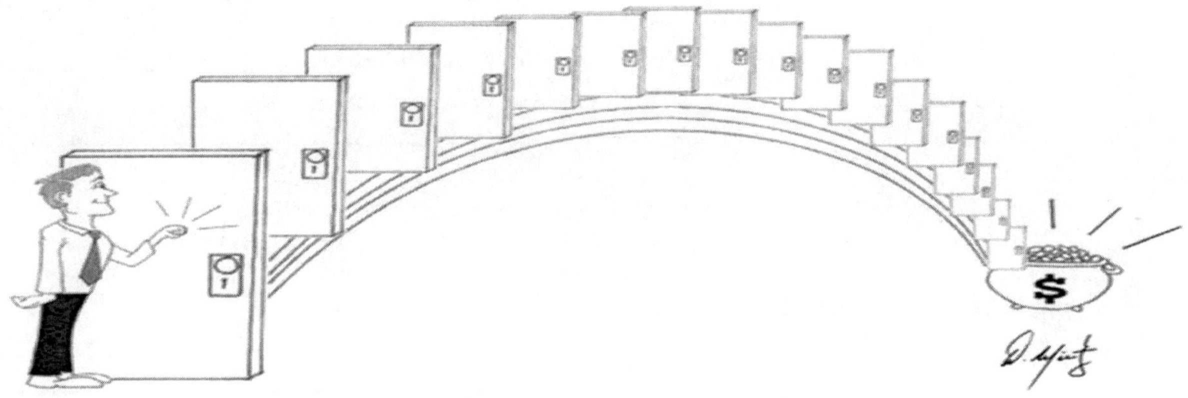

Knock on the Door of Opportunity and Challenge

There are two characteristics needed to persevere. One, you must have enough desire-- you must want it bad enough. Two, you must be willing to pay the price and make the sacrifices necessary to achieve it. As the graphic above illustrates, we need to take risks and knock on many doors of opportunity and challenge before we finally receive our pot of gold. It is not uncommon to experience twenty no's before we get a yes. All successful people across many professions will tell you they have to fail more often in order to succeed.

The Beatles survived over twenty rejections by Decca and other major record labels who judged them by their rendition of “My Bonnie Lies Over” single. EMI did too, but their parlophone label (George Martin), finally gave them an audition and a recording contract only after their audition tape had been hawked around London’s label companies. They persevered despite twenty rejections.

A YOUNG JOURNALIST ASKED A BILLIONNAIRE HOW HE COULD BE MORE SUCCESSFUL AT A FASTER RATE. HE WAS TOLD, “DOUBLE YOUR RATE OF FAILURE.”

Exercise 1

Do sit-ups until the point where you feel uncomfortable. Then visualize yourself doing three more and then physically do them. Feel what it's like to persevere in something...the pain involved during the performance and the rush of joy when you are finished. This physical endurance is the same endurance you need emotionally to persevere toward any goal.

Exercise 2

1. Write down a time when you persevered toward a goal you pursued in the past.

____

____

____

What caused you to keep on going? ______________________________

What sacrifices did you make? How did you manage the obstacles? ______________________________

2. Write down a time when you gave up on a goal you pursued in the past. What caused you to give up? What qualities in yourself do you need to strengthen in order to "hang tough" in challenging situations? What obstacles defeated you?______________________________

Exercise 3

What do you want to persevere in next in your life?______________________________

Why do you want this goal?______________________________

What will you sacrifice?______________________________

What will happen if you don't pursue this goal?______________________________

Strategy 7.6
Practice Moral Goodwill.

Definition: **Goodwill -** the ability to resist the urge to become too selfish and, instead, help others.

Service is the rent we pay for the privilege of living on this earth.
N. Eldon Tanner

Moving Beyond Selfishness

People write bad checks, cheat on their taxes, fib to their insurance companies, yet they don't believe they've done anything that wrong. Many have lost their sense of right and wrong in the quest for self-gain.

The biggest evil historically in humankind is the arrogant belief that one is better than another. The worst wars and individual crimes are those filled with hate and greed. We need to learn to respect other people's cultures as well as their education level, personality differences, personal limitations, and all living things like animals, plants, air, and water. Often, the people who don't respect others are the same people who fear them, and then they discriminate or want to dominate them. You can respect and accept others and their opinions without agreeing with them. This is an important difference!

A study by the National Institute on Aging, called the Terman Life-cycle Study, found that honest and caring people live longer, happier lives than self-centered folks. The report began studying personality traits and attitudes of a group of (1,528) children in 1921. The seven-decade research study is one of the most comprehensive studies in science and psychology. Children who were considered stable, resilient, conscientious, and truthful were about 30 percent less likely to die in any given year than other members of the study group. The encouraging news is that "good guys finish last." (Kathryn Doer Perkins, McClatchy News Service 'Newspaper')

Give Without Expecting a Return

To develop goodwill, learn to give without an expectation of anything in return. People usually verify that it will all come back to you anyway. They will say it's a universal law of physics. Be careful of giving to others out of obligation. Though often it may be appropriate to give out of obligation because you feel lazy at a certain time, try to make sure you give with your "heart" as much as possible.

Why Goodness Trumps Self-Esteem

In developing goodwill it will also be vital to seek goodness first, then self-esteem. Members of the Nazi Party had high self-esteem, but they were arrogant butchers. So what good is self-esteem without goodwill to others? I'd rather have an unsuccessful good child than a successful bad one. It's easier to teach them success than to unteach selfishness and aggression. However, our society has put so much value on success, intelligence, and happiness, that good often only gets in the way.

Answering to a Higher Authority helps us release our inherent selfishness and promote our goodwill. Whether it be your conscience, God, the Ten Commandments, nature, etc., many adults are still acting out their childhood selfish behaviors. As a baby, you were dependent on warmth, food, mother, with the mentality of "give me, give me." As we get older, it is important to move out of this selfish state and into a selfless "Heart" state. When we can do this, we become mature and noble.

A Lesson from Systems Theory

If you don't believe that being good and cooperating with your community are important, learn a lesson from Systems Theory. Imagine if your lungs said, "Ok, body, I don't feel like oxygenating you today; you're on your own." Our being is connected to our outside environment and world just like the organs in your body are connected to your whole body system. When they work together in unison, they are unstoppable.

Learn to develop trust and earn the trust of others. If we can't trust others and vice versa, we'll live very lonely, isolated lives and die like a withered leaf on a branch. If you were to examine the highly competitive politics in big business, you would see that trust is low, and heart attacks and misery are high.

How to Practice Moral Goodwill

What legacy do you want to leave behind after you die? When you die, what do you want people to say about you? Do you live up to that desire today? If your desire is to live a more moral life by doing good to others, perform the following:

You have to want to be good in your heart; otherwise, it won't ever happen.

Monitor your deeds/behavior, not your motives and intentions.

Treat people well, even those who are less important to you or whom you don't know.

Exercise 1

Plan to do one nice thing for somebody you know but whom you don't necessarily get along with that well. Do one nice thing for somebody you don't know.

Below, write what act you will choose. **Example:** For people you know but don't get along with, you could perform a part of their workload, buy them lunch or a snack, buy or make a small gift, compliment them, etc.

People you don't know - open door for them, tell the waiter your appreciation, etc.

Do this every day for 1 month, and you should be cured of your selfishness.

____

____

____

____

____

____

Exercise 2

Think of a time in your life when you did something that hurt somebody else. Write down three different times that this happened to you. Is it possible to make amends and apologize to these people? What was it that motivated you to take that hurtful action? How can you prevent this in the future?

____

____

____

____

____

____

Exercise 3

Regarding the times when you hurt somebody, write down the reasons and characterize it with one word. **Example:** Didn't offer somebody my office = selfishness. Somebody got the promotion over me and I was cold to them = jealousy or envy. Others include greed, anger, etc. What word keeps popping up? Buy a book on it and read all you can about it while applying the techniques to heal that part of yourself. We can only do good to others when we do good to ourselves. Otherwise, it's probably a selfish act. Know the difference between helping somebody in the hopes of getting recognized or attention for it and helping somebody out of the goodness of your "heart," not expecting a return.

Strategy 7.7

Practice Intelligent Moderation.

Definition: Moderation - the ability to resist the urge to abuse life's joys and personal vices.

Using Intelligent Moderation to Enjoy the Ordinary

Learn how to enjoy something for the 300th time. Too many people think they'll excite themselves by finding the new woman or man, traveling to the new place, etc. We often avoid the simplistic and seek the exciting. The ability to find the beauty and the exciting in the ordinary is timeless and most powerful. Be able to enjoy the:

- one donut instead of three
- one See's candy instead of five
- one beer instead of four
- two cigarettes instead of ten
- one shopping spree a month instead of five
- one hour of gambling instead of nine

Addictions are caused by a genetic disposition, family history, need to escape reality, need to numb the pain in our life, desire to purge out unpleasant feelings, and/or stress of a compulsive stressed culture. When you're addicted to something, it controls you instead of you controlling it.

How to be Moderate

Check your Emotional Moderation. Are you excessive in your anger, control of others, criticizing, appeasing, avoiding, denying, etc.? If you are excessive with anything that causes harm to yourself or others, perform the following:

- Identify your vice or issue.
- Be moderate with it.
- If you can't be moderate, drop it all together.
- If you can't drop it, seek professional help.

Exercise 1

Identify your vices.... the things you are most out of control with, e.g. food, drink, spending, gambling, sex, and write them down.

____

____

____

____

____

____

____

____

Exercise 2

During the time when we are excessive, we are in subconscious mode. If we bring complete awareness and consciousness to the excessive moment, we can gain control over the behaviors. Put
yourself into your vice (as long as it doesn't endanger your life or others). Close your eyes and put
your hands over your ears. Try the following: Feel the feelings that arise, hear yourself breathe, and experience the vice as consciously as you can. Do this for 10 minutes. Then write your perceptions.

____

____

____

____

____

Exercise 3

Follow the goal-setting model in the Self-Advancement chapter to set a goal of reducing your vice: either eliminate it or reach a healthy moderation. By doing this successfully for one vice, you'll develop the ability to do it for any other vices that you may have. Examples of compulsions include:

Emotional compulsions: rage, criticizing, avoiding, denying, etc.
Physical compulsions: food, substances, alcohol, etc.
Behavioral compulsions: shopping, gambling, television, internet, etc.

A. Write down something you have a hard time controlling. (pick something that you have the ability to control)____

____

B. Have you tried to be moderate with it?__________________________________

____

C. If yes, how? Were you successful? If no, why not? _________________________

____

____

D. What else could you do to moderate it?_________________________________

____

E. Have you tried to eliminate it entirely from your life? If yes, did you succeed? How? If not, what will you try to do about it?____

____

____

____

____

If you can't eliminate or control it, seek professional help from a counselor or from local resources in the Yellow Pages.

Chapter Insight & Commitment

After completing this chapter, I learned the following about my self-discipline (my perspective, patience, attachments, performance, perseverance, goodwill, moderation):

Example: I learned that my Type A personality while often serving me, hurts my performance and puts my health at risk. I am also having a hard time being moderate with fast food.

I can take active steps to help attain my future goals & become more of the person I strive to be:

Example: I will schedule relaxing times and fun into my calendar. This will help me stay balanced to meet the demands of my job as I try to achieve my sales goal this year. I will bring my lunch to work.

CHAPTER 8

Self-Assertion

Using your **Voice** to **Assert** your needs, desires, boundaries, and feelings to others.

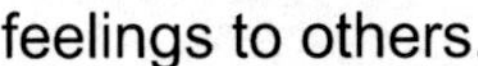

Purpose: To communicate effectively to enhance harmony in relationships and spur goal attainment.

Rewards: Getting Needs Met, Convenience, Pleasure, Intimacy

Obstacles: Fear of Others' Disapproval, Shyness, Suppression of Emotions

Consequence: Being Taken Advantage of, Bad Luck, Missed Opportunities, Sadness, Isolation

Symbol: Microphone

Related Web Sites: http://www.queendom.com/communic.html
http://www.mindtools.com/index.html

Self-Assertion

In a study of how top management in corporations rate job skills, the two most desired capabilities were communication skills and interpersonal skills (Daniel, 1998). Being able to effectively assert and communicate your thoughts will either make or break a person's career success (Carrig, 1999). Assertive people handle conflicts skillfully by expressing their thoughts and feelings clearly and directly, but without judging others or dictating to them. Standing up for yourself or your character is the most powerful way to protect and honor the Self while it encounters a wide assortment of invalidations. These invalidations include insults, manipulations, blame, disrespect, control, and "guilt trips" from others. Strengthening the Self to cope and set boundaries with these forces is achieved by being assertive.

All of us have experienced some form of invalidation throughout our lives that has wounded our Self. When we experienced invalidations in childhood, we often did not have the tools, power, or the knowledge to be able to set boundaries with others and assert our thoughts and feelings clearly and directly. We did, however, create and learn infantile ways of responding to invalidation. This includes subject changing, aggression, joking, revenge, etc… Unfortunately, most of us still use a similar package of infantile responses today. When we do not learn to respond correctly, these invalidations can continue to hurt us. Our development takes a step backward and our pain, forward. This leads to rampant adult passive-aggressive behaviors that make it difficult for people to ask for favors, say no to requests, complain about service, and confront others. In addition, passive-aggressive behaviors destroy most of our relationships.

Some people believe that they are assertive because they can get people to act the way they want them to by being aggressive with them. But aggression and the cruelty and judgment that accompany it not only make the aggressor unpopular, but they facilitate the pain within the aggressor as he/she desperately tries to control others. This can never truly be done. Aggressors are usually very unhappy and depressed people. Therefore, we need to unlearn our present infantile ways of resolving conflicts and learn how to communicate our thoughts and feelings clearly but without resentment or dictating.

In this chapter, you will learn specific methods that make it easier to take risks and assert your thoughts and feelings to all people including the most difficult personalities. You will be able to identify why you attract to others and distinguish between healthy and unhealthy people for both romantic and non-romantic relationships. Further, you will be able to utilize a technique used by top executives to build rapport with anyone you come in contact with by identifying their personality style and creating win-win solutions. Finally, you will be able to identify roadblocks to communication that humans have been using for thousands of years. With practice, you will be able to gently confront and remove these roadblocks and resolve conflicts in your relationships at home and on the job.

Strategy 8.1

Improve your relationships by clearing inner obstacles for assertive communication purposes. Learn what to avoid and what to look for in love and romantic relationships.

No one can make you feel inferior without your consent.
Eleanor Roosevelt.

Clear Inner Obstacles by Assessing Yourself and the Situation Before Asserting

Two of the most common inner obstacles and reasons why we don't assert our selves as often as we should is because **one**, we fear that we will hurt the other person's feelings, and **two**, we fear that we won't get the approval from that person if we upset him/her in some way. Therefore, we play it safe and either don't say anything or we have a funny way of going around the problem, which never addresses it. The approval we need is, unfortunately, tied up with our self-worth. We say to our selves, "If he is upset with me and ends up not liking me, then I'll feel bad about myself."

As adults we need to practice getting approval from ourselves and go on a *fast* (like not eating) from others' approval. If we assert ourselves, firmly, kindly, and with patience, then the other person will probably respect you more whether agreeing with you or not. That's all you could ever ask for. And if the person doesn't, then the person may be the one that has the personal problem; it shouldn't be your worry. You might even think that person is your best friend. However, if the person is only your friend when getting their way, this person doesn't respect a good number of your needs and probably shouldn't be a best friend!!

After assessing yourself, assess the situation. Many situations in which there is a conflict can be loaded with dreadful conditions. Hence, with difficult personalities, we fear revenge or a major conflict as a result of our being assertive. Fear is not a red light! It's a yellow light telling us to adjust our approach, proceed slowly, and be cautious. Two techniques will help. **One**, assume this person will understand your point of view before you start talking. This will put you at ease and will help him/her to be at ease. **Two**, give the person an out! Follow this process:

A. During a conflict, or after you assert yourself, if that person is upset, fake retreat by backing down a tad and this will put him/her off guard. You can say something like, "yet, I can see your point too,"

B. Then, verbalize your assertive statement directly, yet tactfully.

C. Give the person an honorable surrender/out so they don't feel a blow to their pride or ego.

The Three-Step Assertion Punch

Before confronting somebody about a conflict, another common fear that arises is the fear of making mistakes, like distorting our message or forgetting the most important parts of our message. Three points, if practiced, will solve this problem. **One**, when you speak from your "heart" as opposed to your head, you will come off more sincere and genuine. People will appreciate that in you, and they will probably not feel like you're trying to get something from them. **Two**, practice, practice, practice to eliminate most jitters before you assert yourself because you will feel ready and clear about your message. Practice with a friend, spouse, or anyone you feel safe with. Role-play so you can get into the state of mind, like a practice test in school. **Three**, before you assert yourself, ask yourself these questions:

A. What is the worst that could happen? We usually exaggerate to a worst-case scenario but that rarely happens.
B. What is likely to happen? The answer to that question is what usually does happen.
C. Is what you're asking for, reasonable? If not, you can change your statement to reflect fairness and respect of yourself and others. Whenever you risk something, be prepared beforehand to be criticized and second-guessed by others even though you can still assume they will understand you. Negativity may come from your colleagues, friends, family, spouse, etc., but don't let it stop you. Make sure you are asserting for the right reason. Ask yourself, "Am I doing this to get approval from someone else?" The best motivation is an inner force. Once you can let go of the approval, it's amazing how that frees you up to be yourself.

Do You Know If You're Really "In Love?"

In the book "Are you the one for me?" by Barbara DeAngelis, she outlines things to look for in a relationship and what to "stay away" from. She is a psychologist who has counseled thousands of people in love relationships. Below are some ideas about love and ways she helps people determine who is right and who is wrong for each of her clients.

What were your beliefs about romantic love in the past? Circle Mostly True or Mostly False

1. If it is really true love, I will only feel complete and whole when I'm with my partner? *Mostly True or Mostly False*
2. The right relationship will always be interesting and exciting. *Mostly True or Mostly False*
3. If it's really true love, I would know the moment I see the person for the first time. *Mostly True or Mostly False*
4. If my partner and I love each other enough, it's unlikely none of our problems or personality differences will threaten our relationship and break us up. *Mostly True or Mostly False*
5. If I am finally with the right person, I shouldn't be attracted to someone else, because I will be so in love. *Mostly True or Mostly False*
6. If I am in the right relationship, we won't have to work that hard to make it work. *Mostly True or Mostly False*
7. If in love, I'll feel excited and nervous each time I see my partner. *Mostly True or Mostly False*
8. My love partner will give me everything I need and fill all the empty spaces in my life—I won't really need anyone else. *Mostly True or Mostly False*
9. The sex in a relationship can't be really awesome unless it's true love. *Mostly True or Mostly False*

If you circled mostly true, your ideas about romantic love are so low that you have likely gotten your heart broken over and over again in relationships. You likely have an unrealistic and a distorted view of love probably received from watching television, movies, romance novels, or never being taught about the realities of love. You probably put your partners on a pedestal and are more "in love with love" than with your partner. You may be afraid of conflict, which needs to be addressed in relationships. You probably blame your partners who have let you down and have set up relationships to fail from the beginning. Don't worry, many people fall into this category and you can adjust your thinking and behavior on these matters.

If you circled mostly false, you have a realistic understanding of love relationships and realize that love is not enough to make a relationship work. It takes common values, communication, hard work, and compatibility.

Compatibility refers to how you "resonate" with your partner in different areas or styles of your life. *Compatibility is a must for marriage.* These areas include how well both people like each other's

1. Physical Style (appearance, personal fitness, and hygiene)
2. Emotional Style (attitude toward romance, affectionate, supportive, faithful)

3. Intellectual Style (educational background, enjoys learning, attitude toward world affairs, creativity)
4. Social Style (personality traits, interaction with others, sense of humor)
5. Sexual Style (enjoys sex, likes to cuddle, easily aroused with no hang-ups)
6. Communication Style (verbally articulate, good listener, attitude toward communication, expresses thoughts and feelings)
7. Spiritual Style (believes in God or higher power, has moral views, open to the mystical and different philosophies of life, compassionate toward less fortunate)
8. Personal Growth Style (attitude toward self-improvement, wants to learn about self and change for the better, sees own shortcomings, attends seminars)
9. Financial Style (relationship with money, attitude toward success, hard worker, ambitious career, honest and ethical, financially responsible)
10. Interests and Hobbies (enjoys music, dance, movies, travel, or whatever you are interested in).

For compatibility to occur, the majority of these styles would have to mesh between both people.

Romantic Love Myths

1. **Love Conquers All.** – One often thinks that no conflict, problem, or set of circumstances is bad enough if there is enough love; "if I just love him or her more." But the truth is love is usually not enough in younger relationships when one or more of the following circumstances takes place: there is abuse, there is no sexual chemistry, there are no common values about how to raise the kids, type of religion to follow, constant criticism, infidelity, non-communication, one wants children and the other doesn't, age differences, and living in different states. Yet, just because you see one of these problems in your relationship, doesn't mean it is doomed. It does mean you need to pay close attention to the problem rather than ignoring it and hoping it just goes away.

2. **There is only one true love or soul mate in the world who is right for you. –** One will sometimes stop relationships with others because they are not measuring up to the perfect guy or gal. This perfect picture of no flaws and no fighting is unrealistic. The human heart has a tremendous capacity for loving and we can limit this love because of this romantic love myth. There are millions who have experienced love the third, fourth, or fifth time around. Arranged marriages used to be the norm in many cultures and each person often grew to love their partner over the years even though they didn't at first. So finding love along with ***compatibility*** (how the two of you resonate on several areas of life: physical, emotional, social, sexual, intellectual, spiritual, interests, etc.) is the best goal in finding a mate.

3. **Love will happen when I experience "Love at first sight." -** Though this can happen, it is not the norm. In fact, believing in it can blind one from examining the rest of the relationship for compatibility. Love at first sight junkies often look for all the wrong qualities in a mate and overlook the right qualities. Often it is lust at first sight. Or it can be infatuation with one's image, how one looks, one's profession, how much money one has, the car one drives, the uniform one wears, achievement, while they ignore the real person. One can have a strong attraction to someone at the first meeting, but true love grows over time.

4. **Your true love will fulfill you completely in every way. –** Many people walk into relationships expecting their partner to fulfill their every need, and when they do not, they become resentful and disillusioned. They unconsciously set their partner up to fail. Distinguish between what you would like in a partner and what you really need. There are

needs women have that men can't usually fulfill and vice versa. This myth breeds resentment and ends a lot of relationships.

5. **When you feel powerful sexual chemistry with someone, it must be love.** – Unfortunately, sex has nothing to do with true love. You can feel intense physical pleasure with somebody and yet, it doesn't mean you love each other. It could be the absolute wrong person for you. It often occurs like this. First, you feel (lust) powerful sexual chemistry with someone. Then you act on those urges and have sex with that person. Then you experience some guilt or discomfort having been so sexually intimate without the emotional connectedness. Finally you develop a relationship with that person to validate your lust. Then, after some time, you realize you are not compatible because he or she is too critical, negative, controlling, lazy, etc., has unpaid bills and used sex to "hook you in," and you don't share common values. Now, you stay in the relationship longer than you should because of the investment you have put in even though you know they are the wrong person. Some people take more time to analyze their emails than a current partner.

These romantic love myths contribute to:

1) Choosing the absolute wrong people.
2) Helping ruin relationships because these lies or myths promote unfair and unrealistic expectations we put on our partners.

Why We Attract To the People We Love

Have you ever wanted a committed relationship but you ended up falling in love with someone who was unavailable or not capable of making a commitment? Have you ever wanted a mature, responsible partner and ended up with an immature, dramatic, irresponsible person who you resented? Have you ever vowed to never get involved with someone who was emotionally unavailable, but found yourself infatuated later on with someone who couldn't love you back the way you deserved?

Harville Hendrix, in his New York Times bestseller book "Getting the love you want" explains that we choose a life partner based on the personality traits that are similar to our parents or our caretakers. The idea is that we unconsciously have this "Love Image" of all the people who positively and negatively influenced us at an early age, which was likely, a mother and father, one or more siblings, or a close relative. Your brain recorded everything about them, the sound of their voices, the amount of time they took to answer your cries, the way they loved you or hurt you, their moods, talents, and their personality traits like being nurturing, critical, invalidating, loving, etc. Though we consciously seek out the positive qualities of our caretakers, unconsciously, our brain seeks out the negative qualities as well so that it can ultimately heal itself and become whole. Because incidents of neglect, abuse, criticism, or indifference affect our survival, they are **more** deeply etched on our "Love Image Template" than our memories of caring and attention. They are the aching sores that we want healed. In adulthood, even if we seek the positive qualities in others without the negative traits, we would not be attracted in the first place. If your mother's "critical" ways wounded you in childhood, then your unconscious will seek out a critical person like your mother in order to heal.

Do you ever wonder why the beautiful girl stays with the awful guy that abuses her? Because she was more than likely abused as a child and her unconscious brain says she can't be whole unless this new abuser type shows her the love she so desperately needs. **So if childhood home life = abuse, then love = abuse.** You associate love with home. If you weren't shown much love and affection, your equation might be **home = loneliness**. Then one would unconsciously seek out someone who doesn't give much love and affection, even though consciously, we seek out a loving person. The could equal disappointment, denial, suppression of feelings, betrayal, abandonment, etc.

Usually our Imago partner will bear a rough likeness to the original (our parents) with at least a few of the most critical negative traits. But in order to get a good enough match to enable us to complete our unfinished business and become whole when we meet somebody new and exciting, we rework the image. We exaggerate the likenesses, diminish the differences, and distort the truth of who our partner really is so we can paint the ideal image we have.

The good news is, if we seek self-understanding by identifying our own picture of this image (imago) we created to heal our childhood wounds, and we try to get some of those needs fulfilled by ourselves, friends and loved ones, we will then attract to a healthier partner. This healthy partner may have some of the negative traits, but will have more of the positive to offset the negative. This will lead to a healthier relationship and/or marriage. If one remains blind to one's childhood wounds and the imago, then one usually attracts a person at the same level of health that one is at. If one is decent and emotionally unhealthy, one is likely to attract to a decent or indecent, unhealthy person as well. If we don't get our needs met in the relationship, we often try to fill this emptiness with food and drugs and activities. Yet, what we yearn for is our original wholeness, our full range of emotions, an inquisitive mind, and the joy we experienced as very young children. If you are already in a relationship, both of you can begin this journey of uncovering the Imago, and bringing more realistic expectations to fulfilling personal needs in the relationship.

Think of the Imago as the map showing where the buried treasure lies. Remember your judgments or decisions about yourself and others are made from your past experiences. Psychologists estimate that between birth and five years of age, you receive 50% of your emotional programming. Between five and eight years of age, you receive 30 percent more of your emotional programming. So by eight years old, 80% of your decisions about yourself and others have already been made. By eighteen, they estimate, 95%. You can use the other 5% in the Thinking Mind Model to change your emotional programming or Imago for healthier choices of love partners. Common examples include:

Childhood Experience	Decision/Attitude and Love Choices
-Mom and Dad always fought	-I have to be good/not get angry so I don't make people mad
-My parents were divorced.	-I'm not lovable enough and it is my fault.
-I was overweight and often teased.	-I'm not okay as I am. I have to try extra hard to be liked.
-Dad was never home and cheated.	-Men can't be trusted and women are doormats.
-Mom was a rageaholic and moody.	-It's not safe to express myself. I can't make people upset.

In the example where Mom was a moody rageaholic, and the decision was that it was not safe to express oneself, lead to that person choosing a partner who is moody with bad tempers.

By the time we are in a relationship, we further make the problem worse by projecting what we don't like in ourselves onto our partner. Some couples go through their whole marriages as if they were strangers sitting in a darkened movie theater, casting flickering images on each other. They don't even turn off their projectors long enough to see who it is that serves as the screen for their home movies.

The Six Wrong Reasons for Starting a Relationship

1. Pressure from family and friends. Whether it is age pressure ("time is running out") or family and friends telling us who to settle for, we are not listening to our own heart and we are giving our power away ensuring an unhappy end to our love story.

2. Loneliness and Desperation. This is the time when we make poor love choices and end up in unfulfilling relationships.

3. Distraction from Your Own Life. Instead of working on dreams and projects that are best for us, or instead of dealing with the pain of past relationships, we often jump right into the next relationship because we either don't want to deal with the pain, or are bored with the lack of passion and purpose in our lives.

4. To Avoid Growing Up. Many people get into relationships not because they are ready to experience the joys of a mature relationship but because they want to be "taken care of." Many will choose partners because they make a lot of money like the gold digger! Or, they admire their career, power, or reputation. Therefore, one stays in a childlike, irresponsible state and the relationship never grows.

5. Feelings of Guilt. We sometimes get into relationships because we didn't want to hurt the other person's feelings by rejecting them. When you let guilt "run the show," you are ripping your partner off and yourself.

6. To Fill an Emotional or Spiritual Emptiness. We want to feel connected to the universe and feel loved. But getting into relationships so the other person can fill us up, instead of filling ourselves up, will always leave us feeling that emptiness inside.

We often make big mistakes at the beginning of a relationship that create havoc later on. When we feel the love, **we often don't ask enough questions** about their values. We don't ask if they are happy, if they are resentful, have low self-esteem, and so on because we are to busy looking for the right reasons to be in the relationship. Or we think it is not romantic to ask. But AIDS is not romantic, unwanted pregnancy is not romantic, and herpes is not romantic. We also **ignore warning signs** of potential problems like he/she won't discuss the past, or uses too much alcohol or drugs, or is too intrusive, or hates their parents, or flirts with others, or has credit problems and debts, or is controlling, etc. Problems arise when we also have sex to early in the relationship which blinds us from who they really are. Also living together too early causes problems of emotional blindness. Commitments are often made too early as well as wedding plans only later to find out "they were the wrong one for us."

The Eight Categories of Relationships that Won't Work

I know as you are about to read the following material, and the material after it, you may be uptight because you fear that what you read may place doubt about your current relationship. Know that sometimes, it is better to find somebody you are more compatible with, and often, you can work things out if both people are committed.

1. You are in love with your partner's potential. When you start telling yourself the following, it is a sign you are in the wrong relationship. You may tell yourself my partner is trying and just needs a little more time to get him or herself together, or you believe in your partner more than he believes in him or herself, or you don't want to give up on them because that will validate their feelings of worthlessness, or since no one loved them enough, your love will change them, or you feel everyone else misunderstands your partner and only you know the "real" person inside, or you make excuses to family and friends for your partner's problems or problems in the relationship. Having a relationship with a person means loving them for who they are today, not ho out ink they'll become.

2. You care more about your partner than he or she does for you. Or, Your partner cares more about you than you do about him or her. Are you usually the one who, reaches out first for affection, wants to be intimate, makes most of the togetherness plans, is more excited about the relationship, or you fit into their schedule as opposed to their sometimes fitting into yours?

Then you are probably "settling for crumbs" and pretending it's enough. You will end up feeling controlled by your partner, feeling hungry for love, feeling angry, cheated, and/or miserable. *If your partner loves you more than you love him or her*, you will probably feel, defensive when accused of not loving your partner enough, and/or pressured by your partner, and/or smothered by them like they are too clingy and needy. These are relationship red flags.

3. You are on a Rescue Mission. If your partner has serious emotional, physical, or financial problems, and/or feels victimized from the past, and you play a parental, psychologist role to solve their problems, and/or tolerate and excuse bad behavior, you are probably headed for a crash with lots of guilt. You also probably attracted this Imago type because of your childhood. *If you saw one of your parents or siblings ignored, unloved, or mistreated, you will find that person in the form of a partner in need, and will work hard to give them the love and strength you feel you failed to give your family member.*

4. You are in Love with Your Partner for External Reasons. Was it her brown eyes, the way he looked in uniform, the way he played the guitar, the way she danced that made you "Fall in love?" Ask yourself, if they didn't have this one quality, would you still be "In love?"

5. You Choose a Partner in Order to Be Rebellious. This is of the worst reasons for being in a relationship. To see if you are being rebellious, make a list of all of the qualities your parents or family would want you to find in a mate. Then make a list of all the qualities in your partner. If the two lists are opposite each other, you may be in a relationship as a way of rebelling against your parents, not because you are with the right person. Examples include: your parents have always insisted on your marrying somebody Jewish, and you only go out with people who are Catholic or Protestant. Your parents emphasize money, and you attract to the broke, anti-establishment type. Your parents are conservative white people and you've had three black boyfriends. As you try to define yourself as separate from your parents, you are not making choices based on your own thoughtful choices but by your compulsion.

6. You Choose a Partner Who is the Opposite of Your Previous Partner. Examples include: your ex-husband was prudish and uncomfortable with sexuality and your new boyfriend is a raunchy, sex maniac. Or, your ex-girlfriend was needy and overly dependent, and your new girlfriend suppresses her feelings and keeps you guessing. Or, your ex-boyfriend was not ambitious and your new boyfriend is a workaholic who cares more about money than he does about you. So we make the mistake of looking *only* for those missing qualities rather than making them an important but incomplete part of the entire list of traits you want in a partner.

7. Your Partner is Unavailable. This is the partner that is in another relationship, but promises to leave soon. They often say "I don't really love her and we're not having sex anymore," or he/she knows about you and it's all right, or just left somebody but might be going back. If you attract to this type of person, you probably felt abandoned by a parent when you were a child. You repeat this pattern as an adult by finding people who can't be there for you either – the perfect Imago! Remember home = love. Or you are avoiding intimacy, or may have low self-esteem and don't feel you deserve to have somebody all to yourself.

8. You Have Partial Compatibility. Have you ever thought you met the right person because you had something in common like yoga and great sex for two months, and later found that is all you had in common. Look back a few pages on Compatibility and you will see the full list of areas and styles.

The following are compatibility destructors that can destroy a relationship. *If there is a significant age difference (over 10 years), different religious backgrounds, different social, ethnic, or educational backgrounds, toxic ex-spouse, toxic in-laws, toxic stepchildren, or a long-distance relationship, the relationship is not doomed, but has a higher chance of failing. Problems start to*

surface overtime as opposed to at the beginning of the relationship. Deal with it as soon as possible.
I am discussing scenarios that assume the person in a relationship has the problem, knowing full well that the reader could have the very same problem. Stay open to learning and adjusting.

The Eight Character Defects That Will Ruin a Relationship

1. **Chronic Anger**. Do you find yourself saying, "I have to tiptoe around the house and I live in fear everyday." Or, the person might be warm to you until they don't get their "way" and the screaming begins. He or she may express their anger physically, throwing objects, or verbally "putting you down." Chronic anger is a terrorist because it holds the people it comes in contact with hostage. The angry person was either physically, verbally, or sexually abused as a child and stored up the rage inside, letting it out as an adult when they finally feel safe. They may have also felt unloved, abandoned, or powerless as a child and compensate as an adult by controlling others with their anger.

2. Addictions. You are "playing with fire" and will probably "get burned" when you are in relationship with an addicted person. Whether it is an addiction to alcohol, drugs, or whatever is unhealthy, it will take the person's time, attention, and spirit away and ruin intimacy between the both of you. You will see unpredictable behavior, anger, irresponsibility, emotional deadness and unavailability, bad moods, and a lack of sexual desire. Need to hear anymore? Tell your partner, you refuse to live with an addict unless they get help immediately and stick to a plan.

3. Victimhood. This is an attitude that blames others for their problems. Does your partner often complain and pout about things? Do they blame parents, ex-mates and friends for their misfortunes?
Do they have "it's just no use" attitude? Victims are experts at blaming others and not doing something to change a situation. They don't get angry but make you feel guilty by looking upset and hurt. They need to be confronted with their state of mind and make changes to their thinking/behavior.

4. Control Freak. Do you feel criticized, judged, and constantly "under the microscope" by your partner? Do you live in fear of displeasing him or her by doing things the "wrong way?" Does your partner become upset when he or she can't have their "way?" While the Victim often avoids making decisions, a control freak must make all the decisions. They become irritable, impatient, and are highly possessive and jealous while being compulsive about their living habits. You might attract to a control freak because you had a very controlling mother or father and you associate love with control. Home = Love. Or, you are a victim looking for someone to tell you what to do. Or, your last partner was passive and you chose the opposite this time. Or, you were abused as a child and only see yourself relating to others when they're in control and you're afraid of them. Again, confront them and give them consequences for not changing. They can sometimes be dangerous.

5. Sexual Problems. Sexual problems can fall into three categories. Category one is sexual addiction and obsession. Pornography, too much masturbation despite active sex life, and their needing sex one or more times a day regardless of whether you're in the mood all end up causing major problems with intimacy. Category two is lack of sexual integrity. This occurs when the partner flirts with others, touches others' private parts, makes sexual comments to friends and strangers, stares at other people's bodies, and infidelity. If your partner doesn't treat you with respect in the beginning of the relationship, he or she won't suddenly learn respect later. Category three is sexual performance problems. These include impotence that lasts, premature ejaculation, and lack of interest in sex. Suppressed anger and rage can cause impotence as well as physical factors. Resolve to resolve these sexual problems that damage intimacy or, they won't go away.

6. Immaturity. This is the person that can't hold down a job, is careless with finances, undependable, unmotivated, or wants to shop, watch TV, eat, drink, do everything but grow up. You end up becoming the "parent" to this person, which builds resentment. Reminding them of do things, doing things for them, making excuses for them, gets old quick because it kills the passion. These people are usually angry with their controlling parents and rebel against all authority figures, rules, etc.

7. Emotional Unavailability and/or Damage from Childhood. Many people are emotionally blocked and need serious healing before they are capable of giving and receiving love. This person cannot or will not talk about feelings and won't communicate with you about emotions, which causes problems with intimacy and trust. With regard to emotional damage from childhood, find out how severe, are they aware how it affects relationships, and are they actively working on themselves (therapy, reading, seminars) to heal. Severe damage includes sexual abuse; physical or verbal abuse; eating disorders; parental abandonment from divorce, death, adoption, and suicide; parental addiction to alcohol and drugs; and religious fanaticism where the person was taught they were evil, bad, and sex was dirty and sinful.

8. Resentment From a Past Relationship. They usually don't take responsibility for their part in the previous relationship. They often are still traumatized from being hurt or abused from the past relationship and nothing can make them happy again. The unresolved anger and resentment from the past relationship may eventually be projected onto you. Rescuers beware! Give the person time to heal before jumping into a relationship with them.

All of us have emotional baggage we carry with us into relationships. The intent of this writing is to not scare you away from having relationships but to learn about the emotional background of your partner, as well as your own, so you can know what to expect in the relationships.

The Eight Qualities to Look For in a Partner

Some people look for personality traits such as a good sense of humor, loves traveling, affectionate, warm, when they should really be looking at character traits. Character determines how one will treat oneself, how one will treat you, and one day, your children. Instead of asking, "Does my partner love me?" ask, "How capable is my partner of loving, period." Below are eight character traits or qualities to look for. Part of self-assertion is asking questions to get to the truth so you can make the right decisions. The key questions under each quality are what you are to assert to a partner or potential partner. Make sure you've spent time answering these questions so you can also communicate them.

1. Commitment to Personal Growth and Emotional Openness. When you have someone committed to their own personal growth, your relationship can grow and become an adventure as opposed to a power struggle while each try to be right and make the other wrong. The person committed to personal growth strives to see his or her blind spots and the emotional baggage brought into the relationship. This person has personal goals for his or her own self-improvement and sees positive changes over time. Whether it is becoming more patient, dealing stress, treating you better, stopping smoking, or being assertive, you will ultimately respect them.

Key questions to ask them include: "What have you learned about yourself emotionally in the past?" What are your greatest strengths and weaknesses? No, it's not a job interview but almost. What have you learned from past relationships that you don't do now? If I asked your past partner their biggest complaint about you, what would it be and would you agree? What feelings are difficult for you to talk about? What sources of help have you used in the past and how do you cope with challenges? How would you like to change in the next five years? What qualities would you like to acquire in the next few years?"

2. Integrity. Have you ever had a partner that lies and never admits he or she is wrong? The person who is dishonest hides parts of themselves and only tells you what you want to hear to protect themselves so they can have the "upper hand." This will destroy intimacy. Look for someone who is honest with themselves, honest with others, and honest with you.

Key questions to ask them include: Have you ever been lied to or betrayed in a relationship? How did it make you feel? Have you ever lied to or betrayed someone in a relationship? Would you do it again? Why? Do you think partners should be honest about everything in a relationship, or do you think some things should be kept private? If not, what for instance? If I asked your past partners if you were honest and trustworthy, how would they answer and why? What kinds of things do you feel are inherently wrong? (cheating on taxes, stealing, etc.) Are you telling me the truth right now? (watch their eyes closely for reactions).

3. Maturity and Responsibility. A person is more mature when they can earn enough money to support themselves, know how to feed themselves, and know how to keep their living space relatively clean (not a neat freak). If not, you may have stumbled upon a child in an adult's body; lovable, but not ready for a mature relationship. Make sure the person is respectful of your feelings, your time, your possessions, your boundaries, their co-workers, and others people's feelings.

Key questions to ask them include: In what areas of your life would you say you are the most irresponsible, e.g. health, finances, late for events, returning phone calls? Have you been fired from your jobs and for what reasons, and have you quit and why? Do you act more as the caretaker in your relationships or as the one who's taken care of ? If I asked your past partners, would they say you were very responsible, irresponsible, or in between and why?

4. High Self-Esteem. Someone with low self-esteem may be able to show love. But it is a hungry love in order for them to feel good as opposed to loving because he or she feels good about themselves. They don't love themselves. As a result, they criticize themselves, procrastinate because they are afraid of failing, embarrassed by who they are, take suggestions as condemnations, and allows others to abuse them. People with high self-esteem take pride in who they are and treat themselves, others, and their health very well.

Key questions to ask them include: What are you most proud about in yourself and your life? (Does he or she have a difficult time responding?) What do you do to pamper yourself? What kind of emotional abuse have you tolerated in the past and why? What are your worst health and living habits? D you procrastinate often, sometimes, or not at all? What risks have you taken in your life? Are there risks that you have been avoiding?

5. Positive Attitude Toward Life. There are two types of people, positive people and negative people. It makes a huge difference if you fall in love with a negative person. Negative people focus on problems, not solutions. They complain a lot, they don't trust easily, they are cynical and pessimistic, and allow fear and worry to rule them. Positive people turn obstacles into learning lessons and opportunities, they trust their ability and believe that things can always get better. They use their creativity and vision to change their reality. Positive people work through conflicts faster, with less blame and more cooperation.

Key questions to ask them include: "What are some of the most important lessons you've learned about pain in your life? If you cold sum up your philosophy of life in a few sentences, what would it be? If you had to explain why the world is the way it is to your children, how would you explain it? Do you believe things usually turn out for the best? Why or why not? How do you react when things go wrong all at once?

6. Sexual Chemistry. Sexual chemistry is your ability to get aroused by your partner. You either feel an energetic vibration or resonance or you don't. Unfortunately, we often feel it with the wrong people under the wrong circumstances and not enough under the right ones. Over the course of a relationship, it will fluctuate between hot and not hot. It can get cold as you build emotional walls between each other. But, it needs to exist in some form so you can distinguish your relationship from a friendship. It is not compatibility but a small part of compatibility among the other areas. If you meet someone and aren't instantly attracted to the, it doesn't mean that you won't become attracted to them as you get to know them better over time. Gradual attraction occurs when the attraction is not just based on your partner's looks, but by who they are and how you feel about yourself when you're with them. Studies report that couples who were friends before they became romantically involved have more successful and satisfying marriages. It doesn't mean that you stay in a passionless relationship for years waiting for attraction to happen. If you wonder why you attract or stay with people who you aren't attracted to, consider the following. You may be avoiding intimacy and sex for reasons such as, being sexually raped or molested in the past; felt sexually controlled in the past; you don't want to give up control because you fear they will control you; and/or you were brought up with negative messages about sex. People who rationalize to themselves that it isn't a big deal they don't have sex or aren't attracted to their partner are in a situation that makes them ripe to have an extramarital affair.

7. Compatibility. Look again under Compatibility on the past few pages under the title, *how do you know if you're really in Love?* Write down the qualities you seek in a partner in the following ten categories: their Physical Style, Emotional Style, Intellectual Style, Social Style, Sexual Style, Communication Style, Spiritual Style, Personal Growth Style, Financial Style, and Interests and Hobbies. In you want more details look back onto that page. As you talk with the person you can mention, "Tell me more about yourself. What were your relationships like and what when on, and then I'll tell you my love history." If the person can't talk about these things, you deserve better!

8. Commitment. One can have all of the above qualities but if they are unwilling to commit to only
you, and you want to get married, it won't work out. A successful committed relationship needs three things: sexual chemistry, compatibility, and commitment. Without commitment, your relationship will be superficial and directionless. **What is commitment? It is commitment to fully loving one another each moment, as long as the relationship allows you to also love and respect each other.** This is better than committing only for a lifetime because if the person in the future is not willing to stop abusing you or your children, or whatever else, then you have kept your commitment because there is no longer respect on both sides.

Commitment gives your relationship purpose allowing it to move forward, rather than round and round in circles. It is an investment of attention and energy. Moving forward implies that you make a commitment to only each other that will last a lifetime. The first level of commitment before getting married is not to date anyone else and be monogamous. The second level is committing to a future together (engagement) which should last at least within a year or two. The third level is cementing that commitment by either getting married, having a no legal ceremony, or any other ceremony that consecrates the relationship.

Commitment creates emotional safety where you can communicate your vulnerabilities knowing that you'll still be loved and maybe healed in return. Commitment can free you from spending your emotional energy in many different directions of people and allows you to focus on one person. *If you commit to the right person it will liberate you, if you commit to the wrong person, it will imprison you.*

There are three basic reasons for fear of commitment. One, is the fear of being hurt again. Know that if you learn from the past and use the compatibility list, you have a great chance. Two, is fear of choosing the wrong person. Again, look at the past few pages to determine if you are with the right partner. Three, is fear of turning out like your parents. Your parent's definition of communication and commitment are probably different than yours. You now have a lot more tools for success than they did.

There are also those who are commitment-hungry and want to rush into a marriage before developing a strong, mature, relationship. Many commitment-hungry people rush into having children before they have stability in the marriage.

The real act of marriage takes place in the Heart, not in a church, synagogue or outdoors somewhere. It is treating one another with love and respect

Barbara DeAngelis' Sixty-Second Compatibility Test (DeAngelis, 1992)
Ask yourself the following four questions about your prospective or present partner.

1. Would I want to have a child with this person?
2. Would I want to have a child just like this person?
3. Do I want to become more like this person?
4. Would I be willing to spend my life with this person if he or she never changed from the way they are now?

If you answered yes to all four questions, you're probably compatible with one another. If you answered no to any of them, examine the reasons in detail and review the above material.

When To Break a Committed Relationship or Marriage

I believe that couples should do everything they can to salvage a troubled, committed relationship. This includes professional counseling, books, support groups, going to seminars, etc. It is time to end a relationship when, one, you realize you have no sexual chemistry between both of you, two, you realize you are not compatible, three, you and your partner have grown in two different directions, and four, your partner refuses to work on themselves and the relationship. Otherwise, there is no relationship. Being successful in working through issues will breathe new life into your relationship where you can experience the highest joys and lessons that love has to offer. This chapter on self-assertion asks you to assert your questions, thoughts, feelings, and opinions for deeper communication and deeper relationships. The adventure of "Love" requires great emotional courage and demands that you risk (assert), change, and grow together through the years and have the best opportunity for happiness and fulfillment.

Exercise 1

To build your self-assertion, practice using assertive behaviors. See examples below.
- Return an item to a retail store and explain why you want a refund or exchange.
- Get one item in the grocery store and ask someone in line if you can go ahead of him or her.
- Introduce yourself to somebody you don't know.

Write below which self-assertive behaviors you will use.
Some people are assertive at work but not at home, and vice versa.
A. Write down which environments are you assertive. Which environments you are not assertive?
B. Write why you are able to be assertive and not assertive in each of those environments.
C. How can you manage being more assertive in the areas that you are not assertive in?

____

____

____

____

____

____

____

____

Exercise 2

A. What romantic love myths do you or have you believed in the past? How have they hurt your relationships?

B. Many people have a fear of intimacy because they associate intimacy with a negative consequence because of a past experience. One may consciously tell oneself, one wants a loving, intimate relationship. Yet, one's emotional programming will pick a partner who is emotionally unavailable or uncomfortable with intimacy so as to protect them from intimacy. *Below, write down any negative words you have associated with intimacy.* Think about why you may have made those decisions about what intimacy means and write if those decisions have affected your choices in partners. Hint: Home =
Intimacy =

C. Which of the six wrong reasons for starting a relationship have you engaged in and why?

D. Which of the eight categories of relationships that won't work have you engaged in and why?

E. Which of the eight character defects have you attracted to and/or which do you have currently?

Exercise 3

1) At the top of each column below, write the name of each romantic ex-partner you've had in your life. If you haven't had any, write the names of your friends to find patterns.
2) Now, for each ex-partner/friend, think about the red flag event when you noticed something wrong such as, she drank too much, or he flirted too often. What did you do about it? Did you ignore/deny that it was happening? State the event and your response.
3) For each person, write their positive and negative qualities using one-word adjectives to describe them. For example, warm, mean, jobless, manipulative, generous, stingy, boring, etc. Think about their compatibility styles to help spark memories.
4) Once you have finished, circle the words or qualities you used more than once or that stood out to you.
5) Are there some patterns of which you need to be aware? Are your relationships getting healthier, worse, or the same? Is your present partner a lot different from past partners?

1) Ex-Partner/FriendName	1) Ex-Partner/FriendName	1) Ex-Partner/FriendName
2) Event & Your Response	2) Event & Your Response	2) Event & Your Response
3) Positive & Negative Qualities	3) Positive & Negative Qualities	3) Positive & Negative Qualities
4) List of Circled Words	4) List of Circled Words	4) List of Circled Words
5) Patterns/Relationships/ Present Partner	5) Patterns/Relationships/ Present Partner	5) Patterns/Relationships/ Present Partner

You now have a preview picture of your Imago, the kind of person to whom you are unconsciously drawn toward.

Strategy 8.2

Define and set your own boundaries with boundary violator types. Accomplish this by anticipating future situations and using request statements.

You get treated in life the way you train others to treat you.
Robert Anthony

Know Your Boundaries and Enforce Them with Others

Why do we and/or others have unhealthy boundaries? What are boundaries?
A boundary can be a physical, emotional, verbal, or behavioral invisible wall that protects us from harm and serves us by empowering the self, thereby providing self-respect and self-integrity. It is also a concept about how far we can go with comfort in a relationship. Many of us were taught, most often by our parents or our culture, which boundaries we should possess. Often, we are not aware of the boundaries or non-boundaries that we possess. Some people's boundaries and walls are up too much while others' boundaries and walls are not up enough. For example, some people have excessive boundaries such as being afraid to let people get close to them because they fear intimacy. Another is being extra sensitive about sexual and verbal harassment when the perceived perpetrator might have been innocently joking and had done it in good taste. And still, there are others who don't have enough boundaries in place in their character. Often, desperate people, people who need too much approval or want too much to be liked at any cost, commit the following behaviors:
- Tell too much about themselves at an intimate level in the first meeting with somebody.
- Fall in love with a new acquaintance or anyone who reaches out to them.
- Preoccupied, infatuated, or obsessed with a person.
- Act on the first sexual impulse.

Know the different types of boundaries and who violates them in your life.

Boundary Exploiters	**Boundary Victims** - tell their heart intimately on first date.
Manipulators	Desperate people or Self Abusers
Control Freaks	Dependent people—falling in love easily
Nasty people	Aloof people

Physical Boundaries -- not allowing anyone to abuse your body
Emotional Boundaries -- not allowing anyone to verbally abuse you, e.g. humiliation, put-downs.
Intellectual Boundaries -- standing up for your ideas and opinions despite who is present.
Spiritual Boundaries -- standing up for your values and beliefs that define you as an individual.

Cells Function Like Boundaries

The healthy boundary acts like a healthy cell in your body. It keeps poisons out, lets nutrients in, and gets rid of waste. It defines the existence of the cell by separating it from other cells. It knows when to allow healthy things in and when to keep unhealthy things out. So, we, like the cell, have a will and a choice to be an active or passive participant in boundary setting (Whitfield, 1993). If you don't set boundaries, it's as if a little self records that information as "you don't stand up for me," and each time you don't, you push back your boundary to make it easier for the exploiter to exploit you more the next time.

Your Personal Bill of Rights

Have you ever been insulted in conversation and not know you were insulted until you thought about it afterwards? We must be fully conscious when dealing with others so our self and our character are not degraded. Difficult people are merely opportunities to practice our skills. When you do assert yourself, speak clearly, briefly, and firmly. Don't use run-on sentences and chatter. Don't manipulate by asking in an over-sweet manner--express your true feeling by speaking from your "heart." Don't agree when you really disagree. Be congruent by using short phrases. After you practice for a period of time, then move to longer phrases. Ask how others are feeling while you do the same. Judge the act, not the actor. Affirm your personal bill of rights: I have the right to grieve over what I didn't get in childhood; I have the right to follow my own values and standards; I have the right to say 'no' to anything when I feel I am not ready; I have the right to have my needs respected by others; I have the right to expect honesty from others; I have the right to forgive myself and others; I have the right to give and to receive unconditional love. The list goes on and on.

Use the Boundary Request Model to Strengthen Your Self-Assertion

Step 1 (Observation Statement) State the observable behavior. Do not mix your observation with your interpretation. State factual information, not your opinion. For example, "When I saw you talking with Lisa it looked like you were 'coming on' to her," is stating your opinion. It would be better for you to say, "When you were talking with Lisa, I saw you putting your faces close together while you were both smiling." So, state the facts first before "getting into it."

Step 2 (Feeling Statement) Stop and feel the feeling and identify it before speaking. Use feeling words only. See the list below. If you say, "I feel like.../that.../it.../you.../I..." - you will be giving your thoughts or opinions and may invite opposition! Also note non-feeling words on the next page.

SAD	MAD	SCARED	APATHY	LOVING	GLAD	OTHER
Blue	Angry	Anxious	Bored	Affectionate	Amazed	Ashamed
Depressed	Bitter	Desperate	Detached	Compassionate	Cheerful	Engrossed
Disappointed	Disgusted	Envious	Distant	Fulfilled	Confident	Impatient
Distant	Disturbed	Fearful	Exhausted	Moved	Delighted	Impotent
Helpless	Enraged	Jealous	Gloomy	Passionate	Excited	Interested
Hurt	Frustrated	Nervous	Helpless	Satisfied	Grateful	Remorse
Lonely	Irritated	Overwhelmed	Numb	Tender	Happy	Selfish
Regretful	Miffed	Terrified	Passive	Touched	Hopeful	Sensitive
Troubled	Resentful	Uneasy	Weary	Trusting	Pleased	Shocked
Unhappy	Upset	Worried	Withdrawn	Warmth	Proud	Surprised

Non-feeling words include: abandoned, abused, attacked, blamed, cheated, cornered, criticized, guilty, ignored, inadequate, insulted, intimidated, isolated, left out, neglected, pressured, provoked, ridiculed, smothered, stupid, threatened, tricked, unheard, unimportant, unloved, unworthy, violated, worthless.

Although these might seem like feelings, they're actually what you think are being done to you.

Step 3 (Need Statement) Identify the basic need within you that is not being met. If you think you are being lied to, you can say, "I feel frustrated because I think I'm being lied to. My need is trust." If you feel like you're being ignored, you can say, "Because I have the idea I'm being ignored, I'm needing consideration." Or you can say, "Since the needs are consideration, I have the idea I'm being ignored." ***Choose from the list of needs:*** *acceptance, closeness, connection, empathy, honesty, safety, appreciation, love, respect, support, trust, meaning, rest, sexual expression, pleasure, fun, harmony, order, peace, fulfill a dream, integrity, protection, self-esteem, beauty, inspiration, warmth, etc.*

Step 4 (Request Statement) Ask for what you want in do-able, specific, action language. Follow it with the statement, **"Would you be willing to………"** and wait for their yes or no reply before continuing. Make sure it is not a demand. For example, "I'm asking that you give me a kiss goodbye whenever you leave somewhere. Would you be willing to do that." If you're not sure what you want, ask for compassion (to hear their understanding of what you've just said) or for their reaction to what you've just said.

Step 5 (Intention Statement) State what you intend to do as a consequence of their behavior, regardless of their answer. Choose a consequence that really impacts the relationship. If you can't think of one, ask yourself, "what do you do for them that they would really miss if you stopped." Make sure you don't state it in the form and attitude of an ultimatum. For example, "if you're not able to show me some consideration, I'm just not going to be able to cook your dinners anymore because that's my way of showing you consideration. Be sensitive but firm.

Boundary Request Model Example: Your friend is usually late and has asked you to pick them up at the mall. She shows up one-half hour late as you wait impatiently. When you see her you could say:

Step 1 (Observation Statement) "I've noticed in the past that when you say you'll be on time, it is rarely the case."

Step 2 (Feeling Statement) "I feel (frustrated) when you show up 1/2 hour late because I don't feel you are being considerate of me and my time."

Step 3 (Need Statement) "Because I have the idea that you value your time more than mine, I need respect from you."

Step 4 (Request Statement) "My request is that when you tell me a time in the future, make sure it is likely to be the case that you'll be on time. Otherwise, be up front with me and say there's a good possibility you'll be late. Would you be willing to make that effort?" Whether they state yes or no, you still state your intention.

Step 5 (Intention Statement) "That's your choice, and next time I will just leave if you are not there within the first 10 to 15 minutes."

Exercise 1

Write down the people you have problems setting boundaries with or whose boundaries you invade. They could be people who intimidate you, people you intimidate, people you need approval from, etc. Also, write the circumstances that surround this scenario with this person.

____

____

____

____

Exercise 2 (The Boundary Assessment)

Take the following assessment to check your boundary health status. Answer "never," "seldom," "occasionally," "often," or "usually" on the line next to each question.

1. I have difficulty saying "no" to people.____________________
2. I feel as if my happiness depends on other people.____________________
3. I find myself getting involved with people who end up hurting me.____________________
4. I would rather attend to others than attend to myself.____________________
5. People take or use my things without asking me.____________________
6. I have difficulty asking for what I want or what I need.____________________
7. I tend to take on the moods of people close to me.____________________
8. I have a hard time keeping a secret.____________________
9. I would rather go along with another person/people than express what I'd like to do.________
10. I put more into relationships than I get out of them____________________
11. I feel responsible for other people's feelings.____________________

Many responses of "usually" and "often" tend to indicate more boundary problems. People who answered "never" may not be aware of their boundaries. People who answered "seldom" and "occasionally" tend to have healthier boundaries.

For those who answered "usually" or "often," practice using the Boundary Request Model from above with those people who violate your boundaries. Record two results below.

____

____

____

____

____

____

____

____

Exercise 3 (The Role-Play Dialogue)

1. You can use your Power Reclaimer from the Self-Observation Chapter or from the exercise above to identify a frustrating relationship you have with somebody in your life.

2. Write out a two-page dialogue that depicts how a typical conversation proceeds between you and this frustrating person. The first half (page) of the dialogue should state the typical conversation of what normally occurs between you two, and the second half (page two) should state what you would like to be able to say to this person. <u>You must choose the Boundary Request Model for page two that</u> maintains your firmness, kindness, and patience. A verbal boundary sends a message to the other person that you will not tolerate a specific behavior. You can guess how the person would respond to your boundary request.

3. Choose a person who will play the part of the frustrating person, and they can appropriately improvise on your dialogue during the role-play if necessary.

Strategy 8.3:

Develop assertive skills in listening, delegating, and asking for what you want.

Ask and You Shall Receive!

There is one strategy made up of only one word that is so powerful it will more than likely help you to get whatever you want in life; it works virtually every time. The strategy/word is.......**ASK**. How many of you reading believe it works? Most people I ask say 'yes,' yet those same people don't use this strategy when pursuing their personal goals. Jesus said, "ASK and you shall ....receive." Now, he didn't say "BITCH, and you shall receive." When asking others for help, we need to do so in a way that respects the other person. The following 5 Ways to Ask will help guarantee that you will usually get the help you need to pursue any goal.

5 Ways to Ask

1. *Ask specifically.* "Don't beat around the bush." Ask directly and specifically what you want. To help you, just ask yourself, who, what, where, when, why, and how. In other words, tell them how they can help you and/or when can they help you. You can say, "I'd like a $3 raise by next month."

2. *Ask someone who knows.* Many times, we ask for things from others who don't have a clue about the specific topic you are asking about. You wouldn't go to a football player and ask him if he can help you with your graphic design project. You wouldn't go to a person who makes $10,000 a year and ask him/her how you can make a million dollars a year, would you? The best way would be to talk to a millionaire and ask, "How did you do it, and what do you recommend that I do?"

3. *Ask, but create value for them in return.* If you are a salesperson and a client of yours gives you a referral for more business, then offer them a referral, service, or something in return so that they will have incentive to help you out in the future. Or in the $3 raise example, you can say, "I saved the company hundreds of dollars when I developed the customer service form we all use now."

4. *Ask with belief and assume they will help you out.* It's funny, but when other people feel you're nervous or unsure about what you are asking, they are more likely to say 'no' to you. Before asking, visualize them nodding their head; with a smile, saying something like, "I'll be glad to help you out." Then you will more likely be calm and collected when asking something from them in the future.

5. *Ask until.* Ask until you get a 'yes' from somebody. Learn to "think out of the box." There are many different ways of asking for what you want. You can always offer something different in return, or ask another company, agency, business, or person for what you want. Keep thinking of different people and different ways of asking until you get what you want. This was another strategy Robert Schuller used to raise money to build the multimillion dollar Crystal Cathedral.

The Empathic Communication Model: Sharpen Your Listening Skills

You can improve your listening skills and resolve interpersonal conflict using this model. The Model asks the receiver to do the following, in order:

RESTATE what was said.
VALIDATE what was said.
EMPATHIZE with what was said.
When using it to solve interpersonal conflict, both people have to agree to use this model before starting. The sender asks to setup a convenient time for both. Then when both parties agree, the following process takes place.
A. The sender begins to respectfully verbalize his/her frustration while the receiver **silently** listens. The sender should use the Boundary Request Model from the last lesson to ensure it is done appropriately. Afterwards, the receiver then RESTATES what was said.... and then asks, *"Did I get it right?"* and if so, the receiver asks, *"Is there anything more you would like to say about that?"* If not, then...
B. The receiver moves to VALIDATION by saying, "You make sense, because.........." and the receiver says a statement confirming the logic the person used to arrive at the feelings felt by the sender. You might use the phrase, *"You make sense," or "I can understand why you feel that way."*
That doesn't mean that you agree with the logic, but you understand the logic they used to draw their conclusion and that it is painful for them. The receiver then asks, *"Did I get that right?"* If so, then...
C. The receiver moves to EMPATHY by saying, *"I imagine you might have felt.........(*guess the feeling)." Try to use a one word feeling word from the list from the last lesson. Then ask, *"Is that what you were feeling?"* If so, ...
D. Then both partners switch, and the receiver becomes the sender and gives his/her point of view, and the process repeats itself until there is mutual understanding between both people. It can usually resolve itself after a few rounds.

BOOST YOUR EMPATHIC SKILLS USING METAPHORS

When trying to help somebody understand how you feel about something, use a metaphor, story, or example to get your point across.
Find out their interest and draw from it. e.g. nature, cooking, cars, history, etc. For example, let's use the example of **Nature.** In the dialogue, you could say, "I've been growing these roots as I work on my own self-esteem, and when you told me that I was stupid, it was like I felt you ripping my roots from my tree of self-esteem out of the ground." This is a powerful means of communicating your thoughts and feelings. For another example, let's use **Service**. In the dialogue, you might say, "Remember how frustrated you were when you got ripped off from that car dealer? You felt taken advantage of, didn't you? That's the way I feel when you don't thank me for all that I do."

Exercise 1

Write below a dialogue between you and somebody else that you have conflict with in your life. Practice using the Empathic Communication Model by creating these sentences now.
RESTATE____

VALIDATE

EMPATHIZE

Exercise 2

Now estimate their reply to you by writing it below. Then write your reply to them.

Exercise 3

Write down the different ways you can ask when talking with this person:

a) Ask specifically ____________________

b) Ask someone who knows the subject you are asking about.____________________

c) Write down how you can create value for each of those people from your list above.

d) How could you ask with belief?____________________

e) What are some different ways of asking for what you want? ____________________

Strategy 8.4:
Learn how to assert yourself to difficult personalities.

"These People are Driving Me Crazy!"

Everyone at different times is irritable, indecisive, or rude. But some people are difficult most of the day because it is imbedded in their personality. Knowing the different personality types and how to manage them can make life much easier when dealing with these people. Believe it or not, these difficult people are in everybody's life to some extent. Learning to cope with difficult people is worth the effort. You'll get more done and be less frustrated if you do learn to cope. Deal with these personality types using the following strategies.

KNOW IT ALLS - These people are "full of themselves" and often condescending.
- Make sure you have all the facts before you meet and talk with them. Raise possible problems and be sure to follow through.

STALLERS - These people put things off until deadlines or until someone else takes over.
- Make sure to listen to the staller. Find out why he/she is stalling and help the person or ask him/her for help.

BULLIES - These people are hostile and angry and sometimes throw tantrums to get their way.
- Make sure you stand up for yourself. Use phrases like, "I believe." Don't engage or fight with them. Instead make your point firmly. They actually respect that more than if you were passive or "wimpy" about it.

GRIPERS - These people complain about things they don't like but rarely try to change their situation or the situation they are griping about.
- Make sure you let them know you hear their concern or worry. Directly ask, "What is it you want or would rather have?" Help them see that there might not be a solution today , but working toward one might be more constructive. Match their tone so they don't see you as opposing their view.

SILENT TYPES - These people don't say a whole lot even if you begged them to. They often don't say more than, a yes or a no.
- Ask open-ended questions to silent types. Start your sentences with why and how. If you do not get a response, let the silent type know your plans.

APPEASERS – These people will agree with you to get you off their back and will follow by not doing what they say they will do.
- Make sure you show them that you like them to some extent. Then dig to find out what is really going on to get at their true feelings of how they feel toward something. Then you can discover their motivations and work from there more successfully.

NEGATIVE TYPES - These people respond to new ideas with "That won't work" or they will "shoot down" anything new. They do not like change.
- Make sure you don't argue with these types. Suggest what won't work before they do so. They will start to respect your point of view before you give it to them.

INVALIDATORS - "There are small Hitlers all around us every day"--Robert Payne.
According to Jay Carter, a psychologist who wrote the book, Nasty People, the following statistics apply. Invalidators make up 1% of the population and commit the following behaviors below, often intentionally, and quite regularly. About 20% of the population invalidates others semiconsciously as a defense mechanism, and the rest of us do it on occasion or unintentionally.

WHAT DO INVALIDATORS DO AND WHO ARE THEY?

The Invalidators will often tell others:

- "You're not going to amount to anything"
- "You're stupid or dumb"
- ignore you as if you don't exist
- they will embarrass you in front of others such as, teachers, friends, and spouse.
- examples include, co-workers that "stab you in the back" and may be jealous of your success, bosses that demean their employees by, a) disrespecting them "behind their back" in gossip, b) not coming to their defense in public, c) not giving them their deserved breaks in the day, d) yelling at them, e) twisting the truth, f) not acknowledging their presence g) icy stares etc.
- they will often rejoice in others' weaknesses or show no concern for their troubles.

If You're Still In Doubt About Who They Are?

They are not always mean and may be overly nice, which makes them so difficult to understand because they are completely unpredictable. If you call them on their behavior, they are likely to say, "Wow, I have no idea what you're talking about." They may pay you compliments that are really double messages, or tell you secrets about the negative things other people are thinking of you. Or, a common behavior they exhibit is they find your most sensitive vulnerability and provoke it to gain control over you by making you feel shamed and degraded. There are nice ways a husband and wife invalidate that can eventually destroy a marriage. It usually starts off with less extreme behaviors such as using defenses as the "silent treatment," or sayings like, "you look so cute when you're angry," and then it moves on to the bigger stuff.

How To Deal With Invalidators

Make sure you don't play their game. Often they will force you to make a decision.

- Mirror what they say to you so they can taste their own venom.
- Try reason first: use humor, respect, professionalism, diplomacy, patience, discretion, firmness, or words that state what you believe.
- Do not generalize, label, judge, blame, make him or her wrong, or be righteous. Do not insinuate, act out of your angry feelings, or make them feel guilty.
- If reasoning and the above strategies do not work, and these people have to stay in your life, Jay Carter recommends the following. The following is a **last resort** for you to get

them to stop degrading you. When all else fails, show them how it feels when they invalidate you.
You can accomplish this by doing something outrageous like......talking loudly, acting crazy, squirting them with a water gun, laughing as if he/she just told you a joke.

- Wink at him/her, make noises, squeeze his/her cheek, raise your eyebrows at them, stare at them, disconnect, quit, or leave. It is highly effective to say nothing while staring them in the face, repeating the invalidation, saying unbelievably, "That's what I thought you said." Or, "I feel put on the spot." No one can argue with how you feel.

Invalidators have low self-esteem but big egos. They invalidate when they feel inferior or out of control, so in order to get that control and power back, they must invalidate others.
The above behaviors will make them uncomfortable and more likely to stop. Try to extract the human out of the evil mechanism, says Jay Carter. Invalidators were likely invalidated as well sometime in their lives. This does not excuse the behavior, but it is the reason they invalidate. Nonetheless, go to work.

Exercise 1

Identify the person from the list above that might fit you. Why do you think you are that way? Bring awareness to it, take responsibility for ending these behaviors that do no good to others, and use the "heart" exercises to help manage these flaws in your personality. Everybody has flaws, so don't feel bad unless you have been cold hearted, in which case it would be important for you to feel healthy shame.

____

____

____

____

Exercise 2

List which people in your life fall into the difficult personality categories listed above. Cross out the names that are not important to you. Make a commitment to call that person and practice the advice that falls under each difficult personality above.

____

____

____

____

Exercise 3

Using the Boundary Request Model, write out what you could say to any individual who is a difficult personality in your life.

____

____

____

____

Strategy 8.5:

Learn how to build rapport with others by identifying their personality or behavioral style and use it to fulfill the platinum rule (treating others how they would want to be treated).

Understanding Those Who are Different From You

Many of us have a tendency to judge others negatively for doing things differently than ourselves. We often judge others negatively because we estimate that they are too serious or not serious enough. They may talk too much or talk too little, be controlling in their ways or too submissive, superficial, or too "down to earth." It is important to understand that people are different not necessarily because they consciously chose the way they are, but, rather, most of their personality was formed genetically and socially by the age of five. You would not fault the rose because it is not an orchid. Therefore, no one personality style is better than the other. Diversity is a fact of life; it would be awfully boring without it. But we often tell ourselves that if he/she could just be little more friendly, serious, neat, caring, and so on...life would be much easier for me.

Learning, appreciating, and valuing differences in other people's personalities have many benefits.

A) It will deepen your understanding and appreciation for diversity and help you respect those who are different than you.

B) This new sensitivity and respect will foster a better attitude and will often correlate to job promotion and being viewed as more likable.

C) You will be able to develop better rapport with virtually every person in your life, which often translates into having a better marriage and being a better parent, relative, worker, neighbor, colleague, and so on.

The Platinum Rule

The Golden Rule says that you should treat others the way **you** would want them to treat you. However, the Platinum Rule holds even more value. It says to treat others the way **they** want to be treated. Since we are all different, the latter suggestion pays off in a bigger way. For example, a warm, amiable person wouldn't want to communicate gratitude to a bold, authoritarian person by telling him/her how sweet, kind, and thoughtful this person were. The amiable person mistakenly estimates that because he/she would want to be treated that way, everyone wants to be treated that way. It would be better for the amiable person to tell the bold, authoritarian "Your action was well-timed, efficient, and to the point...thanks."

Exercise 1

To identify your Behavioral Style, write a check mark next to either the open or self-contained behavior statements below. There are nine statements each. Read across for each statement. Then, write a check mark next to either the indirect or direct behavior statements below.

OPEN BEHAVIOR	**OR**	*SELF-CONTAINED BEHAVIOR*
- shows feelings and enthusiasm freely		- keeps feelings private, minimal contact
- animated facial expressions		- limited range of facial expressions
- more relaxed and warm		- more formal and proper
- conversations include many open tangents		- speaks in specifics, facts, stays on subject
- opinion oriented		- fact oriented
- open to getting to know people personally.		- not as open to knowing people personally
- Decisions are based on feelings and experiences		- make decisions based on facts/evidence
- prefers to work with and through others		- prefers to work alone and dictate conditions
- focus is one person, interaction, and feelings		- Focus mainly on the idea, concept, or result

INDIRECT BEHAVIOR	**OR**	*DIRECT BEHAVIOR*
- infrequent use of gestures and voice		- frequent use of gestures and voice
- infrequent contributor to group conversation		- frequent contributor to group conversation
- reserves expression of opinions		- expresses opinions readily
- patient and cooperative		- less patient and more competitive
- will wait to be introduced at gatherings		- introduces self at gatherings
- reacts slowly and deliberately		- reacts quickly and spontaneously
- wait for others to introduce themselves		- introduces oneself at social gatherings
- contributes infrequently to group conversation		- contributes frequently to group conversation
- minimal use of gestures, facial expressions, and voice intonation to emphasize points.		- often uses gestures, facial expressions, and voice intonation to emphasize points.

Your Behavioral Style is the one in between the two behaviors (Open, Self-contained, Indirect, and Direct). For example, if you're Behavioral Style was Open and Indirect, then your Personality Style would be the Relater.

OPEN

Relater **Socializer**

INDIRECT DIRECT

Thinker **Director**

SELF-CONTAINED

***Now, use the following table to understand how each personality style prefers to be treated.**

	RELATER	**THINKER**	**DIRECTOR**	**SOCIALIZER**
Strengths	Listening/Teamwork	Plan/Problem solving	Admin./Leadership	Persuading
Weaknesses:	Sensitive/Indecisive	Perfectionistic, Critical	Impatient, Insensitive,	Careless/Disorg.
Irritation:	Insensitivity	Unpredictability	Indecision	Routine
Under stress:	Submissive	Withdrawn	Dictatorial	Sarcastic
Decisions Are:	Consultative	Deliberate	Decisive	Spontaneous
Seeks:	Acceptance	Precision	Productivity	Applause
Appearance:	Casual	Formal	Businesslike	Fashionable
Workplace:	Friendly	Functional	Efficient	Stimulating
Security From:	Friendships	Thoroughness	Control	Others' approval
Fear:	Sudden changes	Criticism	Being hustled	Loss of prestige
Motivator:	Involvement	The Process	Winning	The Chase
Goal:	Stability	Accuracy	Control	Recognition
Do it with:	Warmth	Accuracy	Conviction	Excitement
Save Them:	Conflict	Embarrassment	Time	Effort
For Decisions:	Give assurances	Give data/documentation	Give options/analysis	Give testimonials
Like you to:	Be pleasant	Be precise	Get to the point	Be stimulating
Support Their:	Feelings	Procedures	Goals	Ideas
Behave:	Personally	Seriously	Businesslike	Enthusiastically
Your pace:	Slow/relaxed	Slow/Systematic	Fast/Decisive	Fast/Spontaneous
Focus on:	Communication	The Process	The results	Interaction
Write:	Friendly	Detailed	Concisely	Dramatically
Telephone:	Chatty	Organized	To the point	Playful

*Descriptions of the Behavioral Styles

Everyone possesses the qualities of each style to various degrees and everyone has a dominant style. For the sake of simplicity, I will focus only on dominant styles.

RELATERS: Relaters are warm and nurturing individuals. They are the most people oriented of the four styles. They are excellent listeners, devoted friends, and loyal employees. They are approachable and warm and excellent team players. Relaters are also afraid of risk. They may even tolerate unpleasant environments rather than risk change or confrontation. They strive to maintain personal composure, stability, and balance. They are friendly, good planners, and persistent workers.

THINKERS: Thinkers are analytical, persistent, systematic people who enjoy problem-solving. They are detail-oriented and enjoy perfecting processes for tangible results. They're always in control of their emotions and may become uncomfortable around people who are very out-going, e.g., Socializers. Thinkers have high expectations of themselves and others, which can make them over-critical. Their tendency toward perfectionism (paralysis by over-analysis) makes them slow and deliberate decision-makers. Thinkers are also skeptical, so they like to see promises in writing.

DIRECTOR: Directors are driven by two governing needs: to control and achieve. They are goal-oriented go-getters who are most comfortable when they are in charge of people and situations. Directors are not afraid to bend the rules and figure it is easier to beg for forgiveness than to ask permission. They accept challenges, take authority, and plunge head first into solving problems. They work quickly and impressively by themselves and are annoyed by delays. When they are over driven, they become stubborn, impatient, and insensitive to others. They have a no-nonsense approach and they get results.

SOCIALIZERS: Socializers are enthusiastic "party-animals" who like to be where the action is. They thrive on the admiration, acknowledgment, and accomplishments that come with being in the lime-light. Their strengths are charm, persuasiveness, and warmth. They are idea-people and dreamers who excel at getting others excited about their vision. They are eternal optimists with an abundance of charisma. These qualities help them influence people and build alliances to accomplish their goals. They can become impatient, averse to being alone, and have a short attention span. They are risk-takers who base many decisions on intuition which is not inherently bad. They are not inclined to verify information and assume someone else will do it. They are friendly and enthusiastic.

*How to Treat Each Personality Type:

RELATERS: Show how your ideas minimize risk. Show reasoning and proof. Demonstrate your interest in them. Provide outline and instruction as you personally "walk them through." Give them personal assurances. Allow them to service or support others. Provide relaxing, friendly atmosphere.

THINKERS: Approach them in a non-threatening way. Show your reasoning. Give it to them in writing. Provide explanations and rationale. Compliment them on their thoroughness and correctness. Tactfully ask for clarification and assistance. Allow them time to think, inquire and check to find the best or "correct" answer, within available time limits. Tell them "why" and "how".

DIRECTORS: Show them how to win. Display reasoning. Provide concise data. Agree on goal and boundaries, then support or get out of their way. Vary routine. Look for opportunities to modify their work-load focus. If necessary, argue with conviction on points of disagreement, backed up with facts.

SOCIALIZERS: Behave optimistically and provide upbeat setting. Support their feelings and ideas. Avoid involved details--focus on the "big picture." Interact and participate with them. Vary the routine--avoid requiring long-term repetition by them. Keep a fast, lively pace.

**If you want more information about this specific Behavioral Style Model, call Dr. Tony Alessandra at Alessandra & Associates: 1-800-222-4383 or 1-858-459-4515. The address is: P.O. Box 2767 La Jolla, CA 92038. The website is: http://www.alessandra.com and the email is: tony@alessandra.com*

Exercise 2

After identifying your personality style, observe under your category which aspects you appreciate when you are treated with those specific behaviors. Write below how you might *expect* others to treat you when you might not have treated others who are a different style with their preferred type of treatment.

Exercise 3

Identify one person you know who fits one of the personality types above that is different than yours. Treat them using at least three of the behaviors. For example: You might tell a Socializer how wonderful you think her work is, and that you have an idea that would be fun to break her out of her routine. Think of one person in your life that you need to communicate better with or improve the relationship, whether you like him/her or not. Brainstorm strategies using the information above to address his/her needs at your next meeting. Then practice this with other people you know for one week. It will start to become second nature to you and you will have become a master communicator, which will improve your life in many areas. Write below how successful this went with the person.

Strategy 8.6:

Decrease non-direct and increase direct communication approaches. Identify the three modalities needed to enhance communication with others and yourself.

Love reduces friction to a fraction.
Anonymous

Before you Speak!

The Sufis say that every word we speak should pass through these three gates: 1) Are these words true? 2) Are they necessary? 3) Are they kind?

Identify Your Love Modality

You will increase your ability to intimately connect and understand information, yourself, and others when you learn to identify your 3 L's:

A) Learning Style Modality

B) Love Style Modality

C) Lust Style Modality

A) Take the Learning Style Inventory in the Self-Advancement Chapter.

B) It is important to identify your Love Style Modality and your partner's (in a relationship) because you won't feel love in a stronger way than this. We can often feel unloved, alone, unfulfilled, uncared for, and depressed when we do not receive love the way we'd like to receive it. To determine if your Love Style is Visual, Auditory, or Kinesthetic, read the following: Think of a time when you felt most loved by somebody. Take a deep breath, close your eyes, and remember all of the details of the moment when you felt most loved. Who are you with? Now that you can visualize the moment, in order for you to feel those feelings of deep love, is the other person showing you his/her love (taking you to dinner, buying you something like golf clubs or flowers, or writing you something in a card, looking at you in a certain way, or going out of his/her way to do something for you, etc.)? If so, your Love Modality is VISUAL. If not....

In order for you to feel the love that you are feeling/felt, is the other person speaking to you in some way, communicating love to you (telling you how much he/she loves you, using expression in the voice, etc.). If so, your Love Modality is AUDITORY. If not.....

In order for you to feel the love that you are feeling/felt, is the other person touching you in a certain way, communicating love to you (hugging you, kissing you, squeezing you). If so, your Love Modality is KINESTHETIC.

If you saw the movie "Ghost," the character portrayed by Demi Moore said she didn't know if the character portrayed by Patrick Swayze really loved her. He expressed, "What do you mean, I show you that I love you all the time. I take you out wherever you want to go. I arrange to take you out to dinner all the time. I buy you special gifts throughout the year. I'm always showing my love for you." Demi Moore's character, with tears rolling down her face replied, "but you never tell me that you love me. That's why I'm not convinced." She was AUDITORY; he was showing his love VISUALLY, which was nice, but nowhere close to the place that she needed to feel love the most and within the depth of her soul. Powerful stuff!!!

That is why this is so important. Often, our loved ones, whether they are lovers, children, parents, or friends, don't know we fully love and appreciate them because we haven't identified their Love Modality. For example, it is nice that my wife tells me that she loves me, but I really feel it when she hugs and kisses me. That is because I am KINESTHETIC, and she knows that I prefer to receive love in that kind of manner more often, but not exclusively. The trick is to communicate what yours is and identify what theirs is. Then the key is to stretch and go out of your comfort zone to give your love in the way they need it. When you receive yours, you'll love to give theirs.

C) Then we all have a Lust Style Modality. It works the same way as above, only you ask the questions, "In order for you feel aroused, is the other person showing themselves in an erotic way?" if so you would be VISUAL. If not....

"Are they talking to you in a risqué manner (talking dirty for some people)?" If so, you would be AUDITORY. If not....

Are they touching you in a certain way (rubbing, etc., you get the picture). If so you would be KINESTHETIC.

Again, just like with the Love Modality, it is possible to have plenty of sex with our partner yet still feel empty and unfulfilled inside. Be able to identify your Lust Modality and communicate it to your partner as well as identifying his/hers and communicating it back to him/her.
Your Love Modality could be Visual, while your Lust Modality could be Auditory. Good Luck!!!

Self-Assertion Gone Wrong!

There are four ways to respond to conflict when your needs aren't met. The three ways below will be described, and the fourth will be in the following lesson. Let's take an incident of a neighbor's barking dog. It's been bothering you for days, and you are not sure how to deal with it. See below.

1. Nonassertive Behavior - These people usually under-react in several ways: ignoring the problem, closing the windows and trying not to hear it, denying the problem, telling themselves, "A little barking never hurt anyone," accepting the problem, hoping the neighbor will eventually do something about it, or waiting for them to move away. While sometimes, nonassertive behavior might be best (waiting a couple hours for it to resolve itself and giving them a chance to do it on their own instead of being a pushy neighbor), it often is a dissatisfying course of action and leads to greater resentment toward others.

2. Aggressive Behavior - These people usually overreact with anger or defensiveness, causing hurt and humiliation to others. They'd probably handle the dog problem by either yelling at the neighbors to do something about it or threatening to call the dogcatcher. They usually get their goal in the short run but in the long run, they would lose. Their behaviors cause others to terminate the relationship.

3. Passive Aggressive Behavior - These people usually have resentment that they are unwilling to express directly. They send these aggressive messages in subtle, indirect ways helping them to maintain the front of kindness. The person on the other side usually feels confused and angry that they were either fooled or jabbed indirectly. They'd probably handle the dog problem by complaining to the dog pound anonymously, and after the dog has been hauled away, they would express their sympathy. Or they could complain to other neighbors, hoping their hostility would force the offending neighbors to quiet the dog. Some common titles for passive aggressive behavior includes the following examples:

THE LIAR - The liar refuses to face up to a conflict either by giving in or by pretending that there's nothing at all wrong. This really drives the partner, who definitely feels there's a problem, crazy and causes him to feel both guilt and resentment toward the liar.

THE BLAMER - The blamer is more interested in finding fault than in solving a conflict. Needless to say, she usually doesn't blame herself. Blaming behavior almost never solves a conflict and is an almost surefire way to make the receiver defensive.

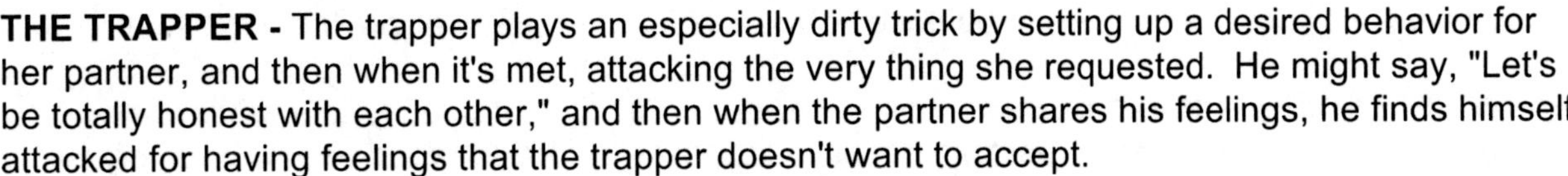

THE TRAPPER - The trapper plays an especially dirty trick by setting up a desired behavior for her partner, and then when it's met, attacking the very thing she requested. He might say, "Let's be totally honest with each other," and then when the partner shares his feelings, he finds himself attacked for having feelings that the trapper doesn't want to accept.

THE DISTRACTER - Rather than come out and express his feelings about the object of his feelings or about the object of his dissatisfaction, the distracter attacks other parts of his partner's life. Thus, he never has to share what's really on his mind and can avoid dealing with painful parts of his relationships.

THE CRISIS TICKLER - This person almost brings what's bothering him to the surface, but he never quite comes out and expresses himself. Instead of admitting his concern about the finances, he innocently asks, "Gee, how much did that cost?" dropping a rather obvious hint but never really dealing with the crisis.

THE MIND READER - Instead of allowing her partner to express her feelings honestly, the mind reader goes into character analysis, explaining what the other person really means or what's wrong with the other person. By behaving this way, the mind reader refuses to handle her own feelings and leaves no room for her partner to express himself.

THE SUBJECT CHANGER – Really, this is a type of avoider. The subject changer escapes facing up to aggression by shifting the conversation whenever it approaches an area of conflict. Because of his tactics, the subject changer and his partner never have the chance to explore their problem and do something about it.

THE GUILTMAKER - Instead of saying straight out that she doesn't want or approve of something, the guiltmaker tries to change her partner's behavior by making him feel responsible for causing pain. The guiltmaker's favorite line is, "It's okay.; don't worry about me..." accompanied by a big sigh.

THE AVOIDER - The avoider refuses to fight. When a conflict arises, she'll fall asleep, leave, and pretend to be busy at work, or keep from facing the problem in some other way. Arguing with an avoider is like trying to box with a person who won't even put up his gloves.

THE JOKER - Because she's afraid to face conflicts squarely, the joker kids around when her partner wants to be serious, thus blocking the expression of important feelings. (Hawkeye on M.A.S.H.).

THE SUBTLE REVENGER - Instead of honestly sharing his resentments, the revenger does things he knows will get his partner's goat - leaving dirty dishes in the sink, clipping his fingernails in bed, belching out loud, turning up the television too loud, and so on.

THE BELTLINER - Everyone has a psychological "beltline," and below it are subjects too sensitive to be approached without damaging the relationship. Beltlines may have to do with physical characteristics, intelligence, past behavior, or personality traits. This person hits below the belt where he/she knows it will hurt the other.

THE CONTRACT STICKLER - This person will not allow his relationship to change from the way it once was. Whatever the agreements the partners had as to roles and responsibilities at one time, they'll remain unchanged. "It's your job to ...feed the baby, wash the dishes, discipline the kids..."

THE KITCHEN SINK FIGHTER - This person is so named because in an argument he brings up things that are totally off the subject ("everything but the kitchen sink"): the way his partner behaved last New Year's eve, the unbalanced checkbook, bad breath, or anything like that.

THE WITHHOLDER - Instead of expressing her anger honestly and directly, the withholder punishes her partner by keeping back something - courtesy, affection, good cooking,humor, sex.

THE BENEDICT ARNOLD - This character gets back at his partner by sabotage, by failing to defend him from attackers, and even by encouraging ridicule or disregard from outside the relationship.

4. Assertive Behavior

The fourth way to handle conflict is using assertive behavior. Assertive people handle conflicts skillfully by expressing their needs, thoughts, and feelings clearly and directly, without dictating them. This is clearly the best communication style to use if you want healthy relationships. The Boundary Request Model is a great illustration of using assertive behavior because it is direct, it communicates how you feel, and it does so without dictating to the other person. More on self-assertion will be discussed in the next strategy.

Avoiding Conversation Mistakes

When conversing with another, makes sure you do not commit the following mistakes.

FIXING EVERYTHING - "I think you should forget about him. He'll never change." This robs the others person's chance of learning it themselves.

ORDERING – “Don't ask me why; just do what I say. Fill this out; then we'll talk.”

THREATENING – “If you do that one more time, I'll never speak to you again."

JUDGING - "You are really a lazy person; you really are." "You'll never make it."

SARCASM - "When did you talk to God?" "Since when are you making the decisions?"

COMPARING - "You are just like your mother." "Why can't you be like your older brother?"

Exercise 1

Identify which nonassertive, aggressive, and passive aggressive styles you use on occasion or regularly. Write an example of what you do when you use it.

____

____

____

____

____

____

____

____

____

Exercise 2

Identify the consequences of using the style that you chose in Exercise 1. Did it work for you? Are you satisfied with this style?
Write down an alternative style that may produce better outcomes in the long run. What fear do you have in putting the alternative style into action?

____

____

____

____

Exercise 3

Write below your Love and Lust Modality. Also write both the results and effects of communicating your modality to somebody else and the results and effects of what you did in response to them telling you of their modality.

Also identify either a lover's (if you have one) Love Modality or an individual who is a family member, friend, coworker, etc. Write below who it is and how you will give your love to him/her.

Strategy 8.7

Create Win/Win Solutions to Resolve Conflict Using the 7-Step Communication Method.

Seek Win/Win Solutions to Resolve Conflict

Assertive people handle conflicts skillfully by expressing their needs, thoughts, and feelings clearly and directly, without dictating them. Subsequently, feelings of discomfort may arise during the resolution, but afterwards assertive people usually feel better about themselves and their integrity than non-asserters.

In the case of the barking dog, you, as the assertive person, may wait a day or two to rule out a fluke situation. Then you could tell the neighbors that they might not have noticed it but the dog is barking excessively at cars and keeps you awake at night. Or, you could tell them you are interested in their answer to the problem. Either way, you have the best chance for a peaceful solution. If not, bad feelings might have to come about by your next appropriate action. Some people are just not reasonable.

Learn how to seek win/win situations. Learn about the different scenarios that take place within many interpersonal relationships.

WIN/LOSE - One person wins and the other loses. We've grown up with an either-or attitude.

Necessary Win/Lose Situations: One job applicant, game/sports opponent, in an unstoppable provoking battle.

Unnecessary Win/Lose Situations: Exerting power over someone else. They're usually in the form of:

- Physical power--parent to a child, "Stop doing that or I'll smack you."
- Authoritative power--The boss who sabotages an employee's work hours, job promotions, gives him/her undesirable tasks, and threatens termination. Teachers who use grades to intimidate and manipulate students is another example.
- Societal power--The majority rules so the other group is left out in the cold.

We are often programmed in childhood to acquire the win/lose mentality. When one child is compared to another, both children get the message that one wins and another loses.

LOSE/LOSE - Neither side is satisfied with the outcome. Compromise is quite common in interpersonal relationships. Though compromise can be a good solution, there are often unexplored solutions waiting to be used. It assumes that both people can't work together for win/win outcomes. Examples include:

- Wars often lead to lose/lose because the winner could come out of it with thousands dead, resources depleted, and a damaged national consciousness.

- Battles of pride between two people striving to win; they can both come out losing their dignity, integrity, and pride.

LOSE/WIN – Some people are taught as they grow, "I lose, you win." The messages may be, "Be a peacemaker, or a good person and let the other person have their way." These people give in too soon, and their permissiveness is a big target for perpetrators. They usually repress their feelings and are people pleasers. Sometimes their anger and frustration will make them swing to win/lose. Then, when they feel guilty, they'll swing back to lose/win.

WIN/WIN - There's a belief that by working together it's possible to find a solution in which everybody reaches his or her goals without needing to compromise. It requires a noncompetitive attitude and an openness and cooperation with the other person.

Example: Carl loved to spend his evenings playing piano, but his wife, Lily, felt cheated out of the few hours of each day they could spend together. Carl didn't want to give up his hobby, and Lily wasn't willing to sacrifice the time she needed alone with her husband. Solution: Three or four nights each week Carl stayed up late to play his piano keyboard through the headphones only after spending the evening with Lily. On the following mornings, she drove him to work instead of his taking the bus, which allowed him to catch up on his sleep.

To Create Win/Win Situations, Perform the Following 7-Step Communication Method.

STEP 1 - *State the problem or your unmet need in the form of a question before discussing it.* Realize that the problem is initially yours even though someone else might be the cause. This attitude will give you a stronger feeling of responsibility and approach the other person less defensively. Also, the unmet need isn't always apparent. If you loaned money to a friend who didn't pay it back, instead of wanting the money back, perhaps the unmet need is more a matter of you feeling victimized by your friend's taking advantage of you.

STEP 2 - *Set a time and date to meet.*
One person might not be ready at a moment's instance to discuss a problem. You can say, "Something's been on my mind; can we talk about it?" If 'yes', great; if 'no', find an agreeable time for both of you. My wife and I use this when one is just too angry at the other.

STEP 3 - *Communicate your problem and needs.*
The other person can't meet your needs if you don't explain why you're upset and what you want. Yet, many of us think the other can read our mind and should know what is wrong. You could state, "We have a situation here that isn't working for either of us. Please tell me what you think the problem is and what is needed to solve it and then I'll share my perspective. Let's talk until we find a solution that works for both of us." Either you can go first, or the other person can. Use the <u>Boundary Request Model</u> from Strategy 8.2 to accomplish this. See next page.

Step 1 (Observation Statement) "I've noticed in the past that when you say you'll be on time, it is rarely the case."
Step 2 (Feeling Statement) "I feel (frustrated) when you show up 1/2 hour late because I don't feel you are being considerate of me and my time."
Step 3 (Need Statement) "Because I have the idea that you value your time more than mine, I'm needing respect from you."
Step 4 (Request Statement) "My request is that when you tell me a time in the future, make sure it is likely to be the case that you'll be on time. Otherwise, be up front with me and say there's a

good possibility you'll be late." Would you be willing to make that effort? Whether they state yes or no, you still state your intention.
Step 5 (Intention Statement) "That's your choice, and next time I will just leave if you are not there within the first 10 to 15 minutes."

STEP 4 - *Get feedback from your partner to ensure he/she understood your message correctly.* A nice way to go about doing this is to ask: "I'm not sure I expressed myself very well just now--maybe you could tell me what you heard me say so I can be sure I communicated it right." After the partner got it, say, "I appreciate that; you got it right on the button."

STEP 5 - *Have your partner communicate his/her needs and then check your understanding.* This is the time to be silent and use your listening skills. It is in your own self-interest to discover and meet your partner's needs so he/she will feel more apt to meet yours. People from different cultures use different methods for solving problems. When it seems to you that other people are sidestepping or escalating a conflict, consider whether your reaction is based on a cultural bias.

STEP 6 - *Negotiate a solution using the 3 Part Method.*
Part 1 - Brainstorm several possible solutions. Write down every thought in a 10-minute time limit, no matter how unworkable because sometimes a farfetched idea leads to a workable one.
Part 2 - Evaluate the brainstorm solutions and agree on three possible solutions.
Part 3 - Decide on the best solution. It needs to be best for both parties and doesn't have to be final. It should look potentially successful.

STEP 7 - *Implement the Solution*
After some time, evaluate how things are going and if anything needs to be adjusted so that both parties are happy. Sometimes, win/win isn't always possible. Some compromise might be in order even with two people who have the best intentions. However, it gives you the best chance of achieving a satisfying result for both parties. Or, agree to disagree. Peacefully coexisting with other people and respecting them even though you don't agree on fundamental issues is a viable option when all else fails.

Exercise 1

Write down a time when you used a win/lose approach that could have been approached as a win/win.

____

____

____

____

____

____

____

____

____

____

____

Exercise 2

Write down a time when you used a lose/lose or lose/win approach or used a compromise when you could have approached it from a win/win.

Exercise 3

Identify a conflict you have with somebody right now. Use the 7-Step method from above to resolve the conflict by yourself first. Then approach the person and go through the 7 steps. Write 7 steps you intend to use below and then eventually write down the results. This will prepare you and keep ideas fresh in your mind.

Chapter Insight & Commitment

After completing this chapter, I learned the following about my communication skills, boundaries, modalities, and conflict resolution skills:

Example: I learned that I attract to the wrong people in life for the following reasons... I learned that I let people cross my boundaries and take advantage of me. I learned that my temper gets in the way of my listening and my ability to assert myself with pride and respect. I learned that I never use a feeling word to communicate how I feel. I always seem to use a thinking or non-feeling word. I can sometimes be passive-aggressive in my communication like the trapper and the blamer.

I can take active steps to help me achieve my future goals and become more of the person I am or strive to be by:

Example: I will make a list of healthy attractive qualities I like in a mate and act accordingly. I will start setting boundaries with Joe, my boss, and my girlfriend by using the Boundary Request Model. I will cool off next time I am angry and then find the right words to say before I speak to them with the help of the Boundary Request Model. I will use the feeling chart so I can express what I feel more clearly.

CONGRATULATIONS!!!
YOU HAVE COMPLETED THE BOOK

Now, refer back to the beginning of the book and complete the Pre-Post Life Skills Assessment to see if you've made progress in each of the life skills areas.

APPENDIX A: Emotional Freedom Technique (EFT)

Emotional Freedom Technique (EFT) is one of many new meridian energy psychology therapies that have evolved over the last 25 years. Founder Gary Craig invented it from the person who discovered TFT, Roger Callahan. The Chinese discovered that the meridian system is a network of energy pathways similar to an invisible circulatory system. The concept of subtle bio-electron energy flowing through the meridians has been understood by asian physicians for over 3,000 years. When illness, injury, chronic stress or trauma interrupts the balance/flow of Qi or energy, the energy is blocked. Qi energy can be un-blocked and healing will result if certain acupoints are stimulated by gentle fingertip tapping while the mind is focused on the memory, problem, stress, trauma, physical pain, etc. EFT is a blend of psychology and traditional Chinese acupuncture.

There have been over fifty peer-reviewed studies from reputable journals conducted on EFT and other Energy Psychology modalities. The research documents the success EFT has had on anxiety, depression, performance, phobias, pain, weight loss, PTSD, and much more. The APA (American Psychological Association) has approved it for psychologists who need continuing education credit to keep their licenses current. The National Institute of Health's Office of Alternative/Complimentary Medicine has endorsed acupuncture as a treatment for pain and nausea. Every year, more and more traditional, cognitive-behavioral trained psychiatrists, and therapists are recognizing the power of EFT and other energy psychology techniques. The mind/body/spirit connection is going mainstream. See my website below or energypsych.org for current research.

The following information allows the user to try EFT on any issue they desire. I recommend to the user to seek professional help when working through deep, traumatic events. An EFT practitioner or professional will know how to untangle the trauma that gets entrenched into the mind and body of the person who has suffered. They know the terrain that is filled with many obstacles that will prevent the healing. Also, a professional will know how to de-stress a person if the user triggers an intense memory that causes more trauma.

The following websites will help you to become more knowledgeable about EFT.

- *tappingintowellness.com (Author Thomas Ventimiglia's EFT website)*
- *eftuniverse.com*
- *attractingabundance.com (Carol Look's EFT website)*
- *masteringeft.com (Pat Carrington's EFT website)*
- *energypsych.org (excellent published research articles and resources on all energy psychology therapies.*
- acestudy.org/files/OriginsofAddiction.pdf
- If after using EFT on an issue, and you don't get much progress, be sure you are persistent and tap every day over and over until you get results.

THE BASIC RECIPE

Founder Gary Craig believes the cause of all negative emotions is a disruption in the body's energy system. When you clear the energy system using the Basic Recipe below, pains, negative emotions, etc., are released from the body and ailments clear up. He says, "Try it on everything!!" Rate the pain on a scale of 1 – 10 before and after the tapping.

1. THE SETUP: Verbally repeat the Affirmation three times while rubbing the Sore Spot or tapping the Karate Chop point.

Affirmation: Even though I have this ______(name the ailment, event, or emotion),______ I deeply and completely love and accept myself.

See the diagram on the page 314. The Karate Chop point is number 13. The Sore Spot is three inches below the your breast bone and three inches over to the left. The Sore Spot works a little better but both work fine. Example: "Even though I have this pounding headache, I deeply and completely love and accept myself." Be as specific as you can about the condition. Is the ache dull or sharp, etc. You can see more examples on page 326 under the title of Beliefs. Connect the positive statement to the negative.

2. THE SEQUENCE: Tap about 10 times on each of the following energy points while verbally repeating the Reminder Phrase at each point.

The Reminder Phrase is a summary version of the affirmation in the setup. For example: "This pounding headache" as you tap the (eb) point "This pounding headache" as you tap the (oe) point, and so on. Emphasize the negative issues and beliefs you have.

Another way to use the Reminder Phrase is to talk about the problem as you focus on the negative. Example: Tap all the points as you say, "This pounding headache when I work," "this pounding headache because Sue is driving me crazy," "this, I don't want to go into work headache," "this dreadful headache," and so on.

See the following points in the diagram on the next page.
(eb, oe, ue, un, ul, uc, ua, R, T, if, mf, lf, sh, g)

3. THE 9 GAMUT PROCEDURE: Continuously tap on the Gamut point (number 14 on diagram) while performing each of these 9 actions below:

1) Close your eyes 2) Open eyes 3) Shift eyes down right 4) Eyes down left 5) Roll eyes in circle, clockwise 6) Roll eyes in other direction, counterclockwise 7) Hum 2 seconds of a song 8) Count to five 9) Hum 2 seconds of a song.

4. PERFORM THE SEQUENCE AGAIN (#2 above). Tap on new issues that arise.

Note: In subsequent rounds (after you completed steps 1 - 4), use the word "remaining" in the Setup Affirmation and the Reminder Phrase.

For example, in the Setup, "Even though I have this remaining headache......." In the Reminder Phrase "This remaining headache." This will address any causes unsaid.

Points on the Body:

EB – Eye Brows, beginning of brows on the bone of the eye sockets.
SE – Side of Eyes, the bone at the outer edge of the eyes.
UE – Under Eyes, the bone that forms the lower eye socket, under pupils.
UN – Under Nose, the crease between nose and upper lip.
UL – Under Lip, between the lower lip and chin.
CB – Collar Bone, where the collarbone meets the sternum.
SS – Sore Spot, a tender spot 3 inches down and to the left across from top of the sternum.
UA – Under Arm, side of the body, 4 inches down from the arm pit in line with the nipple on a man or where the bra strap runs on a woman.

Points on the Hand

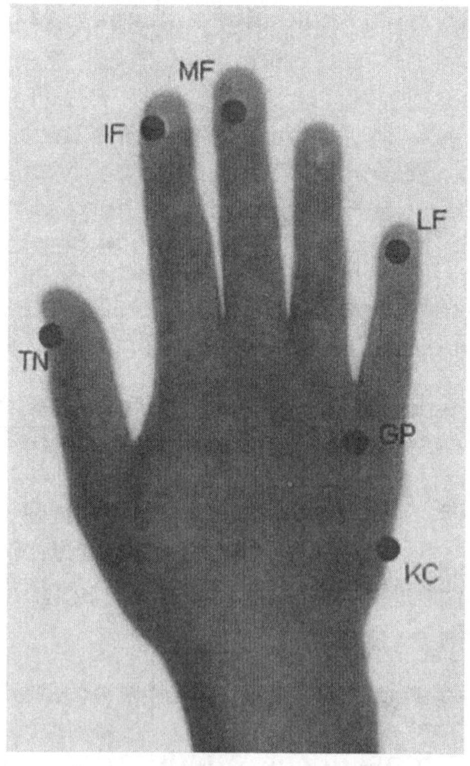

TN – Thumb Nail, the edge point at the base of the nail.
IF – Index Finger, the edge point at the base of the nail.
MF – Middle Finger, the edge point at the base of the nail.
GP – Gamut Point, Indentation between bones of the little finger and ring finger.
LF – Little Finger, the edge point at the base of the nail.
KC – Karate Chop Point, side of the hand, where you would hit performing a karate chop.

ASSOCIATION OF ENERGY POINTS TO OUR BODY ORGANS AND EMOTIONS

Energy Point	Body Organ	Negative Emotion
eb = Eyebrow	Urinary Bladder	Restlessness, Impatience Frustration Tap for Peace and Harmony
oe = Outer Eye	Gall Bladder	Rage, Wrath, Fury, Hostility Tap for Love, Forgiveness, and Adoration
ue = Under Eye	Stomach	Anxiety, Fear, Disgust, Disappointment Tap for Contentment, Calm
un = Under Nose	Spine/Governing Vessel	Embarrassment Tap for healthy sense of Pride
ul = Under Lip	Spine/Governing Vessel	Shame Tap for healthy sense of Pride
uc = Under Collarbone	Kidney	Sexual inhibition, Anxiety Tap for Sexual Assuredness,
ua = Under Armpit	Spleen	Anxiety Tap for Security, Confidence, Trust
R = Rib	Liver	Unhappiness Tap for Happiness and Cheer
T = Thumb nail	Lung	Scorn, Contempt, Intolerance, Tap for Humility, Tolerance
If = Index finger	Large Intestine	Guilt Tap for Self-worth
Mf = Middle finger	Circulation/Sex	Regret, Remorse, Sexual tension, Stubborn Tap for letting go of the past
Lf = Little finger	Heart	Anger Tap for Love, Forgiveness
Sh = Side of hand	Small Intestine	Sadness, Sorrow Tap for Joy
G = Gamut spot Despair	Thyroid	Depression, Grief, Loneliness,
(For 9 Gamut procedure)		Tap for Hope, Lightness

The above was formulated by John Diamond, M.D. and aren't exactly corresponded to Chinese Acupuncture.

Advanced Use of EFT

Only tapping on the pain, emotion, or whatever issue you are addressing will usually give you only partial healing. If the pain is a seven out of ten, you might get it down to a four or a five by just tapping on the issue. These pains and issues are usually associated with a negative event, emotion, or belief. Therefore, if you identify these events, emotions, and/or beliefs and associate it with the pain/issue, you have the best chance of it going to a zero and completely healing for good. See the example in point two.

1. QUESTIONS THAT HELP IDENTIFY THE ROOT ISSUE.

- What is the first or worst time you felt this way?
- What do you think is the possible cause? How old were you?
- What decision or vow did you make about life as a result? Example: "I'll never trust a man/woman again." "I'll never get in an elevator again."
- Is the pain dull, sharp, red, throbbing, etc.
- What is the shape, color, and size of the pain?
- What do you tell yourself about it?
- How does that make you feel? Use a one word emotion…angry, hurt, etc.
- Replay the audio or videotape of the event in your mind and notice where your body feels pressure or discomfort.
- What event or person you would most liked to have skipped in your life?
- What is your biggest regret?
- What do you really want and need to feel happy and secure?
- Who do you need to forgive in order to be completely over this problem? Could it be you? Could it be God?
- What is the major reoccurring pattern in your life?
- Who do you feel powerless with when you are around them?
- Who do you feel inadequate with when you are around them?

2. CREATE A GREAT AFFIRMATION STATEMENT (The Setup)

It is crucial to start with the words, "Even though." Those words will help clear any subconscious reasons for holding on to the issue. After, identify feelings, and connect them to who or what they remind you of in your past such as certain negative people and events. Then, pick a phrase of what you want (I choose to release this anger) and give yourself a good reason to believe your want should come true and put that after the word, "because." The reminder phrase is a short summary version of the negative part of the setup statement.

Even though I have this ______ (name the pain or issue) ______
and I feel ______ (connect it to an emotion like anger, hurt, fear, etc.) ______
which reminds me of ______ (relate it to a past troubling event/person in your life) ______

I allow/choose to ______ (state what you want.....let it go and have peace of mind, etc.) ______
because ______ (give yourself a good reason why you can .....I'm safe now, I deserve it, etc. ______
AND I deeply and completely love and accept myself.

Example: Even though I have this pain in my lower back and I feel fear and anxiety which reminds me of all the responsibilities I'm carrying like my job, the kids, and the bills, I allow myself to let go of the anxiety because I've proven I can manage things and I deeply and completely love and accept myself. *See more examples on page 335.*
Reminder Phrase: this anxious lower back pain.

Now you try! Fill in the blanks in the two samples below.

Sample 1
1. Even though I have this ______
and I feel ______
which reminds me of ______
I allow/choose to ______
because ______
and I deeply and completely love and accept myself.

Reminder Phrase ______

Sample 2
1. Even though I have this ______
and I feel ______
which reminds me of ______
I allow/choose to ______
because ______
and I deeply and completely love and accept myself.

Reminder Phrase ______

3. TREAT DIFFERENT ASPECTS OF THE PROBLEM.

Example: don't just tap on the scary spider, tap a round for fear of being bitten, another for how it crawls, another for how it looks, and so on.

4. IF NO PROGRESS IS MADE......... TREAT PSYCHOLOGICAL REVERSALS, ENERGY TOXINS, BIRTH TRAUMA, AND/OR COLLARBONE BREATHING.

A. PSYCHOLOGICAL REVERSALS: These reversals will literally block your progress with EFT and anything else in your life. It is a form of self-sabotage like having your foot on the gas pedal and the brake at the same time. There are often subconscious reasons why we don't want to heal and progress. Have you ever wondered why.........

- athletes get into slumps?
- addictions are so hard to overcome?
- people get writer's block?
- healing takes so long?
- People have learning limitations like dyslexia?

People often blame it on lack of will power, poor motivation, or spacing out. Physically, the polarity is reversed in the body's energy system which is like having your batteries in backwards; the machine won't work. The energy system runs in reverse. As a result, many people are psychologically reversed against losing weight. They consciously will tell you, "I want to lose weight so bad," but through counseling or muscle testing it's revealed that they don't want to for subconscious reasons such as:

- If they lose weight, they'll gain it back and don't want to spend more money in changing their wardrobe.
- If they lose weight, they won't have anything to medicate the emotional pain from the past that they don't want to deal with.
- If they lose weight, men will want to be with them which means they won't be safe because a man in their past molested them. Staying fat will prevent further trauma.

It is the old brain trying to protect you. That's where EFT can come in and speak to your subconscious mind to say, that was then, you are older and can protect yourself now. It is now safe for you to lose the weight and be okay. EFT works because, one, you are using the phrase "Even though," and two, you hopefully have the insight or your therapist has the insight to reveal these subconscious motivations so they can be tapped on and eliminated.

To clear most psychological reversals, rub the sore spot or tap the karate chop point and repeat all of the following phrases:

- "Even though I have this issue of _________, I am doing the best I can."
- "Even if I fear I won't succeed with this goal, I'm now willing to be pleasantly surprised.
- "Even if part of me fears it is unsafe for me to succeed with this goal, I now give myself permission to succeed anyway, trusting myself to deal with whatever comes as a result."
- "Even if part of me fears it could be unsafe for one or more other people for me to succeed with this goal, I choose to trust others to take care of themselves as they need to, as I now move into fuller integrity with my highest intentions."
- "Even if part of me believes I don't deserve to succeed with this goal, I am now willing to be wrong about this."
- "Even if part of me believes that if I succeed with this goal, one or more people who have hurt me will have gotten away with that, I forgive myself for having a part of me that wants vengeance more than my own success, and I now choose success anyway."
- "Even if some part of me believes I would not know who I am if I succeed, I now trust myself to grow into a more expanded and authentic me anyway."
- "Even though there are risks in both succeeding and failing with this treatment, I now trust myself to be large enough to hold both sets of risks side by side, with compassion and full acceptance."
- "Even if I have any other objections to succeeding, I deeply and profoundly accept and forgive myself for having these, and I now choose success nevertheless, beginning now."

B. ENERGY TOXINS: Remove energy toxins such as moving away from computers, TV, fumes, chemicals on clothes, perfumes, hair spray, cosmetics, food insensitivities, and so on. These block the meridians and will prevent any progress from occurring.

C. BIRTH TRAUMA: On the next page you will find birth circumstances that you would want to tap on to eliminate any psychological reversals. This information comes from rapideyetechnology.com

- <u>Unplanned, unwanted, illegitimate:</u> Even though I feel I don't deserve to live or feel unwanted, I am legitimate and deserving of love and choose to thrive being myself.

- Late – past due date: Even though I feel slow, stuck, and/or afraid to come out, I allow myself to move forward in life trusting I will be safe.
- Fast – the labor was very quick: Even though I have to slow down to survive or I want to rush things, I love and accept the pace and timing of my personality.
- Held Back – labor was slow and long: Even though I feel blocked, stuck, claustrophobic, and/or procrastinating, I am safe and free to move forward
- Wrong Sex – Mom or dad were hoping for the other sex: Even though I'm afraid of disappointing others, being disapproved, confused, unloved, and/or feel unwanted, I am delighted to be a woman/man, am desirable, and a wonderful surprise.
- Induced Birth: Even though I hold myself back and feel others have to push me, I am free and safe to assert myself, and/or do things on my own.
- Cesarean Section: Even though I feel angry at being interrupted, yanked out of relationships, indecisive, confused, and/or not going for what I want, I allow myself to decide on effective ways for my highest good and am safe to complete things.
- Forceps: Even though I feel I'm not good enough, need to be bailed out, fear being touched, want excess control, and/or have difficultly finishing things, I am competent and able to make it on my own allowing support from others and pleasurable endings.

D. COLLARBONE BREATHING: In a small percentage of cases, a unique form of energy disorganization occurs within the body that blocks progress of EFT. The following collarbone exercise will take about two minutes to perform.

Place two fingers of your right hand on your right Collarbone Point. With two fingers of the left hand, tap the Gamut Point continuously while you perform the following five breathing exercises: breathe half way in and hold it for seven taps, breathe all the way in and hold it for seven taps, breathe half way out and hold it for seven taps, breathe all the way out and hold it seven taps, breath normally for seven taps. Then, place the two fingers of your right hand on your left Collarbone Point and, while tapping the Gamut Point, do the five breathing exercises. Then, bend the fingers of your right hand so that the second joint or knuckles are prominent. Then place them on your right Collarbone Point and tap the Gamut Point while doing the five breathing exercises. Repeat this by placing the right knuckles on the left Collarbone Point. Repeat procedure using the fingertips and knuckles of the left hand.

TAPPING FOR THE BODY, ILLNESSES, AND BELIEFS

Often times, our body pain matches the symbolic language we use. For example, jaw pain could be "something gnawing at you." Your setup affirmation could be *"Even though I have this jaw pain which reminds me of Pam's promotion that has been gnawing at me because I deserved the promotion, I choose to let go of the anger once and for all and I allow my jaw pain to disappear starting now."* If you have a pain in your neck, your setup statement could be, *"Even though I have this pain in my neck that reminds me of my husband who the pain in my neck, I allow myself to be pain free and trust I can work out the situation with my husband."*

Also, try to connect medical conditions and illnesses to emotional events and feelings. For example, your headache could be related to emotional upsets, feeling unable to control things, fear and anxiety, or self-criticism. See Louise Hay's book called, "You Can Heal Your Life." Also, author Richard Shane and Karol Truman have material in their books on the subjects above as well.

The words below in bold print are some common beliefs many of us feel throughout our lifetime. Use the associated setup statement for EFT tapping.

I'M NOT GOOD ENOUGH

- Even though I think I'm not good enough and am depressed because I could never please mom and dad, I allow myself to acknowledge my own achievements, choose to only impress myself, and completely love and accept myself from now on.

I MUST ACHIEVE IN ORDER TO BE ACCEPTED

- Even though I'm sad because I can't accept myself unless I achieve greatness, I choose to love/accept myself completely whether I achieve something or not.

I CAN'T DO MATH

- Even though I think I can't do math because I was told girls can't do math by my teacher and parent, I choose to let that belief go and I allow myself to solve math problems easily and successfully starting now.
- Even though I can't do math, which reminds me of when Mr. Clark in eighth grade embarrassed me in the class, I choose to let it go and make math easy and fun now.

I CAN'T SPEAK IN FRONT OF OTHERS

- Even though I can't speak in front of others because if I screw up, their judgment would ruin me, which reminds me of the humiliation I felt in junior high theatre, I release that and trust that my performance will be just as good as my practice session.

I CAN'T BE SUCCESSFUL

- Even though I grew up feeling unworthy and not deserving of financial freedom, I now deem myself very worthy and allow money to flow to me using it for good things.
- Other blocks to success: I must be poor in order to be close to God, I fear success will bring too much pressure and responsibility, I would disappoint God or others, I feel it's unfair to have more money because my parents didn't, I feel guilty for wanting success, I'd feel inadequate and incompetent, I believe I'm supposed to be poor.

I'M NOT SMART ENOUGH

- Even though I think I'm not smart enough because I got bad grades in high school, I allow myself to trust my abilities especially since I'm more disciplined now than before.

I DON'T DESERVE LOVE

- Even though I feel I don't deserve love which reminds me of not getting it growing up, I allow myself to believe I do deserve love as any person of my good nature should.

OTHER NEGATIVE BELIEFS

- Even though I feel like I'm taken for granted………………………..
- Even though things never work out for me…………………………
- Even though I feel like I don't belong or feel left out……………

TRY IT ON EVERYTHING!

abuse, auto accidents, love pain, panic attacks, sports issues, PTSD, war memories, weight loss, phobias or fears such as: public speaking, dentist, spiders, roaches, needles, driving, snakes, heights, water, etc., confrontations, self-esteem, and all the unhealthy emotions like anger, sadness, hurt, grief, frustration, regret, confusion, rage, worry, guilt, etc

APPENDIX B: Preventing Panic Attacks

1. Know that panic attacks can't kill you or make you crazy.

2. Breathe slow breaths into a paper bag...adds carbon dioxide to your blood.

3. Splash your face with cold water...it produces the dive reflex.

4. Toss something like a can of food between your hands back and forth.

5. Count down from 100 as fast as you can.

6. Do math problems or anything that occupies your mind.

7. Listen to your favorite music loudly and sing and dance along.

8. Slap your cheeks and dance around...confuse your thoughts to distract yourself.

9. Do not sit down or look at yourself in the mirror.

10. Use Diaphragmatic Breathing: Rest one hand on the abdomen. Breathe in through the nose for one count, and out through the mouth for two counts. Increase it to two counts in, and four counts out, three counts in and four out, etc. Don't go beyond your breaking point.

11. Get in touch with your senses: touch; hold some ice, smell; sniff some strong peppermint, taste; bite into a lemon, sight; take detailed inventory of everything including colors, counting objects, etc.

12. Disengage and go on a walk outside.

13. Reduce or eliminate: sugar, caffeine, nicotine, alcohol, and lower carbs.

14. Do EFT (Emotional Freedom Technique) on what triggered the panic attack, if known.

Sources

American Cancer Society (1991). *Cancer facts and figures.* Atlanta: American Cancer Society.

Barefoot, J. C., Brummett, B. H., Williams, R. B., Siegler, I. C., Helms, M. J., Boyle, S. H., Clapp-Channing, N.E., Mark, D. B. (2011). Arch Intern Med. 2011; 171(10): 929-935.

Benor, D. J. (1993). *Healing Research* (in four volumes). Munich: Helix Editions, Ltd.

Branden, N. (1992). *The power of self-esteem.* Deerfield Beach, FL: Health Communications.

Byrd, R. C. (1988). Positive therapeutic effects of intercessory prayer in a coronary care unit population. *Southern Medical Journal,* 81 (7), 826-829.

Carrig, M. (1999). Interpersonal skills are key in office of the future. *TMA Journal,* 19(4), 53.

Daniel, A. G. F. (1998, October 26). Success secret: A high emotional IQ. *Fortune,* 293.

Evans, W. (1996, February 15). The benefits of exercise. *The Press Enterprise.* pp. C1, C4.

Farrell, W. (1993). 2nd ed. (2000). *The myth of male power.* New York: Simon & Schuster.

Gardner, H. (1993). *Frames of mind: The theory of multiple intelligences.* New York: Basic Books.

Girion, L. (2001, June 15). Office pressure cookers stewing up 'desk rage.' *Los Angeles Times.* pp. W1, W4.

Goleman, D. (1997). *Emotional intelligence.* New York: Bantam.

Hall, P. D. (1999). The effect of meditation on the academic performance of African American college students. *Meditation*, 29(3), 408-416.

Harju, B. L., & Bolen, L. M. (1998). The effects of optimism on coping and perceived quality of life of college students. *Journal of Social Behavior and Personality,* 13(2), 185-201.

Herbert, N. (1987). *Quantum reality.* Garden City, NY: Anchor/Doubleday.

Hodge, D. R. (2007). A systematic review of the empirical literature on intercessory prayer. *Research on Social Work Practice,* 17, 174-187.

Kohlberg, L. (1981). *The philosophy of moral development: Essays on moral development* (Vol. I). San Francisco: Harper and Row.

Luft, J. (1969). *Of human interaction.* Palo Alto, CA: Mayfield.

Monty, W., & Monty, M. (1981). Exploration of long-distance pk: A conceptual replication of the influence on a biological system. *Research in Parapsychology 1980,* 90-93.

Nolen-Hoeksema, S., Morrow, J., & Fredrickson, B. L. (1993). Response styles and the duration of episodes of depressed mood. *Journal of Abnormal Psychology,* 102, 20-28.

Pearce, J. C. (1992). *Evolution's end.* San Francisco: HarperCollins.

Phares, J. (1988). *Introduction to personality.* (2nd ed.). Glenview, IL: Scott, Foresman, and Company.

Salmela-Aro, K., & Nurmi, J. E. (1996). Uncertainty and confidence in interpersonal projects. Consequences for social relationships and well-being. *Journal of Social and Personal Relationships,* 13(1), 109-122.

Salzberg, S., & Kabat-Zinn, J. (1997). Mindfulness as medicine. In D. Goleman (Ed.), *Healing emotions* (pp. 107-144). Boston: Shambhala.

Seligman, E. P. (1994). *What You Can Change and What You Can't.* New York: Alfred A. Knopf.

U.S. Bureau of Health and Human Services, National Center for Health Statistics (1991). (Vol. 2A). *Mortality.* 51, tables 1-9.

U.S. Bureau of Health and Human Services, National Center for Health Statistics (2009).

U.S. Department of Justice, Office of Justice Programs, Bureau of Justice Statistics. (1987). *Criminal victimization in the U.S.*

U.S. Department of Justice, Office of Justice Programs, Bureau of Justice Statistics. (2010). *Homicide Trends in the United States.*

Bibliography

Bourne, E. J. (2000). *The anxiety and phobia workbook* (3rd ed.). Oakland, CA: New Harbinger Publications.

Boyd, J. (1992). *Musicians in tune. New York: NY Fireside/Simon and Schuster*

Bradshaw, J. (1990). *Homecoming.* New York: Bantam Books.

Carter, J. (1989). *Nasty people.* Chicago: Contemporary Books.

Covey, S. R. (1990). *The 7 habits of highly effective people.* New York: Simon & Schuster

DeAngelis, B. (1992). *Are you the one for me?* New York, NY: Delacorte Press.

Diamond, H.& M. (1987). *Fit for life II.* New York: Warner Books.

Farrell, W. (1993). *The myth of male power.* New York: Simon & Schuster.

Gray, H. (1992). *Men are from mars, women are from venus.* New York: HarperCollins.

Hay, L. (2001). *Heal Your Body A-Z: The Mental Causes for Physical Illness and the Way to Overcome Them.* Carlsbad, CA: Hay House

Hendrix, J. (1990). *Getting the love you want.* New York: HarperPerennial.

Kubler-Ross, E. (1969). *On death and dying.* New York: Macmillan.

Kubler-Ross, E. (1975). *Death: The final stage of growth.* Englewood Cliffs, NJ: Prentice-Hall (Spectrum).

Masters, R. (1978). *How your mind can keep you well.* Los Angeles: Foundation of Human Understanding.

Myss, C. (1996). *Anatomy of the spirit.* New York: Three Rivers Press.

Orman, M. (1991). *The 14 day stress cure.* Houston, TX: Breakthru Publishing.

Ornish, D. (1998). *Love and survival.* New York: HarperCollins.

Parker, J. D. A., Duffy, J., Wood, L. M., Bond, B. J. & Hogan, M. J. (2005). Academic achievement and emotional intelligence: Predicting the successful transition from high school to university. *Journal Of First-Year Experience And Student In Transition.*

Pearce, J. C. (1992). *Evolution's end.* New York: HarperCollins

Phares, J. (1988). *Introduction to personality.* (2nd ed.). Glenview, IL: Scott, Foresman, and Company.

Riso, D. R. (1996). *Personality types: Using the enneagram for self-discovery.* New York: Houghton Mifflin

Sapiro, V. (1994). *Women In American Society.* (3rd ed.). Mountain View, CA: Mayfield

Schuller, R. (1994). *Power Thinking.* New York: Bantam.

Siegel, B. (1988). *Love, medicine, and miracles.* New York: Harper & Row (Perennial Library).

Siegel, B. (1993). *How to live between office visits: A guide to life, love, and health.* New York: Harper Collins.

Truman, K. (1991) *Feeling Buried Alive Never Die* Brigham City, Utah: Brigham Distributing

Weiten, W., & Lloyd, M. A. (1997). *Psychology applied to modern life.* Pacific Grove, CA: Brooks/Cole.

Whitfield, C. L. (1993). *Boundaries and Relationships.* Deerfield Beach, FL: Health Communications.

Yalom, I. D. (1980). *Existential psychotherapy.* New York: Basic Books.

Index

About the Author

Thomas Ventimiglia, founder of Inner Growth Seminars, holds a Bachelor's Degree in Business Administration and two Master's Degrees: one in Counseling and a second in Higher Education. He has counseled college students academically, vocationally, and personally and has taught his own achievement principles in personal growth courses for over twenty-three years at community colleges in both San Diego and Riverside counties and at the University of California, San Diego Extension (UCSD). Thomas Ventimiglia's high-powered Live, Thrive, and Produce Program has received rave reviews from a diversity of participants including educators, business groups, disabled groups, Native Americans, associations like ASTD (American Society for Trainers and Developers), honor societies, diversity conferences, counseling departments, and state agencies. Thomas obtained the "Outstanding Young American" Award in 1998. He won the most prestigious "Telly Award" for excellence in Educational Television in 2005. The 26 module Television series, "Quest for the Empowered Self" utilized this book as the main source of content for the program. Tom and his television series also won a 1st place Western Access Video Excellence Award (WAVE) out of six states competing in 2005.

CPSIA information can be obtained
at www.ICGtesting.com
Printed in the USA
FFOW01n1029031014
7777FF